(Continued on back endsheets)

Dictionary of Literary Biography
Yearbook: 1989

Dictionary of Literary Biography
Yearbook: 1989

Edited by
J. M. Brook

8263

A Bruccoli Clark Layman Book
Gale Research Inc.
Detroit, New York, London

Copyright © 1990
Gale Research Inc.
835 Penobscot Bldg.
Detroit, MI 48226-4094

Manufactured by Edwards Brothers, Inc.
Ann Arbor, Michigan
Printed in the United States of America

Library of Congress Catalog Card Number 82-645187
ISSN 0731-7867
ISBN 0-8103-4569-2

Dedicated to the memory of William Ellis Seawright

Contents

Plan of the Series

The advisory board, the editors, and the publisher of the *Dictionary of Literary Biography* are joined in endorsing Mark Twain's declaration. The literature of a nation provides an inexhaustible resource of permanent worth. We intend to make literature and its creators better understood and more accessible to students and the reading public, while satisfying the standards of teachers and scholars.

To meet these requirements, *literary biography* has been construed in terms of the author's achievement. The most important thing about a writer is his writing. Accordingly, the entries in *DLB* are career biographies, tracing the development of the author's canon and the evolution of his reputation.

The purpose of *DLB* is not only to provide reliable information in a convenient format but also to place the figures in the larger perspective of literary history and to offer appraisals of their accomplishments by qualified scholars.

The publication plan for *DLB* resulted from two years of preparation. The project was proposed to Bruccoli Clark by Frederick G. Ruffner, president of the Gale Research Company, in November 1975. After specimen entries were prepared and typeset, an advisory board was formed to refine the entry format and develop the series rationale. In meetings held during 1976, the publisher, series editors, and advisory board approved the scheme for a comprehensive biographical dictionary of persons who contributed to North American literature. Editorial work on the first volume began in January 1977, and it was published in 1978. In order to make *DLB* more than a reference tool and to compile volumes that individually have claim to status as literary history, it was decided to organize volumes by topic, period, or genre. Each of these freestanding volumes provides a biographical-bibliographical guide and overview for a particular area of literature. We are convinced that this organization—as opposed to a single alphabet method—constitutes a valuable innovation in the presentation of reference material. The volume plan necessarily requires many decisions for the placement and treatment of authors who might properly be included in two or three volumes. In some instances a major figure will be included in separate volumes, but with different entries emphasizing the aspect of his career appropriate to each volume. Ernest Hemingway, for example, is represented in *American Writers in Paris, 1920-1939* by an entry focusing on his expatriate apprenticeship; he is also in *American Novelists, 1910-1945* with an entry surveying his entire career. Each volume includes a cumulative index of subject authors and articles. Comprehensive indexes to the entire series are planned.

With volume ten in 1982 it was decided to enlarge the scope of *DLB*. By the end of 1986 twenty-one volumes treating British literature had been published, and volumes for Commonwealth and Modern European literature were in progress. The series has been further augmented by the *DLB Yearbooks* (since 1981) which update published entries and add new entries to keep the *DLB* current with contemporary activity. There have also been *DLB Documentary Series* volumes which provide biographical and critical source materials for figures whose work is judged to have particular interest for students. One of these companion volumes is entirely devoted to Tennessee Williams.

We define literature as the *intellectual commerce of a nation:* not merely as belles lettres but as that ample and complex process by which ideas are generated, shaped, and transmitted. *DLB* entries are not limited to "creative writers" but extend to other figures who in their time and in their way influenced the mind of a people. Thus the series encompasses historians, journalists, publishers, and screenwriters. By this means readers of *DLB* may be aided to perceive literature not as cult scripture in the keeping of intellectual high priests but firmly positioned at the center of a nation's life.

DLB includes the major writers appropriate to each volume and those standing in the ranks immediately behind them. Scholarly and critical counsel has been sought in deciding which minor figures to include and how full their entries should be. Wherever possible, useful references are made to figures who do not warrant separate entries.

Each *DLB* volume has a volume editor responsible for planning the volume, selecting the figures for inclusion, and assigning the entries. Volume editors are also responsible for preparing, where appropriate, appendices surveying the major periodicals and literary and intellectual movements for their volumes, as well as lists of further readings. Work on the series as a whole is coordinated at the Bruccoli Clark Layman editorial center in Columbia, South Carolina, where the editorial staff is responsible for accuracy of the published volumes.

One feature that distinguishes *DLB* is the illustration policy–its concern with the iconography of literature. Just as an author is influenced by his surroundings, so is the reader's understanding of the author enhanced by a knowledge of his environment. Therefore *DLB* volumes include not only drawings, paintings, and photographs of authors, often depicting them at various stages in their careers, but also illustrations of their families and places where they lived. Title pages are regularly reproduced in facsimile along with dust jackets for modern authors. The dust jackets are a special feature of *DLB* because they often document better than anything else the way in which an author's work was perceived in its own time. Specimens of the writers' manuscripts are included when feasible.

Samuel Johnson rightly decreed that "The chief glory of every people arises from its authors." The purpose of the *Dictionary of Literary Biography* is to compile literary history in the surest way available to us–by accurate and comprehensive treatment of the lives and work of those who contributed to it.

The *DLB* Advisory Board

Foreword

The *Dictionary of Literary Biography Yearbook* is guided by the same principles that have provided the basic rationale for the entire *DLB* series: 1) the literature of a nation represents an inexhaustible resource of permanent worth; 2) the surest way to trace the outlines of literary history is by a comprehensive treatment of the lives and works of those who contributed to it; and 3) the greatest service the series can provide is to make literary achievement better understood and more accessible to students and the literate public, while serving the needs of scholars. In keeping with those principles, the *Yearbook* has been planned to augment *DLB* by reflecting the vitality of contemporary literature and summarizing current literary activity. The librarian, scholar, or student attempting to stay informed of literary developments is faced with an endless task. The purpose of *DLB Yearbook* is to serve these readers while at the same time enlarging the scope of *DLB*.

The *Yearbook* is divided into two sections: articles about the past year's literary events or topics; and obituaries and tributes. The updates and new author entries previously included as supplements to published *DLB* volumes have been omitted. (These essays will appear in future *DLB* volumes.) Included in the articles section are an essay commemorating the bicentenary of the birth of James Fenimore Cooper and extended discussions of the year's work in fiction, poetry, drama, and literary biography. The *Yearbook* continues two surveys begun in 1987, an overview of new literary journals, and an in-depth examination of the practice of book reviewing in America. In addition, the *Yearbook* features an article on the recipient of the 1989 Nobel Prize in Literature, Camilo José Cela, including Cela's Nobel lecture.

The death of a literary figure prompts an assessment of his achievements and reputation. The obituaries section marks the passing of Donald Barthelme, Malcolm Cowley, Georges Simenon, and Robert Penn Warren. An obituary of Samuel Beckett, who died on 22 December 1989, will appear in the 1990 *Yearbook*.

Each *Yearbook* includes a list of literary prizes and awards, a necrology, and a checklist of books about literary history and biography published during the year.

From the outset, the *DLB* series has undertaken to compile literary history as it is revealed in the lives and works of authors. The *Yearbook* supports that commitment, providing a useful and necessary current record.

Acknowledgments

This book was produced by Bruccoli Clark Layman, Inc. Karen L. Rood is senior editor for the *Dictionary of Literary Biography* series.

Production coordinator is James W. Hipp. Systems manager is Charles D. Brower. Photography editor is Susan Brennen Todd. Permissions editor is Jean W. Ross. Layout and graphics supervisor is Penney L. Haughton. Copyediting supervisor is Bill Adams. Typesetting supervisor is Kathleen M. Flanagan. Typography coordinator is Sheri Beckett Neal. Information systems analyst is George F. Dodge. Charles Lee Egleston is editorial associate. The production staff includes Rowena Betts, Anne L. M. Bowman, Teresa Chaney, Patricia Coate, Sarah A. Estes, Mary L. Goodwin, Cynthia Hallman, Susan C. Heath, David Marshall James, Kathy S. Merlette, Laura Garren Moore, John Myrick, Cathy J. Reese, Laurrè Sinckler, Maxine K. Smalls, John C. Stone III, Jennifer Toth, and Betsy L. Weinberg.

Walter W. Ross and Parris Boyd did the library research with the assistance of the following librarians at the Thomas Cooper Library of the University of South Carolina: Gwen Baxter, Daniel Boice, Faye Chadwell, Cathy Eckman, Gary Geer, Cathie Gottlieb, David L. Haggard, Jens Holley, Jackie Kinder, Thomas Marcil, Marcia Martin, Laurie Preston, Jean Rhyne, Carol Tobin, and Virginia Weathers.

Dictionary of Literary Biography
Yearbook: 1989

Dictionary of Literary Biography

The 1989 Nobel Prize in Literature
Camilo José Cela
(11 May 1916 -   )

Lucile C. Charlebois
University of South Carolina

BOOKS: *La familia de Pascual Duarte* (Madrid &
Burgos: Aldecoa, 1942); translated by John
Marks as *Pascual Duarte's Family* (London:
Eyre & Spottiswoode, 1946); translated by
Anthony Kerrigan as *The Family of Pascual
Duarte* (Boston: Little, Brown, 1964);
Nuevas andanzas y desventuras de Lazarillo de Tormes
(Madrid: La Nave, 1944);
Pabellón de reposo (Madrid: Afrodisio Aguado,
1944); bilingual edition, with English transla-
tion as *Rest Home* by Herma Briffault (New
York: Las Americas Publishing, 1961);
*Pisando la dudosa luz del día: poemas de una adolescen-
cia cruel* (Barcelona: Zodíaco, 1945; revised
and enlarged edition, Palma de Mallorca:
Ediciones de los Papeles de Son Armadans,
1963);
Esas nubes que pasan (Madrid: Afrodisio Aguado,
1945);
Mesa revuelta (Madrid: Ediciones de los Estudian-
tes Españoles, 1945; enlarged edition, Madrid: Taurus, 1957);
El bonito crimen del carabinero, y otras invenciones
(Barcelona: José Janés, 1947) republished in
part as *El bonito crimen del carabinero* (Barcelona: Picazo, 1972);
*Las botas de siete leguas: Viaje a la Alcarria, con los ver-
sos de su cancionero, cada uno en su debido*

Note: Translations in the text are by the author.

Camilo José Cela (copyright 1989 Horst Tappe)

lugar (Madrid: Revista de Occidente, 1948);
translated by Frances M. López-Moullas as

3

Journey to the Alcarria (Madison: University of Wisconsin Press, 1964);

San Juan de la Cruz, as Matilde Verdu (Madrid: Hernando, 1948);

El gallego y su cuadrilla y otros apuntes carpetovetónicos (Madrid: Ricardo Aguilera, 1949; revised and enlarged edition, Barcelona: Ediciones Destino, 1967);

La colmena (Buenos Aires: Emecé, 1951; Barcelona: Noguer, 1955); translated by J. M. Cohen and Arturo Barea as *The Hive* (London: Gollancz, 1953; New York: Farrar, Straus & Young, 1953);

Avila (Barcelona: Noguer, 1952); translated by John Forrester (Barcelona: Noguer, 1956);

Santa Bárbara 37, gas en cada piso (Melilla: Mirto y Laurel, 1952);

Del Miño al Bidasoa: notas de un vagabundaje (Barcelona: Noguer, 1952);

Nuevas andanzas y desventuras de Lazarillo de Tormes, y siete apuntes carpetovetónicos (Madrid, 1952);

Timoteo el incomprendido (Madrid: Rollán, 1952);

Baraja de invenciones (Valencia: Castalia, 1953);

Café de artistas (Madrid: Tecnos, 1953);

Mrs. Caldwell habla con su hijo (Barcelona: Destino, 1953); translated by J. S. Bernstein as *Mrs. Caldwell Speaks to Her Son* (Ithaca: Cornell University Press, 1968);

Ensueños y figuraciones (Barcelona: G. P. 1954); republished in the enlarged edition of *Mesa revuelta* (Madrid: Taurus, 1957);

Vagabundo por Castilla (Barcelona; Seix Barral, 1955);

Historias de Venezuela: La catira (Barcelona: Noguer, 1955);

Judíos, moros y cristianos: Notas de un vagabundaje por Avila, Segovia y sus tierras (Barcelona; Destino, 1956);

El molino de viento, y otras novelas cortas (Barcelona: Noguer, 1956);

Mis páginas preferidas (Madrid: Gredos, 1956);

Cajón de sastre (Madrid: Cid, 1957);

La rueda de los ocios (Barcelona: Mateu, 1957);

Nuevo retablo de don Cristobita; invenciones, figuraciones y alucinaciones (Barcelona: Destino, 1957);

Historias de España: Los ciegos, los tontos (Madrid: Arión, 1957); enlarged as volume 1 of *A la pata de palo* (Barcelona: Noguer, 1965);

La obra literaria del pintor Solana (Madrid: Papeles de Son Armadans, 1957);

Recuerdo de don Pío Baroja (Mexico City: De Andrea, 1958);

Primer viaje andaluz: notas de un vagabundaje por Jaén, Córdoba, Sevilla, Segovia, Huelva y sus tierras (Barcelona: Noguer, 1959);

La cucaña: memorias (Barcelona: Destino, 1959);

Los viejos amigos, 2 volumes (Barcelona: Noguer, 1960-1961);

Cuadernos del Guadarrama (Madrid: Arión, 1960);

Cuatro figuras del 98: Unamuno, Valle-Inclán, Baroja, Azorín, y otros retratos y ensayos españoles (Barcelona: Aedos, 1961);

Tobogán de hambrientos (Barcelona: Noguer, 1962);

Gavilla de fábulas sin amor (Palma de Mallorca: Papeles de Son Armadans 1962);

Obra completa, 14 volumes (Barcelona: Destino, 1962-1983);

Garito de hospicianos; o, Guirigay de imposturas y bambollas (Barcelona: Noguer, 1963);

El solitario, de Camilo José Cela, y Los sueños de Quesada, de Rafael Zabaleta (Palma de Mallorca: Papeles de Son Armadans, 1963);

Toreo de salón: farsa con acompanamiento de clamor y murga (Barcelona: Lumen, 1963);

Once cuentos de fútbol (Madrid: Nacional, 1963);

Las compañías convenientes y otros fingimientos y cegueras (Barcelona: Destino, 1963);

Izas, rabizas y colipoterras (Barcelona: Lumen, 1964);

A la pata de palo, 4 volumes (Madrid: Alfaguara, 1965-1967)–volume 1: *Historias de España*; volume 2: *La familia del héroe; o, discurso histórico de los ultimos restos (ejercicios para una sola mano)*; volume 3: *El ciudadano Iscariote Reclús*; volume 4: *Viaje a U.S.A.; o, el que la sigue la mata*; republished in one volume as *El tacatá oxidado: florilegio de carpetovetonismos y otros lindezas* (Barcelona: Noguer, 1973);

Viaje al Pirineo de Lérida: notas de un paseo a pie por el Pallars, Sobirá, el Valle de Aran y el Condado de Ribagorza (Madrid: Alfaguara, 1965);

Páginas de geografía errabunda (Madrid: Alfaguara, 1965);

Nuevas escenas matritenses, 7 volumes (Madrid: Alfaguara, 1965-1966); republished in one volume as *Fotografías al minuto* (Madrid: Sala, 1972);

Madrid (Madrid: Alfaguara, 1966);

Calidoscopio callejero, marítimo y campestre (Madrid: Alfaguara, 1966);

María Sabina (Madrid: Papeles de Son Armadans, 1967); republished with *El carro de heno; o, El inventor de la guillotina* (Madrid: Alfaguara, 1970);

La bandada de palomas (Barcelona: Labor, 1969);

Víspera, festividad y octava de San Camilo del año 1936 en Madrid (Madrid: Alfaguara, 1969);

Homenaje al Bosco, I: El carro de hero; o, el inventor de la guillotina (Madrid: Papeles de Son Armadans, 1969);

Al servicio de algo (Madrid: Alfaguara, 1969);

Barcelona (Madrid: Alfaguara, 1970);

La Mancha en el corazón y en los ojos (Barcelona: EDISVEN, 1971);

Obras selectas (Madrid: Alfaguara, 1971);

La bola del mundo: escenas cotidianas (Madrid: Sala, 1972);

Diccionario secreto, 2 volumes (Madrid: Alfaguara, 1968-1972);

Oficio de tinieblas 5; o, novela de tesis escrita para ser cantada por un coro de enfermos (Barcelona: Noguer, 1973);

A vuelta con España (Madrid: Semanarios y Ediciones, 1973);

Balada del vagabundo sin suerte y otros papeles volanderos (Madrid: Espasa-Calpe, 1973);

Cuentos para leer después del baño (Barcelona: La Gaya Ciencia, 1974);

Prosa, edited by Jacinto-Luis Guerena (Madrid: Narcea, 1974);

Rol de cornudos (Barcelona: Noguer, 1976);

Enciclopedia de eroticismo (Madrid: Sedmay, 1977);

Los sueños vanos, los ángeles curiosos (Barcelona: Argos Vergara, 1979);

Album de taller (Barcelona: Ambit, 1981);

Las compañias convenientes y otros fingimientos y cegueras (Barcelona: Destino, 1981);

Los vasos comunicantes (Barcelona: Brugera, 1981);

Vuelta de hoja (Barcelona: Destino, 1981);

Mazurka para dos muertos (Barcelona: Seix Barral, 1983);

El juego de los tres madroños (Barcelona: Destino, 1983);

El asno de Buridán (Madrid: El País, 1986).

OTHER: *Homenaje y recuerdo a Gregorio Marañón (1887-1960)*, edited by Cela (Madrid: Papeles de Son Armadans, 1961);

Fernando de Rojas, *La Celestina puesta respetuosamente en castellano moderno por Camilo José Cela quien añadió muy poco y quitó aun menos*, adapted by Cela (Barcelona: Destino, 1979);

Miguel de Cervantes Saavedra, *El Quijote*, edited by Cela (Alicante: Rembrandt, 1981).

By many Hispanists and fellow writers, Camilo José Cela is considered the dean of the post-Spanish Civil War novel, yet of himself he has said that "he is nothing more than somebody who has the spirit of a junk dealer, a writer who knows how to pick, choose and accumulate," while acknowledging that, "for him, literature is the very practice of humility" (*Del Miño al Bidasoa: notas de un vagabundaje*, 1952). Cela's career has been marked by controversy since the publication of his first novel in 1942, and he still sparks heated debates in literary circles, as the article entitled "Cela 'versus' the Rest," which appeared on 24 November 1989 in the leading Spanish newspaper *El País*, might indicate. Shortly after the announcement that he had been awarded the 1989 Nobel Prize for Literature, he issued a provocative pronouncement flatly chastising young Spanish novelists for being too obedient and catechetical in their works ("Y sin embargo, colegas," *El País*, 12 November 1989).

In his multifarious works Cela gives only a surface depiction of characters, places, and events; he never really delves into the metaphysical aspects of life, the hermeneutics of literary theory, or the demythicizing of various Spanish prototypes, as do many of the novels of such predecessors and contemporaries as Miguel de Unamuno and Luis and Juan Goytisolo, respectively. Cela utilizes a detached and objective tone, clearly evident in his first (and most controversial) novel, *La familia de Pascual Duarte* (1942; translated as *Pascual Duarte's Family*, 1946), as well as an experimental approach to novelistic form in his unabashed attempts at baring the foibles, characteristics, and virtues of his fellow Spaniards and, by extension, all human beings.

Camilo José Manuel Juan Ramón Francisco Santiago Cela was born on 11 May 1916 just a short distance from what is known on the Iberian Peninsula as "finisterre"–land's end–in the small town of Iria-Flavia in the Galician region of Spain. Cela's ancestors included a great-grandfather who was governor of Parma (Italy), an English candle-factory owner, and yet another distant relative who supposedly descended from an old family of British pirates. Of Cela's varied heritage, Alonso Zamora Vicente quotes Cela himself: "It is these three bloodlines–the Spanish, the English and the Italian–which made me who I am . . . That inherent feeling of being tied to various geographies doesn't seem to me, as a writer anyway, to be an obstacle. It is those very bloodlines which soften the rough edges of such lineages, the combination of which allows one to see things concretely and with the objectivity and perspective that are so necessary. Feeling thoroughly and unequivocally Spanish, I believe I see and know and love Spain with a lot more common sense than many of my Spanish friends."

Cela's father, Camilo Cela y Fernández, worked as a customs official, and since his mother, Camila Enmanuela Trulock y Bertorini, had many close relatives in England, Cela began his travels at the early age of three when he first visited the British Isles. He also accompanied his parents on their trips throughout Spain and lived in such places as Barcelona, Vigo, and Madrid. While it was in Vigo that he first enrolled as a student in a school run by the nuns of the order of St. Joseph of Cluny, it was from the Marist-run institute of St. Isidro that he graduated high school in 1933 in Madrid, where his family had settled permanently when he was nine years old. Shortly after his graduation, he fought the first of two bouts with tuberculosis from which he recuperated initially in a sanitarium in the nearby mountain area of Navacerrada, then once again in 1941 in the Hoyo de Manzanares sanitarium located in the Guadarrama mountain range north of Madrid.

A notoriously impervious student, Cela made various attempts at college life. He studied medicine at the Central University of Madrid for approximately one year (1934-1935) and later, in 1939, enrolled in the law college at the same university. Both endeavors to find a suitable career were overshadowed by Cela's interest in literature. It was during this same course of study that Cela wandered into the renowned Spanish poet Pedro Salinas's literature class at the university. Having already immersed himself in the reading of the seventy-one-volume collection of the *Biblioteca de Autores Españoles* (Library of Spanish Authors) during his period of convalescence from tuberculosis in 1934, Cela found immediate satisfaction under Salinas's tutelage and, in 1936, at the height of the many aerial bombings that characterized the three-year Spanish Civil War (1936-1939), Cela wrote his first volume of poetry, entitled *Pisando la dudosa luz del día: poemas de una adolescencia cruel* (Treading the Uncertain Light of Day: Poems of a Cruel Adolescence), which was later published in 1945. The young man who admittedly "never studied grammar" and who finagled his way through a capricious high school course of studies had stumbled upon something that was to be both a way of life and an inordinate source of diversion.

Cela is without a doubt one of Spain's most versatile manipulators of language. He is also prolific, having produced, by age seventy-three, ten novels, several novellas, two plays, fourteen collections of short stories, numerous travel books, dictionaries, and illustrated travel guides of cities and regions of Spain.

The cataclysmic Spanish Civil War, which erupted when Cela was twenty years old, became one of the dominant themes of his later and most noteworthy novels: *La colmena* (1951; translated as *The Hive*, 1953), *Víspera, festividad y octava de San Camilo del año 1936 en Madrid* (Eve, Feast and Octave of San Camilo's Day 1936 in Madrid [1969]), and *Mazurka para dos muertos* (Mazurka for Two Dead Men, 1983). Cela experienced the war firsthand as a Nationalist soldier. During his two-year stint in the army, he saw active duty, was seriously wounded, and subsequently discharged as a corporal in 1939.

The years immediately following the Civil War provided significant turning points in his personal as well as his public life. In 1942, after two years of work, *La familia de Pascual Duarte* was published, only to be confiscated in 1943 by government censors (the ban was lifted in 1946). In 1944 Cela married María del Rosario Conde Picavea, and in 1946 his only son, also named Camilo José, was born. By 1946 Cela had begun what were to be his famous walking tours through various regions of Spain and had written five rough drafts of his novel *La colmena*, which was not published until five years later in Argentina. (*La familia de Pascual Duarte* had been published in Argentina in 1945).

Cela came of age during the highly politicized, unstable, and chaotic period of the second Republic (1931-1936), which culminated in Spain's civil strife. Despite the detached tone and objective characterization of his novels, Cela is nonetheless preoccupied in his best fiction with the war, its causes, and its effects on his countrymen. However, in *La novelística de Camilo José Cela* (1971), Paul Ilie astutely affirms that Cela's novels engage in a structural manifestation of problems common to humankind and thereby serve as cornerstones of philosophical speculation.

Cela and his work are nonetheless products of an epoch from which Spain was to emerge irrevocably changed. It is not surprising, then, that *La familia de Pascual Duarte* had such an impact on its readers. Cast in the early decades of twentieth-century Spain, the novel takes the shape of the memoirs–discovered in manuscript form by the fictitious "transcriber" who accidentally stumbled upon them in 1939 in a pharmacy in Almendralejo–of a young man who wants to leave with his readers what seems to be a confession of how his life was thwarted, warped, and ruined by the primitive, rural Spanish society in which he lived. Pascual's account of life in "a village lost somewhere in the province of Badajoz" begins in rather typical picaresque fashion when he says, "I, sir, am not bad, although there are certainly plenty of reasons why I should be." His recollections lead inexorably to a graphic blow-by-blow description of how, having finally summoned up the courage to brutally stab his mother to death, he is then able to "breathe. . . ."

The importance and the shock that such a naturalistic novel produced in Spain at the time of its publication were profound. It represented the first significant novel to emerge from the war-torn Spain of the 1930s; this in turn gave Cela immediate recognition, if not necessarily positive and laudatory. Nonetheless, Pascual Duarte's grotesque recounting of the sordid details of his childhood and adolescence provided ample opportunity for critics to label the novel *tremendista* (scandalously shocking), thereby crediting Cela not only with reviving the creative process that had been brought to an abrupt standstill with the Civil War, but, moreover, with initiating a new framework within which other Spanish novelists might also work.

An avowed enemy of prescriptive labels, Cela repudiated those critics who had coined the *tremendista* approach, in the prologue (which can be seen as Cela's own critique of his first four novels) that preceded *Mrs. Caldwell habla con su hijo* (1953; translated as *Mrs. Caldwell Speaks to Her Son*, 1968). While Cela's admonitory words should be heeded, the vigor with which Pascual Duarte recounts the incidents of his youth is indeed shocking and attests to the barbarism he knew early in life; for example, his little brother Mario's fate at having both ears bitten off by a pig and the boy's subsequent death by drowning in a huge jug of olive oil. If not convincing as an excuse for Pascual's self-confessed criminal behavior (he has murdered at least three people), the novel's success depends on its symbolization of the rampant chaos that immediately preceded and followed the outbreak of the war.

In the decade following the publication of *La familia de Pascual Duarte*, Cela established the three main areas of his literary productivity: novels, short stories, and travel books. *Nuevas andanzas y desventuras de Lazarillo de Tormes* (1944; The New Episodes and Misfortunes of Lazarillo of Tormes) is the first-person narration, set in con-

temporary times, of Lazarillo de Tormes, the Spanish archetypal rogue first brought to life and subsequently immortalized in the fifteenth-century anonymous picaresque novel that bears his name. Like his predecessor, Lazarillo is engaged in peripatetic roaming in search of prosperity, but Cela's novel is marked by realistic detail characteristic of the picaresque novel.

Based on Cela's personal history of tuberculosis, his third novel, *Pabellón de reposo* (1944; translated as *Rest Home*, 1961), is virtually devoid of action and plot lines. It is, to put it simply, the account of how seven anonymous patients suffering from tuberculosis in a sanitarium face life with the growing realization that their disease is indeed terminal. In an effort to highlight the passivity of its characters and *fábula* (plot), the novel takes on a quasi-epistolary form in which the reader finds himself confronted with the diary entries and interior monologues of the invalids. Interspersed throughout the second of the novel's two parts is the recurring symbol that further poeticizes the lyrical nature of the narrative discourse in addition to suggesting the only concrete movement in the novel; that is, the unassuming and indiscriminate rolling along of the small wheelbarrow used to transport the caskets of the patients as they inevitably fall prey to their impending deaths.

In 1948 Cela published his first travel book, *Las botas de siete leguas: Viaje a la Alcarria* (translated as *Journey to the Alcarria*, 1964), a collection of notes taken during his first walking trip in the mountainous region northeast of Madrid between the provinces of Guadalajara and Cuenca. Filled with descriptions and personal reactions to the sights and sounds of life in rural Spain, Cela's masterful art of the character sketch takes root in this book and flourishes in similar future works, including *Del Miño al Bidasoa* (From the Miño to the Bidasoa, 1952), *Judíos, moros y cristianos* (Jews, Moors and Christians, 1956), *Primer viaje andaluz* (First Andalusian Journey, 1959), and *Viaje al Pirineo de Lérida* (Journey to the Pyrenees of Lérida, 1965). Of equally captivating appeal for their poignant character sketches are Cela's collections of short stories, especially *Esas nubes que pasan* (The Passing Clouds, 1945), *El bonito crimen del carabinero y otras invenciones* (The Neat Crime of the Carabiniere and Other Tales, 1947), and *El gallego y su cuadrilla y otros apuntes carpetovetónicos* (The Galician and His Troupe and Other Carpeto-Vettonian Notes, 1949).

Notwithstanding the diverse reactions that Cela's early novels, short stories, sketches, and travel notes provoked, most of his critics agree that all of these creative undertakings culminate in what is still considered by many to be his major work, *La colmena*, which was published first in Argentina in 1951 before the Spanish censors lifted their ban and allowed it to be published in Spain in 1955. *La colmena*, set in December 1943, is a complex novel of meticulously ordered vignettes about everyday life in Madrid. The pathos with which many of its characters are forced to eke out a living in order to simply survive from day to day attests to the dastardly state of affairs in Spain immediately following the Civil War. If *Pascual Duarte* addresses, among other things, the nefarious socio-economic conditions of early twentieth-century Spanish life, *La colmena* gives testimony to the harsh realities of life after the war.

Despite the presence of some 296 fictional characters and 50 references to individuals who have authentic historical counterparts, the many accounts of their comings and goings, the frequently overheard conversations between the fictional characters, and the numerous places that file past the reader, the action takes place in less than forty-eight hours, with the entire novel hardly encompassing more than three days. Not capriciously does Cela in the prologue to *Mrs. Caldwell* call *La colmena* a "novela reloj"—clock novel—for the fictional three days together with the compactness of each character's function and activities within the limited time frame make for the structuring of a carefully orchestrated plot that ends in the murder of Doña Margot, the mother of Suárez, a homosexual.

To further complicate matters, there are over two hundred changes in scenery that are distributed strategically throughout the novel's seven chapters. Little by little order is established as one begins to recognize those gathering places that serve as focal points in the narration and nooks of refuge in the characters' lives, in particular, Doña Jesusa's brothel, Doña Rosa's café, and Don Celestino's bar.

The reader who finishes the novel feeling more than disappointed at not knowing if and how he missed the solution to the crime committed against Suárez's apparently innocent mother has undergone much of what Cela intended to transmit in this work. Aware of his failure, the reader has entered a fictitious world where mere subsistence demands of the hivelike dwellers radi-

cal compromise and betrayal of whatever ethic has been traditionally held in esteem within the context of the unmitigated Catholicism that Spanish life presupposed for centuries. The only way the characters can survive is to become active participants in the subculture of lying and trickery that are part of the fabric of rampant poverty, prostitution, neglect, and destruction. Such is the titular beehive's world where reality begets denial and half-truths, and apathy, disappointment, and hopelessness slowly vitiate the vitality of human existence. Being wholly impractical, if not altogether ludicrous, hopes and dreams filter down to the viability of only the most basic of needs: eating, sleeping, sexual satisfaction, and more of the same, over and over again, day after day, year after year. Frustration abounds, but life goes on.

Thirty years after the end of the Spanish Civil War, Cela published *Víspera, festividad y octava de San Camilo del año 1936 en Madrid* (commonly referred to as *San Camilo 1936*). Of hermetic proportions—matched only, according to Darío Villanueva, by *Oficio de tinieblas 5* (Hell's Work 5), which Cela published in 1973—because of the second-person narrative that its anonymous main character carries on with himself, the novel is imbedded in the first ten days of the outbreak of the Spanish Civil War. Its title alludes to the saint whose feast day is commemorated on 18 July, the day on which the military troops of Francisco Franco initiated the revolt in Morocco that quickly spread to Spain and plunged the country into three years of bloodshed, hunger, and death. For the first time since the beginning of his career, Cela chooses to address, albeit via fictive discourse, very directly the topic of his country's civil struggle. Whereas *Pascual Duarte* depicts prewar years, and *La colmena* postwar years, *San Camilo 1936* is the Civil War manifested in one ordinary, unnamed Spaniard.

The novel is divided into four parts: the night before 18 July 1936, St. Camille's feast day itself, the octave of the saint's day, and an epilogue. The interior monologue by a twenty-year-old man, who has an incessant fixation on his own reflection in an ever-present mirror, is preceded by three short introductory comments by Cela. The first is a biting explanation that the saint being honored is remembered on 18 July and is the patron of hospitals; the second a bittersweet dedication where, while the author mournfully remembers all those young men who in 1937 were used as reinforcement troops, he very pointedly says that this is not meant to be a tribute to the "foreign adventurers, Fascists and Marxists, who got tired of killing Spaniards like rabbits, and whom nobody had remembered in our own burial"; the third remark is a quote from Benito Pérez Galdós–the foremost of Spain's nineteenth-century novelists–that emphasizes the lack of stability and security that seem to be endemic to Spanish life. Following these ominous textual indicators, one is faced with the novel's stream of consciousness. The reader is immediately immersed in the narrator's schizophrenic mind precisely because confusion, uncertainty, terror, insanity, and self-doubt were all but outward manifestations of the feelings of citizens who suddenly found themselves engulfed in a civil war. The man who is constantly looking at himself in the mirror does not need a name because he is everyman. The reflection he sees reminds him of the three archetypal figures that will become a part of the narrative tapestry: Narcissus, Napoléon, and King Cyril of England. In this way, he learns that neither martyrdom, heroism, nor self-indulgence will bring him any true knowledge or inner peace.

The reader who is familiar with the comings and goings so typical of *La colmena* soon feels very much at home with this novel's frenzied weaving of the three primary levels of discourse: the narrator's own explorations into his self-consciousness, life, and background; the daily activities of those people who, with him, live in the same bellicose time and place; and the interwoven names, dates, and events that actually comprise the true history of the Spanish Civil War. As in the process of bonding that took place between the reader and the characters of *La colmena*, a similar pattern is determined through the repetition of names of people and their daily habits and practices; these, in turn, become oases of sanity in an all too voracious ebb and flow of line after line of unseparated ideas, facts, impressions, doubts, and rhetorical questions where such textual markers as paragraphs and quotation marks are absent. As the monologue accelerates to its most heightened pace–the day the Civil War began–all punctuation ceases and the segment itself ends in a half-uttered word.

What was virtually unimportant before assumes subtle meaning as precise clock-time is reiterated and more and more of the characters from the earlier part of the novel begin to turn up dead as a result of the diverse aspects of the first days of the war. Such is the case with, for

Cela in Stockholm, December 1989 (photograph by Lüfti Özkök)

example, Engracia, Matías, Virtudes, Victoriano, and even Joaquín Calvo Sotelo, the actual right-wing Spanish government official who was assassinated in 1936. A woman dies in childbirth as her husband is shot in the back when he runs out into the street in search of help; a well-known Nationalist lawyer cleverly escapes being apprehended when officials come looking for him in his middle-aged fiancée's boardinghouse; a man catches his wife with a man the reader knows to be her lover and consequently punishes them both by forcing the two of them to sit in scalding chocolate. And the retinue of vignettes that are characteristic of Cela's narrative art continues, serving both as a network of symbolic leitmotifs and an incentive for the reader to plod on in what is the virtual debacle of the narrator's quest for self-knowledge and direction in life. While he never seems to be as directly affected as his fictional counterparts by the Civil War repercussions as they manifest themselves in Madrid–the city where he lives–the novel ends with his Uncle Jerónimo, a paragon of wisdom for the confused young man, telling him to be careful, to rebel against the Spaniard who dwells within, and to take heart, for it is not the end of the world, but rather a time to trace for oneself a path of faith, hope, and charity. With that, he beckons him finally to go to bed and get some well-deserved rest, reassuring him that what really surrounds him is mere foolishness.

In 1983 Cela published *Mazurka para dos muertos* (Mazurka for Two Dead Men), which gained for him his country's National Prize for Literature in 1984. *Mazurka para dos muertos* deals once again with the Spanish Civil War. This time, however, the action takes place in the rural setting of Cela's own home soil of Galicia, where the rain that naturally keeps the countryside endlessly green also becomes one of the dominant leitmotifs for the story. The vignette-type style begun in *La colmena* is present, and once again Cela has chosen a title steeped in irony: the deaths mentioned in the title stand in direct contrast to the rhythmic and usually gleeful meter of "Ma petite Marianne," the mazurka played by the blind accordionist Gaudencio Beira at the outset of the novel and at its conclusion, and are but a simple anticipation of the death that encompasses what life remains in the novel's Galician homes, villages, and countryside. To this end Cela prefaces his work with a quote from Edgar Allan Poe's *Ulalume*: " 'our thoughts they were palsied and sere, Our memories were treacherous and sere.' "

Ostensibly well-informed and dauntless in the narration of the *fábula*, the narrator's factual account of the daily habits, practices, likes and dislikes of the inhabitants of this region is reminiscent of a chronicler who has been an active witness to much of what is being told. His care with regard to the transmission of the genealogies of the Moranes and Guxindes families, together with his constant reminders of the rainy days, transports the reader to what resembles a very primitive world, where the repetition of actions, motifs, and names suggest a mythic circularity that is characterized by the satisfaction of only the most basic of human needs and desires. The strict division between the roles of men and women in the novel further exacerbates the primal ambiance of women, who are consistently and submissively satisfying men's sexual drives.

Another very basic and integral aspect of life in this rural Galician setting is death. As the narrative begins to unfold, almost all the numerous female characters are heard speaking of their husbands', lovers', brothers', and cousins' deaths.

After a while, however, the reader begins to realize that the unrelenting genealogical information regarding the nine Gamuzo brothers and others is part of Cela's impeccable narrative plotting, which eventually gives way to the basic dilemma of the story: revenge by the Moranes and Guxindes families for the murders of two men in particular, Baldomero and Cidrán, if not for those of all the other victims of the polarization within families, neighborhoods, regions, and Spain itself.

With pristine specificity, the narrator's voice is very clear toward the end of the novel where that isolated Galician world takes its place in the world community: "On All Souls' Day in 1939 the Second World War had already begun, St. Charles' feast day comes a little after All Souls' Day, on St. Charles' day in 1939, the twenty-two men, all related by blood, summoned together by Robín Lebozán, met in Miss Ramona's house . . . ." They came together to decide upon avenging the deaths of their friends and relatives. After Robín Lebozán–who bears the full name of Robín Lebozán Castro de Cela–tells them that it was Moucho Carroupo who murdered them, the women's timely question, "¿Cuándo oímos la bomba?" (When will we hear the bomb?), signals the inevitable dénouement: Moucho Carroupo is viciously attacked and killed by two of Tanis Gamuzo's canines. The figurative bomb is heard far and wide, and the novel ends with the forensic report of the state of the cadaver: death by accident. The blind accordionist plays his mazurka for the second and last time, and retribution, though not necessarily justice, prevails.

When Sara Suárez Solís wrote her book *El léxico de Camilo José Cela* (Camilo José Cela's Lexicon) in 1969, one of her closing comments seemed to be a direct challenge to Cela. It said that his readers were waiting for him finally to write a novel that would at last reflect the maturity of his literary talent and experience. Although Cela continued to stay in the public eye with his directing of the prestigious journal *Papeles de Son Armadans* (which he founded in 1956; one year later he became the youngest member ever to be elected to the Royal Spanish Academy), he was becoming less known as a novelist, though his popularity as a travel writer and celebrity remained undiminished. For many years after *La colmena* both critics and the reading public either disregarded him as a serious novelist, especially after his ill-received Venezuelan novel *La catira* (The Blonde, 1955), were unable to grasp the complexities of such novels as the surrealistic *Mrs. Caldwell habla con su hijo, San Camilo 1936,* and *Oficio de tinieblas 5,* grew tired of his travel and somewhat commercialized tour books, or were not amused any longer by works such as the *Diccionario secreto* (Secret Dictionary, 1968-1972) and *Rol de cornudos* (List of Cuckolds, 1976). With *Mazurka para dos muertas,* Cela's literary public was once again positively awakened, as was the world at large with the awarding of the Nobel Prize for Literature. It is, then, with renewed enthusiasm that his current novel in progress "Madera de boj" (Box-wood) is awaited. Of perhaps equal interest is his son's recent book, *Cela, mi padre* (Cela, My Father), which was published late in 1989 in Spain. Cela has pleased, shocked, tricked, and surprised his readers since he began writing in 1942. His legend lives on, as one cannot help but wonder what strategy he will employ next.

References:

José Homero, "*San Camilo 1936* o cómo escapar del espejo," *Siempre!,* 1902 (6 December 1989): 42-43;

Paul Ilie, *La novelística de Camilo José Cela* (Madrid: Gredos, 1971);

D. W. McPheeters, *Camilo José Cela* (New York: Twayne, 1969);

Olga Prjevalinsky, *El sistema estético de Camilo José Cela* (Valencia: Castalia, 1960);

Gonzalo Sobejano, "La novela ensimismada," *España Contemporánea,* no. 1 (1988): 9-23;

Sara Suárez Solís, *El léxico de Camilo José Cela* (Barcelona: Alfaguara, 1969);

Eduardo Trives, *Una semana con Camilo José Cela* (Seville: Gráficas Vidal, 1960);

Darío Villanueva, "La intencionalidad de lo sexual en Cela," *Los Cuadernos de la Literatura,* no. 51 (octubre-noviembre 1988): 54-58;

Alonso Zamora Vicente, *Camilo José Cela* (Madrid: Gredos, 1962).

NOBEL LECTURE 1989
Camilo José Cela

Translated from the Spanish
by Mary Penney

EULOGY TO THE FABLE

Distinguished Academicians:

My old friend and mentor Pío Baroja—who did not receive the Nobel Prize because the bright light of success does not always fall on the righteous—had a clock on his wall. Around the face of that clock there were words of enlightenment, a saying that made you tremble as the hands of the clock moved round. It said "Each hour wounds; the last hour kills." In my case, many chimes have been rung in my heart and soul by the hands of that clock—which never goes back—and today, with one foot in the long life behind me and the other in hope for the future, I came before you to say a few words about the spoken word and to reflect in a spirit of goodwill and hopefully to good avail on liberty and literature. I do not rightly know at what point one crosses the threshold into old age but to be on the safe side I take refuge in the words of Don Francisco de Quevedo who said: "We all wish to reach a ripe old age, but none of us are prepared to admit that we are already there."

However one cannot ignore the obvious. I also know that time marches inexorably onwards. So I will say what I have to say here and now without resorting to either inspiration or improvisation, since I dislike both.

Finding myself here today, addressing you from this dais which is so difficult to reach, I begin to wonder whether the glitter of words—my words in this case—has not dazzled you as to my real merit which I feel is a poor thing compared to the high honour you have conferred upon me. It is not difficult to write in Spanish; the Spanish language is a gift from the gods which we Spaniards take for granted. I take comfort therefore in the belief that you wished to pay tribute to a glorious language and not to the humble writer who uses it for everything it can express: the joy and the wisdom of Mankind, since literature is an artform of all and for all, although written without deference, heeding only the voiceless, anonymous murmur of a given place and time.

I write from solitude and I speak from solitude. Mateo Alemán in his *Guzmán de Alfarache* and Francis Bacon in his essay *Of Solitude,*—both writing more or less at the same period—said that the man who seeks solitude has much of the divine and much of the beast in him. However I did not seek solitude. I found it. And from my solitude I think, work, and live–and I believe that I write and speak with almost infinite composure and resignation. In my solitude I constantly keep in mind the principle expounded by Picasso, another old friend and mentor, that no lasting work of art can be achieved without great solitude. As I go through life giving the impression that I am belligerent, I can speak of solitude without embarrassment and even with a certain degree of thankful, if painful, acceptance.

The greatest reward is to know that one can speak and emit articulate sounds and utter words that describe things, events and emotions.

When defining man philosophers have traditionally used the standard medium of close genus and specific difference that is to say reference to our animal status and the origin of differences. From Aristotle's *zoón politikón* to Descartes' *res cogitans* such reference has been an essential means of distinguishing man from beast. But however much moral philosophers may challenge what I'm going to say, I maintain that it would not be difficult to find abundant evidence identifying language as the definitive source of human nature which, for better or worse, sets us apart from all other animals.

We are different from other animals, although since Darwin we know that we have evolved from them. The evolution of language is thus a fundamental fact which we cannot ignore.

The phylogenesis of the human species covers a process of evolution in which the organs that produce and identify sounds and the brain which makes sense of those sounds develop over a long period of time which includes the birth of Mankind. No subsequent phenomena, neither *El Cantar de Mío Cid* or *El Quijote*, nor quantum theory, can compare in importance to the first time that the most basic things were given a name. However for obvious reasons I am not going to dwell here on the evolution of language in its primeval and fundamental sense. Rather I will deal with its secondary and accidental but relatively more important meaning for those of us who were born into a society whose tradition is more literary than secular.

Ethnologists such as the distinguished A. S. Diamond believe that the history of language, of all languages, follows a pattern in which at the very beginning sentences are simple and primitive but go on to become more complicated in terms of syntactic and semantic variations. By extrapolating from this historically verifiable trend,

it can be deduced that this increasing complexity evolves from the initial stage where communication relies mainly on the verb, building up to the present situation where it is nouns, adjectives and adverbs that give flavour and depth to the sentence. If this theory is correct and if we apply a little imagination, we might conclude that the first word to be used was a verb in its most immediate and urgent tense, namely the imperative.

And indeed the imperative still retains considerable importance in communication. It is a difficult tense to use. It must be handled with care since it requires a highly detailed knowledge of the rules of the game which are not always straightforward. A badly-placed imperative can bring about the exact opposite of the desired objective. John Langshaw Austin's famous triple distinction (locutionary, illocutionary and perlocutionary language) is an erudite demonstration of the thesis that perlocutionary language tends to provoke specific behaviour on the part of the interlocutor. It is useless to issue an order if the person to whom it is addressed dissembles and ends up doing whatever he likes.

Thus from *zoón politikón* to *res cogitans* sufficient distinctions have been drawn between the beast that grazes and the man that sings albeit not always in well-measured tones.

In Plato's *Dialogue* which bears his name, Cratilus hides Heraclitus among the folds of his tunic. The philosopher Democritus through his interlocutor Hermogenes speaks of the concepts of fullness and emptiness. The same can be said of Protagoras the anti-geometrician who irreverently maintained that "Man is the measure of all things": what they are and how they are, what they are not and how they are not.

Cratilus was concerned with language–what it is and what it is not–and developed those ideas at some length in his discourse with Hermogenes. Cratilus believes that what things are called is naturally related to what they are. Things are born or created or are discovered or invented. From their very beginning they contain essentially the exact term which identifies them and distinguishes them from everything else. He seems to be trying to tell us that this distinction is unique and comes from the same ovum as the thing itself. Except in the reasoned world of the etymologist, a dog has always been a dog in all the ancient languages and love has been love since first it was felt. The boundaries of paradox in the thoughts of Cratilus in contrast to Heraclitus' hypotheses is hidden in the dovetailed indivisibility or unity of opposites, their harmony (day and night), the constant movement and reaffirmation of their substance. The same is true of words as things in their own right (there is no dog without the cat and no love without hate).

Conversely Hermogenes thought that words were mere conventions established by humans for the reasonable purpose of understanding one another. Man is confronted with things or they are presented to him. Faced with something new, man gives it a name. The significance of things is not the spring in the woods but the well dug by man. The parabolic frontier of the senses, and of expression, as expounded by Hermogenes and concealed by Democritus and at times by Protagoras, comes up time and again: is man who measures and designates all things generic or individual? Is the measurement of those things a mere epistemological concept? Are things only physical matter or are they also feelings and concepts? By reducing being to illusion, Hermogenes kills off truth in the cradle; the contradictory conclusion that the only possible propositions are those which man formulates by himself and to himself, renders real what is true and what is not true. You will recall that according to Victor Henry's famous aporia man can give a name to things but he cannot take them over; he can change the language but he cannot change it any way he wishes. Referring in perhaps overcautious terms to the exactitude of names Plato seems to sympathise obliquely with Cratilus' position: things are called what they have to be called (an organic and valid theory that is on the verge of being acknowledged in pure reason as a principle) and not what man decides they should be called according to which way the wind is blowing at any given time (this being a changing or even fluctuating corollary, dependent on the changing suppositions present at the same time as, or prior to, a given thing).

This attitude, originally romantic and consequently demagogical, was the starting point for the Latin poets, headed by Horace. It gave rise to all the ills which have afflicted us in this field since that time and which we have not been able to remedy. *Ars Poetica*, verses 70 to 72, sings of the prevalence of usage in the evolution of language (not always a welcome development):

Multa renascentur quae iam cedidere cadentque
quae nunc sunt in honore vocabula, si volet usus,
quem penes arbitrium est et ius et norma loquendi.

This time-bomb, however pleasing in its charity, had several complex consequences leading finally to the supposition that language is made by the people–and inevitably by the people alone–and that it is futile to try and subject language to the precise and reasonable rules of logic. This dangerous assertion by Horace that usage determines what is right and acceptable in language created a rubbish-dump clogged with overgrown efforts in which the shortcut became the highway along which man progressed bearing the banner of language blowing freely and trembling in the breeze, obstinately continuing to confuse victory with the subservience inherent in its very image.

While Horace was partly right (and we should not deny that), he was also wrong in a number of ways and we should not try to hide that either. But we should also acknowledge the contribution of Cratilus and Hermogenes by refining their principles. Cratilus' position falls within what is referred to as natural or ordinary or spoken language, which is the product of the constant use of an historical and psychological path, while Hermogenes' proposition fits into what we understand as artificial or specialized language or jargon, deriving from a more or less formal arrangement or from some formal method based on logic but with no historical or psychological tradition behind it–at least at the time it is conceived. The first Wittgenstein, the author of the *Tractacus* is a celebrated modern exponent of Hermogenes' proposition. Thus in that sense it would not be illogical to talk of Cratilian or natural or human language and of Hermogenian or artificial or parahuman language. Like Horace my point of reference is obviously the former, the language of life and literature, without technical or defensive obstacles. Max Scheler–and indeed phenomenologists generally–is also referring to what I will now call Cratilian language when he talks about language as an indication or announcement or expression, as is Karl Bühler when he classifies the three functions of language as symptom, signal and symbol.

It goes without saying that Hermogenian language naturally accommodates its original artificiality. On the other hand Cratilian language does not adapt to extraneous territory where there are often hidden pitfalls alien to its essential transparency.

It is dangerous to admit that in the final analysis natural, Cratilian language is the offspring of a magical marriage between the people and chance. Because people do not create language they determine its development. We can say, albeit with considerable reservations that people solve to a certain extent the puzzle of language by giving names to things; but they also adulterate and hybridize it. If people were not subject to those hidden pitfalls referred to earlier this issue would be much more urgent and linear. What is not put forward but which nevertheless lies hidden within the true heart of the matter is one and the same and already determined; and neither I nor anyone else can change that.

The Cratilian language, the structure or system described by Ferdinand de Saussure as "langue" is the common language of a community (or rather more *in* than *of* a community) is formed and authenticated by writers and regulated and generally oriented by Academies. These three estates—the community, the writer and the Academies—do not always fulfil their respective duties. Very often they invade and interfere in other areas. It would appear that neither the Academies, nor the writers nor the community are happy with their own roles. While not competent to do so they prefer to define the role of others which, perhaps even rightly in principle, will always be unclear and ill-defined and, even worse, end up dissipating and obscuring the subject of their attention, namely the language and the verb which should be essentially transparent. The algebraic and mere instrument with no value other than its usefulness, in the final analysis as in Unamuno's *Love and Pedagogy*.

The final determining factor, the State, which is neither the community, nor the writers nor the Academies, conditions and constrains everything, intervenes in a thousand different ways (administrative jargon, government pronouncements, television, etc) compounding, more by bad example than by inhibition, disorder and disarray, chaos and confusion.

But no-one says anything about popular, literary, academic, state and other excesses. Language evolves not in its own way which in principle would be appropriate, but is rather pushed around by the opposing forces surrounding it.

The community to whom Horace's lines are recited eventually believe that this is how a language should evolve and tries to incorporate phrases, styles and expressions that are neither intuitive nor the product of their subconscious—which at least might produce something valid or plausible—but rather deliberately and consciously invented, or even worse, imported (at the wrong time and against sound common sense).

Writers, obviously with some exceptions, follow the often defective usage in their own environment and introduce and sanction expressions that are cumbersome and, worse still, divorced from the essential spirit of the language.

The Academies' problems stem from the basis on which they operate: as institutions they tend to be conservative and afraid of being challenged.

The erosion of the Cratilian language by Hermogenean influences is becoming more pronounced and there is a danger that it will desiccate that living language and render the natural language artificial. As I have already said, this threat is caused by invented, gratuitously incorporated or inopportunely resurrected or revitalised language.

There seems to be some political reason behind the impetus that now leads as it has in the past gaily to abandon the principles of a language in the face of a blunt attack by those besieging it. In my view the risks outweigh the possible benefits—which are somewhat Utopian—that might accrue at some future unspecified date. While I am far from being a purist, I would like to call on writers in the first instance and then on Academies and on States to a lesser degree to put an end to the chaos. There is undoubtedly a continuity in language that supersedes any classifications we wish to establish but that does not constitute grounds for tearing down the natural frontiers of language. If we allow that we would be admitting to a defeat that has not yet taken place.

Let us rally our genius in defence of language, all languages, and let us never forget that confusing procedure with the rule of Law, just as observing the letter rather than the spirit of the Law, always leads to injustice which is both the source and consequence of disorder.

Thought is intrinsically linked to language. Moreover, freedom is also probably linked to certain linguistic and conceptual patterns. Together they provide the broad framework for all human endeavour: those that seek to explore and expand human frontiers; also those that seek to undermine the status of man. Thought and liberty are found in the minds of heroes and villains alike.

But this generalisation obscures the need for greater precision if we are to arrive at an understanding of the real meaning of what it is to think and to be free. Insofar as we are able to identify the phenomena that take place in the mind, thinking for man means thinking about being free. There has been much argument regarding the extent to which this freedom or liberty is something concrete or whether it is just another slick phenomenon produced by the human mind. But such argument is probably futile. A wise Spanish philosopher has pointed out that the illusion and the real image of freedom are one and the same thing. If man is not free, if he is bound by chains that psychology, biology, sociology and history seek to identify, as a human being he also carries within himself the idea, which may be an illusion but which is absolutely universal, that he is free. And if we wish to be free we will organise our world in much the same way as we would if we were free.

The architectural design on which we have tried to build successfully or otherwise the complex framework of our societies, contains the basic principle of human freedom and it is in the light of that principle that we value, exalt, denigrate, castigate and suffer: the aura of liberty is the spirit enshrined in our moral codes, political principles and legal systems.

We know that we think. We think because we are free. The link between thought and freedom is like a fish biting its own tail or rather a fish that wants to get hold of its own tail; because being free is both a direct consequence of and an essential condition for thought. Through thought man can detach himself as much as he wants from the laws of nature: he can accept and submit to those laws, for example like the chemist who has gone beyond the boundaries of phlogiston theory will base his success and prestige on such acceptance and submission. In thought however, the realms of the absurd lie side by side with the empire of logic because man does not think only in terms of the real and the possible. The mind can shatter its own machinations into a thousand pieces and rearrange them into a totally different image.

Thus one can have as many rational interpretations of the world based on empirical principles as the thinker wishes primarily on the basis of the promise of freedom. Free thinking in this narrow sense is that antithesis of the empirical world and finds expression in the fable. Thus the capacity to create fables would appear to be the third element in the human status—the others being thought and freedom—and this capacity can turn things round in such a way that things which before they became the subject of a fable were not even untruths became truths.

Through the process of thought man begins to discover hidden truth in the world but he can aim to create his own different world in whatever terms he wishes through the medium of the fable. Thus truth, thought, freedom and fable are interlinked in a complicated and on occasion suspect relationship. It is like a dark passageway with several side-turnings going off in the wrong direction: a labyrinth with no way out. But the element of risk has always been the best justification for embarking on an adventure.

The fable and scientific truth are not forms of thought. They are rather heterogeneous entities which cannot possibly be compared with one another since they are subject to completely different rules and techniques. Consequently it is not appropriate to brandish the standard of literature in the struggle to free men's minds. Literature should rather be regarded as a counterweight to the newfound slavish submission to science. I would go further and say that I believe that a prudent and careful distinction must be drawn between those forms of science and literature which join together to confine man within rigid limits which deny all ideas of freedom and that we must be daring and offset those forms by other scientific and literary experiences aimed at engendering hope. By unreservedly trusting in the superiority of human freedom and dignity rather than suspect truths which dissolve in a sea of presumption, would be an indication that we have progressed. However in itself it is not enough. If we have learned anything it is that science is incapable of justifying aspirations to freedom and that on the contrary it rests on crutches that tilt it in exactly the opposite direction. Science should be based solely on the most profound exigencies of human freedom and will. That is the only means of enabling science to break away from utilitarianism which cannot withstand the pitfalls of quantity and measurement. This leads us to the need to recognise that literature and science although heterogeneous cannot remain isolated in a prophylactic endeavour to define areas of influence and this for two reasons, namely the status of language (that basic instrument of thought) as well as the need to define the limits of and distinguish between that which is commendable and laudable and that which must be denounced by all committed individuals.

I believe that literature as an instrument for creating fables is founded on two basic pillars which provide it with strength to ensure that literary endeavour is worthwhile. Firstly aesthetics, which impose a requirement on an essay, poem, drama or comedy to maintain certain minimum standards which distinguish it from the sub-literary world in which creativity cannot keep pace with the readers' emotions. From socialist reality to the innumerable inconstancies of would-be experimentalists wherever aesthetic talent is lacking the resulting sub-literature becomes a monotonous litany of words incapable of creating a genuine worthwhile fable.

The second pillar on which literary endeavour rests is ethics which complement aesthetics which has a lot to do with all that has been said up to now regarding thought and freedom. Of course ethics and aesthetics are in no way synonymous nor do they have the same value. Literature can balance itself precariously on aesthetics alone–art for art's sake–and it could be that aesthetics in the long run may be a more comprehensive concept than ethical commitment. We can still appreciate Homer's verses and medieval epic canticles although we may have forgotten or at least no longer automatically link them with ethical behaviour in ancient Greek cities or in feudal Europe. However art for art's sake is by definition an extremely difficult undertaking and one which always runs the risk of being used for purposes which distort its real meaning.

I do believe that ethical principle is the element which makes a work of literature worthy of playing the noble role of creating a fable. But I must explain clearly what I mean because the literary fable as a means of expressing the links between man's capacity to think and the perhaps Utopian idea of being free cannot be based on just any kind of ethical commitment. My understanding is that a work of literature can only be subject to the ethical commitment of the person, the author, to his own idea of freedom. Of course no-one, not even the cleverest and most balanced literary author can ever (or rather cannot always) overcome his humanity; anyone can have a blind spot and freedom is a sufficiently ambiguous concept and many blinding errors can be committed in its name. Nor can an aesthetic sense be acquired from a textbook. Thus, the literary fable must be based on both a sense of ethics and a commitment to aesthetics. That is the only way it can acquire a significance that will transcend ephemeral fashions or confused appreciation that can quickly change. The history of man is changing and tortuous. Consequently it is difficult to anticipate ethical or aesthetic sensibilities. There are writers who are so tuned in to the feeling of

their time that they become magnificent exponents of the prevailing collective trend and whose work is a condition reflex. Others take on the thankless and not sufficiently applauded task of carrying freedom and human creativity further along the road, even if in the end that too may lead nowhere.

This is the only way in which literature can fulfil its role of closely identifying its commitment to the human status and if we wish to be absolutely precise in this thesis, the only endeavour that can unreservedly be called true literature. However, human society cannot be linked to geniuses, saints and heroes alone.

In this task of seeking out freedom, the fable has the benefit of the well-known characteristic of the intrinsic malleability of the literary story. The fable does not need to subject itself to anything that might restrict its scope, novelty and element of surprise. Thus unlike any other form of thought it can wave the Utopian banner high. Perhaps that is why the most avid authors of treatises of political philosophy have opted to use the literary story to convey Utopian propositions that would not have found ready acceptance outside the realms of fiction at the time they were written. There are no limits to the Utopianism that the fable can express since by its very nature the fable itself is based on Utopianism.

However the advantages of literary expression are not confined to the ease with which it can convey Utopian propositions. The intrinsic plasticity of the story, the malleability of the situations, personalities and events it creates provide a superb foundry from which one can without undue risk, set up an entire factory, or to put it another way, a laboratory in which men conduct experiments on human behaviour in optimum conditions. But the fable does not restrict itself to expressing the Utopian. It can also analyse carefully what it means and what its consequences are in the myriad different alternative situations ranging from learned prediction to the absurd that creative thought can produce.

The role of literature as an experimental laboratory has been often highlighted in science fiction: speculation about the future that has subsequently been realised. Critics have heaped praise on novelists who have a talent for predicting in their fables the basic coordinates which subsequently have been substantiated. But the real usefulness of the fable as a test-tube lies not in its anecdotal capacity for accurately predicting something technical but as a means of conveying in a timely, direct or negative fashion all possible facets of a world that may be possible now or in the future. It is the search for human commitment, for tragic experiences, that can shed light on the ambiguity of blindly choosing options in the face of the demands placed upon us by our world, now or in the future, that turns the fresco of literature into an experimental laboratory. The value of literature as means of carrying out experiments on behaviour has little to do with prediction since human behaviour only has a past, present and future in a very specific, narrow sense. There are, however, basic aspects of our nature which have an impressive permanency about them and which cause us to be deeply moved by an emotional story from a completely different age to the one we live in. It is this "universal man" that is the most prized figure in literary fable, an experimental workshop in which there are no frontiers and no ages. It is the Quixotes, the Othellos, the Don Juans that illustrate to us that the fable is a game of chess played over and over again, a thousand times with whatever pieces destiny throws up at any given time.

In absolute terms it might appear that this detracts from the so-called freedom I am advocating and indeed that would be the case if one did not take account of the role of that imperfect, voluble and confused personality, the author, the man. The magic of Shylock would never have emerged without the genius of the Bard, whose unreliable memory was of course far more inconsistent than that of the characters to whom he gave life and to whom in the end he denied death. And what of those anonymous scholars and jugglers whom we remember only for the result produced by their talents. There is undoubtedly something that must be remembered over whatever sociology or history tries to impose upon us and that is that thus far and insofar we can conceive of the future of mankind, works of literature are very much subject to the needs of the author; that is to say to a single source of those ethical and aesthetic insights I referred to earlier, an author who acts as a filter for the current which undoubtedly emanates from the whole surrounding society. It is perhaps this link between Man and Society that best expresses the very paradox of being a human being proud of his individuality, and at the same time tied to the community that surrounds him and from which he cannot disengage himself without risking madness. There is a moral here: the limitations of literature are precisely those of human nature and they show us that there is another status, identical in other ways, which is that of gods and demons. Our mind can imagine demiurges and the ease with which human beings invent religions clearly demonstrates that this is so. Our capacity to create fables provides a useful literary means of illustrating those demiurges, as indeed we have done constantly since Homer wrote his verses. But even that cannot lead us to mistake our nature or put out once and for all the tenuous flame of freedom that burns in the innermost being of the slave who can be forced to obey but not to love, to suffer and die but not to change his most profound thoughts.

When the proud, blind rationalist renewed in enlightened minds the biblical temptation, the last maxim of which promised "You will be as gods" he did not take account of the fact that Man had already gone much further down that road. The misery and the pride that for centuries had marked Man's efforts to be like the gods, had already taught Man a better reason; that through effort and imagination they could become Men. For my part, I must say proudly that in this latter task, much of which still remains to be accomplished, the literary fable has always, and in all circumstances proved to be a decisive tool: a weapon that can cleave the way forward in the endless march to freedom.

The Year in Fiction

George Garrett
University of Virginia

To the natural impulse toward measurable summary of the year gone by, measuring by whatever numbers are available, the retroactive overview of 1989 acquired an added significance as the end and summation of a decade. Although, for a variety of reasons, the final numbers will not be available for months, *Publishers Weekly* (5 January 1990) presented a great deal of objective information and, from writers and literary folk, subjective reaction to the decade past. Money, particularly in the form of extravagant advances (soon to be curtailed by a new "austerity," we are advised), was one story. James Clavell's *Whirlwind* (Morrow) brought the author $5 million; Stephen King garnered $10 million from New American Library for paperback rights to two new novels; Mary Higgins Clark was advanced more than $10 million for a five-book contract; Tom Wolfe received $1,522,500 from Bantam for paperback rights to *Bonfire of the Vanities* (1988). *Bonfire* also appears on the *PW* list, "The Top 25 of the 80's: Fiction Bestsellers"–aside from Salman Rushdie's *The Satanic Verses* (Viking), the only other "literary" novel on the list resonant with the names of popular favorites: Tom Clancy, Stephen King, Jean M. Auel, Danielle Steele, Garrison Keillor, Sidney Sheldon, James A. Michener, Robert Ludlum.

Perhaps surprising, the two top books of the decade, in terms of sales, were both brought out in 1989–Tom Clancy's *Clear and Present Danger* (Putnam) and Stephen King's playful mixture of self-reflexive metafiction and horror story, *The Dark Half* (Viking). King led the pack with seven books on the list. Clancy was close behind with four of the decade's best-sellers, all the more impressive in view of the fact that his first fiction of any kind, *The Hunt for Red October* (Naval Institute) was published in 1984. In the short term, serious literary fiction fared better on lists limited to 1989 alone. For example, the accounting in *PW*

George Garrett received the 1989 T. S. Eliot Award for Creative Writing, which is sponsored by the Ingersoll Foundation.

Dust jacket for Rushdie's controversial novel. The Ayatollah Khomeini considered the book blasphemous and issued a fatwa, *or death sentence, against the author.*

of the "Longest-Running Hardcover Bestsellers for 1989" showed that *The Satanic Verses*, Alice Walker's *The Temple of My Familiar* (Harcourt Brace Jovanovich), *A Prayer for Owen Meany* (Morrow), by John Irving, and Anne Tyler's 1988 novel *Breathing Lessons* (Knopf) held their own among the most successful popular fiction. Perhaps most surprising of all is the fact that a first novel, of serious literary intent, Amy Tan's *The Joy Luck Club* (Putnam), led all the other books in this category in 1989, with thirty-five continuous weeks on the list.

Summary accountings of seasons and years gone by seem inevitably to end up as lists, the best and worst of this and that. There are many good and worthwhile books in all that follows. But this time I should like to begin this whole piece with a brief listing of my own special favorites from among the works of fiction published in 1989. The list is, of course, arbitrary and in large part whimsical, in the serious sense that tomorrow or the next day it might well radically change as my own moods and sense of things will change. Critics have moods, too. But if nothing else, my choices will help the reader to understand the sources of my critical judgment, the assumptions and the taste my critical notions are based on. The range of the critic's interests and enthusiasms reveals his limitations even as it asserts his cherished convictions.

Here, then, are my particular and exemplary favorites from the fiction of 1989. Some of these have been already, even widely, noticed and honored. Others are not so well known or, for one reason or another, have been mostly ignored. No matter. On this list, anyway, all are equal and equally favored, though usually for a variety of reasons.

A Court For Owls (Pineapple), by Richard Adicks, tells the story, as carefully researched as it is richly and justly imagined, of Lewis Powell, aka Lewis Paine, who was in fact involved as a conspirator in the assassination of Lincoln. (It was Powell/Paine who wounded Secretary of State Seward.) Young and handsome, brave as can be, and, at the same time a burned-out combat veteran and a zealot, Paine was hanged. Died honorably enough. When the hangman told him, "I want you to die quick, Paine," Paine's last words were: "You know best, Captain." Adicks is a sixth-generation Floridian, and his evocation of Confederate Florida, Paine's home place, is remarkable.

Author of three previous novels and a highly praised collection of short stories, twice honored already as a finalist for the PEN/ Faulkner Award, Richard Bausch has produced his finest work so far with *Mr. Field's Daughter* (Linden/Simon & Schuster). Telling the story of a single parent, James Field, a Duluth banker, his grown daughter Annie, and her daughter Linda, together with a group of closely involved and fully developed characters, adroitly moving from one point of view to another, Bausch presents a credible story of family love that manages to endure its own flaws and, finally, to pass through the crucible of violence and come to something more, a state Annie describes as "free of grief for us all, and still, in the middle of that hunt,

praying for what was mine in the world–asking that I might be blessed enough to appreciate it. . . . " Powerful and moving work.

Soldier's Joy (Ticknor & Fields) is Madison Smartt Bell's fifth novel and the first one set in his native South. The time is the early 1970s and the place is Tennessee. *Soldier's Joy* is both larger and longer than Bell's earlier books, rich with a detailed poetry of place and crowded with interesting characters. At the center of the story are two Vietnam veterans–Laidlaw (white) and Redmon (black), friends since childhood. These two are forced by circumstances to put their combat skills to work one more time, in the woods of Tennessee, in an apocalyptic sequence about as violent as any to be found in recent fact or fiction.

Since *Crazy in Berlin* (1958), Thomas Berger has published sixteen novels without repeating himself, while, at the same time, establishing his own voice as for all practical purposes inimitable. In *Changing the Past* (Little, Brown), a middle-aged copy editor, Walter Hunsicker, is allowed to do just that–to change his past and his identity as it pleases him. And so he becomes in swift succession Jack Kellog, rich slumlord; Jackie Kellog, stand-up comic; John Kellog, author; and Dr. Jonathan Kellog, radio call-in host. Needless to say, Hunsicker learns a thing or two, enough to send him back to his own, old life and his own wife, to whom he is able to lie with new sincerity–"I couldn't even imagine another life."

Rough and ready Charles Bukowski, who has been called "the ring around the collar of American literature," can always surprise and does so with his first-rate, very funny, and very authentic novel *Hollywood* (Black Sparrow). It is, in fact and fiction, an almost entirely undisguised account of the making of the movie *Barfly* (1987). Only the names have been changed and these only slightly. It is about as good and complete a record of how a movie is made, with far more emphasis on the intricacies of the Deal than on the art and craft of cinema and Production, as anything in the genre of the Hollywood novel. And it is much funnier than most. Appropriately, it builds toward a kind-of happy ending where Bukowski, called here Henry Chinaski, responds to a reporter's question about "the way the movie turned out," immediately following the world premiere: "It's a better than average movie. Long after this year's Academy Award movies are forgotten, *The Dance of Jim Beam* [fictional title for *Barfly*] will be showing up now and then in the Art houses. And it will pop up on T.V. from time to time, if the world lasts." That's Bukowski, all aglow with optimism.

Winner of the National Book Award, John Casey's second novel, *Spartina* (Knopf), tells the story of forty-year-old fisherman Dick Pierce of Galilee, Rhode Island, his life and loves and times, and the passion he has for a fifty-foot fishing boat he is building in his backyard, the *Spartina*, named for the tough grass of the salt marsh. This story demonstrates a superbly realized sense of place, a keen eye for details and for the rhythms and textures of dailiness. There are solid characters and entirely credible (if sometimes surprising) events. *Spartina* also has what must be the best storm-at-sea sequence since the work of H. M. Tomlinson and Joseph Conrad.

Brighten the Corner Where You Are (St. Martin's) is Fred Chappell's sixth novel and, including his poetry and *The Fred Chappell Reader* (1987), his twentieth book in an important literary career. (Among other things, Chappell won the Bollingen Prize in Poetry in 1981 for *Midquest*.) This novel follows one May day in the life of Joe Robert Kirkman, science teacher and a good man and true, who begins his day before dawn up a tree after the mythical devil-possum, and ends it cheerfully dreaming about the public hanging of Charles Darwin. In between, in a slender and resonant book, is every kind of story, from "magic realism" to something much like folk tunes for a steel-string guitar. This is a warm and loving novel without one false note or clumsy move.

The eleventh novel by North Carolina's brilliant and gifted John Ehle, *The Widow's Trial* (Harper & Row), tells by adroit multiple narration the story of love and death involving a young woman, Winnette Plover, and her dangerous and glamorous husband, Lloyd. Ehle brings the old and new South into direct confrontation and somehow manages to give them both their due. It is Blue Chatham, a fine country musician among other things, who has the last word on Lloyd in those terms: "He wanted his own world, mind, and there was a time up here a man could have that, could live in his cove, in his cabin, be his own man, have his own family to himself, as he saw fit. Now it's all invaded with schools and governments, trucks and planes, radio and TV and movies and magazines, frowns and opinions and criticisms, highways and airports. . . ."

The year 1989 has been a fine one for first-rate suspense fiction, with new work by Parker and Higgins, Hillerman and Leonard, and others catching the eye and holding attention. Worthy of inclusion with the best of them is James W. Hall's *Tropical Freeze* (Norton), which brings back into action Thorn, the Key Largo fisherman who starred in *Under Cover of Daylight* (1988). Hall is already a master of the moves and counters of the suspense thriller; and he here puts Thorn through a well-mapped course of guns and mayhem, sex and violence, disappearances, murders, and double-dealing. But, above and beyond that, Hall recreates the ambiance of the Florida Keys with an authenticity and authority second to none. He has his man and his place, and chances are we shall be seeing more of both of them.

One of the trends of the times and, especially, of this year past has been the exploitation of the autobiographical in fiction and, perhaps more important, the exploitation of the various and sundry ways to mingle facts and fiction to present a valid self-portrait. If there is a trend in sight, or just behind the bushes, Barry Hannah will sure enough be aware of it and will be involved in it, too, albeit always with a wink and a strong nudge of irony. Hannah likes the latest things, and his latest book, *Boomerang* (Houghton Mifflin/Seymour Lawrence), mixes the facts of his life with some pure and simple fictions and fabrications as smoothly as if it were done in a blender. Somewhere in there is a portrait of the artist as a man pushing fifty. And thinking thoughts like: "I'm looking straight ahead to pussy and shelter and thirteen dollars. With that and a pencil, I can rule the world." For 150 pages he does precisely that. Which is just right. As long as any kind of sleight of hand should last. After that, thundering applause.

William Harrison has already written three fine African novels, each different from the others in both ends and means; and so it comes as no surprise that *Three Hunters* (Random House) should have a remarkably accurate and sophisticated sense of place. More surprising, perhaps, is how successfully Harrison grafts onto the solid sense of place a genuine adventure story involving three celebrated safari guides, father and sons, from the old East Africa safari days, who came together for one last wonderfully dangerous hunt—to track down a marauding leopard. Traditional, clean-cut, popular fiction is given depth and dimension by the integrity of place, the living picture of old and new Africa. This one is ready for translation into film.

Another kind of novel, a complex, neatly plotted suspense story, that could *not* be translated into film except at the risk of losing its perfectly realized ambiance and the inimitable glory of its vernacular language, is *Trust* (Holt), the latest in the chronicles of crime and punishment by the prolific George V. Higgins. This one centers chiefly on Earl Beale, an ex-con (he threw basketball games, playing at St. Vincent's), a super and conscienceless car salesman, and a scam involving an expensive automobile. ("I got a small problem. It's a car, is what it is. Mercedes fucking Benz. It's got to disappear. Can you make it do that?") Set in late 1967 and early 1968, with the Vietnam War flashing on the story's horizon like distant heat lightning, this one is a parade of deadly sins as practiced by a richly various cast of characters, high life and low life, different, really, only in their accents and habits of style. Nobody writes about these people and places (northeast corridor along I-95, New York to Boston to upper New England) with more sophisticated art and craft than Higgins. He has long since jumped the fences of genre writing to join the mainstream. Proof of this was his induction on 10 November 1988 as a Literary Lion by the New York Public Library.

After a forty-year delay since its first publication in Dutch in 1949, during twenty years of which the manuscript of the English translation was somehow lost and forgotten, Hella S. Haasse's huge novel of medieval France in the Hundred Years War, *In a Dark Wood Wandering* (Academy) arrived, revealing itself to be a rich and decorative tapestry of stories of all kinds, from magic fables to earthy fabliaux and including among its cast of characters such great historical figures as Henry V, Joan of Arc, and François Villon. The sprawl and slope of time and event are large, but the author's attention to vital details is meticulous.

Kaylie Jones's second novel, *Quite the Other Way* (Doubleday), did not receive the critical attention it deserved, both on its own merits and on account of its subject, which has become increasingly relevant throughout the year. Jones tells the story of twenty-five-year-old Clinton Gray, who goes to study for a semester at the Gorky Institute in Moscow. There are friendships and love affairs, cultural clashes and a steady, cumulative awareness of the complex truths of life and these times in the Soviet Union. Like her late father, novelist James Jones, the author does her best work with a plain style and a straightforward story line, trusting that the substance of things, told with honesty, will speak for itself. Her trust is

well founded. What we have been given is a fascinating picture of a place and a people just on the eve of glasnost and all that has followed.

Last Things (L.S.U. Press) is the distinguished novelist Madison Jones's eighth novel and is joined by a new trade paperback edition of his 1971 novel called "a masterpiece of fictional art" by Allen Tate–*A Cry of Absence*. It is good to have the latter book in print. Better to have the former, *Last Things,* arrive on the scene. It is the story of the rise and fall (or vice versa) of Wendell Corbin, college-educated country boy from Bliss County. An affair soon leads him into the drug business and its attendant nightmares of violence. An itinerant country revivalist is able to save what is left of his body and soul. Jones is a master craftsman, and so it is all fully realized and fully credible. It is a pleasure to see younger writers such as Allen Wier and Fred Chappell speak out in celebratory support of this novel. Youngest of them all, Madison Smartt Bell, calling *Last Things* "at once a profound and an accessible book," says: "His strong powers of language are undiminished, and come together here with a gift for satire seldom previously deployed." There are precious few second chances in American literary life. Madison Jones seems to be enjoying one now, all the sweeter because he has earned it.

Ward Just's latest novel continues his authoritative exploration of the way things really work in our society and how things came to be that way. *Jack Gance* (Houghton Mifflin) gives us forty years, the first-person story of Chicagoan Jackeson Gance, senator from Illinois. Chicago and Washington, among other places, are superbly depicted. But even more elegantly evoked are the corridors of power, the ways that the modern American political machine works and the costs it exacts from all its servants, even essentially good men like Gance. Gance arrives at a kind of sad wisdom, in one sense a compromised man, but still, thereby, a player in the game and able to say to a young and innocent audience of home-state students–"In the Senate as in life you yielded conceding ground; and your opponent did likewise and from the struggle came something durable and true-speaking." Just's novel is durable and truth-speaking.

Author of several odd cult classics (including *E. T.* [1982] and *Doctor Rat* [1976]), William Kotzwinkle has a wild swing, and he hits and misses. His latest, *The Midnight Examiner* (Houghton Mifflin/Seymour Lawrence), takes on the already-fantastic worlds of tabloid publishing and the continued decay and decline of New York City with a crew of crazies for characters adding slapstick to a surreal situation. Maybe not everyone's cup of tea, but for me one of the funniest stories I have read in a very long time.

With *Strickland* (St. Martin's), his sixth novel, Hilary Masters completes his Harlem Valley Trio, including *Clemons* (1985) and *Cooper* (1987). *Strickland* begins with the sounds of gunfire (hunters) in upstate New York and ends with a moving scene at the Wall, the Vietnam memorial in Washington. Carrol Strickland, a celebrity radio and TV announcer, loses much, indeed almost everything he desires, but gains more through his love of and for Robin Endicott, a girl half his age. This is a story about changing and growing up, closely shadowing the recent history of the nation. It is successfully ambitious, elegantly controlled, and strongly evocative.

Some of the best short stories of the past decade have been the work of Kent Nelson. He has published one collection of stories, *The Tennis Player* (1977), and a novel, *Cold Wind River* (1981). Now with his second novel, *All Around Me Peaceful* (Delta), Nelson writes of his native Colorado, here and now and in the hardscrabble days of the past. The story is mainly concerned with a group of young people who have ended up living in Gold Hill; chief among them Neil Shanks, Becky Carlsson, and her husband–Finn. Becky disappears, and the story shifts into the suspense mode, plot playing off against the size and weight of the landscape and wounds of the careless past. Nelson is an extremely gifted writer who moves his narrative forward by well-constructed scenes. Here and elsewhere he has done some of the best writing about the contemporary American West.

May Sarton is the author of many books, poetry, and journals and now, with *The Education of Harriet Hatfield* (Norton), of some nineteen novels. This one uses the story of a woman just past sixty who "comes out," almost inadvertently, as a lesbian and is then persecuted for her preference by one side and taken into a minority community by the other, to make a larger point, really, something beyond the limits of sexual preference. What clearly interests Sarton most here is the discovery that human beings have the capacity for change, to change for the better even in old age. At the beginning Harriet Hatfield, still interested if not entirely innocent, tells us: "How rarely is it possible for anyone to begin a new life at sixty!"

Near the end of her account she is more alive in the world than ever and able to tell a friend: "I am carried along on a kind of excitement. I never know what is going to happen next."

Mary Lee Settle's *Charley Bland* (Farrar, Straus & Giroux) adds distinction to her reputation and new dimensions to an important body of work. Not directly a part of her Beulah Quintet, the new novel nevertheless includes the same West Virginia setting and some of the same characters, handsome Charley Bland among them, who appear in the quintet and other related novels, especially *The Clam Shell* (1971). The narrator of this slender and evocative novel of obsessive and profane love, who shares many details of the "real" life of the author, frees herself from her obsession and her past, having learned that "the profane love I bore as my burden has left its residue like a pebble in my hand, shaped by an unknown sea. It has shown me what it is to love and has become in time a hope without illusion, the recognition of a light glimpsed through the glass, darkly, which is all we were ever promised."

Writing under his own name as well as several pen names, poet and translator David Slavitt has been, for more than twenty years, one of the most productive novelists in America. His newest, *Lives of the Saints* (Atheneum), may be his best work so far. In the loose guise of a kind of thriller set in southern Florida, it follows the story of its protagonist and narrator (unnamed) who is investigating the story of a mass murderer for a tabloid. He sees these checkout tabloids with their lurid headlines and improbable tales as the contemporary equivalent of hagiography. Before he is finished he, himself, enjoys a kind of miracle that results in the healing of deep and hidden wounds, the gift of love and, at last, some sense of purpose: "Work and love will keep us going. . . ." The writing and the concept are brilliant and accessible.

Through its Noonday imprint Farrar, Straus & Giroux has brought out a new and "definitive" English edition of *August 1914* by Aleksandr Solzhenitsyn, the first volume, or "knot," in the epic *The Red Wheel*, which Solzhenitsyn has been working on for years. The new version is revised and expanded and includes more than three hundred pages dealing with the 1911 murder of the tsarist prime minister Pyotr Stolypin by anarchist Dmitri Bogrov. *August 1914* is now twice the size of the original 1972 English translation. The American Left has never been enthusiastically supportive of Solzhenitsyn, and it appears that many of our book reviews paid only perfunctory attention at most to the appearance of the new edition, downplaying its literary significance. (An exception was *Time* magazine of 24 July 1989, which published "Russia's Prophet In Exile," pages 56-60.) With the sudden changes in all the Eastern Bloc, Solzhenitsyn and his works are again much discussed in the Soviet Union and are likely, in the future, to be even more influential.

Life With a Star (Farrar, Straus & Giroux), by the Czech writer Jiri Weil, is a masterpiece. It is told in the form of a first-person monologue by one Josef Roubicek, a former bank clerk struggling to survive during the occupation of his city by aliens, known here only as "they" and "them." Although in many details the conditions and events of the story closely approximate the Nazi occupation of Prague, Weil makes it all somehow more sinister by being (perhaps in the tradition of Kafka) unspecific. It is Prague, to be sure, but could be anywhere. Style helps to create a maximum impact by its constant conflict with substance and terrible meaning. All things are told, from beginning to end (as Philip Roth writes in a preface), "with the matter-of-factness of the journalist and the disarming simplicity of the family anecdotalist." It is a story unbearably true and strongly laced with numbing irony, as in this exchange between Josef and his friends, the grave-diggers:

> "You get used to it," I said. "That's the problem. We shouldn't become used to it. Is it supposed to be normal to carry corpses? Did you ever in your lives think that you would be going to morgues and mortuaries?"
>
> "A person can do anything if he's ordered to," said the former owner of a fabric shop. "I've seen people do even worse things."
>
> "A horse will do all sorts of things if a man forces him to," said the bookie. "But there are things a horse won't do even if you whip him from morning till night. Man is powerful. He'll do anything."

Weil, who managed to survive the occupation, published this novel in the few free years right after World War II. It was later denounced by the Communists (the next Occupation) as "pernicious existentialism." Weil died in 1959, and this great novel remained unnoticed by the West until now.

The prolific and adventurous Paul West, author of eleven novels and nine books of nonfic-

Dust jacket for Bausch's fourth novel, the story of a single parent trying to reestablish a relationship with his grown daughter, who has returned home, with her own daughter, after a five-year absence

tion, weighed in with a brilliant literary tour de force, *Lord Byron's Doctor* (Doubleday), which purports to be the unexpurgated diary of Byron's real doctor, J. W. Polidori, and concerns the extravagant ménage assembled by Byron and Shelley at Villa Diodati in 1816. Polidori, though gnawed with envy and, finally, a suicide, was no Salieri. He moved for a time among the greatly gifted, and that experience undid him. "As by some giant eagle," he writes, "I had been wafted to the heights of Helicon or Parnassus, living there on nectar and ambrosia, having what we used to call the time of my life, and then down, tumbling awry to the level of *The Morning Chronicle,* in due time to be known as 'A person whose name finds mention': no more than that." A fine book about the literary life, then and, most likely, now as well.

Allen Wier, young author of two lyrical novels and a collection of stories, surprises with his large-scale (sixty years of the history of one family) accounting of the life of a good woman, Julia

Marrs, with one ineradicable weakness–"There would always be, in Julia's heart, a place for outlaws–a place her mind could not rule." *A Place For Outlaws* (Harper & Row) is Wier's most complex book to date, joining his lyrical, often tender voice and his deep and abiding sense of the power of place to the world of a very contemporary story of sex and violence and of sorrow, early and late. Julia Marrs endures much and finally prevails, able at the end to stand alone on a hilltop and say her piece: " 'The Widow Marrs,' she shouted, 'has no regrets.' She waited, but there was no echo. Good. She'd said it, it didn't need repeating."

In *Sort of Rich* (Harper & Row), his fourth novel about the little New South town of Tula Springs, Louisiana, James Wilcox, who is surely one of the funniest of the whole crew of new southern writers, offers a more refined kind of comedy than most. By and large, he lets his characters, silly as they may be, take themselves as seriously as anybody else. He depends more on context and situation than one-liners, and he is mercifully liberated from the perennial, perhaps terminal cuteness which afflicts so many young southern novelists. In this novel he brings a Manhattan Yankee, and a Radcliffe graduate to boot, fortyish Gretchen Peabody Aiken-Lewis, as the impulsively new wife of widower Frank Dambar, into an eccentric household that seems like a hybrid of Saroyan and some of the stories of Eudora Welty. Everybody misreads everybody else for a good comic while. Then, with the sudden death of Frank and with some surprising revelations, the tale takes a new, more serious turn. It is this turn and the more mixed reaction it calls forth that seems to have confused some reviewers. Too bad. For it is the mixed and mingled moods of *Sort of Rich* that lift it well above the ordinary.

With first novels, justly or unjustly, our expectations are somewhat different. We expect, and usually get, good writing, sentence by sentence. If the novel is assertively autobiographical, as many are, we can at least hope more for a lively and interesting life (so far) than for any distillation of hard-earned wisdom. In any case, we look for engaging subject matter and perhaps some fresh ways and means of telling a story, neither too conventional on the one hand nor too insistently or outrageously "original" on the other.

Here are four excellent first novels that, in one way or another, stood up to all the tests, satisfied expectations. Cathryn Hankla's *A Blue Moon*

in Poorwater (Ticknor & Fields), published in 1988, is skillfully crafted in large and small as might be anticipated from a prizewinning young writer who has already published a volume of poetry and a collection of short stories. Except for a prologue in 1942, the novel is set in 1968 and is the story of Dorrie Parks growing up in the Virginia town of Poorwater. Here, with the gritty and authentic evocation of life in a coal town, Hankla is superb, writing like a seasoned professional. The story has an unanticipated turn when it shifts from Dorrie's point of view to the "Blue Horse Notebook," the journal of her older brother, Willie, a chillingly dangerous religious fanatic. Willie becomes completely believable in his own confused words. One critic noted the benign influences of Italo Calvino and William Goyen on this work, and these and other influences may very well be there. But, still, Hankla's words and work are very much her own.

Julian's House (Ticknor & Fields), by Judith Hawkes, arrives with a strong endorsement from Annie Dillard, praise of which Hawkes is certainly deserving. Taking the traditional ghost story and bringing it up-to-date, Hawkes sends a pair of contemporary, high-tech parapsychologists, David and Sally Curtiss, to the old Gilfoy house in a sleepy, rural Massachusetts village. The results are as instructive as they are delightful.

Randall Kenan is a young writer from Chinquapin, North Carolina, who is now an assistant editor at Alfred A. Knopf. His first novel, *A Visitation of Spirits* (Grove), explores four generations of a black family, the Crosses of Tims Creek, North Carolina, a family saga given a freshness of vision by a complex but accessible structure and by the introduction of hallucinatory episodes. All this is accomplished without the loss of touch with the reality of the subject. This is a work with sophistication and integrity and with, as writer Gloria Naylor noted, "a great deal of courage about personal and communal strife within the black community."

Jeanne Larsen's *Silk Road* (Holt) is one of those accomplished and special books that it seems almost irrelevant to think of as a first novel. Poet, translator, and story writer, Larsen is a knowledgeable specialist in the period of her novel–eighth-century China in the Tang dynasty– and she brings together in harmony bits and pieces of the "real" China with all the marvels of the imaginary kingdom. This is achieved so effortlessly that the two are inseparable so long as the story lasts. It is, in fact, many stories, a whirling of prayer wheels, but chiefly always the magical adventures of the beautiful Greenpearl and her two great quests. Critic Jay Parini is more accurate than amusing when he describes Jeanne Larsen as "Kipling come back to haunt us in the cloak of García Marquez."

Finally, *Up Through the Water* (Doubleday), by Darcey Steinke, listed by the *New York Times Book Review* among the "Notable Books of the Year" (3 December 1989) and highly praised for the lyrical beauty of its writing and for its realized sense of place, the island of Ocracoke off the North Carolina coast, has another virtue worth acknowledging. For lack of a better critical term, call it the *concentration* of the story on its people–sixteen-year-old Eddie, his mother Emily, his girlfriend Lila, and the two men in Emily's life, John Berry and Birdflower–and the events of their lives, a tight focus that gives the world of the novel an authority rare in any fiction. While the reader is within the story, engaged from first line to last, nothing else is real or important. It is a kind of magic spell.

The list of outstanding collections of short stories published during 1989 could easily be longer, not because there were many more short-story collections published during the year, though it seems there were plenty. The high quality of the books of stories, and their extraordinary variety, are directly related to a couple of factors. First, that a very large number of writers are, for many sound reasons, creating short fiction. Even the least known of the literary magazines in America receives thousands of stories in submission each year from which perhaps a dozen or so are accepted. Similarly, there are hundreds of completed book-length manuscripts of short stories–these composed of stories most of which have already made it through the strait gate and winnowing process of the magazines–making the rounds of the book publishers. The quality of these manuscripts is very high, and, within limits, the book editors can pick and choose as they please. Beyond a certain point the choice of the book editor may be purely whimsical or personal. Yet another factor increasing the number of collections published and enhancing the quality of one and all is the active publication of short fiction by university presses and small presses. Time was when the commercial publishing houses published (if at all) only the top line of short fiction. The leftovers, the works of lesser-known or idiosyncratic authors, found a place on the lists of the smaller presses. Nowadays there is apt to be less difference between the books coming from small presses and the big houses, except perhaps in appearance. And in many cases even that sort of distinction is blurred; well-designed, well-made, and handsome books are coming from even desktop publishers. There remain two tracks, one reserved for "well-known" writers (which usually means well-known, at least in the publishing or literary worlds, for something else, usually novels), the other for writers who must stand or fall on the basis of the excellence, or lack thereof, of a particular book. The irony of the situation is that the author of some reputation risks more by publishing a collection of stories, both for himself/herself and the publisher. Therefore there are, inevitably, more inhibitions at work on the well-known than the lesser-known writers.

All this and other things considered, the year was an exciting one for short fiction. And here are some special favorites singled out for special attention.

One of the major events in the publication of short fiction came near to the end of the year and celebrated the lifetime accomplishment of one of the most influential story writers–influential as teacher and editor and critic as well as by example–of the whole period since World War II. R. V. Cassill's *Collected Stories* (University of Arkansas Press), though in truth highly selective, is huge, 39 full-scale stories filling some 643 pages. Cassill, author of 22 novels and of 3 previous collections of short stories, offers enough restless variety of form and content for this to serve as a textbook on the potential and the limits of the contemporary story. All his stories are united by two things; first, an identifiable voice, once described in the *New York Times Book Review* as a "bumpy, difficult, ambitious style, able to redeem and enrich what may appear unpromising or overworked subject matter, capable of moving effects and sudden illuminations"; second, by subject matter itself that, as Cassill says, "has its roots in places and circumstances in which I have been passionately involved."

You have to love T. Coraghessan Boyle, with his wildly adventurous and imaginative novels and stories, his widely publicized (in fashion magazines) outrageous wardrobe of thrift shop and Good Will clothes, his stand-up antics: as when, for example, in accepting the PEN/Faulkner Award in 1988 for his novel *World's End* he offered, instead of a conventional acceptance speech, a comic monologue of a demented press agent whose purpose is to improve the image of the Ayatollah Khomeini. This monologue appears as "Hard Sell" in Boyle's latest (his third so far) collection–*If the River Was Whiskey* (Viking), composed of sixteen widely various stories that have appeared all over the lot from the *Antioch Review* to such shiny and coated-paper havens as *Gentleman's Quarterly* and *Playboy*. Boyle is boldly uneven, but at his best he is purely fun and games with some dark undertones. And as a member in good standing of a generation of writers who, on the whole, would rather be rock stars (along with Jay McInerney, Brett Easton Ellis, Ron Hansen, Richard Ford), Boyle is already the real thing.

Frederick Busch is a more serious and more prolific writer. Author of two books of nonfiction and twelve books of fiction, Busch brings out *Absent Friends* (Knopf), sixteen stories produced since 1984. These are fully developed (nothing minimal here) stories out of literary magazines, quarterlies, and the *New Yorker*; solid, well-made, various. The longest, really a novella and evidently published here for the first time, is "From the New World," a mocking and moving sequence from the family ("The Swiss Family Nutcake") of a film producer–Norman Tauber. It, like all the other stories, demonstrates Busch's good ear and sharp eye and above all his quiet sense of humor in surprising places, as when Norman says to his wife, after successfully invoking the aid and comfort of the Savior: "I'm not converted, Tess. Just grateful."

Carole L. Glickfeld won the Flannery O'Connor Award for Short Fiction for *Useful Gifts* (University of Georgia Press), ten stories and a novella, "Relics of Stars," all dealing with Ruthie Zimmer, youngest child of deaf-mute parents. The first ten stories treat Ruthie's childhood and their fourth-floor apartment on Arden Street; in the novella Ruthie is twenty years older, newly divorced, and very lonely. The stories are all good but are specially enhanced by the language created to represent the sign language used between deaf parents and the child. Deeply moving without being in the least sentimental.

Tom Hawkins writes both fiction and poetry, and his work has appeared in many of the leading literary magazines and quarterlies. His collection *Paper Crown* (Bookmark) presents twelve lean and quick and powerful stories, honorable realizations of the battered outcasts of our times. Hawkins does with grace what a lot of other writers have tried and failed to do. He is utterly convincing.

The High Spirits (Godine) is David Huddle's third collection of stories. He has also published two volumes of poetry. This collection offers a thematic unity; each of the eleven stories concerns itself with love or, more aptly, what the publisher defines as "the politics of love." The stories are otherwise various in setting, subject matter, technique of telling. The centerpiece, the title story, novella-length, is a first-person account of a Charlottesville band ("We were a band of very low quality.") called The High Spirits and a love story that ends in sudden violence. It is a wonderfully straightforward story, clearly observed, thoroughly examined, exact in all details. A beautiful piece of work by a writer of great promise. Another poet of distinction (she was Consultant in Poetry to the Library of Congress, 1971-1973) is Josephine Jacobsen, whose *On the Island* (Ontario Review) brings together twenty new and selected stories, widely ranging in setting, subject, and technique, but each and all bearing, in the words of critic and editor William Abrahams, "the stamp of an artist: humane and masterly."

Since the appearance of *Shiloh and Other Stories* (1982) Bobbie Ann Mason has been something of a star in the literary world, honored with prizes and fellowships, promptly and seriously reviewed and, perhaps most enviable to other working writers, regularly published and (apparently) widely read. The temptation of the critic is to call attention to the sameness of her stories, both in form and content. And here and there something has been made of her seemingly snobbish condescension, if only in an aesthetic sense and in terms of their unsophistication, toward many of her characters and her use of flashcard, superficial stereotypes to both label and judge people. And all of these things are true and are present in *Love Life* (Harper & Row), consisting of fifteen stories, six published in the *New Yorker* (the book is dedicated to Roger Angell), all about the protean shapes of love in the lives of Americans. But there are strong positive virtues that make mere quibbles of critical reservations. These stories are simply better and surer and deeper than the earlier, prizewinning stories of *Shiloh*. The language is exciting. She has refined an already trained mastery of the nuances and rhythms of American speech, both in dialogue and, more subtly, in narration. Even if she still sometimes condescends to her characters, there is an undeniable sense of authorial love for these her creatures. Mason is a highly productive and highly gifted writer, and this is her best work so far. Not to be ignored, not to be slighted.

Peter Matthiessen is another writer, yet another *kind* of writer, whose work since the early 1950s has been of such distinction and importance, in the fields of both fiction and nonfiction, that everything he writes deserves full attention. Of the ten stories, chronologically arranged from "Sadie" (1950) to "Lumumba Lives" (1988), making up *On the River Styx* (Random House), seven appeared in his only other collection of stories— *Midnight Turning Gray* (1984). Taken together, the stories show that, not surprisingly, the author of that amazing oral novel *Far Tortuga* (1975) has a superbly tuned ear for all kinds of speech, and that Matthiessen's compassion and his sensitivity to the complexities of race relations shine through his work, early and late. ("Lawyer Burkett don't care none for no 'Hey nigger,' Speck. Round here, we're integrated good. We say, 'Hey Nigra!' ") The good news is that the most recent story, "Lumumba Lives," poetic, hard-edged, haunting, and mysteriously sad, is the best story in the book. Perhaps there will be more in days to come.

Another collection spanning and representing a lifetime's art is *Acts of Worship* (Kodansha) by the enormously prolific and admired Japanese writer Yukio Mishima, who killed himself in November 1970. (*Has it been almost twenty years?*) These seven stories have been selected from the twenty volumes of short fiction he published in his lifetime. They are characteristic of Mishima, at least as he comes to us in the West, marked by a strongly defined sense of order and structure and by clarity and beauty of style and imagery. They also have an unbreakable mystery at the center, reminding us always of his fascination with Zen. The longest story in the book, and evidently one of Mishima's favorites, is "Act of Worship," in which a professor takes his student with him, both of them riddled with complex motivations and baffled by misunderstanding, while he performs a ritual act of worship at the Kumano shrines. Near the end she hears him tell a story through and by which she suddenly discovers or, anyway, believes that his whole life has been a kind of fantasy. "At this moment," Mishima writes, "she made a firm resolution on one thing: that from the moment of hearing the story until her dying day she would never betray, whether in front of the Professor or other people, the least sign of not believing it."

Small presses continue to publish most of the more experimental writers, so it is no surprise to find *Thirteen Stories,* by Ursule Molinaro, coming from McPherson in a handsome trade paperback edition. (McPherson simultaneously published a paperback edition of the author's 1983 experimental novel–*Positions with White Roses.*) These stories have all the appearance of the familiarly experimental: unusual spacing and spelling, frequent smatterings of ampersands, a grammar of broken and run-on sentences. But beneath this camouflage uniform are the firm and solid, naked bodies of stories that are funny, grotesque, violent, and deeply imaginative. They are various, to be sure. "Sweet Cheat of Freedom" is set in ancient Rome and deals with the paradoxes of slavery. "Rumors/Murky Haloes" concerns a French executioner (the man who dispatched Anne Boleyn) in 1536. One of the strongest stories is the straightest, "Xmas Tryst," in which an American girl in Hawaii is pursued and killed by a crazed Samoan. Here she is running for her life: "The pale-haired pale pale pale haole woman is fleeing along Kuhio Avenue. In the opposite direction she walked with her mother before. On stocking feet. With a bleeding face. Pursued by the Samoan with the Godzilla doll under one arm."

Gladys Swan is a very different kind of writer: her *Of Memory and Desire* (L.S.U. Press), eleven stories published between 1980 and 1987, is neither outwardly experimental nor (still) fashionably minimal. These are strong stories, patiently worked out and through, cumulative in effect, set mostly in the Southwest and in Mexico. You respond to and remember her people most, characters who, even in ordinary circumstances, are, in the words of the publisher, "at odds with themselves and the world." Swan is more than a little like her own character Alta of the traveling carnival in "Carnival for the Gods." Here Alta takes in two runaways to her trailer and her table: "Here they were, just another pair among the number she had seen, in the procession of all the misbegotten things headed out of the world onto the road, moving from town to town, never calling any place their own. They were her family, if you could call it that–they were her fate."

Antic, determinedly oddball, leading us into a world of TV, rock music, commercials, funny punctuation, and deranged high tech, mixing real and fictional characters like a shuffled and dealt hand of cards, David Foster Wallace begins his creative writing for *Girl with Curious Hair* (Norton), a novella and nine good-size stories, with this statement on the copyright page: "Where the names of corporate, media, or political figures are used here, these names are meant to denote figures, images, the stuff of collective dreams; they do not denote, or pretend to private information about, actual 3-D persons, living, dead or otherwise." We are talking a cross between Max Apple and T. Coraghessan Boyle. Actually, Wallace sounds like himself, usually textured and intelligent, and simply and youthfully smart-aleck (a risk that goes with the territory) at his worst. Basically, it is all summed up in this exchange between two show-biz types in "My Appearance":

> "This is the man, Ed Lyn, who publicly asked Christie Brinkley what state the Kentucky Derby is run in."
> "That's part of what makes him so dangerous," my husband said, lifting his glasses to massage the bridge of his nose. "The whole thing feeds off everybody's ridiculousness."

Besides the old standbys there were any number of interesting anthologies of short fiction in 1989. But the old standbys got that way by earned repute and deserve to be dealt with first. William Abrahams's *Prize Stories 1989: The O. Henry Awards* (Doubleday) has some excellent stories, some by "names" in the field–Alice Adams, T. Coraghessan Boyle, John Casey, Susan Minot, Joyce Carol Oates, James Salter, Charles Simmons, and the much-anthologized Rick Bass; but presents, as well, stories by less well-known writers and even newcomers: Charles Dickinson, Millicent Dillon, Starkey Flythe, Jr., Ethel Herman, Jean Ross, Francis Sherwood, and the virtually unknown Banning K. Lary, whose contributor's note allows that he "cannot be located." The first prize was won by Ernest J. Finney for his story "Peacocks," which appeared in the *Sewanee Review*. This time, surprisingly in spite of the drift of things in that direction, Abrahams found the majority of the best stories in the little magazines and quarterlies. The three prizewinners are all from that league. There are two stories from the *New Yorker,* but there are also two fine stories from the *Greensboro Review.*

Meantime, Margaret Atwood, acting in concert with series editor Shannon Ravenel, mined the literary magazines as well, though somewhat less adventurously and widely than Abrahams. Given a choice, given the example of her choices, it seems that Atwood would generally prefer to follow an established trend or fashion than to take

real risks or go against the safe, familiar grain. Still, *The Best American Short Stories 1989* (Houghton Mifflin) contains exciting and memorable stories, including work by Charles Baxter, Madison Smartt Bell, Frederick Busch, Mavis Gallant, Alice Munroe, and Bharati Mukerjee. And there are some promising "discoveries," especially the work of David Wong Louie, Dale Ray Phillips, and Arthur Robinson, whose first published story, "The Boy on the Train," has found its way here.

Doubling up as, also, the editor of *New Stories From the South: The Year's Best 1989* (Algonquin), Ravenel has selected some excellent stories by good people found in good places. This time (surprise) there are a couple of stories that appear in both her annual anthologies–Madison Smartt Bell's "Customs of the Country" and Mark Richard's "Strays." It is a pleasure to see work by David Huddle and Kelly Cherry in this book. Both Ravenel and her annual southern anthology took something of a savaging from fellow Southerner Daniel Wallace ("Lite in August," *Nation,* 27 November 1989, pp. 640-644), and some points were scored not only about her choices in general, but also about some of the hardening clichés of the official literature of the New South. But Wallace, too busy playing hardball, misses a significant criticism that needs to be made, namely that Ravenel, like other editors of annual anthologies, seems to miss most of the even mildly experimental literature being written today. Ironically, there are some first-rate experimental writers in the New South whose work cannot be missed and so must be being ignored. One thinks of people, a few among many, who publish regularly in the magazines, people such as Tom Whalen, Fred Chappell, Dana Gibson, Cathryn Hankla, R. H. W. Dillard, Darcey Steinke, Lydia Derrick, and Cedric Tolley.

Since "theme" anthologies of all kinds are a popular fashion this season, it is not the least surprising to find several brand-new anthologies based and built upon the image or the idea of the South or some part of it. Best of the bunch, judged so for the writers on board, for the stories selected, and purely and simply as a handsome example of bookmaking, is *Stories: Contemporary Southern Short Fiction* (University of Arkansas Press), edited by Donald Hays. It has stories by twenty-seven quite different writers, ranging from Barry Hannah to Peter Taylor, from Bobbie Ann Mason to Alice Walker, from Tom T. Hall to Eudora Welty. The reader gets at least a general notion of the large precinct that is southern writing. *New Stories by Southern Women* (University of South Carolina Press), edited by Mary Ellis Gibson, with twenty-one contemporary stories, misses out, as it must, on some of the best women writers of the South. But there are none here who do not deserve to be. And there are some good new voices, people such as Jane Bradley and Marianne Gingher, Mary Hood and Jill McCorkle. And, maybe best of all, there is a kind of bibliography, "Suggestions for Further Reading," which, even if it doesn't pick up all the people it ought to and sometimes gives important writers short shrift (Mary Lee Settle and Ellen Douglas noted for only one book each), does present a broad and inclusive listing of the literary scene, notably including a lot of small-press writers. Typical of the more localized southern gatherings is *Florida Stories* (University of Florida Press), edited by Kevin McCarthy. Here are seventeen stories by Floridians or about Florida, from Stephen Crane to Harry Crews, from Sarah Orne Jewett to Donald Justice. In historical time they range from Andrew Lytle's "Ortiz's Mass," set in sixteenth-century Tampa, to the first chapter, set in 1970, of Crews's *Karate Is a Thing of the Spirit* (1971). And there is a selected bibliography of work by the authors included. It is good to see Edwin Granberry, whose literary career began in 1927 and continued into the 1960s, rediscovered and included. But there are any number of significant voices left out. This critic is particularly distressed by the absence of native Floridian George Garrett from these pages.

All theme anthologies smack of gimmickry one way or another, but some are better than others, usually more because of the quality of the work included than the unifying idea. In its own terms *The Invisible Enemy: Alcoholism & The Modern Short Story* (Graywolf), edited by Miriam Dow and Jennifer Regan, is odd, to say the least. It is hard to argue, as the editors try to, that stories written about or in some way involving drunks can be taken as case studies of the dangers and sorrows of alcoholism. Nevertheless, their scheme has allowed them to assemble fifteen very good stories, published from 1946 to the present; and these are placed in a handsome edition by Graywolf. A more likely candidate for pure and simple gimmickry is *Love Stories For the Time Being* (Pushcart), edited by Genie D. Chipps and Bill Henderson. It may, indeed, be intended as a hustle for the unwary; but there are too many good stories here (twenty-six) by good people, includ-

ing some who are not yet as familiar in anthologies as they ought to be–Bo Ball, Ellen Wilbur, H. E. Francis. Following their editorial success with *Sudden Fiction: American Short-Short Stories* (Perigrine), editors Robert Shapard and James Thomas have produced *Sudden Fiction International* (Norton), some sixty short-short stories from all over the planet, including a scattering of Americans. Limitation on length allows for a wider and more representative selection of recent world writing than is usual. Another unusual anthology is *Best Stories From New Writers* (Writer's Digest), edited by Linda S. Sanders. Here there are twelve stories that are the first published fiction of the authors involved. Each story has an afterpiece consisting of the editor's reaction to the story and also the reasoning and reaction of the original magazine editor who published the story. In that sense it is a "how to," directed to other beginning writers, but it is an interesting collection of quality fiction in its own right. Oddest of all anthologies in 1989 was one produced in a different medium. *The Wedding Cake Stories*, consisting of original stories by six writers built around a common image, a wedding cake in the middle of the road, was commissioned and assembled by National Public Radio's Susan Stamberg for her "Weekend Edition" show. The six stories were broadcast, together with interviews with the writers, from 11 June to 23 July.

Prominent novelists of the elder generation continued to be productive contributors to the literary scene. Louis Auchincloss was represented by his forty-first book–*Fellow Passengers: A Novel in Portraits* (Houghton Mifflin). Berry Fleming, who died on 15 September 1989, at age ninety, witnessed publication of *Captain Bennett's Folly* (Permanent Press), a visionary story of Captain Nolan Bennett, old soldier and former history teacher. The novel was written in 1979, but it took Fleming ten years to find a publisher. Meantime, Second Chance republished his 1938 novel, *To the Market Place*, a story of four Southerners seeking their fortunes in New York. Howard Fast's forty-sixth book, *The Confessions of Joe Cullen* (Houghton Mifflin), is a crime story of cocaine and corruption starring Mel Freedman, a Jewish police lieutenant in New York City. Published posthumously, Bernard Malamud's *The People and Uncollected Stories* (Farrar, Straus & Giroux) consists of sixteen chapters of an unfinished novel, with notes for the five remaining chapters, plus fourteen previously uncollected stories. The novel is deftly described by its editor, Robert Giroux, as "a comic-tragic narrative of a persecuted and doomed people, a tribe of Indians in America's northwest in the post-Civil War period who put their hopes for justice in an itinerant peddler and occasional carpenter named Yozip." Though *The People* was a long way from finished when Malamud died, there are flashes of the unmistakable Malamud way with things: "Yozip believed he could be somebody if he tried, but he did not know what or how to try. If a man did not know what to do next, could you call that a destiny?" The late David Grubb is represented this year by *You'll Never Believe Me* (St. Martin's), eighteen violent and Gothic tales. A remarkable example of the continuing creativity of the elders is *And Again?* (Birch Lane), the first novel in thirty-nine years by the distinguished Irish story writer Sean O'Faolain. This, his fourth novel, boldly tells the story of Bobby Younger, a man actually reliving his life backwards to the womb, thus a unique being, a living man with no future. Finally, the persistence of earlier generations is splendidly represented by *The Short Stories of F. Scott Fitzgerald* (Scribners), which includes forty-three stories edited by Matthew J. Bruccoli, twenty-three of which did not appear in Malcolm Cowley's 1951 collection.

Some of the most highly regarded members of the middle generation of American writers brought out new books in 1989. One that appeared on every published list of "the best" books of the year and was a nominated finalist for most of the public prizes was E. L. Doctorow's *Billy Bathgate* (Random House), in which the eloquent fifteen-year-old Billy tells of his coming of age under the tutelage of gangster Dutch Schultz in the Bronx in 1935. True to his form Doctorow has other "real" figures, including Thomas E. Dewey and Walter Winchell, as characters in this story. John Irving's *A Prayer for Owen Meany* (Morrow) is narrated by one John Wheelwright (a character with many parallels and similarities to his author), who tells us, "I am a Christian because of Owen Meany." Meany, cruelly described by one unconvinced critic as "a morally cute dwarf," is a kind of modern saint and prophet in this tale of the 1950s and early 1960s. Perhaps in homage to Maine author Carolyn Chute, Irving permits Meany to speak only in capital letters. No question that Irving was serious about all this. Speaking of his subject and theme, he told the *New York Times:* "I've always asked myself what would be the magnitude of the miracle that could convince me of religious faith." Mixed

reviews greeted *Meany*. Another well-publicized book by an author writing out of the New England experience is *Affliction* (Harper & Row), by Russell Banks, a story of domestic violence and brutality in rural New Hampshire. It is the sad story of Wade Whitehouse, forty-one-year-old town policeman who wants to be a good man, but who is the doomed victim of an alcoholic, abusive father. The story is told by his younger brother, Rolfe, a high-school teacher who can articulate much that Wade has no words for.

All My Friends Are Going to be Strangers (1972) was Larry McMurtry's fifth novel and introduced us to the young writer Danny Deck. Now, in *Some Can Whistle* (Simon & Schuster), set twenty-two years later, Danny is fifty-one, a huge commercial success as creator of a TV sitcom, "Al and Sal," and bored to death, living in reclusive luxury and relative loneliness; until (to set the story going full speed) Danny's daughter, T.R., whom he hasn't seen since her birth, enters his life, bringing plenty of trouble but also the gift of life itself. Although *Some Can Whistle* is largely set in Texas, it confirms, as *Los Angeles Times* book editor Jack Miles noticed, that McMurtry is, in a serious sense, just as much an L.A. novelist as a Texan.

The amazingly productive Joyce Carol Oates brought out two novels this year. *American Appetites* (Abrahams/Dutton), the nineteenth novel published under her own name, is the realistic story of a violent murder in an apparently happy family. *Soul/Mate* (Abrahams/Dutton), published under Oates's pseudonym, Rosamond Smith, tells of a psychopathic killer, Colin Asch, who is in love with art historian Dorothea Deverell.

Extensive publicity and equally widespread praise greeted the publication of Thomas McGuane's eighth novel, and his first in five years—*Keep the Change* (Houghton Mifflin/Seymour Lawrence). McGuane's story, which in a sense is a shadow of his own, is about Joe Starling, painter, who leaves Key West to go back home to Montana and to take up an old/new life trying to run the family ranch. Critical reception, while not unmixed, was mostly a welcome home to McGuane. "He has always been one of our best novelists," wrote Robert Wilson in *USA Today,* "and *Keep the Change* is up to his best work."

Other notable efforts include William Wharton's seventh novel, *Franky Furbo* (Holt), an unusual combination of fable and metafiction set in Perugia and Bavaria and involving painter-writer William Wiley and his family and a telepathic, talking fox named Franky Furbo. Bruce Jay Friedman's *The Current Climate* (Atlantic Monthly Press) is about Harry Towns, fifty-seven-year-old writer, and cuts back and forth from the present to the 1950s in New York and Hollywood. Both Eric McCormack's *The Paradise Motel* (Viking), a story in which all the characters tell horror stories, called "brilliant and unsettling" in the *New York Times Book Review*, and Patrick McGrath's first novel, *The Grotesque* (Poseidon), whose narrator is the relentlessly unreliable Sir Hugo Coal of Crook Manor ("I have come to believe that to be a grotesque is my destiny"), qualify as somewhat spoofing, high-reflexive horror tales. A little different, at once spookier and funnier, is Jack Butler's second novel, *Nightshade* (Atlantic Monthly Press), set on Mars in the twenty-second century and told by Jack Shade (same name as Nabokov's poet in *Pale Fire*), an imaginary vampire who is telling a real story about a future conflict between Wetbrains and Janglers. Writes Butler, "I am interested in border conditions, the way the old meets the new." Butler is dean of students at Hendrix College.

Alan Lelchuck's fifth novel, *Brooklyn Boy* (McGraw-Hill), is set in the 1940s and early 1950s and follows adolescent baseball fan Aaron Sclossberg. Jackie Robinson, Pee Wee Reese, Duke Snyder, Roy Campanella, and others from the Old Dodgers appear. Howard Frank Mosher's *A Stranger in the Kingdom* (Doubleday) takes place in the summer of 1952 in Vermont and details the dramatic conflicts arising from the arrival of a new minister in town–Rev. Walter Andrews, who is black. Craig Nova's *Tornado Alley* (Delacorte) begins as the story of young Marie Boule, who runs away from home in rural Pennsylvania to find herself in Marlowe, California, with types like Ben Lunn who can predict the weather and the epileptic Faith Wheeler and other wounded characters from small-town America. Some critics labeled Nova's writing in this, his sixth novel, as "Faulknerian." Veteran Seymour Epstein published his tenth novel, *Light* (Holt), a modern love story told by TV personality "George Light": "My present intention is to really think about, and no doubt write about, the man-woman thing." C. E. Poverman's fourth novel, *My Father in Dreams* (Scribners), takes protagonist Jed Hartwick from his childhood to the present. *Apes and Angels* (Putnam), by poet Philip Appleman, is a story of small-town hypocrisy and violence set in Kenton, Indiana, just before Pearl Harbor. A novel that found its place on many

lists by various critics and reviewers of the best fiction of 1989 was the story, set in the islands of Kauai and Manhattan, of two sisters and their search for sexual identity and fulfillment. *The Whiteness of Bones* (Doubleday) is Susanna Moore's second novel and follows *My Old Sweetheart* (1987), which won the PEN/Hemingway Award.

Whether or not the publishing business was really in a slump, it was a year in which many first novels received significant attention, and some, widely advertised and promoted, were among the more successful books of the season. Much praise, attention, and promotion were lavished on *Oldest Living Confederate Widow Tells All* (Knopf), by Allan Gurganus. Told in first-person by Lucy Marsden, a ninety-nine-year-old widow (who had married Willie Marsden, fifty-one, when she was only fifteen) ending her days in the Lane's End rest home, the novel is a grab bag of stories, anecdotes, and memories, her own and those of others she listened to, covering the years 1850 to 1984 from the southern perspective. Most reviewers accepted Lucy's judgment of herself: "My English may be ugly as a mud fence but I know what a story is." Unconverted, Peter Prescott of *Newsweek* called it "as slick as your grandmother's darning egg," adding that it is "not a bad book, just an unendurable one."

Two first novels were among the finalists for the National Book Award. Katherine Dunn's *Geek Love* (Knopf) told the story, in the voice of Olympia Binewski, an "albino, hump-backed dwarf," of her carnival family and their freak show–Binewski's Fabulon. *Geek Love* received mixed notices, though those who liked it were highly enthusiastic. Novelist Paul West praised the author's "forceful, sulfuric, lucid imagination"; and Thomas McGonigle, writing in *Chronicles*, named it as "one of the most exciting and bizarre novels to be published in a long time." Amy Tan's *The Joy Luck Club* (Putnam), a group portrait of four elderly immigrant Chinese women and their American daughters, built around a mah-jongg game, played over forty years, where the women remember and "say" stories, proved to be a surprise best-seller, hugely successful.

Not as successful at the box office, but uniformly awarded serious critical attention, was Maxine Hong Kingston's Chinese-American story– *Tripmaster Monkey: His Fake Book* (Knopf). Kingston, whose previous works are nonfiction, including the celebrated *The Woman Warrior* (1976), here tells many kinds of stories through the me-

Dust jacket for Bell's fifth novel, the story of two Vietnam veterans (one white, one black) who join forces in the Tennessee woods in the early 1970s

dium of a twenty-three-year-old, fifth generation Chinese-American playwright, Wittman Ah Sing. Set in San Francisco in the heady 1960s, it is the story of the life of the larger-than-life Wittman, whose dream is to create "an enormous loud play that will wake an audience for us." In some ways this complex and high-energy novel is that very play. Another side of the coin is found in *Silk Road* (Holt), a first novel by poet and translator Jeanne Larsen that tells many stories while following the life and times of Greenpearl, a courtesan of eighth-century China. A delightful puzzle, *Silk Road* reads as though Ursula K. Le Guin, Umberto Eco, and Maxine Hong Kingston had collaborated to bring ancient China magically to life in the form of a Möbius strip with a double twist.

Jane Vandenburg's *Failure to Zigzag* (North Point) is the story of three generations of a Southern California family plagued by insanity, with the action covering the 1940s to the 1960s. Rejected by most commercial publishers, it was finally and handsomely brought out by North Point. Scott Bradfield's *The History of Luminous Mo-*

tion (Knopf) was widely reviewed and either well-praised or damned. A Southern California story also, it is told by the brilliant and brilliantly verbal psychopathic eight-year-old Phillip Davis, a child with an alcoholic, wandering mother and an absent father. Troubling the negative reviewers was the voice of the child. "He sounds like a very big boy," wrote Merle Rubin in the *Los Angeles Times,* "who's taken one too many creative-writing classes."

African-American writers continued to make a significant impact on the consciousness of the reading public. Alice Walker's ambitious and unusual *The Temple of My Familiar* (Harcourt Brace Jovanovich), an angry book composed of many stories interlaced with Walker's ideas and unsupported notions on many subjects, annoyed many reviewers. Lee Lescaze of the *Wall Street Journal* described the work as "untempered by wit or art." David Nicholson concluded in *Book World:* "One may applaud her cuteness but it is hard to take her seriously." Walker, herself, described the novel as a story that "moves from contemporary America, England, and Africa to unfamiliar primal worlds, where women, men and animals socialize in surprising ways." Ishmael Reed's eighth novel, *The Terrible Threes* (Atheneum), is a slapstick and surreal comedy set in the United States in the near future, a future in which, as Reed sees it, former President Reagan will be viewed as a left-winger. Its fictional format has been described as a parody of a collection of op-ed pieces.

Somewhat more straightforward were Marita Golden's *Long Distance Life* (Doubleday), which follows the lives of a black family in Washington, D.C., from the 1920s to the present, and Nettie Jones's generational saga *Mischief Makers* (Weidenfeld & Nicolson), accounting for a mother, Raphael de Baptiste, called Peaches, who can easily "pass" for white, and her three daughters. Terry McMillan's *Disappearing Acts* (Viking) turned some clichés of the contemporary black novel inside out by telling a genuine love story, in alternating points of view, between an urban male, Franklin Swift, and Zora Banks, a Brooklyn schoolteacher. Al Young's latest, *Seduction By Light* (Seymour Lawrence/Delta), a lively and often funny story of a middle-aged black woman who works as a maid in Hollywood, was well-received by reviewers. Tina McElroy Ansa's *Baby of the Family* (Harcourt Brace Jovanovich) begins in 1949 in Mulberry, Georgia, and is chiefly concerned with the family life of Lena McPherson, who, born with a caul, has second sight and can converse with spirits. Melvin Dixon's *Trouble the Water* (University of Colorado/Fiction Collective II) is a brief (194 pages) first novel of the younger generation of African-Americans, telling of Jordan Henry, a southern black who attends Groton and Harvard and returns to the South in search of his roots. Barbara Chase-Riboud turned to history to retell the story of Joseph Cinque's rebellion on the Spanish slave ship *Amistad* in *Echo of Lions* (Morrow).

Black history also figures prominently in the title story of John Edgar Wideman's collection of twelve short stories–*Fever* (Holt), Wideman's ninth book. Told in several voices and based on the 1794 narrative by Richard Allen of the yellow-fever epidemic in Philadelphia in 1793, it is an advocacy piece based upon an original of the same nature; but its high energy and brilliance of writing offset its sometimes simplistic argument and substance. The other stories are widely various, including racial erotic fantasy ("The Statue of Liberty"); folktale ("When It's Time To Go"); "Concert," a rewrite of or homage to Eudora Welty's "Powerhouse"; "Valaida," a Holocaust story; and "Sur Fiction," intellectual satire, fun and games: altogether demonstrating an authentic artistic virtuosity. Two other outstanding story collections by black writers were Caryl Phillips's *Higher Ground* (Viking) and *The Amoralists & Other Tales* (Thunder's Mouth), by Cyrus Colter, a seventy-nine-year-old writer from Chicago.

Africa figured as a place and a force in many books published in 1989. Mongane Serote, in exile from South Africa since 1974, produced *In Every Birth Its Blood* (Thunder's Mouth), whose hero is a poet, Tsietsi Molope, and whose setting is the black township of Alexandra, near Johannesburg. Afrikaner writer Karel Schoeman presented another view in *Promised Land* (Summit), a futuristic novel in which the blacks now govern and the Boers are a beleaguered minority. Narrator George Neethling, returning to his homeland from Europe, finds "desolation nowhere interrupted." V. Y. Mudimbe, in his second novel, *Before the Birth of the Moon* (Simon & Schuster), set in Zaire in the 1960s, tells the story of "the Minister," the protagonist, and his complicated love affair with Ya, a prostitute. Thomas Kineally dedicated *To Asmara* (Warner) to "the brave Eritrean People's Liberation Front." It is a highly polemical novel dealing with the conflict between the Ethiopians and the Eritreans as witnessed by an

Australian journalist named Darcy and a little group of Westerners, all looking for something or someone. Stuart Stephens's *Malaria Dreams: An African Adventure*, purports to be a nonfiction journal of a wild journey in contemporary Africa, but is so strongly and selectively narrative in design as to be, obviously, a blending of fact and fiction. In *The Setting Sun and the Rolling World* (Beacon) Zimbabwean writer Charles Mungoshi has brought together seventeen stories from the past twenty years. Interestingly, very little racial conflict occurs in any of these stories. Mainly they deal with the clash of pastoral versus urban life.

Breyten Breytenbach, Afrikaner anti-Apartheid writer and activist who once served a long prison sentence for his political actions, writes of an African couple living in exile in Paris–Mano, a mulatto actor, and his pregnant wife, Meheret. Most of the novel is addressed by Meheret to her unborn child. The narrative is complex and multifaceted ("The night is long. In Africa we burn slow branches of our stories to keep the night at bay."), some of it set at a Pan-African film festival near Ouagadougou in Burkina Faso and some in the "No Man's Land" of contemporary South Africa. Widely reviewed, the novel was sometimes faulted for its elaborate and intricate style. Another Afrikaner writer, André Brink, in his eighth novel, *States of Emergency* (Summit), which he calls "notes towards a novel," asks himself the question–can he write a love story, set in times like these? His protagonist, a professor named Philip Malan, has two love affairs, one in Paris with Claire from Martinique, later in South Africa with twenty-three-year-old Melissa Lotman. Paralleling this latter is the love affair of Jane Ferguson, a twenty-three-year-old writer, with Chris de Villiers, an A.N.C. fugitive.

Bryce Courtenay, an Australian writer, set his first novel, *The Power of One* (Random House), dealing with the coming of age of a young English boy, in the South Africa of World War II, when the passionately anti-British Afrikaners hoped Hitler would win the war. In *Middlepost* (Knopf), Anthony Sher goes back a little earlier to 1901 in South Africa to tell the tale of Smous, a Lithuanian Jew. There are many odd people of various races in his life, most importantly his Bushman companion–Naoksa. Another novel, set early in this century and dealing with the place of the Jew amid the Boers, is *Far Forbidden Plains* (St. Martin's) by Christina Laffeaty. In *The Whales of Lake Tanganyiko* (Grove) Swedish novelist

Lennart Hagerfors retold the story of Henry Morton Stanley and David Livingstone as a variation of and homage to Joseph Conrad's *Heart of Darkness* (1899). The story is narrated by John Shaw, who was "real," but about whom little is known. Hagerfors grew up in the Congo.

Coming Home and Other Stories (Heinemann), by Farida Karodia, presents a South Africa relentless in cruelty. No less moving, yet slightly different in emphasis, are two collections of short stories about South Africa published by Readers International. *Renewal Time*, by Esikia Mphahlele is, in fact, all taken from an earlier collection by the same celebrated author published in Nairobi in 1967, but is worth republishing if only for the sake of the famous "Miss Plum," a liberal white lady of South Africa who "loves dogs and Africans." Ahmed Essop's *Hajji Musa and the Hindu Fire-Walker* is exclusively concerned with the underclass of Johannesburg's Indian community–Fordsburg. Tony Eprile's stories in *Temporary Sojourner* (Fireside), concerned with contemporary South Africans, black and white, living in the United States as well as in South Africa, are reported to be at least partly autobiographical in the several stories centered on a young Jewish protagonist–Mark Spiegelman. Just at year's end came the highly praised *Advance, Retreat* (St. Martin's) by Richard Rive, twelve stories of South Africa more concerned with the grotesque and the banality of racism than its atrocities, told in a manner that has reminded some critics of both Kafka and Flannery O'Connor.

One of the most highly praised books dealing with Africa and African experience was *Stars of the New Curfew* (Viking) by Ben Okri, a Nigerian writer living in London. The basic setting of these stories is the city of Lagos; and the basic drama, often strange enough to pass for "magic realism," is the conflict between the old tribal Africa of forests and daemons and inexplicable nightmares and the waking nightmares of the new Africa where nothing seems to work, and very little makes much sense.

The University Press of Virginia has developed the Caraf Books series devoted to Caribbean and African literature translated from the French. Two novels from the series, published in 1989, are set in Africa. Alioum Fantouré's *Tropical Circle*, the first-person narration of Bohi Di, who leaves his rural village for a life in the city, where he bears witness to the sorrows of a brutal dictatorship, won the Grand Prix de Litterature d'Afrique Noire for 1978. Congolese poet, novelist, and dramatist Tchicaya U. Tam'Si brings together the most ancient ways and means of African storytelling and the most sophisticated French literary innovations in *The Madman and the Medusa*. Set in the final week of June in 1944, the story is about three men–Elenga, a railroad engineer; Muendo, who works at a lumber mill; and Luambu, a clerk. "Death struck down the first two men at their workplace. But where do you think they found the third one almost dead? In the graveyard! Yes, lying between the tombs of his friends." The world of this novel is part magic, part surrealism, and part a "real world of facts and hard knocks." Very soon the three are inextricably joined together. Finally, St. Martin's Press brought out an anthology of African poetry and prose, offering an introduction to the work of African writers–*Ourselves in Southern Africa*.

With major British publishers buying into the American publishing industry and vice versa, it is not unusual that significant transatlantic interchange continues. With *Difficulties With Girls* (Summit), Kingsley Amis came back with a hit, picking up the story of Jenny Bumn and Patrick Standish from *Take a Girl Like You* (1960). Criticized by some for its anachronistic view of London life, it was nonetheless irresistibly funny. In the *New York Review of Books* Amis was called "the W. C. Fields of English letters." A. N. Wilson's *Incline Our Hearts* (Viking), a major critical success, tells the story of the narrator, Julian Ramsay, who was orphaned in the Blitz. The villain of the piece is scholar Raphael Hunter, who allows: "One accomplishes nothing so stylishly as the thing in which one has no belief." David Attoe's *Lion at the Door* (Little, Brown), in the story of Hazel Sapper and her friend Rosko, growing up in the 1950s, made art out of the tricky topic of the abusive father. Set also in 1979, when Hazel is a mother herself, the novel won high praise from critic Bruce Bawer in the *Wall Street Journal:* "In an age of arid brat-pack minimalism, 'Lion at the Door' is a welcome relief, and a most promising debut." A somewhat different tone and attitude is expressed by young Jessie, who has sex with her father in Alexander Stuart's first novel, *The War Zone* (Doubleday): "Incest is brilliant. It's scarier than shagging some Adam in a pub car park or stroking another girl's thigh in some Fulham cafe." (American author Joan Chase, in her second novel, *The Evening Wolves*, published by Farrar, Straus & Giroux, deftly handled the same difficult subject.)

Haydn Middleton, who lectures at Oxford, offered a mix of quotidian and mythological characters, doubling and blending with counterparts, in *The Lie of the Land* (Ballantine). Middleton's Jungian method and mind-set have invited comparison to Robertson Davies. The productive Peter Ackroyd fared less well with reviewers, who were generally confused by his mixture of archeologists and mythological beings in *First Light* (Grove). Michael Moorcock's *Mother London* (Crown), his first "main-stream novel" after an even hundred fantasy and sci-fi books, has London itself as the author of three characters during the Blitz. John Collee, in *A Paper Mask* (Arbor/Morrow) tells a kind of horror story as a medical orderly borrows the identity of Dr. Simon Hennessey and goes to work in a Bristol emergency room. Stanley Middleton writes of the contemporary British art scene in *Entry Into Jerusalem* (New Amsterdam). So, with a difference, does Mary Wesley in *Second Fiddle* (Viking), her sixth novel since she began writing fiction at the age of seventy-one.

It was a notable year for British women writers. Margaret Drabble's *A Natural Curiosity* (Viking), a sequel to *The Radiant Way* (1987), carried on with two of the three heroines of that earlier story–teacher Alix Bowen and psychotherapist Liz Headland (art historian Esther Brewer makes only a cameo appearance). This account of England as changed under Margaret Thatcher opened to mixed reviews in America. Some critics found the subject matter simply depressing. Others found Drabble's latest technique of active authorial intrusion to be annoying. To which the narrator answers in advance: "Life is more like an old-fashioned melodramatic novel than we care to know." Another grim view of life in Thatcherite Britain is to be found in Helen Flint's *In Full Possession* (St. Martin's), in which a TV repairman plans and executes a terrible revenge on a tenant in his house who will not move out. This, too, employs the self-reflexive intrusions of the narrator: "Not to worry; Ben is no psychopath."

"Our existence, if you pay any attention, is unbearably distressing," writes the prolific Fay Weldon in *Leader of the Band* (Viking), her fifteenth novel, story of a forty-two-year-old astronomer, Sandra, who runs off to France with a trumpet player named *Mad Jack*. Weldon also brought out a collection of twelve stories–*Polaris* (Penguin). Part send-up and part scream in the night, *Ducks* (Harmony) is a brief (121 pages) and experimental novel about London by Australian writer Helen Hodgman, replete with sex, violence, and general confusion, a host of characters in brief episodes, and multiple narration. Other novels by British women writers include Mavis Cheek's *Parlor Games* (Simon & Schuster), a comedy of marital infidelity featuring Celia Crossland and her lawyer-husband Alex; Ruth Rendell's latest mainstream thriller, *The Bridesmaid* (Mysterious); Sybille Bedford's *Jigsaw* (Knopf), an intensely autobiographical novel set in Europe in the 1920s that tells the story of a young woman who will become a writer; and *Queen Lear* (Obelisk/Dutton; published in England as *Loving and Giving*), by Molly Keane, an odd, sad story of a family of Irish country gentry in the years before World War I, "always singing, not knowing that they say a dirge."

At least several truly outstanding story collections came to these shores from Britain. *The Devil's Mode* (Random House), Anthony Burgess's first collection of stories, which *Publishers Weekly* described as "a mix of imaginary historical tales and fictional travel pieces," has some celebrated figures for its central characters, among them Shakespeare, Cervantes, Browning, Mallarmé, Debussy, and Sherlock Holmes. A just cause for celebration was the publication, in the author's eighty-ninth year, of V. S. Pritchett's *A Careless Widow* (Random House), six carefully crafted tales in the traditional mode, all concerning older people who have to deal with the past. Young American story writer Richard Bausch, reviewing the book for the *Washington Post Book World*, made this judgment: "Luxuriously intelligent, mercilessly observant and yet compassionate, written in a brilliantly even-handed and governed prose, exact and precise and unintellectual as the notes in a Mozart concerto, these stories are the work of a true master–a man who has seen almost everything and has had the character and the grace to remain interested." The anonymous reviewer for the *Virginia Quarterly Review* was equally effusive about the thirty-four stories in Penelope Lively's *Pack of Cards* (Grove): "This may be the perfect book to take on a long weekend visit, but the thoughtful hostess will leave a copy on the bedside table just in case." Welsh writer Gwyn Thomas is represented by *Selected Stories* (Dufour), twenty-three stories, all but one set in Wales. In *A Link With the River* (Farrar, Straus & Giroux), Irish writer Desmon Hogan gathered a series of stories about Dublin and its neighborhoods, a book that the *Washington Times* praised as "one of the most serious story collections you will read this year."

Earned second chances and recapitulations include *The Doris Lessing Reader* (Knopf), with short stories, novel excerpts, and various nonfiction by Lessing; *Where Joy Resides: A Christopher Isherwood Reader* (Farrar, Straus & Giroux), consisting of two short novels and various essays and reminiscences; and, finally, the publication in America for the first time of John Mortimer's *The Narrowing Stream* (Viking), which was that English man of letters' first novel, published there in 1954.

From neighboring Canada we received two significant novels: Robertson Davies's *The Lyre of Orpheus* (Viking), the final volume in his Cornish trilogy, this one concerned with the production of an opera, *Arthur of Britain*, by E. T. A. Hoffman. Hoffman's words to Planche, his librettist, are the key to the Jungian novel and trilogy: "Let us, I entreat you, explore the marvelous that dwells in the depths of the mind. Let the lyre of Orpheus open the door of the underworld of feeling." In Margaret Atwood's seventh novel, *Cat's Eye* (Doubleday), the narrator, a close surrogate for the author, is Elaine Risley, a middle-aged painter returning to Toronto for a retrospective show. The return awakens complex and troubling memories of a childhood friendship. Does Elaine speak for Atwood when she says, "Eminence creeps up my legs like gangrene?" Also out of Canada, at least originally, is expatriate writer Mavis Gallant, whose newest collection, *In Transit* (Random House), contains twenty *New Yorker* stories set in the 1950s and 1960s.

Foreign fiction, most of it in translation, remained an important and active part of the American literary scene. Although this piece is almost exclusively concerned with the range and variety of the year's hardcover publishing, appreciative mention must be made of the Vintage International series, devoted to trade paperback editions of international modern classics, bringing out works by Kobo Abe, Albert Camus, Friedrich Dürrenmatt, Primo Levi, Vladimir Nabokov, Thomas Mann, Marcel Proust, Italo Svevo, and many more, including new editions of celebrated works by some British (E. M. Forster, Ford Madox Ford, V. S. Naipaul, Doris Lessing) and American (Maxine Hong Kingston) writers. (Vintage books has also separately, as the Vintage Crime Series, been bringing out the work of Dashiell Hammett, James M. Cain, and Chester Himes.)

American public interest and enthusiasm for all things Chinese may have cooled off, at least for the time being, since the shocking events at Tiananmen Square in Beijing; time will tell. Meanwhile there were some Chinese books already in the pipeline. *I Myself Am A Woman* (Beacon) offers a selection, from 1920-1978, of writings by Ding Ling. "All dogs, big and small, bark in the voice they are given," writes Zhang Jie, whose *Heavy Wings* (Grove/Weidenfeld) won China's first Mao Dun Prize in 1985. Zhang Jie did not begin to write until after 1978 and the downfall of the Gang of Four, but she can now be described as "one of China's most popular and controversial writers." Panoramic in scope and cast, this novel centers on the story of the Morning Light Auto Works and depicts a constant struggle between the establishment and the moderate reformers. Another, quite different, novel from China is Wang Anyi's brief story of villagers and village life in *Baotown* (Norton). *6 Tanyin Alley* (China Books), by Liu Zongren, tells what happened during the Cultural Revolution to ten poor families living at one address.

A Wild Sheep Chase (Kodansha), by Haruki Murakami, a young Japanese writer who lives in Rome, was a huge success in Japan and earned serious and favorable international attention. Part hard-boiled thriller, part spoof, part allegorical fable, it tells the story of an unnamed thirty-year-old narrator who works for an advertising agency and is sent on a quest by the Boss to find a mystical sheep with a chestnut-colored star on its back.

In addition to the international work by Indian writers already mentioned, there was the novel *Mistaken Identity* (New Directions), the eighth work of fiction by Nayantara Sahgal. Set in 1929, it tells of Bhushan Singh, who is arrested and held by mistake and tells imaginative tales of his own life to entertain his cell mates. From Iranians came some interesting new fiction. Taghi Modarressi, husband to American novelist Anne Tyler, produced his second novel, *The Pilgrim's Rules of Etiquette* (Doubleday), set in the recent past and chiefly involving Haoi Besharat, an Iranian historian. *Playhouse* (Mage), by Simin Daneshvar, is a collection of stories about women and is said to be a mixture of fact and fiction. From Morocco came Tahar Ben Jelloun's *The Sacred Night* (Harcourt Brace Jovanovich), about a girl named Zahra who is raised as a boy named Ahmed.

Until now, and including the books of the year past, Russian and Soviet writers, at home and in exile, have demonstrated two different ways to deal with the weight of sorrow and absurdity in their country–satire or something like a cry in the night. A superb example of the latter is *Goodnight!* (Viking), by Abram Tertz (Andrei Sinyavsky), which is essentially a memoir of Tertz's arrest in 1965 and his imprisonment. Valentin Rasputin's *Siberia On Fire* (Northern Illinois University Press) is a mixture of stories, essays, and literary criticism from a peasant writer from a small Siberian village whose intensely critical work has been taken as prophetic of the desperate need for glasnost and the truth. Another regional Soviet writer of the new thaw is Chingiz Aitmatov, a native of Kirghizia, in Central Asia, whose new novel *The Place of the Skull* (Grove) is half about human beings ("Man") and half about wolves ("Wolf"). Reviewers speculated as to the influence of Jack London, long popular in the Soviet Union. Exemplary of Soviet satire (there were many of these satirical novels) is Vassily Aksyonov's *Say Cheese!* (Random House), a story of photographers in the 1970s and a send-up of Soviet artistic and intellectual life. Another example, this one selected by the *New York Times Book Review* for its annual list of notable books, is Zinovy Zinik's *The Mushroom Picker* (St. Martin's), a satire about a Russian intellectual obsessed with food. Also Vladimir Voinovich's *The Fur Hat* (Harcourt Brace Jovanovich), a satire on the Soviet Writers' Union, where all are issued fur hats according to their rank and reputation. The protagonist, adventure writer Yefim Rakhlin, is allocated a hat made from the pelt of a tomcat. Widely reviewed was *On the Golden Porch* (Knopf), a collection of thirteen stories, all set in Soviet Russia, by the great-grandniece of Leo Tolstoy–Tatyana Tolstoya. These stories, highly sophisticated and original in form, are more "western" in their passionate concern with the idiosyncrasies of individual lives. Poet Joseph Brodsky has called her "the most original, tactile, luminous voice in Russian prose today."

From Hungary there was *The Notebook* (Grove), by Agota Kristof, a parable of young twins in World War II who, faced with the modern world, train and program themselves (successfully) for inhumanity and evil. World War II in Poland is the setting for *Rondo* (Farrar, Straus & Giroux) by veteran Polish man of letters Kazimierz Brandys. It takes the form of a letter to the editor of a quarterly explaining how the writer, "Tom," created an imaginary underground organization called Rondo during the Nazi occupation in order to engage the interest of an actress, and how what began as falsehood led to true consequences. A variety of Czech novels appeared in English. *Catapult* (Catbird), first of Vladimír Páral's books published in English, is a farce about a man who accidentally has an affair and ends up with seven avid lovers to deal with. In *I Served The King of England* (Harcourt Brace Jovanovich) Bohumil Hrabal, author of *Closely Watched Trains* (1981), followed the life of a tiny (4'6") busboy in Prague named Ditie, who marries a Nazi but whose finest hour was serving roast camel to the Emperor of Ethiopia. Leo Perutz, a Spanish Jew who lived in Prague and wrote in German, a contemporary of Kafka, is represented by two novels published in English this year: *Leonardo's Judas* (Arcade), set in fifteenth-century Milan, and his second novel, first published in 1920, *The Marquis of Bolibar* (Arcade), which is set in Spain during the Napoleonic Wars.

Coming from the German, also, were the stories of Doris Dörrie, who is known as the director of the successful film *Men . . .* (1985), in *Love, Pain, and the Whole Damn Thing* (Knopf). Another story collection is *The Selected Stories of Seigfried Lenz* (New Directions), representing the forty-year career in writing of an author the *New York Times Book Review* called "the last gentleman of German writing." Pantheon brought out Christophe Hein's love story, *The Distant Lover*; and Swiss playwright Friedrich Dürrenmatt continued his fictions of crime and punishment with *The Execution of Justice* (Random House).

Dedicated to F. Scott Fitzgerald is Peter Handke's *The Afternoon of a Writer* (Farrar, Straus & Giroux), being exactly that and leading John Updike to conclude (in the *New Yorker*, 25 December 1989): "To an American reader, so reverent an examination, by a writer, of a writer's psyche verges on the pompous and, worse, on the claustrophobic." *Accident/A Day's News* (Farrar, Straus & Giroux), by East German Christa Wolf, is also a writer's story, but with a difference. Set in April 1986, it is a day in which her brother undergoes cancer surgery and the day the news is spread about Chernobyl. Even though she somehow manages to blame the Americans for the latter, the book is of great interest as an accurate portrayal of an intellectual's transcendence over ideology and social piety. *The Survivor* (Little, Brown), by Fritz J. Raddatz, editor of *Die Zeit*, is the quasi-autobiographical story of Bernd-Jorn Walther from 1930 to the present. Dutch writer Harry

Mulisch tells the story, set in 1982, of a seventy-eight-year-old retired cabaret performer, Uli Bouwmeester, who collaborated with the Germans in World War II, in *Last Call* (Viking). Mistress of "the borderland between the fantastic and the real" (often compared to Isak Dinesen), Danish writer Hanne Marie Svendsen, in *The Gold Ball* (Knopf), tells of four centuries in the life of a family on an island off the coast of Denmark.

Winner of the Mobil Corporation's Pegasus Prize for Literature was Norwegian Kjartan Flogstad for *Dollar Road* (L.S.U. Press), a story following the transformation, from the late 1930s to the early 1970s, of Norway from pastoral to industrial nation. Also from Norway, part of a University of Nebraska Press series, was Knut Faldbakken's *The Sleeping Prince,* story of the self-deceptions of a forty-seven-year-old virgin looking for a prince. That series also published Villy Sorenson's reworking of the classic stories of the Norse gods–*The Downfall of the Gods.* Novelist and sister to Swedish director Ingmar Bergman, Margareta Bergman focuses on the devastation of a family by mental illness in *Karin* (St. Martin's).

There were significant works of fiction out of the Italian. Alberto Savinio, brother of painter Giorgio de Chirico, was author of two books published by Marlboro–*Operatic Lives,* fourteen short biographies, and *Speaking to Clio,* which takes the form of a journal in August and September of 1939. Marlboro also published *Nocturne and Five Tales of Love and Death,* by the famous Gabriele D'Annunzio. Published in Italy in 1936, *Maria Zef* (University of Nebraska Press), by Paola Drigo, the story of life in the mountain villages of Friuli in Veneta, has been brought out in the European Women Writers' Series. Natalia Ginzburg, still an active member of Parliament, is represented by her 1961 novel, *Voices in the Evening* (Arcade/Little Brown), also concerned with village life, as well as the love affair of a village woman and a factory owner's son. Tommaso Landolfi's surreal ghost story, *An Autumn Story* (Eridanos), was first published in Italy in 1975. Spanish writer Ana María Matute had a collection of seven short stories–*The Heliotrope Wall* (Columbia University Press).

There were several French novels that received considerable attention in 1989. Jacques Roubaud's *Hortense Is Abducted,* a highly literate and amusing spoof of the modern detective story as well as contemporary French life and litera-

ture, was published as part of a major new translation series from the French by Dalkey Archive. Roubaud is a member of the celebrated experimental literary workshop Oulipo. Daniel Odier's highly self-reflexive *Cannibal Kiss* (Random House) has as its central figure a young woman named Bird who tells us, "I am unreal. I am a character in a novel." Another character, The Indian, tells her: "You smell like paper, ink and death. I like that." Loup Durand's *Daddy* (Villard) is a complex thriller about an eleven-year-old chess prodigy who ends up (with the S.S. in hot pursuit) as the only one alive who knows how to find $350 million of Jewish savings. Marguerite Duras's *Emily L.* (Pantheon) is, typically, slender and spare, an austere mix of realism and the surreal. Daniele Sallenaue's *Phantom Life* (Pantheon), translated by the gifted Lydia Davis, treats an adultery. Claude Simon, 1985 Nobel laureate, brings together the French Revolution, the Spanish Civil War, and World War II in a story in which history, itself, appears as a trickster, *The Georgics* (Riverrun). Guadeloupe-born writer Maryse Condé tells of the ancient African kingdom of Segu (now part of Mali), how it was first conquered by Moslems, then taken by the French, in *The Children of Segu* (Viking).

It was a year during which several Israeli authors made an impact on the American scene. A. B. Yehoshua tells in five chapters, *Five Seasons* (Doubleday), the story of an Israeli widower looking for a new love; he is a man who has witnessed "the sun rise in glory on men in need of mercy." Nobel laureate S. Y. Agnon writes about the adultery of Byzantine specialist Manfred Herbst with a young nurse in the late 1930s in *Shira* (Schocken). In *His Daughter* (Braziller), Yoram Kaniuk has created a suspense story as an Israeli general searches for his missing daughter. Past and present Israeli officials appear as characters. Three important novels treated the inescapable Holocaust story. *For Every Sin* (Weidenfeld & Nicolson), by Aharon Appelfeld, follows a concentration camp survivor on his journey home. Avigdor Dagan's first book in English, *The Court Jesters* (Jewish Publication Society), is about four prisoners in a camp–a juggler, an astrologer, a hunchback, and a dwarf–who were kept alive to amuse a Nazi officer. *See Under: Love* (Farrar, Straus & Giroux), by thirty-five-year-old David Grossman, whose nonfiction book *The Yellow Wind* (1988) was greatly successful, may well be a major contribution to the literature of the Holocaust and its aftereffects. It is a very complex story, told in four distinct parts (with a "Glossary: The Language of 'Over There,'" including such definitions as "Dreck Jude," German for "dirty Jew"), which is at heart the story of Momik Neuman, only child of Holocaust survivors who grows up to be a writer who repeats the stories of his great-uncle Wasserman, whose storytelling saved his life in the camps, and writes stories about the Polish writer Bruno Sculz. "Love conquers nothing," says Momik.

Latin American writing continued to be a growth stock in the United States. And there were any number of contributions to the cultural milieu by Latin American fiction writers. Carlos Fuentes weighed in (at 531 pages) with the near-futuristic (1992) epic novel of Mexico, as told by an unborn baby, *Christopher Unborn* (Farrar, Straus & Giroux). With all of Mexico in deep trouble and even Yucatan ceded to Club Med, things look bad for the five-hundredth anniversary of Columbus's first voyage. Another Mexican writer, Juan García Ponce, presented *Encounters* (Eridanos), consisting of three stories and a novella, "The Seagull," which brings together teenagers Luis, Mexican, and Katina from Bavaria. Benito Pérez Galdós, sometimes called the "Spanish Balzac," was twenty-seven in 1870, when his first novel, *The Golden Cafe* (Latin American Literary Review) was initially published. It is set in Mexico in the 1820s. *The False Years* (Latin American), by Josefina Vicens, is a long dramatic monologue by seventeen-year-old Luis Alfonso spoken at the grave of his father. Two prominent Argentine writers, Adolfo Bioy Casares and Osvaldo Soriano, brought out books in the United States. Casares's *The Adventures of a Photographer in La Plata* (Dutton) reports the misadventures of a young country photographer, Nicolasito Almanz, who falls in with strange folk in the big city. Before his story is done he comes to one kind of wisdom: "Life is one big joke, without any meaning. Of course if we get sick or slip into poverty, the joke becomes an affliction." *Winter Quarters* (Readers International), by Soriano, is his second novel about the garrison town of Colonia Vela and brings a tango singer and a boozy ex-boxer to town and to trouble. Colombian Manuel Zapata Olivella writes of the hard life of blacks on an island near Cartagena in *Chambacu: Black Slum* (Latin American). Claribel Alegría's *Ashes of Izalco* (Curbstone) is a novel of El Salvador in 1966. Cristina Peri Rossi's *Ship of Fools* (Readers International) is the first of the Uruguayan novelist's ten works of fiction to be published in English. *The*

Enigmatic Eye (Available), by Brazilian writer Moacyr Scliar, is a collection of stories in the manner of "magic realism." Perhaps the most significant Latin American work in translation was Cuban writer Alejo Carpenter's *The Chase* (Farrar, Straus & Giroux), first published in 1956 and finally published in English. Carpenter has been called the father of "magic realism," and this brief (122 pages) novel was enormously influential.

As communications and the so-called information revolution have made the world more and more a single entity, transcending many boundaries, visible and invisible, we are seeing writers create fiction not merely of international setting, exotic or mundane, but also offering fully imagined lives of people who, until recently, would have been defined by alien, almost unimaginable qualities. Thus, as if a paradigm of this changing, Bharati Mukerjee's novel *Jasmine* (Grove/Weidenfeld) follows the constantly changing life of a young Indian widow who comes to America and changes her name as her life and situation change, from Jyoti–Jasmine–Jase to Jane Ripplemeyer, Iowa farm wife. It is a deliberately and richly coincidental story, riddled with random violence. Violence is the center of Marianne Wiggins's *John Dollar* (Harper & Row), a rewrite and revision of William Golding's *Lord of the Flies* (1954), involving eight girls, seven English and one Burmese, on an island with a dying English sailor more than seventy years ago. Wiggins, who is an American from rural Pennsylvania and wife to novelist Salman Rushdie, moves easily and imaginatively across time and space. Not all reviewers were convinced, however. Writing in the *New York Review of Books*, Gabriele Annan concluded: "Wiggins' inconsistencies and affectations are absurd."

American Jonathan Carroll set his "fairy tale for adults," the surrealistic *Sleeping in Flame* (Doubleday), in Vienna. The movement of his fiction has been described as "out of the world of *Vanity Fair* and into that of *Weird Tales*." French writer Henri Coulonges, in *Farewell, Dresden* (Summit), has as his central character a young German girl who experiences the firebombing of Dresden in World War II. Canadian Douglas Glover takes on the South from the inside, writing of the small Florida panhandle town Gomez Gap in *The South Will Rise at Noon* (Penguin). Richard de Combray's *Lost in the City of Light* (Knopf), telling the story of a sculptor, Kevin Korlov, and a woman named Lea whom he meets by means of a computer program for sexual messages, is really about Paris, fully experienced and imagined.

One of the most highly praised first novels of early 1989 was Jonathan Burnham Schwartz's *Bicycle Days* (Summit), which, though in part autobiographical in its story of American Alec Stern working in Japan (and in part literary, borrowing some things from Brad Leithauser's *Equal Distance,* 1984, and Jay McInerney's *Ransom,* 1985), is nevertheless audacious in its attempt to render Japanese culture with accuracy. British writer Edward Swift in *The Christopher Park Regulars* (British American) deals with the denizens of Christopher Park in the West Village. *Publishers Weekly* praised the novel as "an elegant hymn to weirdness." The late Bruce Chatwin possessed amazing imaginative empathy with no two books alike except in that he imagined and created them. In the posthumously published *Utz* (Viking) he brought excitement and attention to the story of a Sudetan German porcelain collector in Prague.

Regional transference can be just as daring and successful, as evidenced by James Kaplan's *Pearl's Progress* (Knopf), which tells of the essential assimilation of a Jewish poet, a New Yorker, teaching deep in the heart of Mississippi. More extraordinary, indeed a major work, is A. G. Mojtabai's fifth novel, *Ordinary Time* (Doubleday), a religious fable rooted in a completely credible Texas town called Durance. Perhaps an even more extraordinary example of the liberated international literary imagination, and one that was well and widely publicized, was *The Remains of the Day* (Knopf), created by the young Japanese author, Kazuo Ishiguro, who lives now in England. In this story, set in 1956, he effectively uses the voice of Stevens, butler of Darlington Hall, to tell directly the story of his master, Lord Darlington, and, indirectly, the decline and fall of Empire as viewed by a faithful and enthusiastic servant. Thoroughly credible, in both style and substance, the novel would constitute a genuine achievement even for a skilled and native-born British writer. Just at year's end appeared yet another superior example of the new international novel. Spanish writer Javier García Sánchez, in *Lady of the South Wind* (North Point), sets his novel in northern Germany, has, as his central characters, Olga and Hans, and, as author, offers allusions and homage to the work of Goethe, Hölderlin, and Mann. Robert Roger's third novel, *Mexico Days* (Weidenfeld & Nicolson), treats with equal international ease two families, one Mexican and

Dust jacket for Higgins's highly praised novel about an ex-con and his criminal activities

the other American, linked by business partnership and a good deal more. Not even sci-fi is safe from the trend of imaginative internationalism. Dave Wolverton's *On My Way to Paradise* (Bantam) is a thriller about mercenaries on a Japanese corporate planet.

Simultaneous with the sense of one world has been the discovery of the voices of the many and diverse ethnic strains of contemporary America. Karen Karbo's first novel, *Trespassers Welcome Here* (Putnam), introduces the reader to the Russian émigrés of Los Angeles. Cynthia Kadohata, in *The Floating World* (Viking), tells of the adventures of a Japanese immigrant family crisscrossing the United States in search of a place to call home, told from the point of view of a twelve-year-old Japanese girl. Judith Ortiz Cofer, in *The Line of the Sun* (University of Georgia Press), shows us Marisol Santacruz growing up Puerto Rican in America. *Lone Stars* (Atlantic Monthly Press), by Sophia Healy, is the story of Stas, a Pole, and his Mexican wife, Lupe, living near San Antonio. Virgil F. Suarez describes three generations of a

Cuban-American family in California in *Latin Jazz* (Morrow).

Also recreating the Cuban-American experience is one of the most widely reviewed and highly praised novels (a finalist for most of the year's leading literary prizes) of the year—*The Mambo Kings Play Songs of Love* (Farrar, Straus & Giroux), by Oscar Hijuelos. In this, his second novel, Hijuelos tells the story, from the later vantage point of 1980, of two Cuban brothers, Cesar and Nestor Castillo, musicians (the Mambo Kings) in the 1950s, whose one great moment of showbiz triumph was an appearance with Desi Arnaz on the "I Love Lucy" show. It is an evocative period piece and a story of art and commerce, written with high energy and lyricism.

Two novels treat the immigrant experience in the form of the "generational saga." Although the line of present action in Mary Gordon's *The Other Side* (Viking) all takes place in one day, this story of Ellen and Vince McNamara covers ninety years and involves their children, grandchildren, and great-grandchildren. Marina Warner's *The Lost Father* (Simon & Schuster) covers seven decades in the lives of the Pittagoras family who came to America from Ninfania in southern Italy.

The immigrant experience that, of course, was part of the substance of Rushdie's *The Satanic Verses* is part of the British literary scene as well. Anita Brookner's newest, *Latecomers* (Pantheon), is a story of two German refugees, Thomas Hartmann and Thomas Fibich, old friends, in England. Amitav Ghosh's second novel, *The Shadow Lives* (Viking), follows, from World War II to the present, two families, one in Calcutta and the other in London. Piers Paul Read's *A Season in the West* (Random House), a satirical novel of London in the 1980s, has as one of its central characters Josef Birek, dissident Czech writer. Frederick Raphael's *After the War* (Viking) follows the maturing of semiautobiographical Michael, a boy in World War II and later a playwright in a story centered on Jewishness in England.

The American-Jewish immigrant experience continues to engage the attention of fiction writers, almost inevitably involving, in its contemporary form, the almost ineffable experience and history of the Holocaust. Jerome Badanes's *The Final Opus of Leon Solomon* (Knopf) is narrated in the form of a memoir by Lem Soloman, whose memories awaken Vilna, Auschwitz, and Harlem, and whose simple explanation of the need for song strikes the reader like a knife: "When we

stop singing, the Lord, blessed be His name, begins to slaughter." This is a first novel. Established masters Cynthia Ozick and Saul Bellow published slender and resonant short novels on the subject. Ozick's book, *The Shawl* (Knopf), less than a hundred pages in length, consists of the title story, which won first prize in the annual *O. Henry Prize Stories* collection in 1981, and the novella "Rosa" (1984), both of which originally appeared in the *New Yorker*. "The Shawl" tells of the death of Rosa's infant, Magda, in the camps. "Rosa" picks up the story thirty years later with Rosa Lubin now living and growing old in Miami, quarreling by mail and phone with her other daughter, Stella, desperately sorting out her memories of Magda and attempting to live by the truth—"I don't like to give myself lies." In the end love finds her suddenly, takes her as she is.

Bellow's *The Bellarosa Connection* (Penguin), one of two original short novels he brought out in paperback editions in 1989, is the story of Harry Fonstein, rescued from Nazi-occupied Europe through the offices of Broadway producer Billy Rose (hence the title). This story is complex and typically hard-edged, hard-nosed ("All the world *was* dark and dreary. Fucking-A right!"), but, also typically for Bellow, deeply moving—"God doesn't forget, but your prayer requests him particularly to remember your dead." Bellow's other novella, *A Theft* (Penguin), published earlier in the year, has a different focus, telling of Clara Velde, an executive and "a raw-boned American woman" in New York, mother of three daughters, who has managed to survive four husbands and two suicide attempts and to keep the one great love of her life, with lawyer Ithiel ("Teddy") Regler, alive. And whose emerald ring disappears to start the plot in motion and is returned to end it. The culprit is the Haitian boyfriend of Clara's Austrian au pair, a couple of the latest kind of immigrants. Of the Haitian, Clara, no "bleeding heart," says: "These people came up from the tropical slums to outsmart New York, and with all the rules crumbling here as elsewhere, they could do it."

The novella, which has not been the form of choice favored by many publishers, got a new lease on life in 1989. Near the end of the year Jane Smiley's *Ordinary Love & Good Will: Two Novellas* (Knopf) received rave reviews. These two domestic stories are concerned, the author says, with "the death of dreams." "All life is extremity," says Rachael Ingalls of her collection of four novellas–*The End of Tragedy* (Simon & Schuster)–and Ingalls, an American living in England, has created some extreme situations involving giant carniverous toads and an insatiable mechanical love doll. Harold Burton Meyer's *Geronimo's Ponies* (Council Oak), telling of a few weeks in the life of young Davey Parker during the late 1930s, was winner of the first National Novella Award.

Among other significant works of fiction touching on the ethnic experience are Allegra Goodman's *Total Immersion* (Harper & Row), eleven stories about Jews and the lure of assimilation, mostly set in Hawaii; Larry Woiwode's *The Neumiller Stories* (Farrar, Straus & Giroux), thirteen stories, ten of which appeared in the *New Yorker* before 1975, about the Neumillers of Mahomet, North Dakota, who became the subject of the author's well-known novel *Beyond the Bedroom Wall* (1975); Rohinton Mistry's *Swimming Lessons* (Houghton Mifflin), eleven stories about Parsi neighborhoods in Bombay and Toronto; *Fifty Years of Eternal Vigilance* (Peachtree) by Carolyn Thorman, stories of Polish- and Lithuanian-Americans; E. Annie Prloux's *Heart Songs* (Scribners), nine stories of small-town New England; and Annette Sanford's eleven stories of Texas and Texans, *Lasting Attachments* (S.M.U. Press).

Some regions have, in themselves, an ethnic base. Appalachia is one of these. Two first-rate collections of stories about Southern Appalachia appeared this year. Poet Robert Morgan brought out *The Blue Valleys* (Peachtree), thirteen stories ranging in time from the Civil War to the present. All set in Copperhead, Virginia (Buchanan County), during the 1930s and 1940s, the eleven stories of Bo Ball's *Appalachian Patterns* (Independence Publishers) demonstrate a wonderful sense of place and language. Regionalism and ethnic conflict in Maine form the story of Cathie Pelletier's second novel, *Once Upon a Time On the Banks* (Viking), where the town of Mattagash, Maine, is torn inside out on the occasion of the wedding of Amy Joy Lawlor to Claude Cloutier of Watertown. Fannie Flagg has written that these people "give even Erskine Caldwell's turnip-snatching Jeeter Lester family of 'Tobacco Road' a run for their money." Matter of fact, Caldwell's earliest novels were set in rural Maine. Southern California by now must surely qualify as a region sufficiently stereotypical to claim a kind of ethnicity. *Daddy Boy* (Algonquin), by Carey Cameron, is a story of growing up in Hollywood in the 1960s. David Shields's second novel, *Dead Languages* (Knopf), concerns a radical-chic family in L.A.

and centers on Jeremy Zorn, twelve, who has a terrible stutter. Another childhood view of Los Angeles is found in the highly praised *The Year of the Zinc Penny* (Norton), by Rick De Marinis. This is set in 1943 and is about Trygve Napoli, age ten, and his coming of age: "I had discovered something about myself. I knew I was now capable of mustering any necessary lie at will."

It seems altogether possible that the creatures who create rock-and-roll music (as distinct from the mass of creatures who listen to it by choice or otherwise) represent a different tribe with its own totems and taboos, signs and symbols. If so the world of rockers is depicted in a couple of 1989 novels. Michael Vertura's *Night Time Losing Time* (Simon & Schuster) is narrated by a rock-and-roll keyboard player, Jesse Wales, in the town of Quartzsite, Arizona. In *After Roy* (Knopf) Mary Tannen tells us what happened, separately and together and very differently, to the members of the rock band Abiding Light (Roy, Eddie, Sparks, Yolanda, and Maggie) ten years after they broke up. Also after the fact is the time scheme of *Rolling Stone* writer Marcelle Clements's first novel, *Rock Me* (Simon & Schuster), which finds Casey, a female rock star of the 1960s, on the island of Kaulani in Hawaii, and is basically a love-triangle story involving Casey and old flame Michael and present boyfriend Anthony, a writer. Casey says: "Except in your songs, the best affair is the affair you don't have." But, fortunately for the reader, she doesn't live by her motto. The publisher is more to the point in the jacket copy: "Driven by erotic tension, *Rock Me* explores the dark side of creativity."

The long experience and memory of Native Americans continues to fascinate our fiction writers. Pulitzer Prize-winner N. Scott Momaday, basing his compendium of myths and stories on an epigraph from Borges ("For myth is at the beginning of literature, and also at its end.") and on the Kiowa myth of the Bear Boy and the seven stars, tells of the return of San Francisco artist Locke Setman to his Native American roots, with more than a little help from a mystical Navajo medicine woman, in *The Ancient Child* (Doubleday). The distinguished novelist William Humphrey published *No Resting Place* (Seymour Lawrence/Delacorte), which recounts the removal of the Cherokee Nation from Georgia to Texas in the 1830s. It tells the story of Amos Ferguson (also *Noquisi*), a blond Cherokee, beginning from the vantage point of the present, and a descendant–Amos Ferguson Smith IV. Perhaps the most intricate and subtle literary context for the myths and stories of the Indians comes to us in translation in Mario Vargas Llosa's *The Storyteller* (Farrar, Straus & Giroux), which tells the ambiguous story of Saul Zaratas (also *Mascarita*–"Mask Face"), anthropologist-turned-teacher and storyteller to an ancient Amazon tribe–the Machiguengas. In *There's Something in the Backyard* (Viking), by Richard Snodgrass, two middle-aged academic couples, next-door neighbors, have their tedious lives altered for the better by the arrival in their yard and lives of a Hopi Indian kachina.

Speaking of which–the academic . . . surely the academic novel is a modest genre in its own right, and surely the conventions of its characters have become stereotypical enough almost to merit ethnic status. In any case academic fiction continues to be written and, evidently, read. Top of the line and the work of the man who has, for better or worse, given new energy to the academic novel is David Lodge's *Nice Work* (Viking), last of his trilogy about academic life. This one involves "real life" as well, putting Vic Wilcox, managing director of a factory, in confrontation and more with Robyn Penrose, thirty-three-year-old lecturer and feminist at the University of Rummidge. He teaches her much about modern industry and business practices. In return she teaches him about poststructuralist theory in bed. Lodge fans (many) will be pleased to discover that the sleazy American academic wheeler-dealer Morris Zapp makes an obligatory cameo appearance.

Anne Bernays's *Professor Romeo* (Weidenfeld & Nicolson) offers a trendy story of sexual harassment at Harvard, featuring Jake Barker, predatory professor of psychology, who tells his students before having his way with them: "I don't want us to do this if I have to persuade you. It's got to be something both of us want in the same loving way." *A Bliss Case* (Coffee House) by Michael Aaron Rockland, Chair of American Studies at Rutgers, permits four narrators, each with a vested interest, to tell how Rutgers English professor Sidney Kantor evolved into Swami Anudaba, faithful follower of Babadahs. In Rebecca Goldstein's *The Late-Summer Passion of a Woman of Mind* (Farrar, Straus & Giroux), Eve Mueller, a philosophy professor, is awakened to life and, with that, bitter suppressed memories by Michael, a young student. Yet another academic story is a British first novel, *The Cartomancer* (St.

Martin's), by Anne Spillard. This account of the academic community of Avalon comes to us via the unreliable narrator, May Knott, who tells fortunes and claims to be writing this selfsame novel. Finally, closer to home is Jane LeCompte's first novel, *Moon Passage* (Harper & Row), the story of two women in love with the same man, creative writing teacher Jay Ellis. The women are Anne Ellis, his forty-five-year-old wife, and Ellen Cassidy, student-girlfriend. In an unusual fictional device, the man never appears directly in flesh and fact in the novel. Possibly more purely literary than academic is Carol Shields's fifth novel, *Swann* (Viking), of four people searching for the whole truth about Mary Swann, who had been called "the Emily Dickinson of Upper Canada" and was murdered in 1965.

It was an excellent year for various and sundry kinds of genre fiction, more and more becoming a reputable part of the mainstream, in fact as well as marketing. With *The Killing Man* (Dutton) Mickey Spillane reintroduced Mike Hammer after a nineteen-year vacation. And Mysterious Press produced the first American publication of Kingsley Amis's *The Crime of the Century* (1975), which first appeared as a serial in the *Sunday Times*.

John le Carré (David Cornwell) struck gold and stirred up a certain amount of controversy with *The Russia House* (Knopf), earning himself the cover of *Newsweek* (5 June) in the process. A complex plot, taking glasnost very seriously ("The old isms were dead, the contest between Communism and Capitalism had ended in a whimper."), the story offended some American critics by putting most of the blame for the long life of the Cold War on the United States. As C.I.A. agent Russell Sheriton puts it in a moment of candor: "How do you peddle the arms race when the only asshole you have to race against is yourself?" Martin Cruz Smith scored another success with his latest adventure of Arkady Renko, hero of *Gorky Park* (1981). In *Polar Star* (Random House) Renko solves a murder on a factory ship in the Bering Sea. James Lee Burke gave us his detective, Dave Robicheaux, a forty-nine-year-old Cajun widower and Vietnam vet, in *Black Cherry Blues* (Little, Brown). A remarkable posthumous collaboration created *Poodle Springs* (Putnam), by Robert B. Parker and the late Raymond Chandler. When he died in 1959, Chandler left four chapters and some notes for *Poodle Springs*. Parker, author of the popular Spenser novels, gave us the remaining thirty-seven chapters. Chandler fans will find Philip Marlowe married, but not mellow: "I married you because I love you and one of the things I love you for is that you don't give a damn for anybody—sometimes not even for me." Spenser stars in another novel by Parker, *Playmates* (Putnam), which concerns point-shaving in college basketball. Elmore Leonard's *Killshot* (Arbor) pits hard-muscled Wayne Colson and his good wife Carmen against a couple of hit men, including one splendid Leonard creation—Armand ("Blackbird") Degas, a cold-blooded, yet sympathetic, Canadian Indian.

Haughton Murphy, in *Murder Keeps A Secret* (Simon & Schuster), follows Wall Street lawyer Reuben Frost as he solves a murder case. Robert Campbell's hero in *Juice* (Poseidon), Eddie "Panama" Heath, a Los Angeles vice cop, takes us on a tour of downside L.A. as he handles a loan-sharking case. Douglas C. Jones adroitly brought two genres together with *Come Winter* (Hutter/Holt), which, set in rural Arkansas in the last years of the nineteenth century, is part western, becoming a murder mystery that can be solved by his protagonist, banker and former cavalryman Roman Hasford. More purely western was Warren Kiefer's *Outlaw* (Fine), a picaresque tale of one Lee Garland and including a mix of fictional and historical characters, stretching in time from the days of the Apache raids to the Vietnam War.

Lindsey Davis brought the historical and the suspense story together in *Silver Pigs* (Crown), set in ancient Rome and Britain. His detective, Falco, solves a murder and finds some missing ingots. "If home was where the heart was," says the hero, jockey Derek Franklin, in former jockey Dick Francis's twenty-eighth novel, *Straight* (Putnam), "I really lived in the windy Downs and in the stable yards and on the raucous racetracks." This crime novel ("I inherited my brother's life and it nearly killed me.") was not surprisingly a longtime best-seller in 1989. Thomas Sanchez's first novel in sixteen years, *Mile Zero* (Knopf), is a superior example of the marriage of the thriller and the literary. Set in a palpable and authentic Key West, it has as one of its central characters the Cuban-American cop Justo Tamarindo, and is tightly threaded with crime and punishment, racial and cultural conflict and is evocatively written in an energetic, "literary" style.

Ed McBain's *Lullaby* (Morrow) is a new 87th Precinct novel; Peter Maas's *Father and Son* (Simon & Schuster) is about gunrunning to Ireland; Lawrence Block brings back Matt Scudder,

Manhattan-based hero of six previous novels, in *Out On the Cutting Edge* (Morrow); West Coast writer Robert Craig presents the second appearance of Elvis Cole and his partner Joe Pike, searching for a Japanese manuscript and battling the Japanese gangsters (Yakuza) in *Stalking the Angel* (Bantam); another example of the international crime scene is James Melville's *A Haiku for Hanse* (Scribners), his tenth in the series featuring Inspector Tetsuo Otanni of the Hyogo prefecture; Japanese detective novelist Seicho Matsumoto produced another in his series concerning Imanishi Eitaro of the Tokyo Metropolitan Police and his youthful sidekick, Yoshimura Hiroshi, with *Inspector Imanishi Investigates* (Soho).

Miami Herald writer Carl Hiaasen puts his detective hero into dangerous conflict with a six-foot-nine-inch hit man and an inept plastic surgeon in *Skin Tight* (Putnam); Patrick Anderson's *Busy Bodies* (Simon & Schuster) is a Washington story of murder and big campaign money, involving his detective, Tommy Tullis, gossip columnist for the *Capital Vindicator;* Bartholomew Gill's *The Death of a Joyce Scholar* (Morrow) begins with a Bloomsday celebration during which a professor at Trinity College is killed, bringing the attention of Chief Inspector Peter McGarr, his eighth published case. Gill is a pseudonym for the American writer Mark McGarrity. Another "literary" detective story, ninth in a series, is *A Trap For Fools* (Dutton) by Amanda Cross (Carolyn Heilbrun). Once again we have Kate Fansler, feminist English professor and amateur detective, who can tell the murderer when the time comes: "In absolute contradiction to Freud, I have simply developed a very acute moral sense. And you offend it."

Major attention was awarded to Tony Hillerman and his latest—*Talking God* (Harper & Row). Set mostly in Washington, D. C., but also on a Navajo reservation, this story pits Lieutenant Joe Leaphorn and Officer Chee ("We are like two dogs who followed two sets of tracks to the same brush pile.") against a mad hit man—Leroy Fleck. That the genre novel, specifically the thriller, allows for the flexibility of increasing eccentricity is evident from two examples from 1989. Martha Grimes's latest, the elegantly parodic *Send Bygraves* (Putnam), set in the quaint English village of Little Pudly, is written in 108 pages of verse. Iris Weil Collett (pseudonym for Larry Crumbley, a professor at Texas A & M) produced a story of high finance and gem smuggling, *Accosting the Golden Spire* (Thomas Horton), which can double as a business textbook and, as the *Wall Street Journal* put it, "teaches basic accounting and taxation in a thriller format."

A couple of odd and interesting examples of the *what if* genre were Frank Deford's *Casey on the Loose* (Viking) and John Byrne Cooke's *South of the Border* (Bantam). Deford, formerly of *Sports Illustrated,* tells what might have happened in "Casey at the Bat" if the catcher had dropped that third strike. Through the voice of Charley Stringo, cowboy and movie actor, Cooke gives us a Butch Cassidy who lived on into the 1930s. Horror novels continue to be created, and two that received serious notice were Anne Rice's *The Mummy Or Ramses the Damned* (Ballantine) and *The Wolf's Hour* (Pocket) by Robert R. Mc-Cammon, his tenth novel, this one set in World War II and featuring Michael Gallatin, definitely a werewolf and probably the illegitimate son of Rasputin.

The enormous popular success of the work of Tom Clancy, continuing with *Clear and Present Danger* (Putnam), which puts his man, Jack Ryan, in violent conflict with Colombian drug lords, as well as the usual wimp bureaucrats inside the beltway in Washington ("Men were still men. They knew what justice was, courts and lawyers to the contrary."), has helped to create a whole new industry in the techno-thriller. The results of glasnost have somewhat complicated the world of the techno-thriller and clouded its future, but there were a number of outstanding and successful examples during the year. J. C. Pollock's *Payback* (Delacorte) has his hero, Jack Gannon of Delta Force, going against "a think-tank academic with no hands-on experience who had never put his ass on the line in his life" and, more seriously, Malik, a rogue KGB agent. In Stephen Coonts's *The Minotaur* (Doubleday) Jack Grafton struggles with the problem of a "mole" in the Pentagon. Guy Durham's *Stealth* (Putnam) and Dean Ing's *The Ransom of Black Stealth One* (St. Martin's) both trade in the secrets of the new "Stealth" bomber. Steve Shagan's *Pillars of Fire* (Pocket Books) concerns Israel's secret service–the Mossad. Sarah K. Wolf brings a feminist perspective to the techno-thriller with *The Harbinger Effect* (Simon & Schuster), whose central character is Molly Davison, a relief-agency wonder.

The techno-thriller is, of course, close and sometimes indistinguishable kin to the classic futurist sci-fi novel. Some of them earned the attention of readers and reviewers in 1989. Isaac Asimov brought out *Nemesis* (Doubleday), set in

the year 2236 and dealing with colonists in a remote solar system. Joan Slonczewski, in *The Wall Around Eden* (Morrow), placed survivors of a nuclear war in contact and conflict with aliens called "angel-bees." In *Total Recall* (Morrow) Piers Anthony tackled the subject of memory transplants in the twenty-first century. Whitley Strieber, who has published two earlier nonfiction books about UFOs, turned to fiction with more success. His *Majestic* (Putnam) begins on a sheep ranch near Roswell, New Mexico, in 1947 and tells a story of UFOs and aliens. Truman and Eisenhower and other historical characters have cameo roles. Poet and novelist (and winner of a MacArthur "genius" award) Brad Leithauser set *Hence: A Meditation in Voices* in the near future of 1993 and 2025. With touches of metafiction it is essentially the story of a contest between Timothy Garner and a chess-playing computer named Anndy.

For some reason, perhaps the continuing bookstall success of the romance, there seemed to be less serious historical fiction this year than usual. Among the better examples of the genre were the following: Don Robertson's fourth novel about the Civil War, this one about its final days, *Prisoners of Twilight* (Crown); Bernard Cornwell's continuing story of Richard Sharpe, a soldier in the Napoleonic Wars, in *Sharpe's Rifles* and *Sharpe's Revenge* (Viking); Catherine MacCoun's story of Ingrid Fairfax, a failed saint of fourteenth-century England, in *The Age of Miracles* (Atlantic Monthly Press); Maria Bellonci's *Private Renaissance* (Morrow), winner of Italy's Strega Prize, told from the point of view of Isabella d'Este, Duchess of Mantua; from Spain, Llorenc Villalonga's story of the end of the noble house of Bearn in nineteenth-century Mallorca–*The Dolls' Room* (Deutsch); Alain Absire's *God's Equal* (Harcourt Brace Jovanovich), winner of the prestigious Prix Femina, a complex tale of eleventh-century Normandy; *Anne Boleyn* (Overlook) by Vercors, which takes an unusual, possibly unique view of Boleyn as a rising stateswoman ahead of her time; Robert Goddard's *Painting the Darkness* (Poseidon), set in Australia and Britain in the 1880s; Jim Grace's *The Gift of Stones* (Scribners) is credibly set in the late Stone Age; David Raphael's *The Alhambra Decree* (Carmi House, 1988), telling the story of the expulsion of the Jews from Spain in 1492; Walter J. Boyne's *Trophy for Eagles* (Crown), about the aviation world from 1927 to 1937.

Basing his novel on someone mentioned three times in the Bible, Leslie H. Whitten, Jr., has rewritten the Gospels in *The Last Disciple: The Book of Demas* (Atheneum). Reviewing this novel for the *Washington Times*, Michael Hedges warned: "Persons who believe strongly in the virgin birth, the resurrection and the miracles of Jesus will find Demas's rendering of the Christian doctrine misguided at best." With *Fire Down Below* (Farrar, Straus & Giroux), his twelfth work of fiction, Nobel laureate William Golding concluded his trilogy of Edmund Talbot's 1815 voyage on an old warship from England to New South Wales. John Banville, literary editor of the *Irish Times*, who has earlier created memorable and original historical fiction dealing with Kepler, Copernicus, and Newton, told the Faustian story of Gabriel Swan, a mathematical prodigy, in *Mefisto* (Godine). Centering her story *Raj* (Simon & Schuster) on Jaya, daughter of the Mararajh of Balmer, Gita Mehta wrote of India from the time of Queen Victoria's Diamond Jubilee through the bloody civil wars of independence. Lebanese author Amin Maalouf, in *Leo Africanus* (Norton), tells the life story of Hasan al Wazzan, aka Leo Africanus, his childhood in Moorish Granada, youth in Fez, Timbuktu, and Cairo, and maturity at the center of power in Constantinople and Rome. Finally, not to be ignored is James A. Michener's latest blockbuster fictional study of a region from prehistory to the present–*Caribbean* (Random House).

Vietnam novels continued to be written and to appear. West Pointer Lucian K. Truscott IV, author of *Dress Gray* (1979), this time told a story of illicit dope-running by the C.I.A. in *Army Blue* (Crown). Ronald Argo's *Year of the Monkey* (Simon & Schuster) concerns a court-martial for murder. Story writer Larry Brown surprised some readers with his grim first novel, *Dirty Work* (Algonquin), told in alternating monologues by two veterans in a VA hospital–Braiden, who is black and has no limbs, and Walter, white, with no face. *The Deuce* (Simon & Schuster), by Robert Olen Butler, is a postwar story of a teenaged Vietnamese boy growing up in Point Pleasant, New Jersey. Barry M. Taylor's *Shadow Tiger* (Walker) is a somewhat more conventional thriller involving the C.I.A., the U.S. Navy, an American ambassador, and a North Vietnamese hit man named Jia Lazar. In something of a tour de force, Susan Fromberg Schaeffer, known for popular fiction of the blockbuster kind, told the gritty and authentic story of a working-class Brooklyn boy in Vietnam–*Buffalo*

Afternoon (Knopf). Another Vietnam novel, commercially successful, was Mark Berent's *Rolling Thunder* (Putnam), reporting the role of fliers in that war. Partly concerned with the war in Vietnam is *White Badge* (Soho), by Korean writer Ahn Junghyo. The title refers to the badge of the Korean 9th "White Horse" Division (in which the author served), which joined the Americans fighting in Vietnam. Judging by the account of it in this interesting novel, the war was much the same for the Korean soldiers as for the American grunts.

With the whole problem of homosexuality and gay rights now an open part of national discussion, it is no surprise that there was a good deal of overtly gay fiction this year. Armistead Maupin produced his sixth and final volume of the "Tales of the City" series (the first five having been successfully serialized in the San Francisco newspapers), dealing with the residents, gay and straight alike, at 28 Barbary Lane. A good many of the works of gay fiction inevitably had to come to terms with the fact of the AIDS epidemic. Highly regarded, veteran novelist James Purdy published *Garments the Living Wear* (City Lights), story of Jared Wakemen and "the Pest" (AIDS). John Weir's *The Irreversible Decline of Eddie Socket* (Harper & Row), dodged no harsh facts, but created a memorable young hero, Eddie, and produced a story aptly described by Raymond Sokolov in the *Wall Street Journal* as "an elegantly written, even witty book." Gary Indiana, columnist for the *Village Voice*, published *Horse Crazy* (Grove), a story of gay life in New York. Joel Redon's *Bloodstream* (Lyle Stuart) closely follows four months in the life of Peter, an AIDS victim. Holly Uyemoto's *Rebel Without a Clue* (Crown), not strictly a gay novel, nevertheless deals chiefly with a death by AIDS. Sam D'Allesandro's *The Zombie Pit* (Crossing Press), thirteen stories told in the first person of gay life in the 1980s, was published after the author's death from AIDS. David B. Feinberg's first novel, *Eight-Sixed* (Viking), is about the AIDS epidemic in New York City. Jonis Agee's collection of stories *Bend This Heart* (Coffee House), which was named by the *New York Times Book Review* as one of 1989's "Notable Books," while not a gay book, is concerned with varieties of erotic experience and presents an explicit account of a gay relationship in "Private Lives." Two overtly lesbian works of fiction were Nisa Donnelly's *The Bar Stories: A Novel After All* (St. Martin's), set in and around Babe and Babe's Bar in San Francisco, and Shay Youngblood's *The*

JULIAN BARNES

A HISTORY
OF THE
WORLD
IN 10½
CHAPTERS

A NOVEL

Dust jacket for Barnes's novel comprised of ten separate, but subtly linked, stories set in various historical periods and written in widely divergent styles

Big Mama Stories (Firebrand).

Although homosexuality figures in David Leavitt's widely reviewed third novel, *Equal Affections* (Weidenfeld & Nicolson), it is more strictly a family novel, dealing with a family of four, the Coopers, and the death by cancer of the mother. Death by cancer, his own as it happens, is the unwritten ending to Swiss writer Peter Noll's *In the Face of Death* (Viking), a fictional and autobiographical account of his last year of life. First novel *Dying Young* (Doubleday), by Marti Leimbach, already well publicized on account of its $500,000 advance, tells the story of a love triangle, one of whose characters is dying of leukemia. This one opened to mixed reviews at best. A better critical reception greeted Dutch writer J. Bernlef's treatment of another feared disease of our age, Alzheimer's, in *Out of Mind* (Godine). Brief as it is, this first-person narrative is a work of sensitive virtuosity. Although Bernlef has published more than fifty books in Dutch, this is his first book translated into English.

As if speaking for a whole generation of new writers of the New South, Libby Lampert, adolescent protagonist of Neil Caudle's first novel, *Voices From Home* (Putnam), says: "Sometimes I would like to go someplace where you can tell the truth and not have people go all to pieces." The southern writers keep trying to do just that, and several distinctively southern novels of more than passing interest were published this year. They include Sterling Watson's *Blind Tongues* (Delta); Shelby Hearon's eleventh novel, *Owning Jolene* (Knopf); Valery Sayers's *How I Got Him Back* (Doubleday), continuing the story begun in *Due East* (1987), of Mary Faith Rapple; John Kennedy Toole's *The Neon Bible* (Grove), written when he was a teenager, a first-person story of the small-town South in the 1940s; *The Queen of October* (Algonquin), by Shelley Fraser Mickle (this coming-of-age novel, which includes a parrot named Toulouse, a chicken named Elizabeth Taylor, and a thirteen-year-old named Sally Maulden, all citizens of Coldwater, Arkansas, has been described by novelist Jim Shepard as a prime example of the new genre of "Southern zany"); Kaye Gibbons's *A Virtuous Woman* (Algonquin), a novel about a dying woman, Ruby Stokes, in rural Georgia; Robert Love Taylor's *The Lost Sister* (Algonquin), which takes place in Oklahoma City in the 1920s and 1930s; and Terry Pringle's *A Fine Time to Leave Me* (Algonquin), his second novel and a lively story of a couple of innocents, Chris and Lori Gray, who get married first, then try to learn what marriage means.

One of the more impressive works of fiction that tells truths about the new, post-Faulknerian, urban and industrial South is Paul Hemphill's third novel, *King of the Road* (Houghton Mifflin), in which a seventy-year-old retired trucker and his grown son, Sonny, fire up his old truck, Dixie Redball, for one last cross-country haul. Here we see much the same world found in the fiction of Bobbie Ann Mason, but from a different angle, "where folks still point to the past with swagger and pride." A somewhat more stylish literary version of the new times, but no less lively, is T. R. Pearson's *Call and Response* (Linden), telling the story of Nestor Tudor, middle-aged widower who smokes Old Gold filters, drinks Ancient Age, and has a powerful crush on Mary Alice Celestin Lefler. Ingrid Hill casts a wide net and catches the variety of the New South in her collection of stories *Dixie Church Interstate Blues* (Viking). Like many southern writers, she seems to find the life of these times infinitely fascinating and unfathomable. As one of her characters puts it: "Art can't do anything to make life do anything, but be life, a thing you cannot understand."

More than usual the year witnessed the publication of works of fiction unusual enough to be classified as distinctly oddball. Ernest Callenbach's *Publisher's Lunch* (Ten Speed), for example, consists of a series of dramatic dialogues between an editor, Michelle, and a writer, Jim, here former philosophy professor, on the subject of the publishing business. Menus of each lunch are dutifully presented. *The Cockroaches of Stay More* (Helen & Kurt Wolff/Harcourt Brace Jovanovich) is Donald Harrington's latest fiction about Stay More, Arkansas, this time exclusively from the point of view of the roaches ("roosterroaches") there and featuring Squire Sam Ingledew, whose roachy wisdom is: "You have to see everything in a different language to understand it." Somewhat more conventional, if no less special, is Carl Djerassi's *Cantor's Dilemma* (Doubleday). Djerassi, a distinguished Stanford chemist, tells how prizewinning science works and doesn't work and outlines the scientific establishment.

Lynn Alexander's *Resonating Bodies* (Atheneum) has as its central character a sweet and entirely credible viola da gamba, named Rose, who is 319 years old and is being played, in the present, in the music room in Versailles. Robert Mayer's *I, JFK* (Dutton) is presumably being dictated by the ghost of JFK ("Here, among ghosts, there are no ghost writers.") in 1988, his twenty-fifth year in purgatory. He tells his story, talks to other dead companions, fictional and real (including Robert Kennedy, LBJ, and Martin Luther King, Jr.), and discusses his problem of "Pussymania." Adam Lively's first novel, *Blue Fruit* (Atlantic Monthly Press), may well belong in this category of the oddball, telling, as it does, the story of one John Fields, a ship's doctor and violinist in 1787, who passes through a time warp and ends up playing his fiddle in a Harlem jazz band. Gordon Lish's latest, *Extravaganza* (Putnam), fits in fine, being accurately described in the *New York Times Book Review* as a "collage of old Smith and Dale vaudeville routines, along with more recent gags." The reviewer noted an ineradicable strain of serious angst linking the old jokes together: "Jokes may abound in 'Extravaganza,' but Mr. Lish makes sure that existential despair keeps whistling through the cracks."

Books by celebrities, all better known for things other than their writing, continued to hold a place on publishers' lists. Actor William Shatner's novel, *Tekwar* (Putnam), is optimistically set in twenty-second-century Los Angeles, and the hero is ex-cop Jake Cardigan. Gloria Vanderbilt's *Never Say Goodbye* (Knopf) was gently, if accurately described in the *Washington Post* as "a weird triumph—a grab bag of inspired nuttiness." Dealing with four different women who speak in exactly the same voice (the author's), the novel was sometimes cited for its odd style: "We meet and make love like two trains crashing into each other." Columnist Pete Hamill, in *Loving Women: A Novel of the Fifties* (Random House), sent his autobiographical hero, Michael Devlin, sailor and cartoonist, to Pensacola to learn all about life and love. *New York Times* writer Joel Brinkley brought out *The Circus Masters Mission* (Random House), a *what if* predicating an American invasion of Nicaragua. Television personality Steve Allen offered *Murder on the Glitter Box* (Zebra), a "celebrity mystery novel," starring himself as the detective. Public Television's Jim Lehrer continued the saga of One-eyed Mack, a character from his earlier novel, *Kick the Can* (1988), in a new one, *Crown Oklahoma* (Putnam). Pop singer Jimmy Buffet, with twenty-two record albums to his credit, came forth with *Tales From Margaritaville* (Harcourt Brace Jovanovich), a gathering of fourteen stories, six of which have seen earlier service in the form of popular songs. This book found a place on the best-seller list. Another celebrity, radio personality Garrison Keillor, whose *Lake Woebegone Days* (1985) was sixth-ranking fiction best-seller of the decade, followed up that success with *We Are Still Married* (Viking), a collection consisting of eleven poems and several prose pieces. Another example, from among all too many others, is the vision of a correct Central American policy as promulgated in fictional form by a former president's daughter—Patti Davis's *Deadfall* (Crown).

Finally, there are examples of legitimate literary celebrities, writers of some honorable reputation who are, one way or another, suddenly pushed into the limelight and whose work reaches far beyond any audience for which it can have been intended. In 1989 we were witness to the remarkable event of Salman Rushdie's sly, clever, highly intellectual, and mildly surreal fourth novel, *The Satanic Verses* (Viking), quiet winner of Britain's Whitbead Prize in 1988, a complicated tale involving the comings and goings of innumerable characters, but mainly about Gibreel Farishta, "for fifteen years the biggest star in the history of Indian movies," and his sidekick, Saladin Chamcha, "the Man of a Thousand Voices and a Voice," and set (mostly) in Jahila, the City of Sand, and modern London. When Moslem attention and a death threat caught up with Rushdie he had sold roughly a total of twenty thousand copies of his book, more or less according to expectation. With all the publicity, action, and reaction, sales jumped to almost eight hundred thousand hardcover copies in the calendar year.

Less commercial, but applicable, is the claim to a modest fame in one aspect of the literary scene which can be carried over to another. Thus, for example, a major publishing power and personality, Howard Kaminsky, and his wife, Susan, exposed the world of talent agents in *Talent* (Bantam). Two editors of little magazines brought out first novels–Sydney Lea, with *A Place in Mind* (Scribners), concerning a camp in Maine, and Joe David Bellamy, with *Suzi Sinzinnati* (Pushcart), all about Moke Galenaille, a pre-med student at Duke in 1960. Two poets with good reputations produced first novels. Olive Hershey's *Truck Dance* (Harper & Row) tells the story of Wilma, a big redhead from Little Egypt, Texas, who becomes a trucker. Carol Muskie-Dukes tells a witty story of Willis Jane Digby, who does the correspondence for a feminist magazine, *SIS*, in *Dear Digby* (Viking).

Speaking of which, feminism seems already so acclimated in the intellectual landscape that a type familiar a few years ago, the polemical feminist novel, seems to have become quite rare. Barbara Howell's brief and quiet *Joy Ride* (Viking) is a record of the sisterly friendship of Joy Castleman and Madeleine Gibbons. Marge Piercy's tenth novel, *Summer People* (Simon & Schuster), is more predictably a chip off the old block; not surprising for an author who has written: "Marxism, anarchism, feminism, have shaped and actively shape my political activities, my political thinking and all my writing." Anybody looking for an old-fashioned, unreconstructed male chauvinist pig can find him in the person of this novel's villain–Guy Burdock, financier, exploiter, and stereotypical oppressor.

Although they have careers and voices of their own, at least some part of the interest in the work of Susan Cheever and Lucy Ellmann derives from the inescapable fact that both had famous literary fathers (John Cheever and Richard Ellmann). Susan Cheever's fifth novel, *Elizabeth Cole* (Farrar, Straus & Giroux), is set in the New York art world, and Elizabeth, an artist, is presented as the daughter of a famous painter. Lucy Ellmann's brief (145 pages) first novel, *Sweet Desserts* (Viking), which won Britain's Guardian Fiction Prize, is a postmodern collage centered on the character of Suzy Schwartz, whose well-known father has recently died.

The singular habit of blending fact and fiction, of using "real" characters in a clearly fictional context, often associated by reviewers with E. L. Doctorow's successful novels, but, in truth, deriving more from the traditions of historical fiction and the New World's earlier emphasis on fictional authenticity (and aided and abetted by looser judicial interpretation of the concepts of libel and slander), continues to influence the latest fiction. Thus in Karl Alexander's *Papa and Fidel* (TOR), the chief fictional characters are Ernest Hemingway, Fidel Castro, and Herbert Matthews of the *New York Times*. Steve Erickson's third novel, *Tours of the Black Clock* (Poseidon), features a still-living Hitler and tells the story of the fictional Banning Janlight, from small-town Pennsylvania, who served as Hitler's personal pornographer in the 1930s and 1940s. Cary Grant, Ernest Hemingway, and Zelda Fitzgerald are characters in *The Port of Missing Men* (Morrow), which purports to be the story of Lily Neelan, a fifteen-year-old girl who has just won two gold medals for diving in the 1936 Olympics. Sarah Baylis's posthumously published first novel, *Utrillo's Mother* (Rutgers University Press), is about the historical Suzanne Valadon and includes famous French artists as characters. In Daniel Stern's experimental and highly literary stories, *Twice Told Tales* (Paris Review), George Ballanchine, Agnes de Mille, and Eugène Ionesco, among others, appear as characters. And Serbo-Croatian writer Danilo Kís, in *The Encyclopedia of the Dead* (Farrar, Straus & Giroux), a sequence of stories, anecdotes, and essays on death, frequently treats real historical incidents and characters.

Perhaps more complex is the case of overtly autobiographical fiction. To be sure, all writers (and their publishers), to the extent that the work professes to be "realistic," tend to stress the special knowledge and experiences that confer authority to the writer. But in recent years we have seen an explicit insistence on an autobiographical frame for works of fiction, the tension between the "truths" of fact and fiction becoming part of the suspense and drama of the work. Thus Bruce Chatwin's posthumously published *What Am I Doing Here?* (Viking), extremely personal in many details, is described by the publisher as "a kaleidoscope that offers the many selves that Chatwin created." Chatwin, calling the collection "fragments, stories, profiles and travelogues," adds this cautionary note: "The word 'story' is intended to alert the reader to the fact that, however closely the narrative may fit the facts, the fictional process has been at work." Paul Theroux's latest novel, his eighteenth work of fiction, *My Secret History* (Putnam), presents a hero, writer Andre Parent, whose outward and visible life, at least, is almost indistinguishable from the "real life" (as distinguished from the "secret" one) of its author. Widely publicized and reviewed as an autobiographical account, it placed in question Theroux's ingenuous assertion in an author's note: "Although some of the events and places depicted in this novel bear a similarity to those in my own life, the characters all strolled out of my imagination."

No less intricate in exploitation of the autobiographical self is the earlier mentioned *Charley Bland* (Farrar, Straus & Giroux) by Mary Lee Settle, which represents the third distinctly different, yet distinctly accurate presentation of the facts of her life in fictional form. Foumiko Kometani's *Passover* (Carroll & Graf), which won Japan's Akutagawa Prize for 1986, has two long stories, told by a surrogate, Michiko, who, like the author, is married to an American Jew (writer Josh Greenfeld) and is the mother of an autistic child. Equally personal and intimate is Joyce Johnson's *In the Night Cafe* (Dutton), which converts to fiction many of the facts of the author's affair with the late Jack Kerouac, previously done in the form of the memoir *Minor Characters* (1983). Edward Allen's *Straight Through the Night* (Soho), an accounting and exposé of the American meat industry, gains a special authority from the fact that Allen is involved in that industry as a professional butcher.

At the other extreme are the eleven tales of *The Rainbow Stories* (Atheneum), by William T. Vollman. Self-described as autobiographical, these are tales of skinheads, punks, dropouts, and in one case, "The Blue Yonder: A Tale of Cleanliness," of a zombie who decapitates tramps in Golden Gate Park. More reasonable and/or less ironic is the method of Laura Cunningham in *Sleeping Arrangements* (Knopf), which was published as, in fact and nonfiction, a memoir of her own childhood in the Bronx, but in which she calls herself Lily Moore. Lynne Sharon Schwartz's latest novel, *Leaving Brooklyn*

(Houghton Mifflin), following the life of fifteen-year-old Audrey during and right after World War II and including her sexual initiation by an eye doctor, was described by the publisher as autobiographical, the jacket copy asserting that it "blurs the boundaries between fiction and memoir." Austrian novelist Thomas Bernhard published his memoir of his own close friendship with Paul Wittgenstein (1907-1979), *Wittgenstein's Nephew: A Friendship* (Knopf), as a work of fiction in which the names and all the objective facts are correct. And Tessa Dahl, daughter of actress Patricia Neal and writer Roald Dahl, brought out *Working For Love* (Delacorte), a novel replete with autobiographical elements.

A curiosity about the current American literary scene is how at two extremes, the one labeled purely commercial, the other associated with high, if highly successful, art, the various habits of what might be called postmodern metafiction (that is, in all its forms, fiction that does not pretend to be a record of "real" experience, but, instead, is the presentation of an overtly imaginative, highly subjective experience, a kind of elaborate game engaging both reader and writer) are now commonplace, indeed popular and "accessible." Thus, for example, the number two best-selling hardcover novel of the decade, Stephen King's *The Dark Half* (Viking), which sold a million and a half copies in less than a full year, is in its substance, if not its style, a classic, self-reflexive metafiction as well as a wild and woolly horror story. The plot is too complex for summary, "a dream so bizarre that neither criminal science nor his own sharp mind can make any sense of it"; but it is the story of a writer, Thad Beaumont, who is and is not two people; who is and is not a murderer. It is a paradigm of the creative process, told with energy, fun, and next to no pretension.

Two of the books that most engaged the engrossed attention of critics and reviewers were Julian Barnes's *A History of the World in 10 1/2 Chapters* (Knopf) and Umberto Eco's *Foucault's Pendulum* (Harcourt Brace Jovanovich). Barnes, who surprised the literary world with the success of *Flaubert's Parrot* (1984), here creates a more complex puzzle, ten separate stories (and a "Parenthesis") set in ten different historical periods and written in as many literary styles, linked together subtly but strongly by devices, as described by Michael Dirda of the *Washington Post* as "key words, homologous situations, leitmotifs, thematic repetition." In other words serious playing around; fundamentally serious because the central myth is that of Noah's Ark–apocalypse. As for its connection to "reality," Barnes covers that: "The history of the world? Just voices echoing in the dark; images that burn for a few centuries and then fade; stories, old stories that sometimes seem to overlap, strange links, impertinent connections." Barnes can handle "straight" fiction, also, being, in fact, "Dan Kavanagh," who writes crime novels about a bisexual detective named Duffy.

One is hard put to remember anything like the attention–reviews, articles, interviews–lavished upon Umberto Eco and his huge (641 pages) fiction–*Foucault's Pendulum*. He has followed the enormous surprise and success of the best-selling *The Name of the Rose* (1983) with a book that reviewers have the greatest difficulty even generally describing. Herbert Mitgang, in the *New York Times*, came as close as anyone when he called it "a metaphysical study of the search for an answer to some of the religious and historical mysteries of mankind during the last two milennia." Got it? Mitgang continues: "It is set in modern Milan, Paris and Brazil and reaches back to Stonehenge and Crusader Jerusalem." There is a plot, of sorts, recognized by Richard Locke in the *Wall Street Journal* as "a murder mystery that demystifies detection and denounces all detectives." All this has a philosophical point that is at least parallel to that of Julian Barnes. Eco's narrator eventually puts it this way: "I have come to believe that the whole world is an enigma, a harmless enigma that is made terrible by our own mad attempt to interpret it as though it had an underlying truth."

What effect the success of such brilliant fabulators as Barnes and Eco will have on the future of homegrown American fiction remains to be seen. Writing in the *New Yorker* (10 July 1989), John Updike, noting the threat of "postmodernism," struck a defensive blow for his own kind of fiction. "These books made out of other books," he wrote, "are they what the future holds? To 'read up' on an area of geography or history and then be clever and cool about it–is this all the postmodern novelist can do?" Point well taken. Except that it does not apply to the best of the postmoderns whose work is distinctive not only for its authenticity, but also an account of the breadth and depth and vigor of the imagination of the author taken together with a skilled capacity to waken and fully engage the imagination of the reader as well. Americans who try, sometimes modestly enough, to push and expand the boundaries of native fiction, generally find a silent if not a hard row to hoe. A quiet work republished ten years after its first appearance, told in the loose form of a travel book–*The Volcanoes from Puebla* (Boyars) by Kenneth Gangemi–is certainly a worthy and accessible competitor to the big metafiction blockbusters. More in the manner of the late Bruce Chatwin, though always in his own voice, Gangemi sticks to his motorcycle journey across Mexico even as he tells stories and talks about the world, the flesh, the Devil . . . and everything else.

Also worth noting are Michael Brodsky's *Dyad* (Four Walls) and Gilbert Sorrentino's thirteenth work of fiction and the final volume of a trilogy, *Misterioso* (Dalkey Archive), described in the *Los Angeles Times* as "a game in which ambiguity and enigma masquerade as fact and information." Mark Mirsky's latest patrol for the avantgarde is *The Red Moon* (Sun & Moon), all about Job Schwartz, a Jew whose black magic is at work in a New England mill town. Wonderfully off-the-wall experimentation is both style and substance of *Empire of the Senseless* (Grove) by Kathy Acker. A fairly accurate description of the novel was given by R. H. W. Dillard in the *New York Times Book Review*. Dillard defined the book as "a rock-n'-roll version of 'The Critique of Pure Reason' by the Marquis de Sade as performed by The Three Stooges."

Especially heartening for those who hope to see American fiction open to the example of more and different models and mindsets is the fact that *rediscovery* is still possible. Thus a classic such as Felipe Alfau's *Locos, A Comedy of Gestures*, written in 1928, published and promptly forgotten in 1936, was republished in 1988 by Dalkey Archive with an afterword by Mary McCarthy. It is a sort of detective story framed in a series of picaresque tales involving the same people with different names, centering around the Cafe de los Locos, where bad writers hang out hoping to pick up characters. It is a superior example of what would later come to be the tropes of Nabokov and Calvino.

Second chances have been few and far between in the history of American letters. But there were this year new editions of earlier work by writers living and dead, celebrated or overlooked. Ellen Douglas's 1963 collection of short stories, *Black Cloud, White Cloud*, was republished by the University of Mississippi Press, handsomely illustrated by Elizabeth Wolfe. A new edition of Budd Schulberg's *What Makes Sammy*

Run? (1941) came from Random House, together with a newly published collection of sixteen stories, old and new—*Love, Action, Laughter and Other Sad Tales.*

Now that he has won the Nobel Prize, Naguib Mahfouz has become the subject of some interest to American publishers. Doubleday will publish fourteen of his novels in the future and began the series with three books: *The Beginning and the End* (1949), *The Thief and the Dogs* (1961), and *Wedding Song* (1981). These had been previously published by the American University in Cairo Press in somewhat hasty and flawed translations and are here revised and edited by John Rodenbeck. There were interviews with Mahfouz in many of the slick magazines that, in the absence of much material for criticism, focused on the life and life-style of the elderly Egyptian.

After many years Elspeth Huxley's prewar mysteries set in Kenya's Happy Valley have been republished by Penguin: *Murder at Government House* (1937), *Murder on Safari* (1938), and *The African Poison Murders* (1939). Viking has brought out a fifteenth anniversary edition of John Steinbeck's *The Grapes of Wrath* with an introduction by Studs Terkel. Book of the Month Club Editions brought out a new edition of Nathanael West's *The Day of the Locust* (1939) with an introduction by the ubiquitous Robert Stone, who called it "one of those books that change the world." Luigi Pirandello's story of Vitangelo Moscadara's search for his true identity, *One, None and a Hundred Thousand,* first published in America in 1932, was published in a new translation by William Weaver for Eridanos. Feminist Press brought out a revival edition of Irene Rathbone's *We That Were Young* (1932), an autobiographical novel based on her experiences as a nurse and canteen worker in World War II.

Not even counting the many examples already cited in other contexts in this piece, it was a busy year for the publication of all kinds of story collections. A distinction can be made, not at all in terms of quality, between the collections produced by fiction writers with some sort of established reputation and those books published by writers who are, as yet, less well-known to readers and reviewers. Inevitably the collections of the established writers gain more attention and, to an extent, earn a different sort of response. Examples of the latter fell, easily enough, into the contemporary publishing categories of "popular" and "literary." Mary Higgins Clark's *The Anastasia Syndrome* (Simon & Schuster), a novella and four

stories, exemplifies old-fashioned, well-crafted slick fiction (three of the stories appeared in *Woman's Day*). William Kotzwinkle presented three long stories in *The Hot Jazz Trio* (Seymour Lawrence/Houghton Mifflin). One, "Blues in the Nile," involves an ancient pharaoh and his favorite dwarf; "Boxcar Blues" is a hobo story, the hoboes including a famous astronaut and an orthopedic surgeon; and the longest (99 pages), "Django Reinhart Played the Blues," is set in Paris in the 1920s and includes Picasso and Jean Cocteau among its characters.

The literary story by established masters of the form was represented by Janet Kaufman's *Obscene Gestures For Women* (Knopf), some fifteen stories in the voices of women, hard-edged, minimized, and poetic. Alice Adams worked in softer tones, "the landscape of the heart," in the fourteen stories of *After You've Gone* (Knopf). Bob Shacochis, whose *Easy in the Islands* (1985) won the American Book Award, is more various in setting, period, and tone in the eight stories of *The Next World* (Crown). They are set in the Caribbean, of course, but also in Virginia, Rehobeth Beach, Galveston, Philadelphia's Chestnut Hill, and, in one unusual example, "The Trapdoor," at a performance of *Hamlet* at the Globe, witnessed by a captain who has sailed with Drake and fought against the Spanish Armada. In her fourth collection, *Light Can Be Both Wave and Particle* (Little, Brown), Ellen Gilchrist has some characters carried over from earlier fiction and some brand-new ones—Lin Tan Sing, Chinese geneticist, and Margaret McElvoy, bride-to-be. One of the best-realized new people is Ned McFarland, a Mississippi heavy-equipment salesman who tells his own story in "The Man Who Kicked Cancer's Ass." Gilchrist also here includes a new ending for her first novel—*The Annunciation* (1983). Bette Pesetsky's second collection, *Confessions of a Bad Girl* (Atheneum), offers a variety of fifteen stories from the *New Yorker, Vanity Fair,* and major quarterlies, of which thirteen are told in the first person by various characters with surprisingly similar voices. Susan Minot's *Lust* (Seymour Lawrence/ Houghton Mifflin), following the success of her first novel, *Monkeys* (1986), was eagerly awaited and, though its reception was mixed at best, widely reviewed. Here are twelve lean and spare stories organized in three sections and all built around the title. As the narrator of the title story puts it: "Some things I was good at, like math or painting or even sports, but the second a boy put his arm around me, I forgot about wanting to do anything else, which felt like a relief at first until it became like sinking into a muck."

Among up-and-coming male story writers Robley Wilson, editor of *North American Review* and winner of the 1982 Drue Heinz Prize for *Dancing for Men*, brought out *Terrible Kisses* (Simon & Schuster), his fourth collection, containing fourteen stories set variously in Charleston, South Carolina, New Hampshire, Maine, and Copenhagen. Stephen Dixon brought out two collections in the year–*The Play* (Coffee House), a gathering about driven and defeated men, and *Love and Will* (Paris Review), twenty stylized and "hip" stories that were negatively criticized by Eric Larsen in the *Los Angeles Times* as being "curiously trivial, sluggishly flat, and banal." The distinguished Peruvian writer, Julio Ramon Riberyo, who lives in France, published four stories about old men in Peru and Paris in *Silvio in the Rose Garden* (Lockbridge-Rhodes). Veteran (and prizewinning) story writer Barry Targan brought out six new stories in *Falling Free* (University of Illinois Press). Lee K. Abbott, who has published three collections in a fairly short time, brought out his fourth, *Dreams of Distant Lives* (Putnam), ten stories highly praised by Ann Beattie and even more so by novelist William Harrison, who calls Abbott simply "our major short story writer." Two other highly praised and honored (and much anthologized) young writers brought out their first book-length collections: Ron Hansen in *Nebraska* (Atlantic Monthly Press) and Rick Bass in *The Watch* (Norton). Both these writers have been so firmly a part of the literary establishment that it is surprising to realize they had not published collections earlier. Prizewinning first collec-

tions, by other, lesser-known writers include *Line of Fall* (University of Iowa Press), by Miles Wilson, winner of this year's John Simmons Short Fiction Award; *The Long White* (University of Iowa Press), by Sharon Dilworth, winner of the Iowa Short Fiction Award; and *Cartographies* (University of Pittsburgh Press), by Maya Sonenberg, awarded the 1989 Drue Heinz Literature Prize.

Among other excellent collections of stories, stories of every kind and form, special mention is deserved by Ellen Lesser's *The Shoplifter's Apprentice* (Simon & Schuster); Peter Christopher's *Campfires of the Dead* (Knopf), Lish-like but not without interest; Francis Sherwood's *Everything You've Heard is True* (Johns Hopkins University Press); *Short Skirts* (Dog Ear Press), by Maine's Taffy Field; *The Women Who Walk* (L.S.U. Press), by Nancy Huddleston Packer; Barbara Kingsolven's *Homeland* (Harper & Row); Brett Lott's *A Dream of Old Leaves* (Viking); *Dreaming in Color* (August House), by Ruth Moose; *Kiss in the Hotel Joseph Conrad* (Summit), by Howard Norman; *Lover* (Coffee House), by Harriet Zinnes; M. J. Verlaine's *A Bad Man Is Easy To Find* (St. Martin's); Jane Bradley's *Power Lines* (University of Arkansas Press); *A Matter of Days* (L.S.U. Press), by Albert Lebowitz; *A Gravestone Made of Wheat* (Simon & Schuster), by Will Weaver; Frank Manley's *Within the Ribbons* (North Point); *Soulstorm* (New Directions), by Clarice L. Spector; D. Cymbalista's *Danger* (Dutton); and *We Find Ourselves in Moontown* (Knopf) by Jay Gummerman.

In all probability 1990 will continue to be a boom year for the short story. Already, bound galleys of outstanding new collections are in widespread circulation.

The Year in Poetry

R. S. Gwynn
Lamar University

"Who Killed Poetry?" asks Joseph Epstein in an essay from *Commentary* that was reprinted, perhaps for the benefit of the prime suspects, in the May 1989 issue of the Associated Writing Programs' magazine, *AWP Chronicle.* Epstein, editor of the *American Scholar,* looks back to the 1950s when the "high priests of the cult" of Modernism–T. S. Eliot, Wallace Stevens, Robert Frost, William Carlos Williams–were still alive and modern poetry was "High Church." Even though much of this poetry was difficult, it managed to attract a reverent audience and was treated seriously both by professional critics and by the media, which deemed poets newsworthy and, in the case of Frost, made one of them (with the poet's gracious assistance) a national icon. Today, on the other hand, Epstein finds that "Contemporary poetry is no longer a part of the regular intellectual diet. People of general intellectual interests who feel that they ought to read or at least know about works on modern society or recent history or novels that attempt to convey something about the way we live now, no longer feel the same compunction about contemporary poetry." Quoting and apparently seconding Brad Leithauser's judgment, Epstein contends that poetry has become "a sadly peripheral art form"– flourishing in a "vacuum" with an intact structure of publications, honors, academic positions, and financial awards but lacking both a wide readership outside the academy and a demanding critical establishment within it.

Who are the culprits, then? Epstein points a finger at creative writing programs, which have proliferated in recent years. With barely concealed contempt he argues that, while the high-modernist poets thought of themselves as artists, the typical contemporary equivalent styles himself "a poetry professional" who inhabits the insulated world of the M.F.A. program. These poets "publish chiefly in journals sheltered by universities; they fly around the country giving readings and workshops at other colleges and universities. They live in jeans yet carry a curriculum vitae."

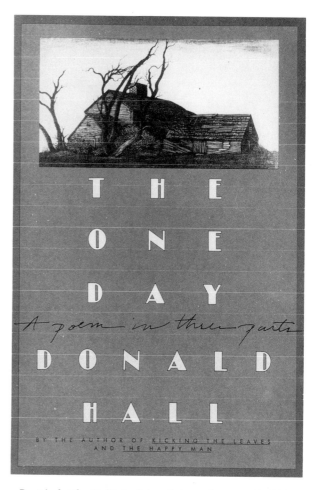

Dust jacket for Hall's book-length poem that won the 1989 National Book Critics Circle Award

Another contributing factor may be the widespread phenomenon of poetry readings; in a given year it is likely that more people *hear* contemporary poetry than *read* it. Because of the generous fees that are paid for such performances, the poet is always tempted to "compose simpler, jokier poems that can be readily understood by an audience." Summarizing a reading by two younger poets, Epstein ironically notes that no great injustice is done in paraphrasing their poems: like much contemporary poetry their work is "slightly political, heavily preening, and not distinguished enough in language or subtlety of thought to be memorable."

A third reason for poetry's decline may be found in the current predominance of the lyrical mode–usually embodied in "a shortish poem, usually fewer than forty lines, generally describing an incident or event or phenomenon of nature or work of art or relationship or emotion, in more or less distinguished language, the description often, though not always, yielding a slightly oblique insight." The chief effect of this hegemony is a narrowing of scope, a neglect of the narrative and dramatic genres that have in the past attracted poets: what is lost is "the power to tell stories, to report on how people live and have lived, to struggle for those larger truths about life the discovery of which is the final justification for reading." In conclusion, Epstein notes that contemporary poetry, despite a few occasional glimmers of light, is in the main "vastly overproduced by men and women who are licensed to write it by degree if not necessarily by talent or spirit."

Since *AWP Chronicle* is read, for the most part, by "poetry professionals" who have a vital interest in the condition of the art, the editors invited responses from one hundred writers and published a selection of them in subsequent issues. Dana Gioia, a contemporary poet who is something of an exception in that he is a business executive, stands in general agreement with Epstein, emphasizing the need for tougher critical standards: "Nowhere are the ill effects of bureaucratic careerism more evident than in the current cowardly state of poetry reviewing. The overwhelming majority of published reviews today are favorable–frequently extravagantly so. Why? Is America currently experiencing an unprecedented poetic renaissance with dozens of new literary masterpieces published each year? I think not." Instead, Gioia sees a not very well concealed public exchange of favors between poets who review one another's books: "The same poets who boast in interviews about 'taking risks' never jeopardize their own professional popularity by finding fault in a peer's volume."

From the other side, former Yale Younger Poet Michael Ryan, currently a faculty member of the "low-residency" (that is, conducted largely by correspondence with some short-term work done on campus) M.F.A. Program for Writers at Warren Wilson College, blasts Epstein by calling his essay "eye surgery with a bulldozer." Saying that the character of poetry in any given age is shaped by complex cultural, social, and technological forces, Ryan calls Epstein's remarks "unhappy, ungenerous, ungraceful, and useless." Charles Simic observes, "Most poetry of any age is no good. To say that is to say precisely nothing. . . . On the other hand, if there's any significant poetry being written today it will be in opposition to the literary and intellectual mediocrity Epstein represents."

However, Robert McDowell, a poet and editor who has been tireless in promoting the revival of narrative poetry, notes that poets in the insular world of the academy have failed to understand "the need to create one's place in our larger community" and have a stake only in perpetuating their own programs, "the grand Hoover that sucks up and contains" contemporary poetry. About all that one can gather from these diverse remarks is that contemporary American poetry's "vacuum" is populated by a large number of inhabitants whose spirited responses deny that there is a corpus delecti for the murder that Epstein alleges has taken place.

Surprisingly, one of the most spirited attacks on Epstein's essay comes from Donald Hall, who responded with "Death to the Death of Poetry" in the September issue of *Harper's*. Hall, who himself has lamented the shortcomings of much contemporary poetry (his remarks on the recent phenomenon of the "McPoem," the standardized product of the poetry workshop, were noted in these pages last year in comments on his *Poetry and Ambition*), attempts to refute some of Epstein's conclusions by citing statistics and by giving the lie to some "pieces of common knowledge" about poetry that many readers are willing to accept without serious argument, particularly the notions that it is "universally agreed that no one reads it" and that poets themselves "are to blame because 'poetry has lost its audience.' " According to Hall, poetry readings and the book sales that accompany them are responsible for the increased size of average trade editions of poetry books. He also notes, referring to the success of the *American Poetry Review*, that "in 1955 no one would have believed you if you had suggested that two or three decades hence the United States would support a bimonthly poetry tabloid with a circulation of twenty thousand copies available on newsstands from coast to coast."

Hall's central point is that "our trouble is not with poetry but with the public perception of poetry." Reviewing has declined just when we most need "a cadre of reviewers to sift through the great volume of material," and the great generation of literary journalists that included Louise Bogan and Malcolm Cowley has not been replaced by younger critics. "Lately, when [the *New Yorker*] touches on poetry, Helen Vendler seems more inclined to write about a translation or about a poet safely dead. . . . People with tenure don't need to write book reviews." Yet despite all this, the diversity and the quality remain. In Hall's view, Epstein's remarks have less to do with an accurate assessment of the situation than with a common phenomenon: "After college many people stop reading contemporary poetry. Why not? They become involved in journalism or scholarship, essay writing or editing, brokerage or solid waste; they backslide from the undergraduate Church of Poetry. Years later, glancing belatedly at the poetic scene, they tell us that poetry is dead. They left poetry; therefore they blame poetry for leaving them."

Whatever the truth may be, it probably lies somewhere between the two poles represented by Epstein and Hall. Perhaps the grim diagnosis of poetry's terminal condition may be partially refuted by the success of "The Power of the Word," a six-part PBS series hosted by Bill Moyers that aired in the fall of 1989. Focusing on poetry readings by such contemporaries as Sharon Olds, William Stafford, Robert Bly, and Joy Harjo, Moyers also used the occasion to interview the poets about the sources of their work. For many viewers, "The Power of the Word" provided a first exposure to the work of contemporary American poets, even if a certain shallowness and posturing were evident. It was also obvious that the poets were selected with a view toward demonstrating the diversity of American poetry; there was a clear attempt to include members of several ethnic groups and to balance male and female poets. Coming on the heels of last year's ambitious series on modern poetry, "Voices & Visions," and coupled with the immense prestige Moyers has gained from his earlier series of conversations on mythology with Joseph Campbell, "The Power of the Word" represents the most serious interest that the mass media have paid to contemporary poetry in recent memory.

It is also interesting to note that popular culture has found some points of contact with poetry in the last year. Television's most poetic monster, Ron Perlman of "Beauty and the Beast," recorded an album of recitations, and David Broza, a singer and guitarist, has recently set poems by Alberto Ríos, Theodore Roethke, and others to music on *Away from Home,* a new release from EMI. Though one is tempted to draw only the worst conclusions, a book of verse *was* on the best-seller lists for most of the year, even if most people who purchased *Jimmy Stewart and His Poems* did so not because of the poems' merit but out of affection for the octogenarian actor.

Assuredly of greater significance as harbingers of new directions in American poetry were a special issue of the literary quarterly *Crosscurrents* (January 1989), edited by Dick Allen, and the publication of *Expansive Poetry* (Story Line), edited by Frederick Feirstein. Both attempt to draw together poets linked to movements called the New Formalism and the New Narrative. As Allen notes, these poets, desiring "to escape the self-absorbed, often narcissistic poems characteristic since the 1960s," have returned to the "traditions of meter and rhyme, to narrative and drama, to poems written from fictional or semi-fictional voices, to poems with a higher informational and thematic content than is contained in the imagistic lyric. Our poetry is Expansive–it moves outward from the Self to reestablish identities with historical, social, religious, and scientific realities."

The special issue of *Crosscurrents* includes poems by Timothy Steele, Dana Gioia, Jack Butler, Molly Peacock, and Mark Jarman; essays by Robert McDowell, Robert McPhillips, David Dooley, and Wade Newman; and an enlightening symposium of eight poets, including some of the above and Brad Leithauser, Mary Jo Salter, Frederick Turner, and Charles Martin. While the participants quibble over individual points concerning influences, approaches to form, and the relationship between the New Formalism and the New Narrative, there seems to be general agreement that American poetry is suffering from an oversupply of short, subjective, free-verse lyrics and needs desperately to rediscover variety.

Expansive Poetry, a collection of critical essays, republishes several of the *Crosscurrents* pieces and gathers together others that appeared in various publications, most prominently Frederick Turner and Ernst Pöppel's "The Neural Lyre: Poetic Meter, the Brain, and Time" from *Poetry.* In this essay, the authors conclude that the universal attractions of poetic meter result from the manner in which the brain processes amounts of information; thus, they find quantitative similarities among the basic metrical line lengths of many cultures otherwise separated by linguistic and historical distances. While not, strictly speaking, confined to a discussion of the New Formalism, "The Neural Lyre" does offer a strong counterargument to those who propound that free verse, under its various names, is somehow more "natural" than metrical poetry.

It is significant that only two poets prominently mentioned in *Expansive Poetry*, Brad Leithauser and Molly Peacock, are represented in *The Morrow Anthology of Younger American Poets* (1985), though partisans of the movement may see this as simply a manifestation of the orthodoxy they claim to be resisting. Also there is not automatically any common ground between a movement promoting a genre (the New Narrative) and one favoring a certain technique (the New Formalism), and this leads to some uncertainties of definition in several of the essays. Nevertheless, both movements have been growing in importance for well over a decade now, and their roots can be easily traced. The New Formalism owes much to Lewis Turco, who chronicled its rise in earlier installments of these pages and whose *The Book of Forms* (1968) and *The New Book of Forms* (1986) have provided a generation of younger poets with handbooks to metrical and formal strategies. Such older poets and editors as John Frederick Nims, X. J. Kennedy, Anthony Hecht, and, of course, Richard Wilbur have provided leadership and encouragement, and anthologies such as Philip Dacey and David Jauss's *Strong Measures* (1986) and Robert Richman's *The Direction of Poetry* (1988) have given clear evidence that metrical writing in the United States is alive and well. This latter, published late in 1988, has occasioned some lively debate about how far the definition of "metered verse" can be extended when it is applied to some of the selections in the anthology.

The strength of the New Narrative movement can be gauged by the number and variety of recent books in the narrative mode. Most traditional are Frederick Turner's two science-fiction epics, *The New World* (1985) and *Genesis* (1988). *Genesis*, a 303-page poem about a future attempt to propogate life forms in the Martian environment, skillfully manages to combine the ancient "machinery" of the epic with the conventions of contemporary science fiction. Following the lead of Vikram Seth, whose novel-in-verse *The Golden Gate* was a surprise success in 1986, several poets have published book-length narratives, among them Brooks Haxton, whose *Dead Reckoning* (Story Line) is a contemporary retelling, complete with Vietnam veterans and drug dealers, of

the ancient Irish legend of Conn-Eda (Haxton's *Traveling Company*, a collection of shorter poems, was published by Knopf this year). William B. Patrick's *Roxa: Voices of the Culver Family* (BOA Editions) combines dramatic monologues, letters, diaries, and newspaper clippings to chronicle a year of life in rural New York in the middle of the nineteenth century. Reprinted in paperback for the first time is George Keithly's 1972 historical epic, *The Donner Party* (Braziller), which relates a horrifying episode of cannibalism among the survivors of a snowbound group of California settlers in 1846. Edward Dorn's "anti-epic," *Gunslinger* (Duke University Press), republished with a critical introduction by Marjorie Perloff, combines elements of the wild-West tale with much talk about drugs and a mythic quest for Howard Hughes—in all, a rather dated relic of the psychedelic 1960s. In all of these diverse books, one notes the increased willingness of publishers to take the financial risks entailed in bringing out long poems.

Given these observations, it is appropriate that a book-length poem (though not a narrative in any conventional sense), Donald Hall's *The One Day* (Ticknor & Fields), should be the 1989 winner of the National Book Critics Circle Award (the book was published in late 1988). Hall has for years been contemporary American poetry's most tireless advocate and, at times, its severest critic. As an anthologist (alone or with, variously, Robert Pack and Louis Simpson) his work ranges from both selections of *New Poets of England and America* (1957 and 1962), which were in their day praised by some and damned by others as epitomes of so-called "Academic" poetry, to this year's *The Best American Poetry 1989* (Scribners); as a memoirist and critic his *Remembering Poets* (1978) and *Poetry and Ambition* (1988) are only two among many volumes that are essential for any poet's bookshelf.

Hall's poetry, however, has never quite managed to excite readers as greatly as that of his Harvard contemporaries Adrienne Rich, Robert Bly, and John Ashbery. His early work, exemplified by such well-known anthology pieces as "My Son, My Executioner," is typical of the fashionable formalism of the postwar generation, and, in changing his style to open forms and the surrealism of the new work that appeared in his 1969 collection, *The Alligator Bride*, Hall seemed to lose his poetic direction for a decade or more, publishing such memorable poems as "The Man in the Dead Machine" only infrequently and having to face some of the most unequivocally bad reviews that any poet has had to suffer ("Donald Hall's *The Town of Hill* is terrible," began a review by Roger Dickinson-Brown in the *Southern Review*).

Following his resignation from teaching and a move to a family farm in New Hampshire in the mid 1970s, he began to reestablish himself with *Kicking the Leaves* (1978) and *The Happy Man* (1986). *The One Day* is subtitled *A Poem in Three Parts,* and its ten-line stanzas are spoken by at least two distinct voices, a middle-aged man who lives on an apple farm ("who will be taken for the author," says Hall) and an elderly woman sculptor whose acclaim late in life will remind readers in some respects of the late Georgia O'Keeffe. The voice of the male persona obviously draws heavily on Hall's familiarity with the New Hampshire landscape:

Smoke rises all day from two chimneys above us.
You stand by the stove looking south, through bare
    branches
of McIntosh, Spy, and Baldwin. You add oak logs
to the fire you built at six in the castiron stove.
At the opposite end of the same house, under
    another chimney,
I look toward the pond that flattens to the west
under the low sun of a January afternoon, from a
    notebook
of bushels and yields.

This seems poetry utterly without affectation, as if Hall has been working toward this style through all of his earlier manners. The middle section of the book, "Four Classical Texts," includes one part, a polemic against the times called "Prophecy," that strikes me as vastly superior in passion and force of language to anything Hall has recently produced. Here are two of its remarkable stanzas:

I reject Japanese smoked oysters, potted
    chrysanthemums
allowed to die, Tupperware parties, Ronald
    McDonald,
Kaposi's sarcoma, the Taj Mahal, Holsteins wearing
electronic necklaces, the Algonquin, Tunisian aque-
    ducts,
Phi Beta Kappa keys, the Hyatt Embarcadero, car-
    penters
jogging on the median, and betrayal that engorges
the corrupt heart longing for criminal surrender.
I reject shadows in the corner of the atrium
where Phyllis or Phoebe speaks with Billy or Marc
who says that afternoons are best although not reli-
    able.

Your children will wander looting the shopping
    malls
for forty years, suffering for your idleness,
until the last dwarf body rots in a parking lot.
I will strike down lobbies and restaurants in motels
carpeted with shaggy petrochemicals
from Maine to Hilton Head, from the Skagit to
    Tucson.
I will strike down hang gliders, wiry adventurous
    boys;
their thigh bones will snap, their brains
slide from their skulls. I will strike down
families cooking wildboar in New Mexico back-
    yards.

Hall has said that *The One Day* represents almost twenty years' writing and revision–effort that seems well spent. Those who are heartened by *The One Day* will also welcome the publication of *The Day I Was Older* (Story Line), a collection of interviews and commentary on Hall's poetry edited by Liam Rector and including critical essays by, among others, Louis Simpson, Robert Bly, and W. D. Snodgrass. It is to Rector's credit that he also includes a fair amount of negative criticism. As Hall enters his sixties his reputation as a poet of the first rank seems, for the first time in a long career, unquestionable.

The 1989 Pulitzer Prize for poetry was awarded to Richard Wilbur for his *New and Collected Poems.* Reviewing the collection in these pages last year, I said, "Wilbur's work is a national treasure, and any attempt to praise it further becomes a futile exercise in trying to find new adjectives; nevertheless, it should be noted that the labels that have too often been applied to him in the past–elegant, witty, graceful, and so on–have become, with some critics, no more than reflex actions by which his work may politely be dismissed." The fifty-page selection of new poems provides ample proof that Wilbur's talents are undiminished.

While no poet of Wilbur's stature produced a similar retrospective in 1989, several collected and selected volumes from poets with a wide range of reputations were published. The most impressive of these, if size alone is counted, is *John Logan: The Collected Poems* (BOA Editions), which stretches to an even five hundred pages. Logan, who died in 1987 at the age of sixty-three, was one of the then-young poets included by Donald Hall in his 1960 Penguin anthology *Contemporary American Poetry.* In retrospect, his seems one of the weakest voices in that volume even if "A Trip to Four or Five Towns," an anecdotal account of a literary tour of the East Coast, still retains the freshness of a young man's love affair with poetry. The most memorable lines describe a visit to William Carlos Williams:

> That old father was so mellow and generous—
> easy to pain,
> white, open and at peace, and of good taste,
> like his Rutherford house.
> And he read, very loud and regal,
> sixteen new poems based on paintings by Breughel!

This poem must have been a breakthrough for Logan, rejecting as it did the involuted catholic hermeticism of his early work; unfortunately, he did not develop any range beyond the relaxed, rather slack phrasing in evidence here. In the mid 1960s, after establishing his academic career and fathering nine children, he divorced his wife and wrote over the next two decades touching, if ultimately sentimental, poems to his sons and daughters that reveal a distant father's love and guilt. He also relentlessly explored themes of sexual ambivalence—"the androgynous / life we each of us live out, the man in the woman / and the woman inside the man"—and his orientation is increasingly homoerotic from *The Anonymous Lover* (1973) to the end of his career. In the future, the chief claim to attention of Logan's work, like Adrienne Rich's, may well reside in how well it documents what it was like to have lived through and been radically changed by the sexual revolution of midcentury. Logan's poetry is undemanding in its idiom, occasionally insightful, and remarkable primarily for its naive sincerity, not for its command of technique—qualities it unfortunately shares with a great deal of contemporary poetry.

Margaret Walker's name will not strike a chord of immediate recognition with most readers, but she remains one of the most distinguished black poets of this century. Born in 1915 and thus two years older than her great peer Gwendolyn Brooks, her first book, *For My People*, was selected for the Yale Series of Younger Poets Award by Stephen Vincent Benét in 1942, eight years before Brooks won the Pulitzer Prize. In many ways, the two women's careers have paralleled each other, but Brooks, to some degree because of her longtime residence in Chicago, where she befriended and championed a younger generation of black poets, and because of her extensive touring, has overshadowed Walker, who taught English at Jackson State in Mississippi for thirty years until her retirement in

Dust jacket for a retrospective selection of Williams's poetry, often praised for its concision and deceptive simplicity

1979. *This Is My Century: New and Collected Poems* offers a fascinating glimpse into what it has meant to be a black American poet who has lived in the South ("Medgar Evers was assassinated on the street where I live," Walker tells us) through an era of social upheaval. In many ways Walker's poetry reveals the changing consciousness of the black artist in general. Her early poems, which must now be read as period pieces, alternate between the stridency of Carl Sandburg's populism ("I sing of slum scabs on city faces, scrawny children scarred by bombs and dying of hunger, wretched human scarecrows strung against lynching stakes. . . .") and the folk ballads of an earlier generation of Negro dialect poets:

> Old Yallah Hammuh lay his jive
> On mens on every side
> And when it come to women folks
> His fame was far and wide.

Walker's verse is admittedly old-fashioned and even embarrassingly awkward at times, but her lines have the clear moral force of righteous outrage. As she writes "For Malcolm X":

> Beautiful were your sand-papering words against
>   our skins!
> Our blood and water pour from your flowing
>   wounds.
> You have cut open our breasts and dug scalpels in
>   our brains.

Miller Williams's *Living on the Surface: New and Selected Poems* (Louisiana State University Press) collects work from eight volumes published since 1964, including an earlier selected edition, *Halfway from Hoxie* (1973), a quarter century's worth of poems that consistently delight and surprise. Born in Arkansas, Williams is as complete a Southerner as one could wish, but his regionalism is most apparent in voice and tone, not, as is the case with many southern poets, in a single-minded focus on landscape or local customs. This grounding in a regional sensibility is balanced by a strong internationalism; Williams has lived in Mexico, Chile, and Italy, and is a distinguished translator of poets as diverse as Giuseppe Belli and Nicanor Parra.

The mixture of incongruous elements is perhaps what gives Williams's poetry its unique qualities; thus, his speech ranges from a consciously rhetorical level, perhaps reflecting his childhood as a Methodist minister's son, to a heightened version of the demotic. Compare these lines from "Vision and Prayer":

> Christ that as the maggot
> Comes from the grave and grows wings
> Cleanse us now and in the hour of our death. . . .

with these from "The Friend":

> He could put his hands between the wall
> and a light and make a rollercoaster
> a kidney machine a split T
> running a double reverse.

In much of Williams's poetry, the boundaries between the real and the surreal are often barely distinguishable, reminding us that every light creates its own realm of shadow. Among his recent poems, which seem to me to profit from longer line lengths and more resonant sonic patterns than his earlier work, I would particularly direct readers to such narratives as "Rubaiyat for

Sue Ella Tucker," which tells the tragicomic story of a country girl who is impregnated and abandoned by her worthless lover:

> She had the baby and then she went to the place
> She heard he might be at. She had the grace
> To whisper who she was before she blew
> The satisfied expression from his face.
>
> The baby's name was Trahan. He learned to tell
> How sad his daddy's death was. She cast a spell
> Telling how it happened. She left out
> A large part of the story but told it well.

Among the new poems gathered here, one that stands out is "The Book," which tells of a shocking discovery made by a former soldier who has kept a diary in an empty book he found in a German bunker:

> He learned years later, when he showed the book
> to an old bookbinder, who paled, and stepped back
> a long step and told him what he held,
> what he had laid the days of his life in.
> It's bound, the binder said, in human skin.

Williams's conclusion, as he holds the book in his own hands, manages to go beyond the immediate revulsion to imply something even larger and perhaps more frightening:

> I stared at the changing book and a horror grew,
> I stared and a horrow grew, which was, which is,
> how beautiful it was until I knew.

Lewis Turco seems most secure in his art when he is describing; one section of *The Shifting Web: New and Selected Poems* (University of Arkansas Press) is called "American Still Lifes" and includes poems that attempt to capture places that may soon vanish from the American scene. Here are some lines from "The Tobacco Shed":

> September comes smoking over the hills
> to lie on the fields smoldering.
> Dust puffs among dry stalks and weeds.
> The sun is old fire upon the clouds.
>
> In the shed August hangs
> sere and golden,
> leaves browning among the slatted walls.
> Shadow is thick in the heavy air.

Despite their surface objectivity, there is an almost ominous quality in these poems; one feels that these places have been empty a long time and must be seen with something like Stevens's "mind of winter." Turco often works in sequences; the book includes a set of poems inspired by Robert Burton's *Anatomy of Melancholy* (1621) and another group of "Monsters" with such folkloric names as "Dybbuk" and "Sasquatch." This delightful poem is from a section featuring a comic alter ego named Pocoangelini:

> "You have many wrinkles,"
> Pocoangelini told the mirror.
> *But my wrinkles are of glass,* the mirror
> replied. "And your hands, Mr. Glass, look like
>   the talons of a bird."
>
>   *That is true,* the mirror
> said, *but my hands* **are** *made of glass.* It smiled
> at Pocoangelini. "Yet glass can
> wither too," Pocoangelini said.
>   "My heart is a glass heart:
>
>   "in it a crystal world
> spins out its hours in little figures. Snow
> falls when one tilts it. Bright fish swim among
> coral clouds. Glass can wither," Poco said.
>   "My heart is a glass heart."

Those who know Turco chiefly from such critical works as *Visions and Revisions of American Poetry* (1986) and *The New Book of Forms* are likely to be surprised on two counts: first, that Turco, whose critical prose is strongly opinionated and often cheerfully idiosyncratic, is restrained in his poetry and, in his refusal to write in the confessional mode, sometimes reticent to a fault; and second, that his formal strategies are eclectic, using anything from prose poetry to traditional accentual-syllabics in an attempt to match content with form. He often works in syllabic stanzas, and his poetry is best when he finds a subject that matches his natural capacity for energetic play of rhythm and sound. These lines are from a poem that asks where the "Failed Fathers" go:

> After the slow slide down the drain,
>   where do they go? After the last
> lay-off, the class reunion where they're shown
>
>   kissing the matronly Queen
> of the Prom, where do they go? Where
> do they go, these old young men, these
> paunchy guys with the eyes that squint
> into the lens at the family picnic,
>
>   the fishing expedition
> near the falls, the baseball game where
> they played second?

It is perhaps significant that this exuberantly sad poem is followed by one titled "Farewell to Melancholy."

Robert Wallace's *The Common Summer: New and Selected Poems* (Carnegie-Mellon University Press) looks back at thirty-five years' worth of work from a poet who is perhaps best known for his editorship of the *Light Year* anthologies, which have done a great deal to revive a tradition of American comic verse that has been almost moribund since the death of Ogden Nash. As one might expect, there is a great deal of wit here, especially in such poems as "The Author," which meditates on aging by examining the dust jacket photographs of John Updike's first four books of poems, and "Chez T. S. Eliot," which retells an anecdote about a night Sir Herbert Read spent on the Eliots' sofa. At seven in the morning the guest is wakened by the sight of a groping hand removing a bowler hat from its hook, a signal of the poet's departure:

>   It was my host,
>
> of course, who with a burglar's tread
>   and manner circumspect and nervous
> was setting off, prayer-book in hand,
>   to go to early Sunday service.

Wallace has considerable range and can often move the reader, especially when he speaks of love and its loss. Consider these deceptively simple lines on the end of a marriage:

> Love fails.
>   It is
>   as natural
> as the falling of the leaves.
>   The mystery
>   is
> going on when love has failed.
>   The going on
>   is love.

Wallace is a resourceful poet who is always mindful of the reader's need to be *interested*.

Would that the same could be said about Patricia Goedicke, whose *The Tongues We Speak* (Milkweed) includes work from eight earlier books. Goedicke's chilly decorum is rarely shaken, even in a postcoital poem that concludes:

> After lovemaking you might think you had turned
>   into a stiff
> Polished oak statue of lovers everyone admires
> Because it is so beautiful now, and dead

But it's not, even lying down here like a log
It keeps feeling around with its toes, it's a live tree
And you made it, and it breathes.

The pointless repetition of "it" enforces a vagueness that seems a drawback to easy enjoyment of Goedicke's poetry; her typical poem is a two- or three-page meditation that begins with airy lines like "I walk to the corner of the beautiful building of the present" or "The bird of music pokes holes in the air" and concludes with such workshop-style "deep images" as these:

All that is other comes

As the secret leaves of the lungs open,
Then close, then open again, idly

Under the distant fingers of the sun.

These lines seem so lifeless on the page that I can't conceive of their being read out loud for the pleasure of an audience.

Anne Waldman, on the other hand, is a flamboyant performance artist whose repetitive chants and rants seem diminished in *Helping the Dreamer: New & Selected Poems 1966-1988* (Coffee House). A well-known example such as "Fast Speaking Woman" has a weird force when *heard* but little vitality when seen in print:

I'm the fish woman
I'm the blue fish woman
I'm the woman with scales
I'm the woman with fins[.]

And so on for five hundred lines. Waldman, who has strong ties to both the Beats and the New York School, often indulges in the kind of free associating that was considered daring thirty years ago. "Sun the Blond Out" begins, "That's my mind out nines in coke / blue boxes of Ralph Waldo, the PEOPLE people / A year ago I smelled the wild columbine / & the Lutherans have built 'Anne! Anne!' "–an appropriate degree of coherence from a poet who bills herself as "Co-director and founder of the Jack Kerouac School of Disembodied Poetics" at the Naropa Institute. Since Waldman's poetry so resolutely denies the validity of traditional critical assessment, it is pointless to attempt to praise or damn it. It is simply there. Those who have enjoyed her work in the past will want this book; those who have not will not.

Two large collections by poets previously unknown to me bear brief mention. *Star in the Shed Window: Collected Poems* (New England Press) assembles work by James Hayford, a Vermont native who studied writing under Robert Frost at Amherst College. Hayford's single influence is clear enough; unfortunately, his poems, for the most part epigrammatic stabs at the Great Truths ("Observatories in the merest shacks / Open upon the universal deep"), imitate that pseudo-profound aspect of Frost that seems his least attractive trait.

Leo Connellan's *New and Collected Poems* (Paragon House) has as its centerpiece *The Clear Blue Lobster-Water Country,* a trilogy exceeding one hundred pages that was first published in book form by Harcourt Brace Jovanovich in 1985. This poem defies easy summary; its autobiographical sections deal with the poet's demanding and difficult father, the mother who died when he was seven years old, and a period spent in an alcoholic detox center. Weaving through the poem is a fragment from Richard Wilbur's poem "Running," which seems to have struck a lost chord in the speaker's unconscious mind, dredging up an essential if fleeting memory from his painful childhood. The result is maddening and obsessive, yet the poem occasionally reveals flashes of hard-won wisdom:

But standing in
dusty alone you die
as best you can absolutely
no good at it, with style
and a flair if this is
your last song you try then
to change your character
to be what the appalling
situation seems to require[.]

There are also some strong narrative sections in "Crossing America," a sequence that will remind many readers of the down-and-out ambience of Charles Bukowski's poems.

Three collections by senior citizens are worthy of notice. Despite having published in almost every periodical imaginable, eighty-five-year-old Mildred Cousens has published no books prior to *Time to Consider* (William L. Bauhan). Her clear eye and precise diction have garnered praise from Philip Booth and Maxine Kumin. Here is the conclusion of "Marsh":

In such essential slime
the dance of cells began,

amoeba, protozoa,
newt, snail, and mammal,
source of men and marvels,
myths, dreams, and time.

A. L. Lazarus's *Some Light: New & Selected Verse* (Bellflower) includes work by a retired Purdue professor that ranges from classical meditation to this delicious classroom catalog of "Girls' Heads": "Tobacco boll, Orange roll, Charcoal / Sienna clay, Ice soignée, Straw soufflé / Copper dipper, Sevenupper, Chili pepper. . . ." Ernest Sandeen, professor emeritus at Notre Dame, has some thoughtful poems about aging in his *A Later Day, Another Year* (University of Notre Dame Press). I particularly admire the comparison that is implicit in "At the Kitchen Sink":

After the last dinner dish
is rinsed and dried,
the faucet, turned off,
continues to drip.
It should not be allowed
to tick away the seconds
of something as precious
as a lifetime. Yet it does,
it does, it does.

Briefly noted are James J. McAuley's *Coming and Going: New and Selected Poems* (University of Arkansas Press) and Frederick Seidel's *Poems, 1959-1979* (Knopf). Dublin-born McAuley is particularly sharp in some of the *aors*, Irish poems of satirical invective, which are found in the book's final section. "Aor Against the Warmonger" ("Look at him, hair a black cowl, as odd / As a bishop's mitre or a dowager's / Tiara, his tireless tongue / Chewing on those hoary lines: / This creature, this incomplete / Reptile awaiting fulfillment / In the wreckage of Eden.") is directed at "R. R."

In Seidel's case, those who have followed the poetry wars for a good while may recall the controversy that surrounded the publication of his first book, *Final Solutions,* in 1959; publication was held up while possible libel charges were investigated (the poem in question has not been republished), and the judges who selected the book for the Y.M.H.A. prize resigned in protest; Seidel's early work is heavily derivative of Robert Lowell, one of those judges ("Now the green leaves of Irish Boston wither / Into blood-red Hebrew, Cotton Mather's fall"). *Sunrise,* his second collection, won the 1980 Lamont Award. *Poems, 1959-1979* has been released to coincide with the publication

Dust jacket for Carver's posthumously published volume of previously uncollected poems

of *These Days* (Knopf), Seidel's third collection, which, despite some good passages, too often sounds like ersatz Ashbery:

We were discussing the arms race when the
    moderator died,
Presumably a performance piece, was
What it's called. He said it is.
It actually wasn't so political was only
Broadcast without a live audience.
The telephone is warbling.
The secretary has allowed the call through which
    means the President
Herself is on the line.

What this has to do with the poem's title, "AIDS Days," is beyond me.

Three collections of work by deceased American poets also appeared. Anne Sexton's *Love Poems* (Houghton Mifflin), the largest seller of all her collections, was republished on its twentieth anniversary with a curious introduction, apparently aimed at members of a younger generation who are likely to think of Sexton as a contemporary of Emily Dickinson. "In Sexton's New England," Diane Wood Middlebrook explains, "the margins of towns have been transformed into suburbia, and adultery looms as the next horizon of sexual destiny, once marriage and childbirth have ripened a woman's body and mapped her pleasure centers. In 1969 this was new...."

John Ciardi's *Echoes* (University of Arkansas Press) includes poems that seem to have been left unpolished at the poet's death in 1986 and a couple of real gems that seem to me as good as anything to be found in his other collections. "Thinking about Girls" relates a chance meeting with an old acquaintance "a grandmother I had thought about once / as something else." After a cup of coffee and a few shared memories, Ciardi records their parting:

A single blink froze us a millennium dead.
I studied us one instant from my own death.
Then left some money, kissed a ghost we know,

a dryest peck, then blinked it off in a taxi
to a street below two temples one on the other.
Then back to today in which I thought about girls.
Which came to nothing really. Where it began.

Raymond Carver's *A New Path to the Waterfall* (Atlantic Monthly Press), with an introduction by his widow, poet Tess Gallagher, collects the poems written by the great short-story writer in the last years of his life. It is almost impossible to judge the merits of these poems; looked at objectively, they probably fail most of the tests of good poetry. Yet for those who loved Carver's fiction and mourn his untimely death, they speak with a familiar voice, one that we had hoped would go on for years. "Gravy," which appeared in the *New Yorker* shortly after his death, sums up the writer's gratitude for the long-delayed success that finally arrived in his forties: "He quit drinking! And the rest? / After that it was *all* gravy, every minute / of it, up to and including when he was told about, / well, some things that were breaking down and / building up inside his head." About this plain yet affecting style Gallagher notes, "The truths he came to through his poetry involved a dismantling of artifice to a degree not even Williams, whom he had admired early on, could have anticipated.... Ray used his poetry to flush the tiger from hiding."

The year was not notable for new anthologies. *An Ear to the Ground: An Anthology of Contemporary American Poetry* (University of Georgia Press), edited by Marie Harris and Kathleen Aguero, is

another "politically correct" attempt to reject "the myopic notion of center (European, male literary tradition) and periphery (all other cultural influences) in favor of the more accurate representation of contemporary U.S. literature." If, in an attempt to showcase the cultural and ethnic diversity of American poetry, both the center and the periphery are abandoned, what are we left with? Out of over a hundred poets included, the work of a few professionals–Edward Field, Robert Peters, Gwendolyn Brooks, Vern Rutsala, Joy Harjo, and others–mercifully leavens the proceedings and almost undoes the damage done by the majority of mediocrities.

Somewhat closer to the mainstream is Ronald Wallace's *Vital Signs: Contemporary American Poetry from the University Presses* (University of Wisconsin Press), an unusual if somewhat pointlessly conceived anthology whose table of contents reads like a Who's Who of the contemporary scene. Wallace makes two curious claims for the collection's purpose: "to preserve poems that might not otherwise be accessible" and to provide comparisons between well-known and still emerging poets. Since the main purchasers of university-press poetry books are public libraries, the first claim is absurd, and the second is weakened by Wallace's selections: almost all of the 168 poets included here are familiar names, and many of the poets appear under the banners of two or more presses.

If there is anyone out there who hasn't heard that the university presses dominate American poetry, he will probably be convinced of the fact quickly enough. For the most part, Wallace chooses well, and his five hundred pages hold a large number of good poems. He also includes an accurate overview of the publishing situation in the United States and a brief history of each press's poetry series and a complete list of books for each. As one might expect in such a complicated undertaking, some errors creep in. Thus, we learn that R. H. W. Dillard, presumably in rompers, published his first book with the University of North Carolina Press in 1940; a poem from Charles Martin's *Room for Error* is included, but the book does not appear in the list from the University of Georgia Press. Quibbles aside, this is certainly a more representative and readable volume than *An Ear to the Ground*, and Wallace's introduction should be required reading for all aspiring poets.

Texas Tech press has republished *Carrying the Darkness: The Poetry of the Vietnam War*, W. D.

Ehrhart's 1985 anthology that was originally published as a trade paperback. Also from Texas Tech and Ehrhart comes *Unaccustomed Mercy: Soldier-Poets of the Vietnam War*, an odd occurrence in that this new anthology's selections are virtually identical to those in the earlier collection, even if fewer poets are represented here. It is useful to have a selection from Michael Casey's *Obscenities,* which won the Yale Series in 1972 amid some controversy over judge Stanley Kunitz's baldly political choice of manuscript; Casey, who has published no subsequent books, would not allow his poems to appear in *Carrying the Darkness* but has relented for the new collection. The editor does not adequately justify the inclusion of work by John Balaban, admittedly one of the best poets who has written about Vietnam but also a conscientious objector (not a "soldier-poet"), and there is a curious reference in John Clark Pratt's introduction to "Dover Beach" as one of several "earlier war poems." The anthology also includes a largely superfluous glossary that identifies "shrapnel" as "metal fragments from any explosive device"; "VD" as "venereal disease"; and "Zippo" as a "type of cigarette lighter."

One anthology must be mentioned sadly. *Nine Years After,* a retrospective collection, marks the end of R. L. Barth's adventurous and idealistic chapbook series from the small press that bears his name. Barth, an independent publisher who has refused any public grant funds to support his endeavors, has been a tireless and at times lonely champion of formalism, publishing many poems that, the introduction notes, "would have, because written in an unfashionable style, gone unpublished." Among the poets, both British and American, included here are Turner Cassity, Dick Davis, Thom Gunn, X. J. Kennedy, Janet Lewis, and Timothy Steele—a list that any *trade* publisher would be lucky to have.

Among books published by American poets of the senior generation, Adrienne Rich's *Time's Power: Poems 1985-1988* (Norton) is valedictory in tone, its title poem describing an old home movie:

> I have seen my mother
> tossing an acorn into the air;
> my grandfather, alone in the heart of his family;
> my father, young, dark, theatrical;
> myself, a six-month child.
> Watching the dead we see them living
> their moments, they were at play, nobody thought
> they would be watched so.

The political themes—sexual and otherwise—that have for the last two decades dominated Rich's poetry, or at least the public's perception of it, are present in the background here, as in "Harpers Ferry," where, in 1859, a white girl abused by her brothers ("they've climbed her over and over / leaving their wet clots in her sheets / on her new-started maidenhair") hears rumors and, not quite understanding whispered terms like *free soil,* runs away to join John Brown's raid. The point, I suppose, is to equate one liberation with another, but this straining for significance strikes me as pretentious, almost as absurd as the poem's "cameo" by Harriet Tubman ("in her blazing headrag, this girl knows her for Moses"), whose "appearance in this poem is a fiction," Rich admits in a note. Despite her reputation as a spokeswoman in the world of ideas, the strengths of Rich's writing remain where they began—in her skills as a lyrical poet: "From here / nothing has changed, and everything."

Richard Howard's ninth collection, *No Traveller* (Knopf), showcases his usual assemblage of bric-a-brac—dramatic poems in the forms of letters, interviews, and monologues with Virginia Woolf, William Wordsworth, and unnamed bystanders ("a local man" who remembers the painter Fuseli) as personae. "Even in Paris," the thirty-page poem that opens the book, consists of five alternating letters from "Ivo" and "Richard," respectively, to "Reynaldo," who has returned to the United States from Paris. The essence of this overlong fantasy is that Wallace Stevens, in 1953, makes a secret trip to Paris and is befriended by Richard, who, eyes aglow in the presence of his Crispin, acts as his guide to the shrines of art and architecture. The high point of the poem occurs when Ivo, at dinner at the Ritz with the Duke and Duchess of Windsor, observes the poet's mistaken reaction to the Duke's remark to his wife: "Really, Wallis! there are times / when I fear your taste is . . . elementary." There may be readers, devotees of Ronald Firbank perhaps, who have the patience to be amused by something as campy as this; though he is usually compared to Robert Browning, Howard has always struck me as American poetry's answer to Walter Winchell. The book includes one rather conventional and satisfying poem, "Triangulations," a three-part game of romantic musical chairs with a tangle of relationships (two men and one woman) that is somewhat reminiscent of the film *Sunday, Bloody Sunday.*

Laurence Lieberman's *The Creole Mephistopheles* (Scribners) should be subtitled "The Triumph of Typesetting," with poems horizontally centered and spread symmetrically across its pages. All of this, which amounts to little more than camouflage, cannot conceal the fact that Lieberman is essentially writing prose and not very distinguished prose at that. I defy the reader to supply the line breaks that chop this sentence into verse: "Soon, I try to synchronize this manic picture with a sound track that issues from unseen thickets overhead, the stream of vile cusswords in high-velocity Spanish; Dominican, Cuban, or Puerto Rican Creole dialect more accessible, oddly, to my uninitiated ears than was Creole English, moments before." As in his previous books, *Eros at the World Kite Pageant* (1983) and *The Mural of Wakeful Sleep* (1985), Lieberman continues his busman's holiday tour of the world (here the Caribbean), incessantly taking notes for poems while trying to keep up with his son and daughter. Written as prose, with some decent regard for the reader and a bit more attention to the niceties of sentence structure, Lieberman's adventures might make a minor contribution to the literature of travel, but as far as poetry is concerned he is no Childe Harold.

Having won the Bollingen Prize in Poetry for *Midquest* (1981), his four-part autobiographical epic, Fred Chappell proves that the vein is unexhausted with *First and Last Words* (Louisiana State University Press), a collection that features several prologues and epilogues to such literary works as *The Oresteia* and *The Death of Ivan Ilych*. Chappell's prologue to *The Fathers* describes an afternoon spent watching football on television with Allen Tate; of a Lombardi-coached team Tate says, "It's their precision I like, like a machine, / . . . like well made poetry." Chappell's epilogue to the U.S. Constitution describes two workers attempting to "raise the roof . . . and lower / the floor" of a hermit's cabin purchased by a Florida buyer who will "put him in an ice machine, / And have him a radar carport and a poodle / He's trained to count his money"–a wise and witty narrative that begs to be read allegorically. No contemporary poet wears his classical learning as lightly as Chappell.

Three other collections from L.S.U. Press display the work of poets of the middle generation who have generally been received with respectful attention in the past. James Applewhite's *Lessons in Soaring* finds the poet at home in the North Carolina locales that have inspired many

of his poems, in touch with how "Feeling becomes narration: / Youth packed away in language, / Fibrous, pungent as tobacco, / Staining our teeth in the telling." *Equinox and Other Poems* by David R. Slavitt, poet and novelist, is a mixed bag, avoiding, for the most part, the classical themes and subjects of his earlier *The Walls of Thebes* (1986). I particularly like these lines on a poet's continuing education in his craft:

Over the years, he learned that by taking pains
he could avoid the obvious pitfalls
of thought, vision, of sensibility,
and of the language. One learns what is not
a poem. What is not not a poem,
may prove perhaps to be of worth.

Brendan Galvin's *Wampanoag Traveler* is most unusual, a book-length poem in the form of letters chronicling "the life and times of Loranzo Newcomb, American and natural historian." This character, who travels the colonies before the Revolution gathering specimens of fauna for his English clients, at poem's end addresses the contemporary reader on the subject of apples:

You,
in your century, will have
Red Delicious, Granny Smiths,
and a few other perfections
for the eye, but mush
on the palate, cores a dog
rejects by ear for their
want of snap.

Much of Galvin's point in writing this poem seems to be directed toward our passion for gassing, spraying, cloning, and hybridizing everything in nature, robbing even the fruits "of such wine / the northern lights swam" in the eater's eyes.

The poems in Robert Pack's *Before It Vanishes: A Packet for Professor Pagels* (Godine) are preceded by a passage from one of Heinz R. Pagels's works on physics. Those who know Pack's work will be reminded of earlier sequences, such as *Clayfield Rejoices, Clayfield Laments* (1987), in which the poet's invention flags before the end of the book. Here are some lines on Einstein trying to comprehend the new physics:

Dazzle of starlight curved across the dome
of Einstein's brain, bewilders me;

rebelling against randomness, he was
determined not to see how such

chance breaking spoke the name of God. How
      could
   one mind conceive so much

yet yearn for more?

Lines that might well apply to Pack's own tireless
energies.

At the opposite end of the scale is James
Laughlin, who specializes in short, humorous impressions (sometimes in French) that will remind
many of e. e. cummings. Now approaching
eighty, Laughlin, in *The Bird of Endless Time* (Copper Canyon), muses on one of the shortcomings
of "The Golden Years": "I belong to the American Association / of Retired People and get 10%
off at // the hardware store but not at the li- /
quor store." Here is a short poem on the carpe
diem theme, "Elusive Time":

In love it may be dangerous
to reckon on time to count

on it   time's here and then
it's gone   I'm not thinking

of death or disaster but of
the slippage the unpredicted

disappearance of days on which
we were depending for happiness.

Aging is also on Maxine Kumin's mind as,
mowing a field, she observes that she is "growing
into one sex, a little leathery / but loving, appreciat-
ing the air of midday." *Nurture* (Viking Penguin)
displays Kumin's varied interests—gardening, marathon running, promoting vegetarianism, and saving endangered species such as the manatee.
These lines are from a poem noting the demise
of the "last pure dusky seaside sparrow":

Tomorrow we can put it on a stamp,
a first-day cover with Key Largo rat,
Schaus swallow tail, Florida swamp
crocodile, and fading cotton mouse.
How simply symbols replace habitat!
The tower frames of Aerospace
quiver in the flush of another shot
where, once indigenous, the dusky sparrow
soared trilling twenty feet above its burrow.

At the center of the book is a poem of personal
and literary concerns, "Marianne, My Mother,
and Me," which parallels Marianne Moore's ca-

reer, Kumin's own, and the life of her mother,
who was born in the same year as Moore:

I claim them both as mine
whose lives began in a gentler time and place
of horse-drawn manners, parlor decorum
—though no less stained with deception and regret—
before man split the atom, thrust the jet,
procured the laser, shot himself through space,
both shapers of my alphabet.

Kumin is one of the few poets writing today who
can handle personal and public poems with equal
success.

Walter McDonald has published several collections of poetry in the last fifteen years, two of
them coming this year. I say "several" by design,
for the note on the jacket of *Rafting the Brazos* (University of North Texas Press) speaks of "eight previously published collections," and its counterpart
says, "*Night Landings* [Harper and Row] is
McDonald's ninth book of poetry. His two most recent collections are *The Flying Dutchman* . . . and
After the Noise of Saigon." McDonald is likely to become some future bibliographer's nightmare,
with identically titled (though different otherwise) poems in both collections. Here are some
lines from the version of "The Songs We Fought
For" in *Night Landing*:

Nothing like
songs could break a man's heart
with the draft and a war in Vietnam
drawing him closer daily. We slumped
under our Stetsons, squinting
in blue smoke layered like gunfire,

and bought pitchers of beer for women
we never hoped to marry.

Both books feature dramatic monologues, either
using the choral "we" as this example does or a
rancher persona who discusses the difficulty of living on the West Texas "hardscrabble." McDonald
knows a limited territory—flying, ranching, hunting, and fishing—perhaps better than any other
contemporary poet, and he makes the most of
his firsthand knowledge. A former military pilot,
he has emerged as one of the most thoughtful of
the Vietnam War poets.

Several other collections by well-established
poets include Peter Davison's *The Great Ledge*
(Knopf), gathering poems written since his new
and selected volume of 1984. The death of his
first wife in 1981 and marriage to his second in
1984 provide, respectively, the occasions for

"Equinox 1980," an account of a last canoe trip ("knowing as we stowed it / that this would be the last time"), and "Second Nesting," two of the best poems in the book. Paul Zimmer's *The Great Bird of Love* (University of Illinois Press), selected by William Stafford for the National Poetry Series, continues the adventures of Zimmer's third-person antihero, "Zimmer," which have been going on for more than two decades now. Even though the poet persona claims, "I detest poems about poetry," he still takes time to deliver the following pronouncement:

> Poetry comes to you
> Like puberty–fervent, perplexing,
> Unexpected, before you know what
> Is happening. It is a humbling process,
> Leading to knowledge that can preserve you.

Barbara Guest, one of the New York poets of the 1950s associated with John Ashbery and Frank O'Hara, offers some rather inaccessible poems in *Fair Realism* (Sun & Moon), her ninth collection. One is not exactly invited into the work when confronted with opening lines like "Time calls hoarsely for sorbets and gestures / of sparrow; when locked in rhyme the door / sways and whines like a thief, / 'the thief of time' was the original fellow / pushed out there on the street, caught beneath a wave, / leaves brushing past and weed tumbled." This sounds like some of the then-avant-garde writing of the poets who were trying unsuccessfully to capture something of the spontaneity of painters such as Jackson Pollock and Willem de Kooning; Kenneth Koch's book-length poem *When the Sun Tries to Go On* (1969), an elegy for Frank O'Hara, remains the most entertaining of these efforts.

The generation of American poets born since 1940, those whose monument among the anthologies will be *The Morrow Book of Younger American Poets*, were active during 1989, led by Rita Dove, who won the 1987 Pulitzer Prize for *Thomas and Beulah*, her affectionate sequence of poems about her grandparents. Her new book, *Grace Notes* (Norton), is her first collection of individual poems since *Museum* (1983). The poems in *Thomas and Beulah* were primarily narratives; those in the present collection are lyrical, most of them less than a page long. The overall effect is one of slightness; one reads a poem, pauses a second to mull its minor resolution ("What I want is this poem to be small, / a ghost town / on the larger map of wills"), and moves on to the next without any lasting impressions having been

made, wondering ultimately if Dove's title does not represent a sort of apology for the book's lack of depth. Here is one example, "Backyard, 6 A.M.":

> Nudged by bees, morning brightens to detail:
> purple trumpets of the sage dropped
> to the floor of the world. I'm back
> home, jet lag and laundry,
> space stapled down with every step. . . .
>
> I swore to be good and the plane didn't
> fall out of the sky. Is there such a thing
> as a warning? I swear
>
> I hear wings, and spiders
> quickening in the forgotten shrines,
> unwinding
> each knot of grief,
> each snagged insistence.

Given the proper context, these images might add up to something, but since Dove only alludes to a journey, a return, and a vague "grief," the reader is left with a description that fails to reach for any larger significance. In much of this book Dove seems to be coasting from poem to poem without investing any real emotion. Occasionally, she lets an idea gather some momentum, as in these lines from a prose poem entitled "Quaker Oats": "And they come, the sick and the healthy; the red, the brown, the white; the ruddy and the sallow; the curly and the lank. They tumble from rafters and crawl out of trundles. He gives them to eat. He gives them prayers and a good start in the morning. He gives them free enterprise; he gives them the flag and PA systems and roller skates and citizenship." But this is uncharacteristically energetic; most of the poems in *Grace Notes* seem overwhelmed by inertia.

Mary Jo Salter's *Unfinished Painting* (Knopf) was the 1988 Lamont Poetry Selection, a prize that supports the publication of a distinguished book during the next year. Salter is a skillful poet, combining a variety of formal strategies with a tonal versatility that keeps her a step ahead of the reader's anticipations with unexpected turns of phrase. Her subjects range from public events ("Chernobyl") and literary speculations ("The Upper Story" describes a visit to Emily Dickinson's room) to personal poems addressed to her husband (poet Brad Leithauser) and an impressive long piece, "Dead Letters," on her mother's death. This last should find its place in the anthologies; its opening section, in which the poet goes through the junk mail that continues arriving long after its addressee's demise, concludes brilliantly:

> From the mail
> today, it seems, you might almost be well:
> *Dear Patient: It's been three years since your eyes*
> *were checked . . .* A host of worthy causes vies
> for your attention: endangered wildlife funds,
> orphans with empty bowls in outstretched hands,
> political prisoners, Congressmen. The *LAST*
> *ISSUE*s of magazines are never last.
> And now you've shored up on some realtors' list,
> since word went out you've "moved" to my address:
> *Dear New Apartment Owner: If you rent . . .*
> Mother, in daydreams sometimes I am sent
> to follow you, my own forwarding text
> *Dear Mrs. Salter's Daughter: You are next.*

Salter is usually included among the New Formalists, and her deft handling of rhyme here and in other poems gives her work the satisfying closures so often lacking in contemporary poetry.

Another poet usually mentioned among the New Formalists is Molly Peacock. *Take Heart* (Random House) has a powerful poem about growing up with an alcoholic father, "Say You Love Me," and several others that relate the traumas of an unwanted pregnancy and subsequent abortion: "I'm in what / I never thought I'd be caught in, / and it's a strong net, a roomy deluxe net, / the size of civilization. To shun / this little baby — how can I?" Peacock's meters are often so deliberately rough, her enjambments so insistent that her rhymes seem to cramp her style:

> The ocean's great to look at
> because there's enough of it.
> It's like music, a substance that
>
> can't be cut up. It has no pit
> to stymie a knife. It's like true laughter:
> even laugh-o-meters can't measure it.

Nevertheless, she can be delightfully inventive with form, as witness "The Spell," a sort of reverse alphabetical acrostic:

> The job in certain lives has been to find **A**
> way to live with feeling—for just to **B**
> the selves they are requires them to **C**
> things they were forbidden to.

And so on through the alphabet.

After finding numerous rhyming poems in this year's batch of books, I begin to wonder if the recent publicity about formal poetry hasn't caused some poets who have heretofore written primarily in open forms to reassess what they are doing. If so, the results are not always gratifying. Here are a couple of attempts at quatrains, from different poems, from Michael Ryan's *God Hunger* (Viking):

> When the little three-note computer tune
> played faster and louder inside my heart,
> if I didn't get the straitjacket on
> my body would start flying apart.
>
> Was it only the new old chemical stirrings
> that made her shoplift purple corduroys
> and squeeze into them out of her mother's hearing
> to discover what noises could come from boys?

When Ryan is working in open forms he is somewhat better, though he does tend to be melodramatic. In "First Exercise" he describes losing his contact lenses while swimming laps in a pool, diving for them repeatedly without success. The poem ends with a huge leap from the trivial to the tragic:

> later, as I walked home,
> the world a blur of dull color run together,
> I thought of my friend diving at dusk
> in that mountain lake for his daughter
> and what came to him when his hands
> sank into the cold mud at the bottom.

If there is an antonym for bathos this must surely be an example of it.

Wyatt Prunty's *Balance as Belief* (Johns Hopkins University Press) also stumbles in its attempts to find form. Note these lumbering couplets from "The Wild Horses":

> They run miles farther than the meadows
> In which he sees them run. They have no shadows,
> Are unceasing, and they never die.
> What he feels when watching them is like a cry
> Heard somewhere else, and neither pain
> Nor happiness in it, but sustained
> Like a long note played in an empty room.

In this and other of Prunty's poems, the unadorned idiom and literal autobiographical treatments seem at odds with the attempts at musicality. That Prunty has recently written a critical study of "precedents for the New Formalism" may have something to do with his style here.

Edward Hirsch's *The Night Parade* (Knopf) follows *Wild Gratitude,* which won the National

Book Critics Circle Award in 1986. Hirsch has been roundly taken to task, most prominently (and unexpectedly) by Helen Vendler, for the sentimentality that pervades his poetry (the book's last poem recalls a grandmother's hug, cookies and milk, and "a time before we knew about time / When the self and the world fit snugly together"), yet it seems to me that lack of precision is his greatest problem. In "Execution," for example, a poem about a high-school football coach dying of cancer, Hirsch begins with these lines:

> The last time I saw my high school football coach
> He had cancer stenciled into his face
> Like pencil marks from the sun, like intricate
> Drawings on the chalkboard, small *x's* and *o's*
> That he copied down in a neat numerical hand
> Before practice in the morning.

I first question why the signs of cancer are "stenciled" and further fail to see how the sun can make "pencil marks." The trope grows more muddled when the reader is asked to imagine that the marks of illness resemble chalkboard diagrams of football plays! And finally, in what sense could the same diagrams be "copied down in a neat numerical hand"? Hirsch is straining for metaphorical significance, and the effect is unfortunate. In another poem, Hirsch describes a chance meeting with a former teammate that is painful for both parties because the friend has risen no further in the world than parking attendant. At first they embrace, but then

>   He held the keys
> To my mother's car and shifted his weight
> Back on his heels–half in anger, half in
>   disappointment–
> As I saw him do on the sidelines against Main
>   South,
> A linebacker's helmet imprinted on my back.

The last line is vague and certainly fails any test of clear prose sense–not always an essential quality of poetry but certainly a necessary one in lines as flat in idiom and rhythm as these. That these two poems were first published in the *Atlantic* and the *Nation*, respectively, does not speak well for the editorial standards of two of our leading magazines.

The Night Parade includes two long poems on historical subjects, "And Who Will Look Upon Our Testimony," which is about the black death of the fourteenth century, and "American Apocalypse," an account of the Chicago fire.

Hirsch employs intricate-looking stanza patterns in both; here is a passage from the latter:

> First, the Tar Works exploded and then came
>   The Gas Works and the Armory,
>   The police station and the fire house,
>   Conley's Patch. There was
> Explosions of oil, crashes of falling buildings,
>
> And down came the Post Office and the Water
>   Works,
>   The impregnable Board of Trade,
>   The Opera House and the Design Academy,
>   The sturdy Chamber of Commerce.
> Down came the banks, the hotels, the churches. . . .

Unfortunately, packaging such undistinguished prose in pretty boxes cannot by itself transform mere journalistic information into poetry.

Lisel Mueller's *Waving from Shore* (L.S.U. Press), her fifth collection, includes poems that look outward on the world from a calm center where the poet has "stopped being the heroine / of my bad dreams." Surfeited with mock-confessional poetry that actually reveals as much as a perusal of the family photograph album, I find it a relief to turn to a poet who can talk about something other than personal life. Among many other subjects, Mueller writes about history, painting, and music but is perhaps most intriguing when she examines the intimacies of biography in "Romantics," a poem about the friendship between Johannes Brahms and Clara Schumann:

> The modern biographers ask
> the rude, irrelevant question
> of our age, as if the event
> of two bodies meshing together
> establishes the degrees of love,
> forgetting how softly Eros walked
> in the nineteenth century, how a hand
> held overlong or a gaze anchored
> in someone's eyes could unseat a heart,
> and nuances of address not known
> in our egalitarian language
> could make the redolent air
> tremble and shimmer with the heat
> of possibility.

This is fine writing, always engaged with its subjects, and marked by intelligence and taste.

A sense of decorum, or the lack thereof, is not likely to trouble La Loca (Pamala Karol), whose *Adventures on the Isle of Adolescence* provides proof that City Lights Books, publisher of *Howl*

(1956) and other controversial works, lies in no danger of going gently into that good night. With such titles as "Why I Choose Black Men for My Lovers" the poet clearly intends to shock, even if the poems are actually more thoughtful than the table of contents would indicate. La Loca does not use many of the resources available to the poet, to put it mildly, but she can sustain long narrative performance pieces; "The Mayan," a teenager's sexual rites of passage story that takes place in a seedy inner-city theater ("The trick seemed to be / to duck the ushers / who patrolled the aisles / with a flashlight"), is an entertaining read, even if little more than autobiographical prose broken into short lines. Here is a short poem with a neat ironic turn, "A Brief Encounter":

My grandmother
ceremoniously devoured
the obituaries
every morning
while she sucked quartered lemons to the peel.
Fifty-three years after divorcing him
she saw his curt paragraph
between a Hula dancer
and a Cantonese mortician.
She spit the pips
on a Melmac saucer
like a sovereign,
folded the Metro section
and later
rolled it
and caused it
to exterminate a fly.

La Loca takes the tradition of the Beats, Bukowski, and her "professor and mentor, Ron Koertge" into a new generation of stoned teenage skaters, L. A. street punks, and heavy metal's "hooliganistic shibboleths / and earsplitting hierograms / wailed to the faithful."

Norman Dubie, born in 1945, is called "a major young American poet" on the dust jacket of *Groom Falconer* (Norton). In an interview that appeared in the November/December issue of *American Poetry Review* Dubie attempts to clarify his curious choice of title: " 'groom falconer' is language lifted out of what must be the title poem of the book. In that poem the doctor, who is visiting this turn-of-the-century asylum, is like a groom to flights of the imagination that have gone horribly wrong in the persons of the insane. In that sense, it is like a groom to a bird of prey, or a groom to a falcon. If you want to discuss this image in terms of my relationship to the world

or to things real or imagined, you'll have to make that case for yourself."

We should be grateful to Dubie for such candor. Along with the title poem, the book includes several examples of Dubie's stock-in-trade, the surrealistic mock-historical poem. Here are the opening lines of "Jeremiad":

After a night of opium and alcohol, Edgar Poe
Walks out of a laundry into the harsh sunlight
Of an affluent Baltimore. From behind, as I see
    him,
He is not
Of experience, and he is without sin—
He waddles
In the archetype of Charlie Chaplin
And crosses the street to the park
Where yesterday evening yellow swathes of poison
Were dropped on the wind
To kill an unprecedented population
Of ground snails.

In the poem's conclusion Poe, climbing to the thigh of an equestrian statue, witnesses a pack of stray dogs attack the "vomiting swans" who "have been feasting / On the tainted snails." Meanings aside, I question the awkwardness of phrases such as "not / of experience" and "waddles / in the archetype of."

Occasionally, Dubie writes descriptive passages of strange, if rather precious, beauty that recall the work of the pre-Raphaelites:

The artisan's daughter laughed
And lay back on the water,
She floated past the green sandbar,
Where her friend was dressing,
Past the dark cranes eating crayfish,
Past the old wharves of my village,
And having joined the eternity of the river—
Evenings of drinking from the wine bowl—
She slowed,
Floating past me forever, her eyes closed.

Dubie's poems are most accessible when some narrative fragment gives the reader a locus for the rest of the poem. Often this may be a memory from his Maine childhood: "we stopped / At a light and watched a procession of cars / Coming down out of the first snow, down / Out of the mountains, returning to Connecticut. Everywhere / Roped to the hoods and bumpers were dead deer." In the *APR* interview Dubie mentions that he does not give public readings, a fact that may reveal something about his occasional disregard of his audience.

Bill Knott's *Outremer* (University of Iowa Press) includes this note: "Some poems in this book may look like personae/dramatic monologs, but I don't intend them as such. Please take this into account when you read them." Thanks for the help, but I frankly can't see the difference it would make when confronted with opening lines such as these, from "Art of the Caresses or the Sphinx (Castration Envy # 36)":

> The Lord Peter Mumsey of Thebes, that yummy
> Oedi-poo dick, advises me, It's no use. To
> Detectify a guilty party will
> Soil the purity of our respective plagues.

It sounds as though Knott is making capital on poetic fashion, attempting belatedly to enter the canon of the L = A = N = G = U = A = G = E poets by reviving the idiom of Ezra Pound. *Outremer* so successfully defies communicating anything that one wonders what the judges of the Iowa Poetry Prize had in mind in selecting it. Knott, it may be recalled, "killed" himself in the early 1960s, writing for several years as "St. Geraud" before resuming his original identity. The work collected in this year's *Poems: 1963-1988* (University of Pittsburgh Press) is, for the most part, more coherent, tracing Knott's work back to earlier phases of more conventional surrealism and the protest poems he wrote during the Vietnam War era.

Nancy Willard, author of award-winning children's poetry, brings off some inspired nonsense in *Water Walker* (Knopf), her eighth collection of poems. One section spins out fables to match the literal sense of newspaper headlines such as "Nets Halt Suns" and "Buffalo Climbs Out of Cellar." This is the opening of "Giants Anxious for Skins":

> They wanted to swim in the raw,
> to slough off
> their warts and bristles,
> bruises and tough
> talk. And scars.
>
> They hid their skins
> in a brake of ferns
> and wrapped what remained
> in scarves of water.

Willard has depths beyond this inspired silliness, though. Perhaps because of her success with children's books, she brings to the mundane a wide-eyed awareness of infinite possibility. The title of "A Hardware Store As Proof of the Exis-tence of God" alone is worth mulling over a long while, as is the poem's conclusion:

> In a world not perfect but not bad either
> let there be glue, glaze, gum, and grabs,
> caulk also, and hooks, shackles, cables, and slips,
> and signs so spare a child may read them,
> *Men, Women, In, Out, No Parking, Beware the Dog.*
>
> In the right hands, they can work wonders.

Willard makes one think of a parallel universe where Father Hopkins acts as a spokesman for Ace.

Rodney Jones is another poet whose inventiveness charges everyday reality with magic. *Transparent Gestures* (Houghton Mifflin), his third collection, is his strongest yet and one of the year's best books. Jones has seemingly solved one of the great problems of contemporary poets— how to get beyond the literal surface of autobiography—by using heightened, though not artificial, diction and a tone that borders on satire but never quite crosses over into it. An example is "Winter Retreat: Homage to Martin Luther King, Jr." The poem does not begin auspiciously: "There is a hotel in Baltimore where we came together, / we black and white educated and educators, / for a week of conferences, for important counsel / sanctioned by the DOE and the Carter administration"; however, after the momentum is established and Jones's voice, not a parody of Dr. King's rhetoric but certainly an echo of it, establishes itself, the poem soars:

> Very delicately, we spoke in turn. We walked
> together beside the still waters of behaviorism.
> Armed with graphs and charts, with new strategies
> to devise objectives and determine accountability,
> we empathetic black and white shone in seminar
>   rooms.
> We enunciated every word clearly and without ac-
>   cent.
> We moved very carefully in the valley of the
>   shadow
> of the darkest agreement error. We did not digress.

Pulpit rhetoric, sociological jargon ("We black and white / politely reprioritized the parameters of our agenda / to impact equitably on the Seminole and Eskimo"), and Jones's own voice seamlessly join in this remarkable performance. Among many other pleasures, the book includes several poems about characters; one gives us the worldview of a Nietzsche-reading small-engine mechanic: "what he likes best / is to break it all

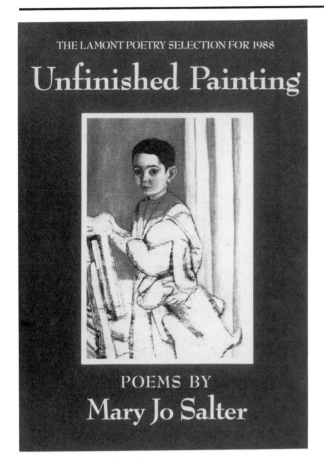

THE LAMONT POETRY SELECTION FOR 1988

Unfinished Painting

POEMS BY

Mary Jo Salter

Dust jacket for Salter's second poetry collection, described by Joseph Brodsky as embodying "the marriage of superb craftsmanship to the tragic sense of reality"

down, to spread it out around him / like a picnic, and to find not just what's wrong / but what's wrong and interesting. . . ."

Annonciade (Viking) by Elizabeth Spires, her third collection, covers a great deal of ground, with poems set in England and France and a couple of unusual dramatic monologues, one of them spoken by the figurehead of a ship sunk in the 1870s ("Learn by looking in my eyes how elements / conspire to drag the living down to never-to-be- / fathomed depths and give new life to the dead") and another representing the meditations of a goldfish sacred to certain Buddhist sects:

> The world
> is a sphere that mirrors my pond, all things
> have order here: the sun rushes
> across the sky, pulling the moon
> on a pale fishing line, and I see myself
> printed among the stars, a great fish
> swimming in the night's black sea.

William Matthews's *Blues If You Want* (Houghton Mifflin) takes its title and many of its free-associative techniques from jazz. "It Don't Mean a Thing If It Ain't Got That Swing" begins with a description of a boy and girl apparently about to make love for the first time. Suddenly, Matthews throws in an abrupt and witty transition:

> From what follows we turn away,
> for we have manners
> and our lovers need privacy to love
> and talk and talk, for love is woven
> from language
> itself, from jokes, pet names and puns,
> from anecdote, from double entendre
> (already invaded by *tendre*), until
>
> our lovers are a kind of literature
> and sole mad scholiasts of it.
> *Inventors at Work*, a sign on the bedroom
> door might say.

From this point we are treated to a mythic account of the invention of language, the poet's memories of "the Montgomery Drive-In thirty years ago," and some entertaining digressions that never quite get back to the starting point. Matthews may seem to ramble, but when, in another poem, he refers to how "the malls and apartment / complexes were named for what had been destroyed / to build them: Fair Meadows Mall, Tall Oaks Townhouses" you know that his jokes have direction. Even if the poem doesn't quite measure up, "Homer's Seeing-Eye Dog" has to be the most intriguing title of the year.

Several other books by established poets are worthy of some brief mention. Stephen Dunn's *Between Angels* (Norton) seems to me filled with what critic Robert Peters labels "workshop poems"–impersonal, unambitious, inoffensive. When, in the book's title poem, the poet says his evenings consist of making "a choice / to read or love or watch, / and increasingly I watch," the reader is not exactly impelled forward into the remainder of its hundred-plus pages. Cathy Song, former Yale series winner and the youngest poet in the *Norton Anthology of Modern Poetry*, is represented by *Frameless Windows, Squares of Light* (Norton), which includes autobiographical poems about the poet's childhood in Hawaii. Song, along with many other poets, could save immense amounts of paper by simply writing her memoirs in prose. Here is her description of her father, a commercial pilot, falling ill: "A year later he suffered a myocardial infarction. / He was flying between two islands / when, like a piece of shrapnel, the pain hit. / When he landed, he drove himself to the hospital." Ira Sadoff's *Emotional Traffic* (Godine) consists, in large part, of lugubrious meditations with such titles as "Summer Solstice in Praise of the Bourgeois": "Tonight's excitement? A walk / around the block, counting inchworms / dangling from the pines. / Watching neighbors clear their dishes, / someone's grandpa tinker in his garage." Charles Simic's *The World Doesn't End* (Harcourt Brace Jovanovich) is a collection of prose poems that begin with lines like "We were so poor I had to take the place of the bait in the mousetrap" or "In a forest of question marks you were no bigger than an asterisk." This ground has already been staked out by Russell Edson, and Simic, for the most part, lacks Edson's saving grace, a bizarre sense of humor that teeters on the edge of sense.

Green Age (University of Pittsburgh Press) by Alicia Suskin Ostriker has at least one gem, "Helium," in which the poet's husband, worried about the approach of years, releases a birthday balloon: "It was still springtime, the sun already high, / And your balloon was either still ascending / Or stopped in the arms of a tree. We couldn't know which, / And we were glad of this." Other poems in the volume are somewhat weightier with mythic, Jewish, and feminist concerns. Susan Gilbert, one of the leading feminist critics and poets, contributes *Blood Pressure* (Norton), which has some surprising moments of high comedy. In "You Meet the Real Dream Mother-in-Law" the expectation is absurdly idealized: "the hair / Atlantic gray, the bone china cups / with blue frost, the silvertipped cane, the misty // voice of Ethel Barrymore, saying, / I've waited so long, *he's* waited so long, / but how glad we are, my dear, / that you're the one!" Carol Muske's *Applause* (University of Pittsburgh Press) focuses on the joys of new motherhood while looking back on a diminished radicalism ("I've always been / surprised to find the world just the way the cynics made it"). The title poem is addressed to Paul Monette, whose *Love Alone* of last year described the death of his lover, Roger Horwitz, from AIDS. In an emotional conclusion Muske remembers a last visit Horwitz paid to her infant daughter: "I wanted to cheer him for going on / like that, for blessing my child when he knew he was dying– / and when the raft hit the swells, one

after the other; / they held on and prayed and God laughed, God gave them a hand."

One of the quickest ways for a poet to establish his or her reputation is to win one of the major open competitions, especially one as prestigious as the Yale Series of Younger Poets, which lists Adrienne Rich, John Ashbery, Michael Ryan, and Cathy Song among past winners (not to mention such forgotten names as Edward Weismiller, Thomas Caldecot Chubb, and Thomas Hornsby Ferril). Selected by James Merrill, Thomas Bolt's *Out of the Woods* (Yale University Press) seems an unusual choice, even in a series marked by idiosyncratic final decisions. Bolt writes a kind of anti-pastoral poetry filled with images of rusted appliances snarled in vines and wrecked automobiles overturned in deserted ravines. Even Merrill, in his foreword, admits that "for a poet to dwell, page after page, upon the same small family of images may argue a certain limitation." A passage from "Unpolluted Creek" is representative of the book's obsessive descriptions:

> All day,
> Iron flecks
> Sprinkle from the shell
> Of a galvanized bucket,
> Its bottom gone,
> The clean sides being slowly punctured.
>
> If anything happens here
> In the changing sun
> Among weeds and stripped metals,
> It is only water
> Picking through junk, gradually
> Enlarging flaws.

Oddly, Bolt does not seem particularly engaged with ecological issues; when, in the book's centerpiece, the twenty-eight page "The Way Out of the Woods," he wanders into an automobile graveyard and says, "I had found / The secret center of America," his voice is strangely detached, his eye cool and painterly. To be sure, there is occasional grandeur in his summations: "We built this city. / Our machinery made this, and demanded / Daily fuel / Of human work and life, / Involving us / To raise its product higher." But the final effect of Bolt's poetry is numbing; the book reiterates its single observation until the reader grows insensate.

The Academy of American Poets' Walt Whitman Award, selected by Amy Clampitt, went to April Bernard for *Blackbird Bye Bye* (Random House). Again, one wonders what made this particular manuscript stand out among hundreds of entries; there is no apparent logic (other than a spurious cuteness) in Bernard's borrowing a title from Wordsworth for her version of "Resolution and Independence," nor is there any conspicuous merit in the broken grammar of the poem's opening stanza:

> Like some spider, orange and brilliant
> to its webs, little clocks that swathe the garden–
> Airy, sticky, precision candy spun again
> until the game assemble.

In another pointless act of homage, Bernard unwisely tries to imitate Emily Dickinson at her most coy: "If blood be wet, and roses red, / and you–my Valentine– / Then does my heart await in me / as rubies–the Pick–in mines?" Admittedly, Bernard has a talent for assembling a collection of clever-sounding ready-mades, a sort of campy collage of "found" lines: "A couch ideally belongs in an office with a door that shuts. / The robot comes complete with one arm. / The yellow cord will double as a belt. / The fringe, which Emilio calls "Garbo," / resembles a veil, a window, a haze." But working them into any coherent design is apparently either beyond her abilities or of no interest to her. It seems perverse to award a prize named after Walt Whitman to a book as willfully uncommunicative as this one.

Sue Owen's *The Book of Winter*, a second collection, is the Ohio State University Press / *The Journal* award winner. The book is filled with short-lined poems whose titles and subjects ("The Onion Poem," "The Knife Blade") will recall Pablo Neruda's "elemental odes" and Charles Simic's work during his "if only I could be a stone" period. This opening stanza is from "A Basket of Buttons":

> Lost eyes, whose sight
> will not be restored.
> What was there to see anyway?
> You saw how the days
> undid you.
> You saw wear wear you out
> and let you down, and how knots,
> told to hold you, didn't.

Owen's apostrophes are clever, but they tend to grow less fresh as one reads further into the book and encounters them on almost every page. Many of the poems dip perilously close to the pathetic fallacy ("Little flies, even if / you buzz that question again, / time will not hear you.") and in some cases leave themselves open to charges of sentimentality:

> But it's a white world
> marred by the tracks
> of squirrels and sparrows,
> little animals in
> a hurry to say nothing.

Without Asking (Story Line) by Jane Reavill Ransom, granddaughter of the poet John Crowe Ransom, is the winner of the Nicholas Roerich Poetry Prize, awarded annually for a first book. Those who come to this collection expecting some vestige of familial reserve are likely to be surprised by the poems' subjects–parental alcoholism, sibling incest, and that staple of contemporary women's poetry, the same-sex love poem ("In the mountains, the snow would not hold us. / We fell, and kissed. Your eyes teared, / your hand moved to touch my face. But I refused, / I stood up. Your eyelashes froze / and snapped, dark fragments of words. I will write, / 'Dear Jo Ann–I remember our vowes [sic]; I still love you. / You must know that.' ").

A sequence about the death of the poet's mother from cancer has one opening line that is a startling example of ineptitude: "Though it was smaller than the coin-sized crabs / molting in the mud slick, your tumor brought the family together that week." Ransom, an international editor of the *New York Daily News* who has been on assignment in Lebanon and Nicaragua, fares somewhat better in the book's final pages, where her journalist's eye confronts such images as these of children torturing a dog in a Palestinian refuge camp:

> How can they? Grip a dog's head the way you do a
>   butternut squash
> to tug it off the vine–and hit it, with a rock.
>   Then the group of children
> uses a razor to open a seam, the way you split the
>   back of Raggedy Ann.

Ransom has centered so many of her personal poems on details intended to shock that the reader is unlikely to sense any change in magnitude when she shifts to larger, issue-related subjects.

The National Poetry Series, in which five established poets annually select a like number of manuscripts for publication, is an idea that sounds promising but has yielded indifferent results in the past. I have already noted Paul

Zimmer's *The Great Bird of Love,* selected by William Stafford. Jorie Graham's choice is Emily Hiestand's *Green the Witch-Hazel Wood* (Graywolf). At over a hundred pages the book is too long, but there are several inventive turns among its contents. A painter (the book's cover design is her own work), Hiestand favors description ("A Bridge with a Fraternity Sign" summons up paintings by Thomas Eakins) and poems written by analogy to visual techniques, like two "bricolages" assembled with bits from the *New York Times Book Review.* "Moving a House" describes a shoreside house being lifted onto a barge: "when they have worked the slimed pilings loose / with the crane that must go for 2K an hour, / Russ brings champagne and they slug it / around like Ripple, swigging bubbles / in the red sun, while the boatmen softly punch / the bronze men with houses and memberships / until they all stand around punching each other. . . ."

Lee Upton's *No Mercy* (Atlantic Monthly Press), selected by James Tate, is more difficult to characterize, its poems occasionally echoing a half-jokey surrealism that belies Tate's own influence, such as "Hog Roast":

> If the town celebrates
> his roasting
> it's their right. He's their hog.
> He's pork now.
>
> His life in the mash has gone sour.
> The bad fairy presides
> over his crispy feet.
> The prodigal has come back
>
> and does not need
> such company.

The two other winners in this tenth year of the series are David Mura, for *After We Lost Our Way* (Dutton), selected by Gerald Stern, and Len Roberts, for *Black Wings* (Persea), selected by Sharon Olds.

The Tyrant of the Past and the Slave of the Future (Texas Tech University Press) by Christopher Davis is the winner of the Edith Shiffert Prize, part of the AWP Award Series. Gerald Stern, in his foreword, praises Davis's poetry "of exaggeration and extremes," singling out his "abandoning traditional (nonpoetic) logic, sentence structure, and punctuation," and citing the influences of, among others, Ashbery, Ginsberg, Zbigniew Herbert, Kafka, Gil Orlovitz, Shelley, Rimbaud, and Hart Crane. These hardly match up with the

Doric narration of the book's opening poem, "Jojo's":

> The night my brother was stabbed,
> but not quite stabbed to death,
> I was drinking wine in a coffeeshop
> called Jojo's with some friends.
> He'd been walking home drunk
> from a party. Two guys who'd shared a case
> of beer had picked him up.
> After stabbing him, they threw him
> down into a canyon.

Whatever virtues Davis's poetry possesses, it apparently has little indebtedness to the forebears cited by Stern.

Other prizewinning collections include Trish Reeves's *Returning the Question,* winner of the Cleveland State University Poetry Center Prize; Mary Ruefle's *The Adamant* (University of Iowa Press), cowinner of the Iowa Poetry Prize (with Bill Knott's *Outremer*); Maxine Scates's *Toluca Street* (University of Pittsburgh Press), winner of the Agnes Lynch Starrett Poetry Prize; Stefanie Marlis's *Slow Joy* (University of Wisconsin Press); and Nell Altizer's *The Man Who Died En Route,* winner of the Juniper Prize from the University of Massachusetts Press.

As is the case with most years, many of the best books of 1989 arrived unheralded from poets whose reputations are not yet established or whose work is not widely known outside a certain region. One such is Robert A. Fink, whose *The Ghostly Hitchhiker* (Corona) collects poems previously published in magazines ranging from the national (*Poetry* and *Triquarterly*) to the strictly local (*West Texas Historical Association Yearbook*). Regional concerns show up in such poems as "Mesquite," where, Fink notes, "The word for *bean* was the same as that for *rain,*" recalling the Indians who gathered the fruit "in baskets woven tight / as that which rescued Moses." Often, though, his subjects are elegiac; during his first Christmas as "a middle-aged orphan," the poet goes through his mother's cedar chest, finding a forgotten photo album of his parents in their courtship:

> Now they're at a table. They lift two empty steins
> as if to toast how naughty they think they are.
> You hurry past the one where she has cocked her
>   hip
> and pulled her dress above one knee,
> where he has taken off his shirt
> and flexed his biceps.

In most of Fink's poetry a sense of irony, projected with the subtlest of inflections, buoys the poems and saves them from sentimentality.

Sidney Burris's *A Day at the Races* (University of Utah Press) displays some lightly worn classical learning ("I'd heard Ulysses sing // in sixth-grade English, the first of my ear-wise, late-century / hallucinations.") and some wry memories of what it was like to have attended high school and have been impossibly infatuated during the height of the period of antiwar activism:

> I was dead-on-my-feet in love.
> She gave me her Marx,
> her Cleaver, her Malcolm X,
> her bologna sandwich with endive.
> She was simply a student of
> a democratic society
> rereading a dog-eared copy
> of *Animal Farm* and thanking the stars above
> for the Berrigan brothers whom I'd learn to like a lot.
> She also shared her pot.

The unobtrusive rhyming, balanced against the varying line lengths, manages to give this a requisite lightness of tone, a quality that Burris's work often exhibits.

Sarah Gorham's *Don't Go Back to Sleep* (Galileo) contains some exquisite moments of lyricism, such as these lines on "Rice":

> At my wedding, throw flowers.
> Each wasted grain
> is a spilled fortune,
> a kiss blown to air.
> ....
> Young woman, finish your rice.
> Your child will be blanketed
> in vernix and goose down.
> He will be healthy and round
> for he too was grown in water.

The death of a parent, pregnancy, and motherhood are among Gorham's subjects, but she is at her best in her nature lyrics: in a well-turned sequence of poems on birds and in this one, which describes a chance encounter with a "Walkingstick": "Hardly as righteous or glaring as the blind / man's cane, this insect blends, fears, / lives patiently as a branch's twin."

From the same publisher comes *Once Out of Nature* by Jim Simmerman, a collection with one moment of sheer inspiration, a one-page poem entitled "Against Derrida" accompanied by a four-page deconstructionist "Glosse" supplied by one Jay Farness. The poem opens, "Terrific, another

post- / structural exegesis of death / as signant or text / as kaleidoscope. Meanwhile, / I'm a romantic with a whale's / eye view of Ahab." Here is the note on the last line: "*Ahab:* the Derridean alterego inscribed with alphabetic laughter ('alphabet' from the Greek a-b); here a-b, a synecdoche for the grapheme, is ruptured by 'Ha!' – *viz.*, the general play of Nietzsche's gay science (for gaiety, see below) as spelled out by the derisive Derrida."

Simmerman's other poems never quite equal this level of brilliance, but the book has many enjoyable moments, including these lines from "Skin Flick," which meditate on the backgrounds of the "actresses":

> Who knows but one
> loved English once:
> the classroom darling
> reciting Hopkins and Frost.
> What she does with her
> lips just now, Modest Reader,
> I don't need to tell –

Simmerman is bright and funny and unafraid to point out absurdity's plain face—qualities that are doubly rare amid the contrived high seriousness that too many contemporary poets mistakenly equate with artistic merit.

Another book with some inspired spoofery is Caroline Knox's *To Newfoundland* (University of Georgia Press), which summons up pleasant memories of Kenneth Koch at his wittiest. Knox consistently comes up with unexpected turns, such as praising "Teeth" by noting, "They pronounce Chidioch Tichbourne for us in committee / and gleam, the foul white radishes of time. / Sometimes help to say, 'Set in 10 on 12 point Palatino,'" or, in the book's wacky title poem, inventing a chorus of Scottish dogs who sing: "Bough! wough! whose dogs are we / whan al our maysters are frae hame / or off to Greenland on the sea." "Exploring Unknown Territory," the longest poem in the book, takes the form of a deconstructionist closet drama populated by characters named "I," "My Husband," "Admiral Peary," and "John Ashbery." Knox's poetry is obviously not for everyone, but those who enjoy sophisticated play with language and allusion will doubtless be amused.

Among other new collections briefly noted, there is precious little levity in Michael Milburn's *Some Silence* (University of Alabama Press), which includes a former student's elegy for Robert Lowell and a somber sequence on the death of a friend from AIDS: "There was this man, and now / there is this lack of him, whose last strength / lies in our grieving cluster, stomping / the earth around his body, leaving him alone." From the University of Arkansas Press comes William Trowbridge's *Enter Dark Stranger* which is marked by meditations on moments when public events touch private lives. Trowbridge watches the network news with his young son: "I think of explanations: why we can't / stop killing, where the 'free world' is, / why our teeth drop out, why I drink more / before dinner than I used to." The book also includes a seriocomic sequence of dramatic monologues as related by one "Kong," unemployed simian actor: "I'm presently looking / for something with more of a future, / like being a poet or a ballroom dancer." Gregory Djanikian's *Falling Deeply into America* (Carnegie-Mellon University Press), as the title implies, includes narrative poems about the poet's arrival in America at the age of eight. One of the best of these is "How I Learned English," which describes the poet, in his first baseball game, being struck in the forehead and crying out, "Oh my shin, oh my shin" while his playmates' "fit / Of laughter overtook me too, / And that was important, as important / As Joe Barone asking me how I was / Through his tears, picking me up / And dusting me off with hands like swatters."

Ralph Adamo's *Hanoi Rose* (New Orleans Poetry Journal Press) includes poems that capture the paranoia of the early 1970s; other poems have superb lyrical moments: "It was once that way for me, the instinct. / I had dreams I could tell without / stopping the conversation." Tom O'Grady's *In the Room of the Just Born* (Dolphin-Moon) includes poems about rural Virginia ("Pastoral Inventory" is one title) that will invite comparisons with the work of Henry Taylor; from the same small-press publisher comes James Taylor's *Artifacture,* a collection of graphics, prose, and poetry that seems to be indebted to European expressionism.

The number of new books published in 1989 by women was large, and, in addition to those already noted, I should mention Maurya Simon's *Days of Awe* (Copper Canyon), which offers, among other pleasures, this description of the perfect "Dress": "It fit me perfectly, and even buttoned itself / in front, without my having to lift a finger. / When I went down the street in this dress / men fell to their knees, sparrows stopped / their small talk to follow me." *When I Kept Silence* (Cleveland State University Press), by

Naomi Clark, has several poems that draw their strength from southwestern locales: "in a landscape of prickly pear and mesquite / I stand still as a lone dead oak." Jana Harris's *The Sourlands* (Ontario Review Press) ranges across the country with such titles as "On the State of Housewifery in Jersey" but focuses in most closely on the seedy inhabitants of a Washington State neighborhood the poet calls "Useless Bay." Beth Joselow's *Broad Daylight* (Story Line) stands out on the merits of two longish dramatic poems spoken by women with few illusions. "The Head Cosmetician Tells a Story" is a *film noir* account of a triangle between the persona, a cop ("Pinkie out of Second District Vice"), and a rich kid named Roger who "wore / three-hundred-dollar suits and smoked some fancy / cigarettes in a holder."

Thylias Moss's *Pyramid of Bone* (University Press of Virginia) is number eight in the Callaloo Poetry Series, which features the work of younger African-American poets. Moss includes a couple of offbeat dramatic monologues spoken by "the undertaker's daughter" and a witty racial revision of Wallace Stevens, "A Reconsideration of the Blackbird": "*Guess who's coming to dinner? / Score ten points if you said blackbird.*" Bonnie Jacobson's *Stopping for Time* (GreenTower) stands out on the basis of such amusing bits of whimsy as "Traffic Light Mandala": "D. M. Thomas says Giotto / could draw a perfect circle in one stroke / but is D. M. reliable? a man / with no first name?" The book's cover also credits Jacobson with a memorably punning clerihew:

Ah, Miss Barton,
before you pack another carton,
meet Mr. Walpole, do—
Clara, Hugh.

Which seems as good a place as any to stop.

In closing I should mention two collections of prose that anyone interested in contemporary American poetry should consider purchasing. Jack Myers and Michael Simms, both poets and professors of English, have collaborated on *The Longman Dictionary of Poetic Terms* (Longman), a reference work that includes *anacoenosis, leaping poetry,* and *euche* among its entries. Some of Myers's and Simms's categories seem merely whimsical (*fill-in-the-blanks-poem*), but the list of rhetorical figures, tropes, and other technical terms is indeed impressive, even if one may cringe a bit at reading that the "New Critics" were "all associated with Vanderbilt University."

Of less practical use but of greater pleasure as a browser's delight is Robert Peters's *Hunting the Snark: A Compendium of New Poetic Terminology* (Paragon House), an attempt to construct a taxonomy of contemporary poetry with such categories as "Feminismo Poems," "Alphabetty Poems," "Academic Sleaze Poems," and "Genteel Bucolicism Poems." Peters, a poet and critic perhaps best known to readers through his two *Great American Poetry Bake-Off* collections of essays, is rarely solemn and views much of the contemporary scene with skeptical contempt. By arranging the poems by types, Peters hopes "that a totality emerges, a creature however beruffled, deplumed, anemic or plump, and noisome." When the critic manages to credit *both* Robert Bly and James Dickey for inspiration and encouragement, the reader can rest assured that he is not going to be a partisan of one camp. Peters can have the reader applauding on one page and pulling his hair out on the next, but he remains our most reliable authority on the world of little magazines, small-press books, and poets who are not likely to get a serious hearing from any other critic. Any aspiring poet should read this book, if only for the many negative models it presents, most of which, we can rest assured, will again be on display in 1990 as we officially enter the fin de siècle.

The Year in Drama

Howard Kissel
New York Daily News

There was a time when a survey of the year in drama might have been likened to entering an art gallery whose walls were filled with fairly large canvases. Nowadays each wall would be crammed with tiny pictures. None of the artists on exhibit seems capable of the grand vision, the sweeping brushstrokes that characterized another era.

It is difficult even to group the pictures under convenient headings, since the artists have so little in common. The general absence of "schools," of course, can be taken as a sign of health, evidence of great individualism. It can also be seen as a symptom of a larger problem, the lack of any agreement on technique. Like contemporary visual artists, present-day playwrights tend to work as if the centuries of accumulated knowledge in their craft were of no value. It is this rejection of traditional structures that may account for the inability of contemporary playwrights to create sizable pieces. (In the case of the visual arts, neither lack of technique nor absence of discernible content seems to deter artists from working in the grand manner.)

It is not entirely accurate to say there are no "schools." There are still numerous examples of a kind of bedraggled naturalism, quasi-autobiographical writing that dwells on details so specific they have no universal interest. Also, parodies of old Hollywood genres appear to be flourishing. (Here the most vital subgroup is spoofs of detective movies, of which there were three.)

In the welter of little canvases it is hard to single any out for special mention. The most honored play of the year, Wendy Wasserstein's *The Heidi Chronicles*, was discussed in the 1988 *DLB Yearbook* drama survey. It had been presented at the Seattle Repertory Company and the Off-Broadway Playwrights' Horizons before moving to Broadway in February. In 1989 it won the Pulitzer Prize, the Tony, and the New York Drama Critics' Circle Best Play awards.

The virtues of the play were even more apparent when the title role, that of an art historian viewing her generation's foibles, was taken over by Christine Lahti late in the year. Joan Allen, who originated the part, made Heidi a dispassionate, somewhat ironic observer as her friends lunged into the political, sexual, and aesthetic frays of the last twenty years. Lahti, by contrast, made the audience aware of the weight of the emotions Heidi repressed to maintain her aloof stance. It gave the play a depth that reinforced the validity of the awards.

Probably the most eagerly awaited event of the year was the revival of Tennessee Williams's *Orpheus Descending* directed by Sir Peter Hall and starring Vanessa Redgrave. The revival had been a great success in London and, had the troubled play been genuinely rethought, the production could have resulted in a major rediscovery for American theatrical literature. The play, after all, had an unusually unhappy history. Originally entitled *Battle of Angels*, in a production that starred Miriam Hopkins, it would have been the first full-length Williams play to reach Broadway. But, after bleak reviews, it closed in Boston just after Christmas 1940. When it was revived in 1957, retitled *Orpheus Descending* and starring Maureen Stapleton, it received equally unenthusiastic reviews. Although it eked out a two-month run, it did not justify its author's declared fondness for it.

In an interview I conducted with him before his production opened, Hall said the problem with the 1957 production, which was directed by Harold Clurman, was that Clurman pared its poetry to bring it closer to the kind of Group Theater naturalism in which he felt comfortable. Hall had worked from Clurman's script and restored the characteristic Williams poetry.

Alas, the restoration of the text was not sufficient to raise the play in anyone's esteem, granted the weaknesses of the production. Chief among them was the performance of Redgrave, who affected an Italian accent that occasionally sounded Scandinavian and which certainly would have sounded ludicrous in the benighted southern town in which the play is set. Her tendency to dominate any stage on which she appears also made it hard to accept her as a woman whose spirit has been crushed by the harshness of her husband and the town whose prejudices and meanspiritedness he embodies. Kevin Anderson, the young actor who played the renegade who rejuvenates her, was quite miscast, destroying any potential chemistry between the two. Convinced that the play verged on opera, Hall staged much of it in a declamatory style that made it irritatingly rhetorical.

The other Hall offering in 1989 was a *Merchant of Venice*, notable because it introduced Geraldine James (familiar to PBS viewers from *Jewel in the Crown*) in the role of Portia. It was not the presence of James that prompted the importation of Shakespeare's play but rather that of Dustin Hoffman as Shylock. The tone of the production was unusually abrasive, stressing the way the Christians of Venice were as mercenary and unpitying as their Jewish enemy. Shylock's reference to Antonio spitting on his Jewish gabardine gave rise to a literal spit-fest. (In London Antonio had spit heartily at Shylock during their first encounter, and Shylock "bettered the instruction" by spitting at the bound Antonio during the courtroom scene. Two more spits were added for New York.)

As for Hoffman, he presented a Shylock without stature, capitalizing on "littleness" much as he did five seasons ago in his unimpressive portrayal of Willy Loman in Arthur Miller's *Death of a Salesman*. It may have been this lack of stature that suddenly made the hoary questions about whether the character is anti-Semitic arise; such questions can only come up when the actor gives Shylock too little humanity. Hoffman's was an effortful interpretation that even the most sympathetic critics were unable to justify. ("A triumph," one declared, immediately modifying it as "a modest triumph"; another characterized Hoffman's delivery of the "Hath not a Jew" speech as Talmudic rather than Old Testament, itself a highly Talmudic distinction.)

Celebrity Shakespeare has become the norm in New York, as Joseph Papp's New York Shakespeare Festival Marathon continues. The marathon is an attempt to present all of Shakespeare's plays by the early 1990s. So far none of the productions has shed any light on the works; they have been notable only for the appearance of inexperienced Hollywood stars who draw equally unprepared audiences to the plays. This merchandising reached its apex in a universally deplored *Twelfth Night* with Michelle Pfeiffer as Olivia, Jeff

Cover of the program for the contemporary staging of Shakespeare's play directed by Mark Lamos

Goldblum as Malvolio, and Gregory Hines as Feste.

In this respect the regional theater has far surpassed New York in its efforts to find contemporary ways to stage Shakespeare. One reads of intelligent productions in cities such as Minneapolis and San Diego that imply a far sharper understanding of the plays than anything presented so far in the highly publicized marathon. One of the more astute regional directors, Mark Lamos, artistic director of the Hartford Stage Company who presented a justifiably acclaimed *Peer Gynt* starring Richard Thomas in Hartford, directed *Measure for Measure* for the Lincoln Center Theater Company. It was a quirky production, mirrored wittily in John Conklin's set, in which what appeared to be latter-day graffiti artfully sketched the outlines of seventeenth-century Vienna. Though the costumes were contemporary, the casting trendily multiracial, the complex rhythms and emotions of the play came through with great force.

Of the Off-Broadway companies that produce new plays, the most successful this year was Manhattan Theater Club, several of whose entries went on to enjoy commercial runs. The most accomplished of these was Brian Friel's *Aristocrats*, a Chekhovian study of an Irish aristocratic family barely able to keep up appearances as it enters the final stages of decline.

A portrait of Catholic aristocrats in Northern Ireland, the play can be seen as a study of one tiny factor in the disintegration of an entire society. But Friel never reduces his subject to sociology. His portraits are never types, but all-too-frail and oddly endearing people, most of whom have the mannerisms of nobility but no sense of what ought to lie beneath. The one exception is the oldest sister, who always seems to be painfully aware of her derelictions of aristocratic duty. But the follies of the family are too many for any one member to cope with. Another sister is alcoholic; yet another seems totally, daftly unaware of what is happening to her, and their brother, who is visiting from Germany, is clearly living in his childish fantasies of the family's glory. The family's future depends on two lower-class men attracted to two of the sisters. Once they would have been entirely unsuitable. Now they are the family's only hope.

At times the play seemed a bit too pat (a stiff storytelling device was the presence of an American sociologist studying the family's associations with Irish history), too predictable, but Friel's elegiac, sadly comic tone made the family's plight genuinely moving.

Another great success of the Manhattan Theater Club was Terrence McNally's *The Lisbon Traviata*. This problematic play was first presented four years ago by an Off-Off Broadway company, Theater Off-Park. There was no disagreement on the first act, both the writing and acting of which were considered brilliant. It concerns an obsessive opera lover, fanatically devoted to pirated recordings (tapes made illegally during performances) of Maria Callas. The appearance of these recordings causes as much excitement in the opera world as auction prices now do in the art world. A third of the way through the first act the fanatic, Mendy, learns of the existence of a *Traviata* taped in Lisbon in 1959 and spends the rest of the act badgering his friend Stephen to bring him the recording. A lot of the humor was specifically operatic (Mendy

tells a telephone information operator that a record store named Discophile is spelled "D, as in De Los Angeles"), but the singlemindedness of a fanatic is funny whether he is obsessed with opera recordings or baseball cards.

In the second act McNally uses Stephen, who, throughout the first, was merely an amused observer, to demonstrate the dangers of obsessiveness in the nonoperatic world. Stephen is desperately unhappy that his male lover of longstanding is leaving him for someone else. By the end of the second act, in a scene that directly parallels the climax of *Carmen*, he stabs his lover and cradles the dying man as *Madame Butterfly* blares from the hi-fi.

The disparity of tone between the two acts, one hilarious, the other stark, made the play a trial. For the MTC revival McNally tried to lessen the disparity. Somber moments were added to the first act, and the still-giddy voice of Mendy made a few more appearances on a telephone answering machine in the second. Still the murder seemed out of place. Nonetheless, the MTC production was so well received a commercial transfer was arranged, and McNally again revised the play, ending with the rupture of the two lovers but no homicide. The strength of the play is still the wild humor of the first act, but now the second is believable and ultimately moving. In Nathan Lane, who played Mendy, and Anthony Heald, who played Stephen, McNally found brilliant interpreters of his highly nuanced, difficult work.

There were four other MTC productions of great interest, an unusually high number for any Off-Broadway group. Two were in the experimental Stage Two, where productions are not always presented to the press. Both were family plays, but iconoclastic in their approach. Lee Blessing's *Eleemosynary* was about three generations of American women. The eldest, an ardent feminist long before such a thing was fashionable, crystallizes her aspirations in her belief that her daughter can fly if she flaps some carefully built wings and believes some psychobabble about centering herself. Blessing takes a basic situation—a mother's determination that her daughter soar in her place —and, unlike many contemporary playwrights who would use it as a pretext for recriminations, he puts it in an imaginative framework with great theatrical potential. The weakness of the play was the needlessly artificial relationship of the daughter and granddaughter. What redeemed the play was Blessing's own eleemosynary (charitable) attitude toward his three characters, never letting their obvious shortcomings outweigh their high aspirations for each other.

Donald Margulies's *The Loman Family Picnic*, an admittedly uneven but very funny play, is about a middle-class Jewish family living in Brooklyn in the 1960s. Lest the parallel with some other Brooklyn dwellers be missed, the younger son is writing a musical based on *Death of a Salesman*. The *Loman Family Picnic* had an admirable playfulness, sometimes repeating scenes several times from different perspectives, cubist fashion. The high point was, of course, a scene from the boy's musical, which drolly parallels his own family's tensions. The major problem with the play was that at its climax it suddenly turned ugly, and this unexpected tone weakened the general whimsy of the rest.

MTC imported from London Nick Deare's *The Art of Success*, an attempt to illuminate the sad grotesqueries of the current art scene by comparing them with the careers of several eighteenth-century Englishmen, particularly the artist William Hogarth, but also the playwright-turned-novelist Joseph Fielding and the politician Horace Walpole. Despite the fact Deare condenses Hogarth's career into the actions of a single day the play is too repetitious for the few points it makes. It raises the important questions: in the very first scene someone asks, "What is art? Is it property or communication? Something to own or to understand?" We see Hogarth commercialize his drawing of a woman he sketches the night before she is to be hanged without too much concern for the ethics of what he is doing. Much of the time Deare seemed too eager to give in to a notion he has Hogarth explain, that audiences love to be shocked: "They take it as proof of their cleverness." Deare shows his own awareness of the limits of art as provocation in the play's final scene, where he contrasts Fielding and Hogarth with their contemporary Handel, whose work overshadows both not by its shock value but its beauty.

The Art of Success is staged in the round, with the audience surrounding a raised platform that can be taken either as a fight ring or, since its surface is heavy paper on which the actors make their mark, a blank canvas. The play—challenging, full of pungent images, even if ultimately tiresome in its adolescent reveling in bawdiness—was a significant import, vibrantly mounted.

The last of the MTC presentations was the first major New York production of Joe Orton's *What the Butler Saw* (1969), one of his wildest, most elegant black farces. A sample of its style is the "expository" speech by the head of a psychiatric clinic in which the action takes place: "My wife is a nymphomaniac. Consequently, like the Holy Grail, she's ardently sought after by young men. I married her for her money and, upon discovering her to be penniless, I attempted to throttle her. She escaped my murderous fury and I've had to live with her malice ever since."

He has confided this to a young woman he is interviewing for a secretarial position. The job, he has told her, requires a full medical examination, for which she has disrobed. Her response to his description of his marital situation is, "Poor Dr. Prentice. How trying it must be for you. I wish there were something I could do to cheer you up."

This combination of absurd, Wildean discourse and blatantly smutty burlesque patter is characteristic of the entire piece, which draws its title from the peep shows Orton remembered seeing as a youth vacationing in Brighton. *What the Butler Saw* is an acid study of the disruptiveness—social and political—of sexuality. (The play ends on a patriotic note, with the nurse displaying a large bronze phallus from a statue of Winston Churchill. In many productions—not this one—a bowdlerized ending is used: Churchill's trademark cigar is displayed, and the fragment of the statue is only alluded to.) John Tillinger's production was exemplary in the way the actors maintained an aloof, dispassionate air as they delivered the ribald, sharply honed dialogue.

Playwrights' Horizons, which had presented *The Heidi Chronicles*, offered Philip Kan Gotanda's *Yankee Dawg You Die*, a somewhat amusing look at how Asian actors face the psychological crises of playing the stereotyped roles Hollywood creates for them. The satirical points Gotanda makes are funny if predictable, but the actual characters he creates for his two actors are less interesting. The group also presented a thoroughly unexceptional play by Peter Parnell, *Hyde In Hollywood*, an attempt to dramatize the plight of gay men in Hollywood during the 1930s. Whatever merit the theme had was lost in the overly complex, ludicrously melodramatic plot.

The one play of distinction Playwrights' Horizons mounted was Albert Innaurato's *Gus and Al*. Innaurato, who is the author of *Gemini* (1976) and *The Transfiguration of Benno Blimpie* (1973), made the play seem, initially at least, brashly autobiographical by setting it just after his *Coming of Age in Soho* opened in 1985. Al, the playwright himself, (adroitly played by Mark Blum) enters carrying the bad reviews. Here autobiography ends and wild, poetic fantasy begins. His roommate, Kafka, an ape who can talk, has invented a time machine. He sends Al back to turn-of-the-century Vienna, where he and his idol, Gustav Mahler (the Gus of the title, played with great authority by Sam Tsoutsouvas) compare their bad reviews. The scene where each tries to top the other with calumny directed at himself–all based on actual reviews–is quite hilarious.

When Gus's friend Sigmund Freud first sees the overweight Al and discovers Gus has taken him in, he remarks that "succoring the overupholstered, underprivileged is a habit we Jews have inherited from our forefathers," an example of the play's richly encrusted style. Among the others Al meets in Gus's Vienna are several historical figures and one personal one, his own grandfather, an Italian day laborer who is Freud's gardener. Innaurato uses this fiction to come to terms with a man he apparently dealt with less skillfully in "real life." The collage of personal and historical elements was both genuinely funny, and in the scenes between Al and the gardener, surprisingly touching. *Gus and Al* is a work of considerable audacity, wit, and poetry, all of which were in short supply in 1989.

Circle Repertory Company, long a supplier of lyrical naturalist drama, has dropped the lyrical in search of gritty material. Paul Zindel's strident *Amulets Against the Dragon Forces* details circumstances so peculiar, so specific, it seems unmistakably autobiographical. Autobiography is the only justification for such a baroque plot. A nurse and her son move in with an elderly woman about to die. Her own son, who cannot take care of his mother himself, is in fact eagerly awaiting her death. He is a middle-aged alcoholic dockworker who lives with a former male hustler and preys on other young men. To add some spice to the already complex proceedings, the dying woman bites the faces of men who get too close to her, and the nurse is a kleptomaniac. The play has notable examples of sharp humor and a poignant moment as the nurse's son tells the alcoholic, "I want to learn how to love; I don't want to be ashamed and angry–like you." But in the end the play has no real resonance.

The same is true of Keith Curran's *Dalton's Back*, in which Dalton is presented as a boy and

as a mature young man. His traumas with his thoroughly unsympathetic mother (many having to do with his refusal to eat lima beans) poison his sexual relationships with young women. However awful his mother was, she had a way of tickling his back that, years afterward, he prefers to sex. Despite a graceful performance by John Dossett as Dalton, the play was too clearly an act of retribution untransformed by art.

Dossett also gave a sensitive performance in Circle Rep's production of William Mastrosimone's *Sunshine*, a play about the age-old subject of the whore with a heart of gold. We are, of course, in the age of AIDS, and Mastrosimone's subject is a woman who works in a porno booth, stimulating the fantasies of her customers, who are separated from her by a glass wall onto which we see one of them ejaculate. In an entirely contrived way we see the woman take refuge in the room of a paramedic (Dossett). In the course of the hour they spend together we discover her wisdom, her vulnerability. We see that he too is used to love behind a glass wall. And so forth. Jennifer Jason Leigh played the girl with great savvy, as did Dossett the paramedic, but neither could disguise the artificiality of the play.

If these Circle Rep entries were samples of honest if dumb naturalism, Cindy Lou Johnson's *Brilliant Traces* was a fatal step in the direction of absurdism. Set in a shack in Alaska in the middle of a blizzard, it begins with a woman banging furiously on the door to get in out of the cold. She enters in her wedding dress and explains that she left her wedding in Arizona several days ago and just drove north. The play made no sense, and its attempts at poetry were hollow.

Of the new plays that opened on Broadway in 1989 most came from London, even *Lend Me a Tenor*, which was written by an American, Ken Ludwig. *Lend Me a Tenor* is a farce set in a Cleveland hotel in the 1930s. It concerns mix-ups between an internationally famous Italian singer and a local boy with operatic aspirations. It had the requisite amount of door-slamming essential for farce; all the zaniness was executed with admirable abandon and intensity.

The most captivating of the imports was Willy Russell's *Shirley Valentine*. Like his earlier play, *Educating Rita* (1980), which was about a working-class woman who takes the idea of education so seriously she changes her life, *Shirley Valentine* is about a woman embracing Life. But this is a more direct treatment of the theme than the earlier one. While it is nice to imagine that exposure

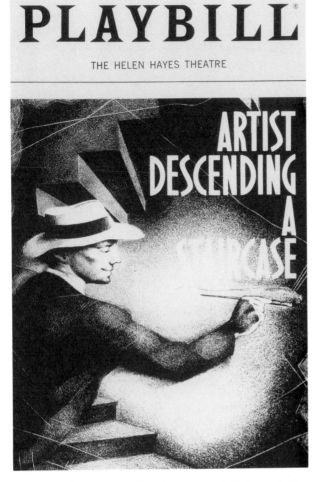

PLAYBILL
THE HELEN HAYES THEATRE

Cover of the program for the stage adaptation of Tom Stoppard's 1972 radio play

to ancient Greek thought can change a woman's understanding, it is easier to accept the changes Shirley undergoes simply contemplating her life in a boring suburb in provincial England and later vacationing on a Greek island.

Remarkably, *Shirley Valentine* is a one-woman show, a genre fraught with artificiality and tenuousness. In its early moments, when the rather proper Shirley is discussing her reactions to the way sex is discussed nowadays, the play verges slightly on stand-up comedy, but once it gains its true footing it never falters. There is a particularly lovely moment midway through the first act. Shirley, while awaiting the arrival of her dreary husband, tells about meeting an old school chum of hers she had not seen in years. The friend invites her to tea in a posh hotel. From the glamorous way her chum dresses, Shirley assumes she must be a stewardess. Her friend laughs and tells her she's a hooker. This awes Shirley. The two

reminisce, realizing that when they were teenagers each wanted to be the other. As the tea ends the hooker kisses Shirley on the cheek. "There was real affection in that kiss. It was the sweetest kiss I'd known in years." Recalling the kiss as she rode home on the bus Shirley cried. It was the beginning of her questioning what had happened to her over the years.

Shirley's closest friend is a woman who became a militant feminist when she discovered her husband in bed with the milkman. The friend offers her a trip to Greece, which Shirley accepts. There Shirley understands what is the matter. " . . . my life has been a crime, really–a crime against God, because . . . I didn't live it fully. I'd allowed myself to live this little life when inside me there was so much . . . That's where Shirley Valentine disappeared to. She got lost in all this unused life."

The play depended, of course, on an extremely powerful actress, which it found in Pauline Collins (another figure familiar from PBS, in this case *Upstairs, Downstairs*). The role offers neither much emotional variety nor the kind of theatricality that blights many one-person shows. To succeed the actress must persuade the audience of the genuineness of Shirley's ability to observe and change. Collins did so with extraordinary naturalness, grace, and radiance.

A Tom Stoppard oddity was imported. *Artist Descending a Staircase* was written in 1972 as a radio play. Several years ago it was successfully mounted in a London theater club, and in November it was brought to New York under the direction of the young Englishman Tim Luscombe, who had persuaded Stoppard to let him produce it as a stage play. The American cast, however, seemed ill at ease playing very English artists contemplating the nature of Art.

Nevertheless, the evening afforded the pleasure of Stoppard's customarily brilliant language. In this play he toys with ideas about modern art. The play is diagrammed in the program: it begins in the present, moves determinedly backward toward 1914, and then rushes forward, showing us what happened just after each scene we have already seen. The diagram bears a resemblance to a staircase. The title, of course, refers to Marcel Duchamp's epochal 1912 painting, *Nude Descending a Staircase*, a suitable reference point for a play concerned with the significance of modern art. On a considerably less profound level the play concerns, quite literally, the descent of an artist down a staircase in a domestic accident that causes his untimely death.

Artist Descending a Staircase is about three artists who have known one another since before World War I, when they shared the belief that art must be "constant surprise." It examines their relationship to each other, to their ideas about art, and to a blind girl two of them loved. The play begins in the present when one of the artists, after a lifetime of producing "groundbreaking" work, has returned to simple pictorialism. He now looks with scathing irony on his former beliefs, declaring "there is something divine about modern art . . . for it is only sustained by faith. That is why artists have become as complacent as priests."

Midway through the play we see the three artists as young men tramping around the French countryside in August 1914, convinced the much-discussed war between France and Germany will not take place. In a sense their aesthetic peregrinations are quite similar, undertaking questions and experiments with no relationship to the real world. One of them later calls avant-garde art "a child's garden of easy victories," and though Stoppard shows enormous sympathy with the struggles his three protagonists have undergone, his own impatience with the limitations of contemporary aesthetics seem apparent.

A very short-lived import was David Hare's *The Secret Rapture*. Hare, the author of *Plenty* (1978), had written an indictment of Thatcherite England whose relevance to American audiences was doubtful. One of the few American plays to reach Broadway was Larry Gelbart's *Mastergate*, an attempt to satirize Washington politics that got bogged down in its own cleverness. The adolescent pun of the title was emblematic of much of the humor, though there were also genuinely witty sallies at the idiocies of Washington English, as when a character declares to a Senate investigating committee, "My involvement was strictly limited to the extent of my participation," or when another speaks of "future and probable deniability." *Tru*, Jay Presson Allen's one-man show based on the life of Truman Capote, drew a first-rate performance from Robert Morse but couldn't transcend the pettiness and bleariness of its subject.

Off-Broadway there were some bright spots, particularly a play about comedians, Jim Geoghan's *Only Kidding*. Geoghan tends to see comedy as an act of aggression. The title is first used by a Borscht Belt comic explaining how he wins over an audience by attacking a fat woman in the front row, adding the phrase "only kidding" to every insult he hurls at her. "I have found the one emotion that binds us together as human beings," he says. "Hate."

Later the same phrase is used by a young comic addicted to cocaine whose drug habit makes it impossible to channel his hatreds into the odd sort of communal "good feeling" that stems from Borscht Belt insult humor. The play used the varying styles of comedy as a way of delineating American social history, showing how much more frenetic and eccentric humor has become as its spiritual center has moved from the Catskills to Los Angeles.

Jerry Sterner's *Other People's Money* (originally presented at Mark Lamos's Hartford Stage Company) is a compelling drama about the takeover of an old New England family-run business by an aggressive New York conglomerate builder. Though extremely well produced and acted, the drama is essentially synthetic, particularly the romance between the crude New Yorker and a young woman lawyer representing the family business. What makes the play interesting is a pair of speeches at the very end, when the audience is asked to be shareholders at the annual meeting. The elderly head of the business asks them to vote for family control of the business. Then his nemesis gives a speech in which he explains in simple economic terms why family-run, old-fashioned businesses are potentially dangerous to the whole economy when competition is no longer local or national but international. In effect the speech is an essay justifying a mentality toward which the average American is likely to be both intellectually and emotionally hostile. But the speech is remarkably persuasive. No one can be surprised that the voters give the vulgar corporate raider control of the company.

One of A. R. Gurney's most graceful plays opened Off-Broadway and, in what may be taken as a statement about the changing tastes of the times, eventually moved into the Broadway theater that had been occupied for most of the last dozen years by *Oh, Calcutta!* The contrast between the two could not be more dramatic. *Love Letters* is the story of a love affair that extends from grade school through middle age, told in letters read by a man and a woman seated behind tiny lecterns set on a huge old-fashioned table. The only "set decoration" consists of a pair of dark blue carafes. Nothing more is necessary.

The carafes conjure up the elegance and orderliness of Gurney's world.

The actors never get up or move around. They simply sit and read their letters. Again, nothing more is necessary. We follow them from puppy love through adolescent anxiety through the storms of college sexual experimentation through their changing relationship as they marry other people—all through their letters. So too do we learn about their marital stress and eventually the woman's uncontrollable alcoholism and her suicide. It is a voyage largely of laughter but also of deep pathos. It was performed by a different pair of actors every week, and the nuances each pair found in the script enhanced one's appreciation of Gurney's writing.

Several writers of note contributed works of considerably less interest than expected. In *Oh, Hell*, David Mamet wrote a skit about hell that constituted little beyond self-parody. It furnished the second half of an evening that began with doggerel by Shel Silverstein about a gambler trying to outfox the devil. Mamet's play, *Bobby Gould in Hell*, took one of his hustling producers from *Speed-the-Plow* (1988), Bobby Gould, and placed him in an elegant library setting that was apparently an anteroom to hell. The devil, irritated that he has to interrupt a fishing trip to interrogate Gould, calls on one of Gould's girlfriends for corroboration. She confounds both Gould and the devil, and Gould is allowed to leave, precise destination unknown. It seemed like a sketch for a play rather than the thing itself but was given a classy production. Tina Howe, who has written such lovely, imaginative works as *Painting Churches* (1983) and *Coastal Disturbances* (1986), tried to grapple with large family issues in *Approaching Zanzibar*, which also seemed like an unfulfilled outline of a play.

Of the failures this year two were especially interesting. Joshua Sobol's *Ghetto* was based on the chilling fact that in the ghetto of Vilna, in the months the Nazis were weeding the population and sending the excess to Auschwitz, the Jewish police chief organized a theater to boost morale. Another phenomenon Sobol used was the fact that the People of the Book, even in times of unimaginable horror, found themselves attracted to books. A lending library, which must have drawn some of its stock from the books left behind by transported Jews, did a thriving business during this period. From these materials Sobol constructed an ungainly play. The production directed by Theodore Mann made the play seem even ungainlier, though a nearly concurrent London production was a huge hit. Having seen another play by Sobol, *Soul of a Jew* (1988), again based on fascinating material, the life and writings of the virulent Jewish anti-Semite Leon Weininger, I am aware of what an unwieldy, unskillful writer he is. But *Ghetto* presented theatrical opportunities the other play did not, and its bungled production seemed a pity.

So did a completely wrongheaded production of a play by Václav Havel, who began 1989 in prison and ended it as the president of Czechoslovakia, the country he refused to leave when other literati saw no hope for it. *Temptation*, Havel's version of the Faust myth, is about a rebel in a totalitarian society. In the Faust legend a medieval magician makes a pact with the devil to win scientific knowledge and worldly experience. In *Temptation* Havel's protagonist, Foustka, is a contemporary scientist who longs to go backward. He is dabbling in the occult. He does make contact with the devil, but in a police state it is hard to distinguish Satan from the System.

In a scientific, materialistic society Foustka's fascination with black magic takes on a subversive coloring. But the play is not just the parable of a questing spirit trying to break free of Soviet constraints. As Foustka says, "Modern man has rejected everything transcendent." This line parallels Havel's own concern with the transcendent, documented in his *Letters to Olga* (1988), the extraordinary letters he wrote his wife during an earlier prison term. "A relatively bearable life on this earth can only be secured by a humanity whose orientation is 'beyond' this world. An unqualified orientation to the 'here' and 'now,' however bearable that may be, hopelessly transforms that 'here' and 'now' into desolation and waste and ultimately colors it with blood," Havel wrote.

In a clearheaded production you might have some sense both of a Soviet man trying to escape the claustrophobic system and of a modern man coming to grips with "the beyond." In the production the Czech director Jiri Zizka did for the New York Shakespeare Festival, it might just as well have been a work of science fiction. Nothing was comprehensible except the director's conviction in his own cleverness.

Havel's concerns with the transcendent parallel those of a 1959 American play revived by the Theater of Lincoln Center, Paddy Chayefsky's *The Tenth Man*, where an elderly, pious Jew chastises a young agnostic: "You are a man possessed by the Tangible. If you cannot touch it with your fingers it simply does not exist. Indeed, that will be the mark of your generation–that you took everything for granted and believed in nothing." Although the play was not well realized, the revival was a reminder that the late Chayefsky, who abandoned the New York theater in disgust twenty years ago, was one of the most promising dramatists of his generation.

Of the slew of parodies of old Hollywood movies, only one had an original idea, Eric Overmyer's *In A Pig's Valise*. This send-up of the hard-boiled style had a detective trailing a gangster who steals people's dreams with an eye to commercial exploitation. The idea has wit, a keen grasp of our cynical times, and a mythical scope worthy of the great Hollywood detective films. There were even some witty lines, such as a blind character who is described as "visually challenged." But instead of developing its fascinating premise the play with music bogged down in silly humor, puns, and campy parody. (Nevertheless, its premise at least gave it more character than a similar entry, *City of Angels*, for which Larry Gelbart strung together jokes about Hollywood with no particular point of view.)

The paucity of original plays that opened on Broadway sent the Tony nominators scurrying for material to fill their categories, and they nominated Bill Irwin's *Largely New York*, a collection of sight gags with no text, for best play. Broadway's closest brush with literature was a mechanical ad-aptation of Franz Kafka's *Metamorphosis* by Stephen Berkoff, in which all the characters are reduced to cartoons. The stage version has been around for many years and is generally trucked out when a celebrity is willing to play Gregor Samsa. In Paris a few years ago the part was taken on by Roman Polanski. In 1989, in New York, Mikhail Baryshnikov assumed the role, but even his dancer's talents seemed wasted by the limited movement required.

One of the more interesting retrospectives in some time was *Jerome Robbins' Broadway*, a recreation of his own Broadway choreography from *On the Town* in 1944 to *Fiddler on the Roof* in 1964. The program was oddly assembled, lacking the momentum that generally characterized shows he directed, but the dancing by a youthful cast was excellent, particularly a suite of dances from *West Side Story* (1957), which have seldom been executed with such throbbing intensity.

In some ways the show was like one of those enormous eighteenth-century paintings that were, in effect, the inventory of a wealthy man's collection. He and his family would be painted in a gallery surrounded by painstaking miniatures of the pieces they owned. Here at last was a large canvas–even if it was created by itemizing many small ones.

The Year in Literary Biography

Mark A. Heberle
University of Hawaii at Manoa

Four enormous volumes are among the most recent contributions to life writing, and together with these weighty biographies of Graham Greene, I. A. Richards, William Faulkner, and Ezra Pound (published in 1988), we should note a second 400-page segment of Bernard Shaw's life, the final 400 pages of Edward Gibbon's, and a study of Ernest Hemingway that comprises 350 pages but covers only five years. The biographies of Faulkner, Pound, and Hemingway as well as the authorized biography of Stevie Smith follow 1987 lives of the writers. And three women biographers present fascinating portrayals of female writers that will do little to advance their subjects' literary reputations even among feminist readers. In general, the most artistically successful biographers have attempted to internalize their narratives by taking on the viewpoint of their subjects rather than defining them from the outside in the guise of biographical scholar or investigator.

Writing the life of a premodern author is problematical for numerous reasons. The most obvious is lack of personal records—letters, notes, testimony by friends and acquaintances, and the like. At the other extreme, so much literary criticism has been produced on any author worth writing a life of that it is difficult to find something new or revelatory to say about the works. In addition, such biographies are necessarily the product of literary scholars, who inevitably submerge the subject within detailed historical, cultural, or literary-critical contexts that may be interesting or comprehensible only to fellow scholars; the recent biographies by Donald Howard (Chaucer), Russell Fraser (Shakespeare), and James Anderson Winn (Dryden) suffer to varying degrees from this uneasy alliance of good life writing and exhaustive scholarship, even though each author intended to reach a general audience. David Riggs's *Jonson: A Life* (Harvard University Press) is the most absorbing and the most successful solution to the problem posed by the premodern subject that I have read. Of course, Riggs's biographical resources are far richer than those available to Winn, Howard, or Fraser, since Jonson left

Dust jacket for the biography that, according to Victoria Glendinning, displays Smith's "frailties without destroying her dignity"

rather full records of his own character, actions, and opinions in the 1618 *Conversations* with William Drummond of Hawthornden, and he comments extensively on his work in the self-justifying prologues and notes to the printed editions of his plays.

Nevertheless, Riggs's *Jonson* succeeds so well as literary biography—both a re-creation of a writer's life and an interpretation of what motivated life and works—by daring to be speculative and even controversial. The author has immersed himself in psychoanalytical theory as well as the new historical criticism that has replaced unexamined cultural and social generalizations with the often microscopic, sometimes subversive details of actual social and material practices. The result is a life that frequently addresses itself to the striking contradictions that marked Jonson's public character in order to powerfully and often convincingly reincarnate the writer in all his large dimensions (Riggs points out that he weighed between 250 and 270 pounds in his maturity).

In much of his poetry, playwriting, and masque writing, Jonson cultivated the persona of a neoclassical stylist, scholar, and moralist, a writer who shunned or satirized vulgar popular taste and sought to please the discriminating palates of the professional classes, aristocracy, and court. Yet, as Riggs notes, "contemporary sources reveal that he killed two men for no apparent reason, went to prison on three separate occasions, was 'almost at the Gallowes' and wore the brand of a convicted murderer on his thumb, enjoyed sleeping with other men's wives (but not with single women), sired one or more illegitimate children, was paraded through the streets of Paris in a drunken stupor, and narrowly escaped having his ears and nose mutilated after collaborating on a play that lampooned King James I." Although Jonson expressed scorn and distaste toward the public theater and attempted to abandon it after 1616 to devote his efforts to poetry and the composition of expensive court masques, it was as a public playwright that he wrote his most enduring and important works, including the comic masterpieces *Volpone* (1606), *The Alchemist* (1610), and *Bartholomew Fair* (1614). Indeed, the latter play, which celebrates the triumph of popular license over attempts to control or inhibit it, was omitted from Jonson's personally supervised collected *Works* of 1616, which attempts to memorialize his writings as if they were already classics of English literature—perhaps a work like *Bartholomew Fair* didn't quite "fit," like the disreputable drives and impulses that seethed below the writer's public persona.

As Riggs emphasizes, the only unquestioned authority for Jonson is Jonson, and we might say that it is with this writer that the concept of "author" first appears in English literature. Shakespeare was indifferent to the publication of his own works, but Jonson not only planned and supervised his but provided copious notes and defenses that are intended to be the definitive interpretation of himself. Perhaps it was in this sovereignty over the world created by his imagination that Jonson satisfied his constant need to

validate himself by condemning social or intellectual inferiors and satisfying his superiors. Riggs rightly points out that Jonson's innovation was liberating in an age of ideological conformity: "authors were not the only, or even the most important, factors in the repression of meaning. On the contrary, the institution of authorship created a context in which Jonson's transgressive texts could circulate freely despite official opposition to his work. The role of author helped to enfranchise displaced intellectuals such as himself; its function was to enlarge, rather than to constrain, the sphere of literary discourse."

Restoration and eighteenth-century literary studies have been enriched recently by the magisterial scholarly biographies by Irving Ehrenpreis (Swift) and Maynard Mack (Pope) as well as Winn's *Dryden*. This year Johns Hopkins University Press published equally definitive lives of two lesser giants of the period: Paula R. Backscheider's *Daniel Defoe: His Life* and Patricia B. Craddock's *Edward Gibbon, Luminous Historian: 1772-1794*, the second and concluding volume of her biography. Both Defoe and Gibbon were masters of English prose, but otherwise their identities seem as widely divergent as their prose styles: while the quasi-aristocratic Gibbon moved inexorably to the achievement of a single great masterpiece and cultivated a public persona as the great historian of Rome, the frenetically entrepreneurial Defoe wrote so many works for so many purposes under so many pseudonyms that scholars are still unable to definitively establish a Defoe canon. *Daniel Defoe* is the first full-length biography of the writer in over thirty years, while Craddock's is the first of Gibbon in half a century; both works supplant all previous biographies of their subjects.

Daniel Defoe is a richly circumstantial, minutely documented study of virtually everything that we now know about this prolific yet elusive writer. Among Backscheider's most important revelations is Defoe's secret relationship with Robert Harley, Queen Anne's secretary of state for the north, who rescued him after he had been imprisoned for seditious libel in 1703 and whom Defoe served as a spy and propagandist thereafter while working as a journalist. In Backscheider's structural scheme, the relationship with Harley divides Defoe's life into three phases: from 1660 to 1703 he first succeeded and then went bankrupt as a businessman before becoming so effective as a Dissenter polemicist that he had to be imprisoned by the new Stuart government. From 1703 to 1714 Defoe was not only Harley's agent but also a highly successful journalist and tract writer who relocated to Scotland in 1706-1711 and helped to effect the government's campaign for the union of the two countries; thereafter, Defoe helped support the Treaty of Utrecht that ended England's long war with France in 1713. Following the downfall of Harley's Tory ministry and the succession of the Whig-directed government of George I in 1714, Defoe's work as a journalist expanded, but he also produced the first important English novels and a series of geographical and trade volumes extolling England's potential as a mercantile empire prior to his death in 1731.

Backscheider provides an impeccably scholarly and comprehensive documentary account of Defoe's tumultuous life; a bibliography of works by or attributed to Defoe goes on for nine pages and lists about 350 titles, all described or discussed in the biography. She quotes generously from letters and memoranda "to let [Defoe] and his contemporaries speak for themselves whenever possible." Too often, however, the sheer volume of minutiae becomes tedious, nearly overwhelming the narrative of Defoe's life. Contemporary political and factional issues were probably confusing even to Defoe's countrymen, and they are too often bewildering despite Backscheider's occasional attempts to define key legal, religious, and political references. Occasional historical outlines would have been helpful. Finally, since her coverage of the works is so admirably inclusive, it is necessarily sketchy, with little interpretation or evaluation.

Partly because the political situation during these years seems so fluid and uncertain, Backscheider's attempts to show that Defoe retained his authorial integrity despite his reliance on Harley are not very convincing—or very clear. He did remain true to some fundamental principles, however—liberty of conscience for all and trust in God's providence—and she shows how both ideas characterized Defoe's own life as well as those of his fictional characters. Her epilogue provides a fine overall evaluation of the writer's life and work; and the opening epigraph of the book, taken from one of Defoe's own self-defenses, epitomizes the bourgeois piety that underlay his indefatigable energy: "The God that gave me brains will give me bread."

In dealing with the relatively circumscribed life of Gibbon, Craddock has a more stable and less complicated story to tell than Backscheider,

and her work is no less authoritative but easier to read, though not as interesting biographically. The first volume had ended with the death of Gibbon's father, the writer's purchase of his own house in London, and initial reading and planning for the *Decline and Fall of the Roman Empire*. Gibbon's one serious love, Suzanne Churchod, had become a friend after marrying Jacques Necker, one of Louis XVI's chief ministers.

Although one of her purposes is to extend Gibbon's identity beyond that of historian of Rome, the *Decline and Fall* bulks so large in Gibbon's life that it necessarily overwhelms everything else (the enormously detailed entry for that work in Craddock's index takes up four full columns of print). Written and published over sixteen years in two cities (London and Lausanne), the six volumes appeared in three installments, each longer than the last, and provided Gibbon enough fame and fortune to support him for the rest of his life, which only lasted for six more years. His *Memoirs* (1796), his only other major work, was left uncompleted and in manuscript upon his death. Indeed, Craddock divides Gibbon's life into phases that correspond to the successive installments of the Roman history: 1772-1776 (volume 1); 1776-1781 (2 and 3); and 1782-1788 (4, 5, and 6). The symmetry of this arrangement almost seems to reflect the order and harmony of Gibbon's own life and his masterpiece: the first three volumes present the decline and fall of the Western Empire, the latter three the growth, decline, and fall of the Eastern, and Gibbon himself moved from England to Switzerland nearly at the midpoint of composition. The fourth section of the biography traces Gibbon's post-*Decline* life in Lausanne to his death in 1794, including a detailed analysis of the *Memoirs*, while part 5 provides a valuable discussion of his posthumous reputation.

Craddock's discussion of Gibbon's great work largely identifies and consecutively traces major emphases and issues in each of its seventy-one chapters. She notes that the writer's increasing self-consciousness within the *Decline and Fall* concerning his role in shaping and creating the past for an audience in the present marks him as the first modern historian. Her discussion of Gibbon's work in the Roman history is clear and straightforward, occasionally incorporating recent critiques of Gibbon's historiography, but it is less interesting as life writing than the rest of the book.

In defense of Gibbon against Boswell and later critics who have regarded him as an upper-class snob puffed up with self-importance, Craddock notes how much he was affectionately admired by friends ranging from the Neckers and the Severys to Lord Sheffield and Lord North to his own servants in England and Switzerland. Unmarried and probably unable to have children himself, he became a foster father for all of his friends' children. Highly clubbable and domestic, he was an inveterate cardplayer. Craddock notes that Gibbon's writing his memoirs was prompted by terrible loneliness after the death of his Lausanne housemate and oldest friend, George Deyverdun, in 1789. Gibbon's hatred of the French Revolution was accompanied by a hardening of his Tory prejudices and opposition to any constitutional innovation in England itself, but it was prompted by what he saw as the widespread destruction and suffering being unleashed by a new barbarism.

His own sufferings were endured with stoical grace. Incapacitated by a potentially fatal leg infection in 1791 and chronically rendered helpless by gout, Gibbon's reaction was to ignore the pain. His failure to attend to the hideous groin tumor that eventually swelled up to a baby's size in his last year led to several unsuccessful operations, and he died of the resulting complications. His sustained work on the *Memoirs* suggests that Gibbon may have been preparing for death ever since finishing the *Decline and Fall*.

Craddock minutely and sympathetically documents Gibbon's relatively uneventful life without overencumbering her narrative with too much detail. Following the work of Patricia Spacks, her analysis of the six drafts of the *Memoirs* provides a new argument about Gibbon's interpretation of his own life. She sees the sixth draft as an entirely new approach by Gibbon and a rejection of its predecessor, the only version completed up to the time of writing and thus the basis of present editions of Gibbon's *Autobiography*. While the fifth draft presents Gibbon's view of his own life as an intellectual quest culminating inevitably in the *Decline and Fall*, Gibbon's final, uncompleted view of his life more freely acknowledges and dramatizes the contradictions, accidents, and personal emotions that made up his existence at every period in order "to see not just what [they] contributed to his achievements, but what it was like to experience that life–what the achievements cost." Patricia Craddock has now

completed that project for Gibbon, and he would probably have been pleased with the result.

In his twenties William Wordsworth enthusiastically welcomed the French Revolution that Gibbon had deplored, yet during the last half of his life England's first great modern poet came not only to repudiate his earlier radicalism but became an active reactionary, campaigning for the parliamentary candidates of Lord Lonsdale, the local Tory magnate, and publicly opposing Catholic Emancipation and the Reform Bill of 1832. Named poet laureate by Queen Victoria in 1843, Wordsworth had not only reversed his political feelings but had completed virtually all of his worthwhile poetry thirty years earlier. One of Stephen Gill's purposes in *William Wordsworth: A Life* (Oxford University Press) is to reexamine and reevaluate the later poetry in the context of Wordsworth's final three decades. The first one-volume biography to take into account extensive new Wordsworth and Coleridge discoveries and scholarship in the last twenty years, this is an objective, lucid, well-organized life intended for the general reader that will also necessarily replace the previous scholarly two-volume life by Mary Moorman (1965), which tended to idealize its subject.

There are no surprises and few revelations in Gill's book, and he admits to being "timid" (but also prudent) in handling such speculative subjects as sexual feelings between Wordsworth and his sister Dorothy or Wordsworth's relationship with Annette Vallon, the mother of his French daughter. Gill uses a straightforward chronological organization and divides the life into three larger periods, 1770-1799, 1800-1822, and 1822-1850. The first culminates with the two-part *Prelude*, Wordsworth's autobiographical account of his childhood in the English Lake Country. Tracing the growth of his imagination as a joint product of nature and his experiences as a schoolboy, it ends with reflections on his identity as a poet now that he has returned to his childhood home and established a household of his own at Dove Cottage with his sister Dorothy.

Gill's treatment of *The Prelude*, Wordsworth's masterpiece but also an unconscious attempt to forestall biography by composing his own, is one of the strongest features of his book. This testament of youth was vastly expanded into a thirteen-book work between 1803 and 1805, and thereafter Wordsworth continued to revise it nearly until his death in 1850; only the final version was published, and posthumously. Rather than adding new material to reflect his life after 1799, however, Wordsworth continually rewrote his youth, recasting the same experiences in light of his achieved success as a poet in 1805 and his increasing conservatism thereafter. Gill notes that much of Wordsworth's poetry and prose of the early 1790s, including his long poem *Salisbury Plain,* is passionately and wholeheartedly radical. But none of this work was published at the time, and Wordsworth did not include that part of himself in *The Prelude,* where he ultimately presents his enthusiasm for the French Revolution as an illness cured by his sister's love and his own love for Nature.

The Prelude was initially addressed to Coleridge, and Gill's detailed study of their sometimes troubled friendship, the most important literary relationship for each writer, is another keystone of this biography. During the great year at Grasmere in 1797-1798, the two were inseparable, Wordsworth discovering his voice as a poet while Coleridge wrote almost all of the poetry for which he is remembered. In tracing the growing tensions and eventual falling off of their intimacy, Gill places most of the responsibility on Coleridge, whose poetical career was eclipsed by Wordsworth's. Unable to create one himself despite his brilliant mind, Coleridge expected Wordsworth to eventually compose a grand philosophical epic; indeed, the 1805 *Prelude* was to have been the introduction to that work, which Wordsworth entitled *The Recluse.* But he only completed the first of three parts, *The Excursion,* a noble but inert nine-book blank verse meditative poem published in 1814 to bad reviews. Ultimately, *The Prelude* would be his epic, and his refusal to have it published during his lifetime must have owed much to the unrealizable plan of *The Recluse:* reviewing the autobiographical poem was more important and more congenial to the poet than resuming the longer work, and as long as *The Prelude* remained unfinished, there was no reason to continue its effectively abandoned successor.

Revisiting, remembering, and reimagining are the characteristic modes of Wordsworth's finest poetry, and Gill emphasizes how important revision and republication were to Wordsworth's identity as a poet. After the collected *Poems* of 1807, Wordsworth spent much of his life changing and reissuing what had already been composed. His insistence on publishing the numerous collected editions of his poems in a thematic rather than chronological arrangement suggests

that no poem was ever truly complete, that they all continued to exist atemporally in the poet's own imagination and could be altered at will.

Gill's account of the years at Rydal Mount from 1813 until the end with Dorothy, his wife Mary, and their children, describes their circumstances well, but it is unsuccessful in salvaging the later poetry from critical oblivion and obloquy. Gill notes that Wordsworth seems to have come to a creative dead end in 1822, publishing no new poetry at all for the next thirteen years, but in the final third of the book he emphasizes the poet's renewed energy after 1834: eight substantial volumes of new or completely revised poetry followed. With the exception of *The Prelude,* however, Gill provides virtually no critical evaluation or interpretation of the poetry in his biography, so the conventional dismissal of the later work remains unshaken. Curiously enough, nearly all of the contemporary reviews cited are negative, which reminds us of the considerable professional hostility toward his poetry during Wordsworth's own lifetime, but this does nothing to validate the later works. Gill argues that Wordsworth finally achieved a satisfying wholeness in his life and work in the last thirty years at Grasmere. This is probably true, though it seems to disregard what had been lost or denied to achieve such harmony. But the biographer's emphasis throughout upon how closely Wordsworth's own identity depended upon inventing or revising poetry suggests why the poor quality of the later poems would not have been evident or even important to Wordsworth: in every poem he recovered or re-created himself, and that was validation enough.

In *Elizabeth Barrett Browning: A Biography* (St. Martin's), Margaret Forster has given us an intimate, fascinating narrative life of this important Victorian poet, whose late poetic melodrama *Aurora Leigh* (1856) has found a devoted audience among feminists in the past two decades. Forster's is one of the most fully internalized biographies of the year, a remarkably convincing view of the poet's life from her own viewpoint that at its best allows us to enter into the daily life of the Barrett and later the Browning household. Forster's success in achieving such immediacy has been generated by her own skill as a novelist and the almost unbelievable wealth of Browning correspondence and diaries discovered by scholars led by Philip Kelley. The result is a lively and coherent intimate third-person narrative of Browning's life. Forster's documentation of her details is rather spotty, however, and one wonders how many of them come from the letters, how many are projected, and how many are simply made up. But the narrative certainly seems authentic.

Elizabeth's furtive marriage to Robert Browning at the age of forty followed by their fifteen-year honeymoon in Italy divides her life in half, of course, and this is mirrored in the two-part structure of Forster's biography. It is in recreating her life before Robert, however, that Forster is most revelatory.

The great weakness of this work is Forster's nearly complete lack of interest in Elizabeth Browning's poetry. None of the poems is evaluated or even described, with the exception of *Aurora Leigh*, and her comments here are somewhat patronizing. Although a separate volume of selected poems was coupled with the English edition of the biography by Chatto & Windus, Forster's failure to consider seriously the work to which Elizabeth devoted her life seems a disservice to the writer whose life she has so fully recreated otherwise.

Michael Holroyd's biography of Shaw is also splendidly internalized in parts, the biographer often merging with the mind and style of his subject to produce a life that is not only brilliantly detailed but Shavian in its wit and intellectual sparkle. Last year's first volume, *The Search for Love: 1856-1898*, ended with Shaw's marriage to Charlotte Payne-Townsend. Volume 2, *The Pursuit of Power: 1898-1918* (Random House), takes Shaw's life through the end of World War I. Holroyd's thesis is that despite his feverish activity as a political essayist, playwright, and speaker, power, like love, proved elusive for Shaw.

The flight from love to power is wittily highlighted at the beginning of this second volume. A series of suspiciously self-repeating accidents confined Shaw to his wife Charlotte's ministrations over his broken limbs, and he was helpless as a baby, so "sex was postponed," Holroyd notes, "until its absence became part of the structure of their lives." Ultimately, "Shaw's own marriage was a masculine contrivance for the procreation of plays and prefaces." Sheltered and financed by his wealthy wife, Shaw was able to evade domestic and sexual entanglements and exercise his potency to influence the mind of England as a whole. Charlotte joined him for a time in Fabian Society work or forced him irregularly to join her on feverish motor tours of the Continent or England. Her unconscious resentment ultimately

Dust jacket for the initial volume of the first full-length biography of Greene, which chronicles his life and career up through the writing of The Power and the Glory (1940)

took the form of mystical and meditative activities that were affronts to her husband's skeptical rationalism. It was a very successful marriage.

The world war itself, a negation of everything Shaw had been working for during these years, registered his ultimate powerlessness conclusively, but Holroyd closes this volume with more specific failures. Shaw's sensible arguments for an Irish federation with England and Scotland only succeeded in uniting England and Ireland against everything that he recommended, and he was not even appointed to the fifteen-man board of famous Irishmen established by Lloyd George to solve the problem in 1917. And his brilliant, quasi-socialist essays in the *New Statesman*, culminating in the farsighted *Common Sense About the War* (1914), made him seem a traitor to many of his countrymen. As Stockton Axson noted, "Shaw is often ten minutes ahead of the truth, which is almost as fatal as being behind the time."

Between the honeymoon and the European catastrophe, Holroyd's second volume traces the evolution of Shaw into one of the first great world media personalities as well as its most well known playwright. In 1898 Shaw was a famous public eccentric who had written nine largely unperformed plays and several forgotten novels. Shaw's reputation had first been made in America in 1897 with productions of *The Devil's Disciple* and *Candida,* and now he worked with translators in Germany, France, and eventually Sweden to offer European productions that spread the Shavian gospel abroad. Shaw's breakthrough in London came with the establishment of the Court Theatre, the first modern repertory company in England, brilliantly managed by Shaw and his surrogate son, Harley Granville-Barker (during its existence, seven hundred of its one thousand productions were plays by Shaw). Characteristically, however, he was upset at his audiences' reactions to the plays, which found them brilliantly entertaining rather than politically enlightening.

Shaw does not occupy Holroyd's panorama as exclusively as he did in volume 1, nor is the author's narrative as fully internalized; partly as a result, this is a more diffuse volume, and the reading of the plays as disguised autobiography, usually Oedipal, is less cogent. But Holroyd fills his stage memorably with the other actors and actresses who helped G. B. S. play his role during these twenty years, friends and critics such as Ellen Terry, Sidney and Beatrice Webb, Barker, H. G. Wells, G. K. Chesterton, and many lesser personalities. Poignant beyond the rest is Shaw's relationship with Mrs. Pat Campbell, the Stella for whom he created the role of Liza Doolittle in *Pygmalion* (1913) and with whom he fell hopelessly in love when he was fifty-six and she was forty-seven. She became his last, unexpected search for love, a passion probably intensified by his mother's death in 1913. He was unwilling to leave Charlotte, and Campbell was unwilling to become his mistress.

As Holroyd's book ends, Shaw's life is uncharacteristically dark: the Great War is over, with appalling casualties; Shaw's success as a playwright seems less significant than his failure as a public conscience; his childless marriage has become a habit, Stella a married friend. At the end of the book, his dear sister Lucy is cremated, a victim of shell shock–from gun testing at Woolwich Arsenal during the war–and resultant anorexia.

Volume 3, *The Lure of Fantasy,* promises a final Shavian quest; scheduled for publication in 1991, it will provide the much-needed documentation for all three volumes and should complete one of the great literary biographies of our time.

In *Stevie Smith: A Biography* (Norton), Frances Spalding narrates a life that was as narrowly circumscribed as Shaw's was publicly flamboyant. Smith worked as a secretary in a publishing house for thirty years, a job that allowed her time for reading and writing, before suffering a nervous breakdown and possible suicide attempt; lived with her aunt in the same house in a London suburb for sixty-five years until her death in 1971; and gained literary fame at thirty-four with the experimental *Novel on Yellow Paper* (1936) and a more lasting reputation through seven volumes of poems. Increasingly in demand in her later years as a reader of her poetry on radio and at public recitals, she scratched out a living as a reviewer and author after quitting as a secretary; less than two years after receiving the Gold Medal for poetry from Queen Elizabeth, she died of a brain tumor that had left her aphasic for her last three months.

Authorized by Smith's literary estate, Spalding's biography follows by two years the full-length life by Jack Barbera and William McBrien (reviewed in the 1987 *DLB Yearbook*). Both are good, well-researched books; nonetheless, it is surprising to see so much attention being devoted to this important minor poet. In her introduction Spalding suggests why Smith seems a significant figure now, noting that the playfulness of her poetry and its subversion of traditional formalism, its undetached and direct social satire, and the poet's unflinching exploration of life as the endurance of pain and disappointment make her work unselfconsciously feminist. Yet Spalding also notes that little has been written about the poetry itself. Smith was exceptionally well read in English poetry, and while she wrote in the tradition of Wordsworth's and Blake's lyrics, her poems freely reflect, parody, or transmute the work of many predecessors and contemporaries. Spalding's careful and intelligent analyses of Smith's creativity and her poems provide an essential foundation for all future interpreters.

By contrast, the poems were identified or briefly described but otherwise left unexplained and uninterpreted by Barbera and McBrien, who were more chatty and anecdotal in their approach than Spalding. As a result, their biography is perhaps more lively than its successor.

They discuss the illustrations that Smith sketched to accompany her poems, while Spalding ignores them, her most serious omission. Otherwise, however, her life is more probing and better integrated in its account of the life than the 1987 biography. As the official biographer, she has had access to unpublished memoirs, diaries, and letters of Smith's friends, including those of her German boyfriend, Karl Eckinger, that have been unavailable to previous writers. Her sleuthing for information from others has been even more productive than Barbera's and McBrien's—indeed, they are included in her long list of direct sources. Spalding has also presented testimony from all her interviews and written sources more smoothly and artfully. While Barbera and McBrien present a comprehensive and interesting character portrait, Spalding provides a more illuminating life of the writer.

Spalding skillfully maps the territory of Smith's imagination, recognizing that a writer's inner world is at least as important as her outward life and acquaintances and that what she reads is the source of what she writes and believes in. *Grimms' Fairy Tales* (an edition was found on her bed table after she died), Browning's "Childe Roland" (a primal poem for Smith, dramatizing a primal scene for her own poetry and her life), Pater's *Marius the Epicurean* (the earliest model for her prose), contemporary American novels (important sources for her breezy, slang-energized unpoetic diction), and many other works left annotated among her papers are well used by Spalding to illuminate Smith's fiction and poetry. Spalding resuscitates many now-forgotten works to explain Smith's own: for example, *John Inglesant*, a nineteenth-century Christian romance that encouraged her movement toward agnostic stoicism, or Geoffrey Dennis's novel *Harvest in Poland* (1925), a source for the mannerisms of her alter ego, Pompey Casmilus, in *Novel on Yellow Paper*.

But Spalding also brings to fuller life the writer's external world by providing substantial, finely etched character portraits of Smith's family and close friends such as the novelists Inez Holden, Olivia Manning, Betty Miller, and Mulk Raj Anand, who reappear in her fiction or recreated Smith in their own. She provides revealing studies of Smith's friends Karl Eckinger and Eric Armitage and authoritative though necessarily inconclusive investigations of her relationships with them and with George Orwell, all reimagined in her three novels and the only men

she may have had affairs with before friendship replaced any hope of romantic love in her life. And a marvelous collection of largely unpublished photographs provides vivid portraits of Smith from three to sixty-three and of the most important people in her life.

Like Frances Spalding's, Norman Sherry's literary biography has been authorized and by the subject himself, for *The Life of Graham Greene Volume I: 1904-1939* (Viking) is the only work in this year's survey that honors a living writer. Sherry has used 725 pages to present Greene's first thirty-five years. At this rate we may well expect two more volumes and over 2000 pages since the biographer has only covered the first fifth of Greene's career as a publishing novelist, and among the eight or ten major fictions only *Brighton Rock* (1938) and *The Power and the Glory* (1940), which concludes this volume, have been covered. And Greene keeps on writing!

Sherry's task is daunting, because while Greene has been one of the most prolific writers in the English language, he has also been one of the most elusive. Although he continues to be an outspoken left-wing polemicist and though parts of himself obviously surface in characters like Fowler in *The Quiet American* (1955), Greene has been jealously protective of his inner life and hard to trace in his peripatetic wandering from one continent to another. The title of his 1974 autobiography, *A Sort of Life*, suggests the slippery indirectness of the narrative, which includes among its casually presented, unexplained revelations Greene's account of how he would sometimes play Russian roulette by himself with his brother's loaded revolver when he was twenty. Although it is certain that he played successfully, everything else about this episode is puzzling. But if assiduous labor and the resourceful unearthing of facts could assure a satisfying life of the mysterious Greene, Sherry would be the right man for the task. Those qualities, in addition to his objectivity in an earlier biography of Joseph Conrad, attracted Greene's attention in 1971 and led to his authorizing Sherry as his official biographer in 1974. After fifteen years of work, including numerous interviews with Greene, his former wife, members of his family, and friends and acquaintances, as well as unprecedented access to private papers and letters never before released and life-threatening trips through Liberia and southern Mexico tracing Greene's own footsteps, Sherry has produced as complete a picture of the writer's circumstances as is possible.

Among the highlights of his research are his portrait of Greene's schooling at Berkhamsted (Hertfordshire), Greene's youthful suicidal depressions, his courtship of and marriage to Vivienne Dayrell-Browning, the overland treks through Liberia and Mexico, and Sherry's meticulous reconstruction of the biographical and geographical contexts of *Brighton Rock* and *The Power and the Glory.* Greene's father was the headmaster of Graham's grammar school, and his son found himself in his midteens being made a scapegoat by his classmates, caught between betraying his father's rule or being betrayed by certain friends. Sherry finds the sources of the typical Greene theme of betrayal and the Judas- and sacrificial-victim figures in these experiences. Impractical attempts at suicide and running away from home were signs of a nervous breakdown, and the boy's loving and surprisingly progressive parents allowed their son to undergo psychoanalysis at sixteen, a possible source of his interest in detached psychological exploration. But at Oxford three years later, depression and ennui set in, possibly prompted by a hopeless love for his sister's governess, and Greene underwent his experiment with the revolver. His great love for Vivienne (now Vivien), which seems to have dissolved those suicidal impulses, takes up the bulk of the first half of the book. This was a very peculiar courtship, conducted through Greene's countless passionately prosaic love letters from 1925 on, which Sherry endlessly reproduces throughout (I assume that Greene destroyed her replies, since none is cited). An ardent Catholic while Greene was not, she was resistant, and among other expedients Graham proposed a marriage without sex before finally converting to satisfy her in 1927. The marriage followed.

The best chapters in the book re-create with painstaking detail Greene's harrowing safari through Liberia with his cousin Barbara in 1935, which resulted in the travel book *Journey Without Maps* (1936), and his caravan by donkey through Tabasco and Chiapas provinces accompanied by native guides in 1938. The suicidal impulse seems not to have been fully arrested in Greene, for he was lucky to survive both adventures. Disappointed to find that the revolution he hoped to cover in Mexico had subsided, Greene produced another travel book, *The Lawless Roads* (1939), but also his early masterpiece, *The Power and the Glory,* a fictional account of the earlier violent

suppression of Catholicism in Mexico. Among other highlights Sherry tries to admire Greene's shrewd but vicious film criticism for the *Spectator,* which led to the delightfully absurd Shirley Temple libel case against the journal after Greene had identified the child actress as a deliberate sexual provocateuress.

Despite Sherry's exhaustive investigation of and admiration for his subject, Greene often threatens to emerge as a self-absorbed, shrewdly self-interested, and unpleasantly cold-blooded figure. He seems to have put on his Catholicism for the wedding but never really grown into it. He and Vivienne produced two children during these years, but Greene really didn't want them and seems to have been uninterested in both after they were born, since they play no part at all in Sherry's massive biography. Greene planned or implemented extended trips abroad during both pregnancies and during each infant's first year of life. Greene's recurrent need to abandon the tedium and the responsibilities of his life through travel and the cultivation of danger is even reflected in some of his titles: *It's a Battlefield* (1934), situated in postwar London, *Stamboul Train* (1932; republished as *Orient Express* [1933] in the United States), *Ways of Escape* (1981). The chill in his soul is indirectly reflected by his cousin's remark after returning from Liberia—"If you are in a sticky place he will be so interested in noting your reactions that he will probably forget to rescue you"—and more directly by Vivien in an interview with Sherry: "He was originally warm and I could make him laugh, that sort of thing—but as he developed into a better novelist the splinter in his heart grew—he became icier. He said writers shouldn't marry, and I daresay that's quite true." Sherry notes that Greene found himself as a novelist when he deliberately abandoned the naive romanticism of his execrable youthful poetry (the 1925 volume was entitled *Babbling April*) and his first three novels, all inferior works, for the bleak scenarios of Greeneland for which he has become famous. Evidently, accompanying the gain in creative power was an inner hardening.

Sherry's work illustrates the formidable problems as well as advantages of having a living subject. Unloading his vast burden of facts he raises all the important and disturbing questions, sometimes rhetorically, but often can't answer them for himself or us, possibly since Greene is around to correct or repudiate him. Page after page of Sherry's elephantine volume is filled with trivial details and often repetitious, matter-of-fact, lengthy extracts of diaries, letters, and interviews, yet Greene remains a puzzle–as Bevis Hillier has noted, Sherry uncovers the mask behind the mask. The researcher and biographical detective is onstage too much, revealing his discoveries without using them creatively to construct an absorbing narrative. The biographer's much-emphasized trips to Liberia and Mexico seem to me wild-goose chases; they haven't uncovered much of anything except a portrait of Greene's (probable) original for the Judas character in *The Power and the Glory,* and it's rather unclear why they were undertaken–Sherry's account of Greene's own experiences are lifted piecemeal from the author's travel books. Finally, Sherry is not a terrible writer, but he is not a good one, disabling his narrative with tedious or banal sentences and transitions (for example, "If 1931 was the worst year of Graham's life creatively and financially, what was it like for his brothers, Hugh, Herbert, and Raymond?" [answer to follow]).

Nonetheless, all of us must hope that Sherry continues and is able to complete his prodigious project. Greene is a masterful and prolific writer–having just completed his twenty-fourth novel last year at the age of eighty-four–and, as one of the very few English novelists to make the Third World his province, he will probably assume even greater significance as time goes on. One fears for his biographer's health and endurance, however, if he continues with the same method at the present pace, one volume every fifteen years with journeys to Zaire, Havana, Hanoi, Saigon, and many other places ahead of him.

Through its publications over the last decade, Johns Hopkins University Press has been in the forefront of the recent theoretical revolution in literary studies in America. It is therefore fitting that Hopkins should publish John Paul Russo's *I. A. Richards: His Life and Work,* the first full-length critical biography of a major Anglo-American literary critic. Russo characterizes Richards as "the most representative critic in the English-speaking world in this century." He finely notes that Richards was also the most future-oriented of all critics, intensely committed to fostering better readers, writers, and teachers of literature now in order to help insure the transmittal and extension of liberal culture and values in an age of mass communication, commercialism, propaganda, and encouraged mediocrity. Richards's scope was universal in at least three senses: he

was a linguist, psychologist, philosopher, teacher, entrepreneur, media performer, translator, and closet dramatist as well as literary critic, each activity complementing the others; he taught, wrote, and lectured extensively in America and China as well as in England, his birthplace; and his own reading, writing, and concept of culture were correspondingly broad–one of his works, *Mencius on the Mind* (1932), was a study of Chinese thought, and he spent thirty years trying (unsuccessfully) to propagate Basic English, a simplified form of the language invented by the linguist C. K. Ogden and expanded by Richards, as a means of universal communication across cultures and nations. His importance within the narrower limits of Anglo-American criticism itself is nearly unmatched: besides being a pioneer in linguistic and psychological criticism, the method of close reading, the distinction between poetic and scientific language and referential and emotive meaning, and the concepts of complementarity, tenor and vehicle, tone, organic unity, and sincerity and sentimentality, are largely his creations. Though he was often regarded as the father of the New Criticism in the 1940s and 1950s, Russo shows that no narrow school or method can define Richards, who would have repudiated the narrow academicism of his imitators and whose ultimate goals were social and moral. Richards bestrode both academia and pedagogy like a colossus between 1920 and 1960; born on the Welsh border in 1893, he died on a lecture tour of China in 1978.

Russo met Richards when the former was a young assistant professor at Harvard in the late 1960s, became a friend, and was authorized by Richards and his wife to prepare a biography. While fully explaining all of Richards's work with implicit admiration, Russo sensibly criticizes his blind spots, including Richards's notorious exclusion of biographical factors in criticism and his disinterest in history, and regrets his exhaustively futile efforts in the Basic English campaign. And occasionally, there were times when even Richards suffered from the myopia of the academic: Russo notes that when Richards and his wife were forced to flee to Yunnan during the Japanese invasion of China in 1937, the professor remained an eternal optimist, regarding the catastrophe as a possible opportunity for introducing Basic English to Japan.

Russo's book will prove a gold mine for literary theorists, for it constitutes virtually an indirect history of twentieth-century English and

American criticism–the summary of New Criticism and its discontents alone is the most comprehensive essay I have read on the subject. Other readers will find the book an intellectual morass, providing exhausting summaries and commentaries upon Richards's two dozen books with criticism and theories of others, too many of them only relevant to Russo's demonstration that the biographer can be a theorist too. Thus, Richards's ideas are criticized from the viewpoint of such writers as Adorno or Jaques Ellul, who have not even written about him.

Plodding on with grim, scholarly discipline for 678 pages of text and 130 pages of closely packed notes extending its scholarship and pedantry, Russo's book is the most self-consciously intellectual literary biography of this or any other year–and the most tedious. The title is a misnomer, since while Richards's work is hermetically analyzed, virtually the rest of his life is absent except for the almost irrelevant photographs of the subject in the middle of the book. This may have satisfied Richards, who did not believe in biography, but it leads to an almost literally lifeless narrative. And Russo's coverage of the works is more than thorough, it is numbingly overextended–he summarizes everything Richards wrote, potentially lively reading if the subject were a novelist or dramatist, but deadly when he is a theoretician. His concept of intellectual biography was apparently to separate Richards's ideas from the rest of his existence and then ignore the latter. The result is not so much a biography as a series of chronologically arranged scholarly articles that deal with I. A. Richards, intellectually impressive but without life.

A far more successful intellectual biography–indeed, one of the finest literary biographies in 1989–is Ernest Samuels's *Henry Adams* (Harvard University Press). Samuels is the author of the earlier massive and magisterial three-volume study of Adams's life and works published between 1948 and 1964 and one of the coeditors of the revised edition of Adams's *Letters,* published by Harvard University Press in six volumes in 1982 and 1988. Although this new one-volume life is necessarily derived from the longer work, it is by no means a simple abridgement, for Samuels has incorporated all that has been learned about Adams in the last twenty years, much of it through the new and fully restored letters now included in the 1982 and 1988 editions. Adams's last final masterpiece was his *Education of Henry Adams,* completed in 1906 but kept back from com-

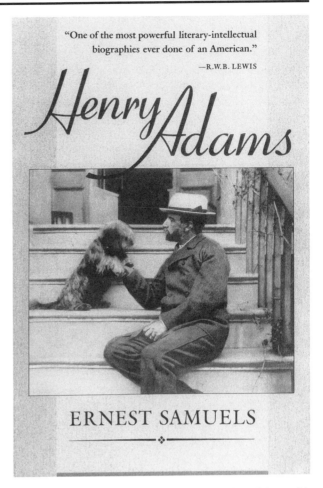

"One of the most powerful literary-intellectual biographies ever done of an American."
—R.W.B. LEWIS

Henry Adams

ERNEST SAMUELS

Dust jacket for the revised and abridged version of Samuels's Pulitzer Prize-winning three-volume biography of Adams

mercial publication by the author until after his death in 1918. As Samuels notes, Adams, "himself a biographer and an insatiable reader of biographers," hoped to preempt future writers of his own life through this thoughtfully dyspeptic autobiography; sending a copy of the *Education* to Henry James, he characterized it as a "shield of protection in the grave." The *Education* was forecast by Adams in an 1888 letter to John Hay, later Theodore Roosevelt's secretary of state and another close friend, after Adams had just finished Anthony Trollope's autobiography: "I mean to do mine. . . . After seeing how coolly and neatly a man like Trollope can destroy the last vestige of heroism in his own life, I object to allowing mine to be murdered by anyone except myself." While Samuels never mistakes his subject for the kind of hero Adams himself most admired, his wonderful biography might arrest even Adams's fine critical irony.

In adapting his earlier works, Samuels has had to shorten considerably his description and analysis of Adams's works themselves and to eliminate much definition of Adams's friends. As a result, the new volume is somewhat oblique in its references. There are no other weaknesses, however, and compensating virtues. The narrative is sharper in its focus, the book a miracle of concision in which virtually every sentence is both necessary and penetrating, and Adams himself occupies much of it, his character more strongly realized than in the original. Samuels skillfully enters into and detaches himself from his subject's own viewpoint, affording intimate yet critical access to Adams's view of himself and the world and providing impressive testimony of a remarkable intelligence without ignoring its prejudices—anti-Semitism, fear of economic democracy, moral snobbery.

While Adams was a universal scholar who claimed to understand very little by the end of his life, Ezra Pound, another American original, confidently proclaimed his opinions on everything from music to economics until it became embarrassingly evident that his competence did not extend beyond literature. In *A Serious Character: the Life of Ezra Pound* (Houghton Mifflin), Humphrey Carpenter adds to the Pound tonnage with the longest biography of the poet yet published. Carpenter's book appeared in late 1988, one year after John Tytell's solid life of Pound (reviewed in the 1987 *DLB Yearbook*). While Carpenter has eschewed Tytell's disdain for nine-hundred-page baggy monsters, his work is not only even more fully researched and comprehensive than his predecessor's but more lively. Extremely readable, everywhere enjoyable, and entertaining for the reader who has world enough and time, it is not only a definitive portrait of Pound but also an artful example of fine life writing.

Carpenter's title, taken from Pound's own expression in letters to his American publisher James Laughlin and the American poet Charles Olson, is not well explained by Carpenter, but part of his own success lies in not taking Pound as seriously as he took himself. While Tytell's work was an earnest and portentous view of Pound as a tragic figure, Carpenter's more externalized, detached tragicomedy presents Pound as a perpetual graduate student and entrepreneur of modern literature and his own viewpoints whose intellectual limitations eventually caught up with him. Constantly issuing impressive manifestos and presenting himself as educator to Amer-

ica as well as to other poets, the "Ezraversity" turns out to be surprisingly incomplete and idiosyncratic, teaching only whatever he had the time to read and publicize himself—Provençal poetry, Robert Browning's *Sordello*, Gaudier-Brzeska's sculpture, George Antheil's music. Pound's brilliant work in delivering Modernism to the world may have been facilitated by his own superficial understanding of what had preceded it.

Tytell had called Pound "a solitary volcano," but Carpenter presents him more fully and accurately as a social whirlwind, constantly surrounded by or egging on other famous writers and artists. Carpenter reveals or highlights previously unexpected or unstressed aspects of Pound's personality, many of them both touching and humorous. The great Bohemian wrote letters religiously to both of his parents throughout his years in Paris and freely discussed his career with them, received their encouragement, and was eventually joined by them in the colony of disciples at Rapallo. As Tytell had suggested and Carpenter explains more fully, Pound's free-spirited attitude about sex was largely theoretical. He dealt with women as intellectual and literary comrades, believing that his sexual potency could be physiologically channeled into his brain. While Olga Rudge was technically his mistress and the mother of his daughter, she was more truly a second wife, while Dorothy Pound remained a friend and companion, the mother of his son. Carpenter subtly straightens out the details of this troika, and his account of the rivalry between the two women in attending to the disgraced "traitor" in America and then the broken-down old man in Italy after 1958 is both funny and sad, and finally moving.

Though Carpenter's emphasis is upon Pound's activities within the social, literary, and cultural world around him, his treatment of the works themselves is much fuller than Tytell's. Here again his judgments are all the more convincing for being so detached. He reveals just how accidental and arbitrary many of Pound's literary movements were: Imagism was taken more seriously by critics than by Pound himself, for example. Carpenter revaluates all of the poetry, praising *Homage to Sextus Propertius* (1934) and the Chinese adaptations and rightly depreciating the adept but sterile versions of Provençal and Neoplatonic love poetry. He shows us that the *Cantos* are variously exciting, boring, illuminating, and opaque—but ultimately a "botch," as Pound finally concluded, for anyone without the time or patience to immerse himself in Pound's private imagination. He points the way for any worthwhile future interpretation, noting that the *Cantos* "do have unity and coherence, for they are autobiography."

With the exception of Tytell's more coherent and less tendentious coverage of Pound's incarceration in St. Elizabeth's Hospital, Carpenter's story is more complete and more exciting. Tytell sensibly disapproves of the later Pound, but Carpenter's externalized panorama of Pound's life allows a more effective evaluation of all its phases. Carpenter constructs his narrative as a series of chronologically arranged fragments, each dealing with a short period or aspect of Pound's life or character, each contributing a new perspective or piece of the picture. The result is a long but nonrepetitive and exhilarating mosaic that dynamically re-creates the features of Pound's character and existence. This portrait by accretion is particularly powerful in chronicling the final ten years of silence and withdrawal in Italy. The fragments become shorter, more incoherent, and less buoyant, dispassionately registering in what is revealed the final tragedy of Pound. Carpenter notes that during his one trip back to his country to be honored at his alma mater, Hamilton College, in 1969, Pound broke away from Olga and James and Ann Laughlin at a roadside hamburger stand; when James Laughlin, his publisher, found him in the woods nearby, Pound gave himself up but only after a terrible suggestion: "Why don't you discard me here, so that I won't be any more trouble to anyone?"

A more limited study of Pound's life is Wendy Stallard Flory's *The American Ezra Pound* (Yale University Press), which attempts to account for Pound's support for Mussolini's fascist government during the years he lived in Rapallo, culminating with his broadcasts for Rome Radio between 1940 and 1945. He was indicted for treason in 1943, tried in 1946, and declared not guilty by reason of insanity but then committed to St. Elizabeth's Psychiatric Hospital until 1958. Returning to Italy in that year, he spent much of the last fourteen years of his life in silence and depression.

In accounting for Pound's broadcasts, which sound like straightforward profascist, anti-Semitic propaganda, Flory constructs a genealogy of psychosis that takes us from Pound's early American upbringing to the final decline in Rapallo. Her title significantly defines Pound as a writer and thinker in the American jeremiad tradition, a stern but patriotic moralist who condemns a corrupt society mercilessly in order to make it see its perverse ways and reform itself. Pound's gospel was the political-economic program of social credit. Spawned by the catastrophe of World War I and stimulated later by the Great Depression, social credit proponents saw the private accumulation of the money markets in the hands of a parasitic and unproductive financial class as the cause of oppression and war in all Western societies. Pound became a fervent prophet of social credit ideology, thought he saw it being successfully introduced by Mussolini in the 1920s, and came to regard fascist Italy as a truly just society. Flory notes that the critical moment for Pound came in 1935, when Italy's invasion of Ethiopia, which might have seemed to discredit Mussolini's regime and Pound's faith in it, was rationalized by the poet as a defensive policy intended to protect Italy against the international moneylenders who wished to destroy her. Thereafter, such rationalization accelerated until it became a true psychosis, an inability to recognize reality, that led Pound to regard Mussolini's ally Hitler as an economic reformer also and the Western allies as a cabal representing corrupt monetary interests, many of them Jewish.

Flory argues that the Rome broadcasts, quoted extensively by her and acutely analyzed, are not fascist propaganda so much as increasingly incoherent and angry attempts by Pound to deny reality, to keep from admitting that he is wrong, and insofar as they have *any* ideological coherence, they are patriotic condemnations of the big-money interests that have led America into this unjust war. In some, Pound is simply babbling to himself, trying to *find* some order, control, or meaning to what he says. His utter divorce from reality is suggested by his comments near the end of the war, when he was sure that Italy would be triumphant but that the small area still under the control of the fascist state should be planted with peanuts so that the war would not be lost after all for want of butter.

With the end of the war and his own commitment to St. Elizabeth's, Flory argues, Pound slowly began to feel that he had been wrong but found his error too terrible and painful to admit to himself—thus, he was quite lucid and perceptive about everything but his ostensible "treason"— whenever that subject came up, he pleaded exhaustion and became silent. Once back in Italy, the growing acknowledgement of guilt took three forms: the depression and endless silences that he fell into between 1961 and 1972; his own oral self-condemnations of his life and work; and *Drafts and Fragments of Cantos CX-CXVII* (1969), which here and there acknowledge his errors. Although some of her evidence depends upon tortuous and obscure wrestings of the Confucian cantos, her overall argument is convincing and her portrait of Pound illuminating.

The classic American modernists continue to draw the attention of literary biographers; like Pound, Ernest Hemingway is the subject of two books written in 1989. Two years after Kenneth Lynn's *Hemingway* (see the 1987 *DLB Yearbook*), Michael Reynolds's *Hemingway: The Paris Years* (Blackwell) provides a season-by-season narrative of the writer's emergence into literary immortality between 1922 and 1925. The work extends Hemingway's life beyond Reynolds's earlier biography *The Young Hemingway* (1986). *Hemingway in Love and War* (Northeastern University Press) reproduces the lost diary of the writer's World War I nurse Agnes von Kurowsky together with her letters to him, selections from his own letters from Italy in 1918, and essays by the coeditors, Henry Serrano Villard and James Nagel.

Reynolds's work begins unsteadily with a map of "Hemingway's Europe" that actually represents Europe after World War II! The maps of Hemingway's Paris on the inside covers are indistinct. And Pound is represented as a sexual gymnast, a misunderstanding that Humphrey Carpenter would correct. I can find no other faults in this superb biography. Reynolds presents a radically internalized, magically absorbing re-creation of Hemingway's experiences as he generated *In Our Time* (1925) and *The Sun Also Rises* (1926) along with the other fiction and journalism of this period. Yet everything is firmly grounded in fact, starting with a detailed and precise chronology of the life from Hemingway's arrival in Paris with his wife Hadley on 20 December 1921 until his return voyage to France from New York on 20 February 1926 with his contract from Scribners in his luggage.

Reynolds's narrative is generated out of these real events—jobs and assignments (from Constantinople to Toronto), business and pleasure trips (including Switzerland and Spain), meetings with others (Ezra Pound, Gertrude Stein, and F. Scott Fitzgerald among them), work on manuscripts, and publications. The introduction to his notes explains Reynolds's method and purpose: "A biographer connects up the dots to draw the picture just as we did as children. First, of course, he must find the dots of data, leaving as little space between them as possible. These notes document as many dots as I thought the reader would want to know about.... Nothing in this book occurs at my convenience. Rain and snow fall as they once fell in another country. My only fiction is the space between the dots." This description of biography might seem commonplace, but in truth connecting the dots is an art that very few biographers even attempt to master. Reynolds has had to be a scholar, detective, interviewer, historian, psychologist, critic, but ultimately an artist, constructing what Steven Oates has called "pure biography," a life narrated as if it were a novel in which the subject is the central character.

The opening of Chapter One, "Losses," graphically exemplifies the method and its results:

> He had twelve hours before the Express reached Paris, twelve hours to feel sorry for himself, to find someone to blame for his losses. At Lausanne, it did not seem possible that his wife had packed all of his fiction, that she trusted a porter with the valise, that it was stolen just like that. It was the sort of thing he expected of Paris in winter. Pick up the paper almost anyday and read about thieves at train stations, stolen bags, stolen jewelry, but never stolen manuscripts that no one wanted to print ... At Vallorbe he filed through the station with other travelers to have his joint passport checked. Yes, he was Ernest Hemingway. No, Mrs. Hemingway was elsewhere, losing things no doubt. No, he was taking nothing out of the country worth mentioning. The uniformed official stamped his papers: December 3, 1922.

Unsettling initially and not often so completely internalized, Reynolds's narrative renders intimately the experience of a writer's life and is utterly authentic: he has checked the weather reports and train timetables and read the Paris newspapers of 1922, looked at the correspondence concerning Hemingway's early rejections, seen the passport. Beginning in medias res, just after Hemingway's Paris manuscripts have been stolen from his wife Hadley on her way to join him in Lausanne, Reynolds's life doubles back to their arrival in France, ultimately revealing that the loss of this early work was actually a blessing, despite Hemingway's own references to it as a tragedy (and his use of it later to help justify leaving Hadley), since he was able to rewrite much of the work but improve it with what he was learning from Pound, Stein, and his own extraordinary creative growth in the year that saw both *Ulysses* and *The Waste Land* published.

Here as elsewhere Reynolds's intimate portrayal authoritatively corrects Hemingway idolaters and subverters. The writer did misrepresent his war injuries as combat-related, filed fake stories on the Greek-Turkish conflict in 1922, continually misrepresented the poor sale of his works upward to impress potentially helpful correspondents, and was automatically anti-Semitic. On the other hand, Reynolds silently corrects Kenneth Lynn's wholly negative view of his treatment of his parents (dismissing his sister Marcelline's vengeful memoir as a fantasy in parts), shows how much he was admired by Pound and Stein personally as well as professionally, and partly justifies Hemingway's slipping out of his contract with Horace Liveright by submitting to him *The Torrents of Spring* (1926), his devastating parody of Sherwood Anderson, Liveright's leading author and Hemingway's former mentor.

Reynolds's treatment of Hemingway the writer is not only properly admiring but revelatory. Beyond showing how voraciously he immersed himself in European and modernist fiction and altered his narrative persona from objective reporter to dramatizing but detached consciousness, Reynolds brilliantly re-creates the actual process of composition, using the "dots" provided by Hemingway's manuscript revisions. Lynn had argued that Hemingway's works are firmly based on his own experiences but never directly autobiographical, but Reynolds demonstrates it, as in his reconstruction of *The Sun Also Rises*.

The novel generated itself out of Hemingway's third trip to Pamplona in the summer of 1925, accompanied now by Hadley, Harold Loeb, Pat Guthrie, and the decadent English aristocrat Duff Twysden, a binge that was creatively combined in Hemingway's imagination with his own war wounds to create Jake Barnes and the lost generation. Reynolds traces successive stages of Hemingway's invention, including the changing manuscript titles—"Nino de la Palma" (the bullfighter would be the fallen hero), "Fiesta, A Novel" (the bullfighter would be idealized as "Pedro Romero"), "The Lost Generation. A Novel" (Jake Barnes would be the damaged, fallen hero), "The Sun Also Rises" (Ecclesiastes 1:5–there it was). Reproducing Hemingway's notebook outline of chapter 18, Reynolds dramatizes how life has been transmuted into fiction until

"The best book about how Hemingway became Hemingway."

Dust jacket for the second volume of Reynolds's biography of Hemingway, which provides a season-by-season account of his life as an expatriate from 1922 until 1925

Hemingway himself confused them: "Looking back over the page, he could not avoid those last lines: 'I go down into Spain to bring Duff back. Get her letter.' Who the hell was telling this story? Did Jake write that or did he? . . . What the hell difference did it make? Someone had to bring Duff back, but he needed to keep some distance between himself and Jake." Only in a later draft would Duff be transformed forever into Brett Ashley.

Reynolds's representations of Hemingway's authorizing himself are the most impressive examples of his own art. More generally, the internalizing of the narrative allows all of his dots to become important because they were significant within Hemingway's life. A weirdly poignant detail closes the book. In the cold winter of 1926, as Hemingway deepened his affair with Pauline Pfeiffer, soon to become the second Mrs. Hemingway, Hadley's own friend and rival promised to send her "robes de nuit" from Paris, since Ernest never bought his wife any clothes. "It was an ironic exchange," Reynolds notes, "nightgowns to Hadley and Hadley's husband to Pauline." Altogether, *The Paris Years* is an extraordinary work; with its predecessor, Reynolds is well on his way to writing the best life of Hemingway and establishing himself as an artist among biographers.

In a still earlier work, *Hemingway's First War* (1976), Reynolds had provided a superb interpretation of Hemingway's masterpiece of 1927, *A Farewell to Arms,* by examining the writer's experiences in World War I when he was nearly fatally wounded while serving as a Red Cross ambulance driver in Italy. During his recovery in Milan in 1918, the twenty-year-old Oak Park adventurer fell in love with Agnes von Kurowsky, a lovely American nurse seven years his senior, who after Reynolds's work is now recognized as a prototype of Catherine Barkley, the tragic heroine of the great novel written ten years later. Henry Serrano Villard, a fellow ambulance driver who was also wounded and became a friend of Hemingway while they were in the hospital together, tracked down the former nurse in the 1960s, reestablished an old friendship, and was given her wartime diary and letters by her husband, William Stanfield, after his wife's death in 1984.

Hemingway in Love and War offers a valuable collection of biographical materials that should extend Reynolds's work. Besides the von Kurowsky diary and letters to Hemingway, including eight never published before, the volume includes Hemingway's letters home during his convalescence, only four of which have been previously published, Villard's own forty-page memoir, "Red Cross Driver in Italy," and a long essay by coeditor James Nagel, "Hemingway and the Italian Legacy." Fascinating period photographs of the three principals, World War I Italy, and Hemingway's x-rays are interleaved throughout–one wishes they had been numbered and indexed. Villard's memoir describes Hemingway's invalidism, Agnes von Kurowsky's professionalism and charm, and generally details the experiences of patients and nurses in the Milan hospital. Agnes von Kurowsky's own diary is rather banal (though it makes clear that she attracted men easily and enjoyed their attention), but her letters to Hemingway show that they had fallen in love and were seriously considering marriage. After Hemingway had been discharged and returned to the United States, however, she became engaged to Domenico Caracciolo, an Italian nobleman, and her last letter from Italy gave Hemingway the bad news (her engagement to Caracciolo was subsequently vetoed by his family but not before he had burned all of Hemingway's letters to her).

Nagel's essay discusses all of the collected material and Hemingway's experiences in Italy generally, drawing largely on Reynolds and correcting him on a few particulars regarding Kurowsky. Though he acknowledges Lynn's charges that Hemingway exaggerated his heroism and importance in the war, he refutes the former's suggestion that Hemingway's war wounds were not very serious–he was very badly hurt indeed, and though his letters and comments to others dismiss the trauma, his fiction would reimagine it, as Nagel's very brief discussion of the World War I-centered fiction demonstrates. It is also clear from the hospital circumstances and Kurowsky's character and testimony that Hemingway never made love to her. The affair of Frederick Henry and Catherine Barkley in *A Farewell to Arms* may derive from his love for Agnes, therefore, but it is not genuinely autobiographical; Nagel's conclusions reinforce Lynn's and Reynolds's cautions about reading Hemingway's life from his fiction.

Another giant who emerged in the 1920s is treated in Frederick R. Karl's *William Faulkner: American Writer. A Biography* (Weidenfeld & Nicolson). This is the largest single volume of the year at 1040 pages of text, but one of its sources, the standard biography by Joseph Blotner, is considerably longer. By contrast, Stephen Oates's radically internalized pure biography (see the 1987 *DLB Yearbook*) is about one-third as long as Karl's. Neither predecessor is fully satisfying: Oates's interesting attempt to re-create the inner life is marred by melodrama and trivialization of the works; Blotner's huge documentary and anecdotal life of his friend and colleague at the University of Virginia seldom penetrates the surface of the man or the writing. Though Karl is not out to replace Blotner's work, his own study is much closer to Oates's in purpose: "By integrating life and work, I have tried to avoid a chronicle or linear life study . . . This study is in the deepest sense a biography; not only a presentation of the relevant facts of the subject's life, but an effort to understand and interpret that life psychologically, emotionally, and literarily. It tries to put Faulkner together . . . as America's greatest novelist of the twentieth century."

Karl's biography begins with a powerful and convincing "overview" of Faulkner. His governing assumption, that Faulkner's life and work were continuously and totally symbiotic and are mutually reflective, underlies several important revisions of both. For example, the heavy drinking was dangerous and almost suicidal, but so were many other activities that flaunted the writer's masculinity–stunt flying, hunting, horseback riding–in compensation for his effeminate professional identity as a writer. On the other hand, Faulkner's binges required and encouraged a maternal nursing by his wife Estelle, Meta Carpenter, and other muses that satisfied him. Most importantly, like his famous silences, Faulkner's drinking was a deliberate choice that cut him off from others so that the strain of imaginative creation could be relieved and its inspiration reactivated. Karl describes in detail the lives of Faulkner's great-grandfather and grandfather before introducing the writer, for they remained alive in Faulkner's own imagination and were transmuted, often critically, into the stories. When he changed the spelling of his name from "Falkner" to "Faulkner," Karl notes, "he could suggest his independence from history and family, but also did not make a change which stressed outward defiance." His fiction is similarly balanced between acceptance and rejection of the southern world within which he lived but which his works transcended.

Karl's treatment of Faulkner as a literary creator is often very fine, particularly his analyses of the writer's modernism and his tendency to withhold, retell, and complicate rather than present information simply. Indeed, withholding was not simply a rhetorical strategy, it was part of Faulkner's way of living. Karl notes that the imaginative world came into being early, as if it had been conceived in his first twenty-five years and was then delivered over the next fifty. One lengthy, unpublished work, "Elmer," was a quarry for *Mosquitoes* (1927), *The Sound and the Fury* (1929), and *The Wild Palms* (1939); another, "Father Abraham," was eventually to reappear as the Snopes trilogy and a source for *As I Lay Dying* (1930); *Flags in the Dust* (1973), the original version of *Sartoris* (1929), "contained nearly everything Faulkner would embrace." Karl's excellent treatment of Faulkner's manuscript changes is particularly illuminating, presenting a pattern of increasing simplicity and coherence but decreasing originality that marks the career as a whole. The later career was both made possible and limited by what Faulkner had learned as a Hollywood writer, and his increasing role as a moral spokes-

man enlarged but also weakened his creative power. Like most American writers, Karl notes, Faulkner lacked the larger intellectual or philosophical consciousness of European authors as a source of power once his own imagination had been exhausted.

Unfortunately, *William Faulkner* is ultimately a dissatisfying work. It is almost unbelievably and unbearably repetitive. Karl notes Faulkner's small, vaguely effeminate physique and his need to compensate for it five times within the first fifty pages. Two direct quotations from *A Fable* (1954) with separate commentary by Karl appear on pages 700-702; the quotations and the commentaries reappear verbatim on pages 881-883. And there are five separate substantial treatments of *Light in August* (1932) between pages 445 and 490. In contrast to the repetition, additional, apparently last-minute footnotes have been huddled into the text. Karl's typically disjointed discussions of Faulkners relationships with others include an all-too-brief reference to his affair with Joan Williams that neglects to mention his marriage proposal to her, so a footnote is added on page 786–and it is added again on page 840. A footnote on page 379, referring to the possibility that Faulkner's stepson Malcolm was illegitimate points us ahead in the text to a *later* discussion that is nonexistent; Malcolm's possible illegitimacy had already been footnoted on page 220 and then discussed more fully on 269.

Although the book would be vastly improved by some editing, Karl's ambitious attempt to press for mutually illuminating significance in every detail of the life and works together with his wise insistence that simple correspondences can't be established create other problems. Since nothing can be proven, anything can be speculated, even uncertainty itself. Thus, the earlier footnote on Malcolm Franklin is typical in its multiplying qualifiers: "At stake is the possibility that Malcolm may not have been Cornell's son. Against the latter supposition is the fact that Malcolm does seem to resemble Cornell Franklin in some photographs." Elsewhere, Karl disables his own argument about biographical implications of the title *As I Lay Dying* by concluding that it "can fit none . . . some or all of these." Although the author wished to go beyond strict chronology, each chapter successively deals with one or more years of Faulkner's life and then proceeds to relate in a rather disorganized fashion what happened externally *and* internally, resulting in much repetition of previous discussions of the latter. And instead of entering into or imitating his subject's point of view as Holroyd, Reynolds, and Oates have done, Karl remains outside, serving not only as Faulkner's critic but as his moral judge, particularly on issues of race and treatment of women. Despite his fine appreciation of his subject as the supreme American modernist and his acute understanding of the writer's inner life, Karl regularly makes Faulkner look smaller than he was.

In *Caroline Gordon: A Biography* (Oxford University Press), Veronica Makowsky has dealt with another southern writer, now almost forgotten, in one more of this year's authorized biographies. Makowsky's work was prompted initially by her utter ignorance of the subject. As a graduate student at Princeton in the 1970s, she found that the university had acquired the author's papers and was then further enlightened by a librarian, who identified Gordon as Allen Tate's wife and then added, "Oh, and she wrote fiction herself." Discovering that she had published nine novels, three collections of short stories, and two critical works, Makowsky wondered why such a productive writer was so little known. Further investigation of the collected papers at Princeton ultimately led to a desire to write Gordon's biography, both to rescue her from relative oblivion and to answer the fundamental question–why *was* she so obscure? Eventually, Makowsky wrote to Gordon in Mexico and gained her approval for a biography. After interviewing her there in 1981, one month before her death at the age of eighty-six, her biographer spent the next seven years acquiring Gordon's letters, interviewing her friends, and reexamining her published and unpublished work.

Granted that a primary goal of Makowsky's life is to interest the reader further in Gordon and her work, this book is a disappointment, although it is successful as an external narrative of the life itself and an interpretive survey of Gordon's writings. The book is well researched and clearly written but cold and unengaging. Even though Gordon met and talked with or entertained most of the major modern post-World War I American writers, there's no larger context to the life than Gordon's works and her relationship to Tate, whom she divorced in 1945 and remarried in 1946. Even this remains muted–we discover virtually nothing specific about their personal relationship, not even the circumstances of Tate's adulteries, which led to their divorce. Gordon herself is occasionally described as a brilliant conversationalist with a wicked wit but the book

is virtually anecdote-free, so there is no evidence to bring her vibrancy to life, and though Makowsky refers intermittently to her vivacious letters, few are quoted. And at the end, the final twenty years of Gordon's life are dispatched in seven pages! Makowsky's detachment from her subject sometimes almost verges on disinterest, and this is a fatal flaw in a life that presumably wants the *reader* to become interested in a neglected author and her work.

Although not directly authorized by Ted Hughes, Sylvia Plath's husband and literary executor, Anne Stevenson's *Bitter Fame: A Life of Sylvia Plath* (Houghton Mifflin) is the first biography produced with the full cooperation of the Plath estate, whose agent, Olwyn Hughes, is not only Ted Hughes's sister but is also described by Stevenson as a virtual coauthor. Stevenson's privileged access to such an authoritative source of information about Plath contrasts with the experience of Linda Wagner-Martin, whose biography (see the 1987 *DLB Yearbook*) was so decisively unauthorized by both Hugheses in manuscript form that she ended up ignoring the Plath estate entirely and limited the extent of her quotations from Plath's works. Her mildly feminist biography sympathetically but critically assessed Plath's life and work but was necessarily limited in its range of written sources and testimony.

Considering its provenance, therefore, we might expect *Bitter Fame* to be a better literary life. Indeed, the extraordinarily contentious book jacket defines Stevenson as the first "fully informed biographer" and the book as "the first authoritative biography . . . as complete, balanced, and objectively written as the facts allow," its goal that of dissolving the "perverse legend" that has grown up about Plath, "the posthumous miasma of fantasy, rumour, politics, and ghoulish gossip" that "her family and friends have been helpless to dispel."

Plath was separated from Hughes, the present poet laureate of England, when she gassed herself in her London flat in January 1963. Hughes's own behavior following her suicide has always angered those who see Plath as a feminist heroine: taking possession of all her unpublished work as literary executor, he had some of them published slowly over the next seventeen years, culminating with the *Collected Poems* of 1981 and the *Journals* of 1982, both of which he edited. The latter constitutes a remarkable but disturbing record of Plath's inner life from 1957 to 1959, comprising not only the laboratory of her imagination but also expressions of anger, despair, and hatred that she repressed in her daily life. Two journal ledgers for 1959 through the fourth day before her suicide also existed, but Hughes burned the first so that their two children would never have to read them and lost the second. The marriage had been troubled for about a year before Plath's suicide, and the loss of the final journals has been seen by some as his attempt at a cover-up. Hughes has refused all requests for interviews about his wife and has never written about her except as a writer. Meanwhile, Plath's mother published her daughter's letters to her, *Letters Home 1950-1963,* in 1975; they reveal another Sylvia Plath who is a loving daughter, positive and optimistic about her life and marriage.

Stevenson's biography is primarily a riposte to all earlier biographical accounts that have treated Plath's husband unfairly. In addition to numerous details of Plath's erratic or malignant behavior toward her husband and others witnessed by Olwyn Hughes and included within the narrative, the book closes with three appendices, memoirs of close acquaintances of Plath and Hughes–the American writer Lucas Meyer, W. S. Merwin's first wife Dido, and the Irish poet Richard Murphy. All describe incidents of ugly behavior by Plath, nearly pathological rudeness, hostility, or dishonesty. The implicit or explicit conclusion of each is that Ted Hughes's marriage to her must have been a living hell for him much of the time, and Murphy blames her for inflicting suffering upon her husband, children, and mother by committing suicide.

Stevenson's life, therefore, largely reveals the truth about its subject by undercutting her. Although she acknowledges Plath's significance as a writer, her choice of detail emphasizes the nearly psychotic side of her character, which is seen to be both the source of her literary power and of her personal failings. Thus, Stevenson draws heavily upon the journals, which Plath never intended to have published, quoting from them nearly as much as from the poetry. The result is twofold: Plath comes across as a seriously disturbed person, and the poetry is quoted primarily to reinforce that characterization–there is little analysis or direct appreciation of the poems as literature. In this respect alone, Wagner-Martin's life is more complete.

Plath's letters to her mother are used to show how she covered up her deepest anxieties and impulses by projecting a false outward self-

confidence and satisfaction with her life and career. The appendix material is paraphrased within Stevenson's text, along with other homely examples of the psychopathology of Plath's daily life. Hughes appears as a long-suffering, patient, and uncomplaining husband. While there are plenty of damning facts about Plath, Stevenson evades at least one other fact: although Plath *was* pathologically jealous of her husband and fiendishly burned up his writings in his study on one occasion because of this, Hughes *did* carry on an extramarital affair with Assia Wevill, yet not only is it referred to elliptically and unclearly, but Hughes's lover is cited as blaming the affair on Plath's jealousy.

No one who reads Stevenson's book can deny afterward that Plath could be a very difficult and unpleasant person, passionately egotistical *and* self-destructive. Nor do Stevenson or the friends of Hughes who have encouraged this biography deny Plath's poetical power. Nonetheless, the book is an odious corrective to the hagiography that has too often marked previous treatments of this doomed writer. Moreover, it seems unlikely that this demolition of his wife will benefit Hughes's own reputation.

To conclude this survey of 1989 biographies we turn from English and American writers to Herbert Lottman's *Flaubert: A Biography* (Little, Brown), the most complete and the only reliable biography in English. Asked about his life in 1868, Flaubert replied, "I have no biography," and on another occasion he asserted, "Madame Bovary, c'est moi." The assumption that Flaubert was little more than a writing machine lay behind Jean-Paul Sartre's massive, influential, and hostile psychobiography, and other biographies have been similarly tendentious or incomplete as well as poorly researched. Lottman, an American who lives in Paris, has assiduously uncovered all the facts and carefully investigated the surmises (Flaubert probably did have epilepsy, but Maupassant was almost certainly not his illegitimate son). His review of documentary material has been exemplary, including the published and not yet published correspondence, contemporary journals and diaries, and Flaubert's manuscripts, and allows full scope for Flaubert's own voice and those of contemporary witnesses such as his discarded mistress Louise Colet and the Goncourt brothers.

Lottman's is not a definitive biography like his earlier massive study of Albert Camus, however. His coverage of the completed works is almost embarrassing, consisting of unexamined generalizations (for example, " 'Saint Julian' was a jewel of a tale") and plot abstracts. In the earlier chapters, there is much amateurish pointing to sources ("And we can actually hold in our hands the petition written . . . by Flaubert"). And Lottman's writing is workmanlike at best and too often banal or even clumsy ("[Champagne] is a countryside of chalky soil whose perfect grape, when dealt with in a certain way, becomes that fizzy wine").

Lottman does, however, valuably revise our notions of Flaubert as simply a human pen by placing his life within the larger context of family, friends, lovers, and admirers who were as important in his life as his art and often contributed to it. In treating the writer, Lottman's detailed examinations of Flaubert's composing his works is revelatory. Privileged by his father's wealth and his mother's indulgence with the leisure to write, he never found leisure in writing: "The erections of the thought are like those of the body; they do not come at Will!" he wrote Louise Colet, and while he also told her that "the author in his work must be like God in the universe, present everywhere and visible nowhere," he had to slave overtime in order to create his worlds. Thirty hours' work on "A Simple Heart" produced a single page. Five years' scholarly research and an excursion to Carthage were necessary to complete *Salammbo* (1862). He observed an operation on a child suffocating from croup for a scene in *A Sentimental Education* (1869). "It was abominable, and I came out of it heartbroken," he reported to his beloved niece Caroline Commanville, "but Art obliges." Flaubert reconnoitered the countryside near Rouen for the house of his middle-class heroes in *Bouvard and Pécauchet* (1881), his final uncompleted novel. He had read 194 books after his first year of research on this satire of modern learning and 1,500 six years later when he complained to Turgenev that his work on the book was killing him; two years later in 1880 he was dead, with one more section to write.

Two excellent biographies not covered in last year's survey should be mentioned briefly. A. N. Wilson's *Tolstoy* (Norton) deals with another, very different master of nineteenth-century European realism, while Lyndall Gordon's *Eliot's New Life* (Farrar, Straus & Giroux) is the sequel to her 1977 study of T. S. Eliot, which ended with his conversion to Anglicanism. Both are provocative reexaminations of their subjects. Wilson, an English novelist who

has been obsessed with Tolstoy for twenty years and learned Russian in order to reencounter him, presents an entirely fresh, lively, frequently witty narrative that sees the author as a monumental egoist motivated by self-dissatisfaction. The apparent autobiographical representations of Tolstoy in his fiction mask his true identity, and even his diaries and memoirs are made-up. The ultimate flight from literature to religion was the grandest self-rejection of all and was typically converted into a moral tyranny both inspiring and deplorable.

In her study of Eliot's inner development, Gordon continues to argue that the true sources of Eliot's art are not impersonal, English, and Anglican, but intensely personal, American, and Puritan. Eliot's relationships with four women–his first wife, Vivienne Haigh-Wood, his friends Emily Hale and Mary Trevelyan, and his second wife Valerie Fletcher, are used to trace the way in which his art actually determined his life rather than the reverse. Gordon's work is vaguely organized and more knotted in its expression than Wilson's, but both are powerful and successful attempts to enter their subjects' work through their psyches and to reveal the egotism that was the source of their power. Although both were literary giants, each was unsatisfied with the ultimate value of literature, and Gordon's characterization of Eliot could also be applied to Tolstoy: "a man who became all the greater as poet for his failure to attain sainthood. He fell back on another goal, to be God's agent, and as public spokesman he achieved an extraordinary authority."

Among notable collections of letters this year is the definitive edition of *The Correspondence of Stephen Crane* (Columbia University Press) in two volumes, edited by Stanley Wertheimer and Paul Sorrentino. A work of superb scholarship, minutely annotated, the edition includes all currently available letters and book autographs written by Crane as well as letters to him and the correspondence of Cora Stewart Crane, his common-law wife, concerning her husband's life and career. Photographs and sketches of Crane and others are included throughout, together with brief introductions to letters written to or from Crane's various temporary homes: military school and colleges, Manhattan, Nebraska, Mexico, Florida, Cuba, Athens, Surrey, Sussex, the sanitarium in Badenweiler, Germany, where he died of tuberculosis in 1900. Read consecutively, these prefaces present a brief but authoritative account of Crane's short and hectic life (unaccountably, they are not included in the index).

Wertheimer and Sorrentino clear away a good deal of make-believe about Crane in this edition, demolishing the 1923 biography by Thomas Beer as unreliable hero worship and consigning all but two of Crane's letters quoted by him in it to an appendix, since all of the rest were probably "composed" by his admirer. Since Beer's biography and letters are an important source for all subsequent Crane biographies, there is currently no reliable life of the author, and this edition of the only genuine extant Crane letters is modestly intended to help any would-be biographer start over again.

With the elimination of Beer's letters, including rhapsodies on baseball (Crane played it well) and Helen Trent (she may have never existed), the Crane correspondence largely comprises matter-of-fact and often banal salutations to family and friends, seven awkwardly romantic letters to an Akron belle, professional correspondence with publishers and editors, and complimentary exchanges with late Victorian colleagues and admirers, especially Joseph Conrad. Clearly, Crane's literary power was fully expended on his fiction and journalism with little time or energy left over for correspondence. In the final year at Brede, the country house in Sussex where he and Cora lived beyond their means, she had to take over virtually all the letter writing while her husband overworked himself turning out second-rate work in order to pay their bills and debts. "Mr. Crane will just deluge you with stuff for the next two months," Cora assured Crane's literary agent on 21 October 1899, and he did, but only seven months later he was dead.

Vladimir Nabokov's *Selected Letters 1940-1977* (Harcourt Brace Jovanovich / Bruccoli Clark Layman) were edited by Dmitri Nabokov, the author's son, and Matthew J. Bruccoli, with appropriately inconspicuous footnotes and translations of the letters in Russian and French by Dmitri and Nabokov's widow Vera. These selections from Nabokov's correspondence have been made according to a rather miscellaneous set of criteria but are intended to give a full portrait of the writer from his arrival in America at the age of forty-one until his death in 1977. Fifteen letters written from 1928 to 1938 introduce the collection proper, ending with Ivan Bunin's recommendation of Nabokov for university teaching positions in England or America. A useful chronology and a group of photographs of Nabokov from his twenties to his seventies are also included.

Nabokov's letters to his wife, son, and sister are affectionate, and those to editors, university colleagues, and other writers and artists who enjoyed his work are courtly and appreciative. Nevertheless, Nabokov seems fully involved only in letters that deal with what Dmitri Nabokov calls "his artistic and personal morality" (one and the same for Nabokov): detailed instructions for improving book jackets of his works, peremptory attacks on unworthy contemporaries (for example, "I detest Pound and the costume jewelry of his verse," a description of Thomas Mann as a "tower of triteness"), endless wrangling with Andrew Field over changes in the latter's critical biography of Nabokov, a letter to Derek Bok politely declining an honorary doctorate from Harvard as a matter of personal honor because "during the last twenty five years or more my firm principle has been to refuse all formal honors, fellowships, memberships, and the like."

Nabokov's wit is most exercised while validating himself on offense or defense, as in a charming rejoinder to Richard Schickel who had celebrated the American publication of *Lolita* (1958) in a review for the *Reporter* but had misidentified the professor's official academic department: "Although I do not teach biology at Cornell, I am in touch with the admirable entomological museum here. Moreover, I discuss in detail beetles and their parasites every year around April, when in my literature course I get to Kafka's 'Metamorphosis,' after which in May, I annually attempt to identify the nocturnal moth that circles around a lamp in the brothel scene of Joyce's 'Ulysses.' And there are three butterflies in 'Madame Bovary,' black, yellow, and white, respectively. So you see that your making me a professor of biology was not only very much to the point, but warmed a cockle which no success in comparative literature can so exquisitely prick."

Nabokov's quarrel with Edmund Wilson is referred to only indirectly in these letters, since the correspondence between the two was published in 1979, but an additional volume of letters between Nabokov and Russian émigré writers, his parents, and his wife is planned as well as a two-volume life by Brian Boyd. Together with the sublime midlife memoir *Speak, Memory* (1951) and the 1973 collection, *Strong Opinions,* these works will provide a comprehensive portrait of this modernist master and lepidopterist.

Finally, 1989 marks the completion of the thirteen-volume edition of the personal journals of James Boswell, a great scholarly enterprise that began in 1950 with *Boswell's London Journal 1762-1763* and now ends thirty-nine years later with *Boswell: The Great Biographer* (McGraw-Hill), edited by Marlies K. Danziger and the late Frank Brady. As noted in the introduction, the title is both fitting and ironic. On 16 May 1791 Boswell's epochal *Life of Johnson* was at last published, won immediate public and commercial success, established its author as "the great biographer," and would gain him literary immortality. On the other hand, despite his triumph as an author, this was probably the worst period of Boswell's life. Lonely after his wife's death in May 1789, unable or unwilling to remarry, and failing to find a suitable position in law or public life, he felt himself a failure, a mere popular writer who had never achieved the importance of his father, a Scottish judge, or the distinction of Samuel Johnson, Edmund Burke, Joshua Reynolds, and the other great men who were his friends. Increasingly depressed despite convivial occasions with friends in London and an energiz-ing tour of Cornwall, Boswell in these journal entries registers somewhat desperate quests for companionship, marriage, and a professional position before his physical collapse in April 1795.

Like its predecessors, this volume is a model of intensive and comprehensive academic scholarship, copiously annotated, with narratives and analyses of Boswell's life prior to and during the period covered by the journals together with lengthy editorial notes linking entries themselves, so that the book nearly constitutes a daily record of Boswell's activities during the last six years of his life. The even larger Yale edition of the complete writings of Boswell (of which this trade series of thirteen journal volumes is only a part) may never be completed within our lifetime: over the past twenty years, only four volumes, research editions of some of Boswell's correspondence, have been published–the entire work will number at least thirty. One would like to know what the father of modern biography in English would have to say about having his own life so exhaustively and even obsessively investigated by his sons and daughters.

Book Reviewing in America: III

"But something strange is happening. In America, which has a history of lapsing into long literary comas, and where even reading a cereal box represents a Promethean effort, people are reading again, and we're not just talking Judith Krantz and Stephen King."

—Will Nixon, *"Big Words in a Small Package,"* Taxi *(April 1989).*

"When publishers send out books accompanied by martinis, moving hands and massage cream, it's not only to single out a particular tome from the pack; it's also a way of signaling that the house believes in the author and plans a muscular sales campaign."

—Joanne Kaufman, *"Martinis, Massage Cream and Other Marketing Ploys,"* Wall Street Journal *(19 January 1989).*

This third piece in a continuing examination of the state of American book reviewing is composed of three general parts: first, a summary accounting of some of the shifts and changes and topics of concern for the year past; second, a study, made by Pulitzer Prize-winning poet Henry Taylor, of the contemporary ways and means of reviewing poetry; third, a brief interview with novelist, historian, and longtime book-review editor Paxton Davis.

I: 1989–Crises and Controversy as Usual, by George Garrett

Book reviewing in America, everywhere except where it may sometimes be found in little magazines and the somewhat larger quarterlies, lives on (where it continues to exist at all) within the context of journalism–news. It is part of that package and inextricable, really, from all the rest of it. Choices are made and judgments are passed, at all levels, on the primary basis of what is possibly newsworthy and what is probably not. On the purest and simplest level, all other things and events being more or less equal, this criterion leads directly to critical choices. In one of several self-reflexive examinations of book reviewing that took place this year ("Book Reviewing in America: A Forum," *Review of Contemporary Fiction*, Spring 1989), Michael Dirda of the *Washington Post Book World* reports: "At newspapers we are obliged to cover books as news, and so we review Stephen King, Jackie Collins, and a lot of high-tech thrillers. These are books, regardless of their varying degrees of literary merit, that people want to know about." With the examination of books as news as the basic mind-set of book-review editors and their various and sundry superiors, it is not at all surprising that whenever there is some real news, hard news of one kind or another involving books, authors, publishers, and the publishing business, this material should capture more space and attention than the limited, strictly literary, or aesthetic event of the publication (or reprinting) of a book.

This was a year that began with big news, on a global scale and with greater than any literary implications, involving a writer, the author of a complex, highly literary, indeed involuted work of postmodernist metafiction, namely Salman Rushdie and his *The Satanic Verses* (Viking). The best and most thorough accounting of the sequence of events, worldwide, is Daniel Pipes's article "The Ayatollah, the Novelist, and the West" (*Commentary*, June 1989). First published in English in Britain in September 1988, the book was legally banned in the author's native India in October and was shortly afterward the subject of public protest and controversy in Pakistan, Saudi Arabia, Egypt, South Africa, and as Gerald Marzorati put it (in "Salman Rushdie: Fiction's Embattled Infidel," a cover story for the *New York Times Magazine*, 29 January 1989), in "every country or city with a sizable Muslim population, including London, where the book had been published in late September and had quickly become a best seller."

By the time Marzorati's article was published a good deal that was newsworthy had happened. Some book burnings, instigated by Muslim immigrants, had begun in England, particularly in the North, in December. And there had been some public denunciations of the book and

Moslem demonstrators in Hyde Park, London, May 1989, protesting the publication of Salman Rushdie's
The Satanic Verses

its author, a few telephone threats, and, as well, the business news that, earlier on, Viking had paid Rushdie an advance of about $800,000 for world hardbound and paperback rights: a very large advance for an essentially literary book unless it was deemed probable that the book and its author would be likely to earn some form of worldwide attention. Which, in fact, is exactly what came to pass, in a hurry and of a size and scope and menace beyond the dreams, the hopes, and fears of publishers, and beyond all the abilities of even the most adroit and cynical publicity agents.

On 12 February there were riots and deaths in Pakistan. Shortly after, the Ayatollah Khomeini saw footage of these riots on television and/or listened to accounts of events in Pakistan on the transistor radio he carried with him everywhere. On 14 February, Valentine's Day, he issued a *fatwa*, an Islamic judgment and directive ordering death to Rushdie and his publishers. A worldly reward of 200 million rials ($170,000)

was soon offered by a private citizen for whoever accomplished this mission, and the Iranian parliament promptly doubled the amount. On 24 February 12 people were killed in riots over the book in India. By March the toll had reached 19 dead and 150 wounded, worldwide, and Rushdie was in hiding under the protection of Scotland Yard.

Actually, Rushdie was already in hiding by 22 February, Washington's birthday, when Viking published the book in the United States, and there was a widely publicized gathering of literary stars in New York, sponsored by the Authors Guild, PEN, and the British anticensorship watchdog group Article 19. Writers read from *The Satanic Verses* and offered expressions of support for Rushdie and for the general ideas embodied in the First Amendment, twenty-one writers such as Robert Stone, E. L. Doctorow, Don DeLillo, Gay Talese, Joan Didion, Larry McMurtry, Susan Sontag, and (of course!) Norman Mailer, among others. That gathering (proud triumph or foolish farce, or both, depending on point of view) and the events that soon followed are accurately described in "The Rushdiad" by Midge Decter (*Commentary*, June 1989), here summing up (not without an edge of sarcasm): "In the end, the drama of Salman Rushdie and the Ayatollah was to play in the press for nearly a month, which is about the span of media attention usually accorded wars, peace treaties, and presidential scandals." In that time a constant rash of random headlines in major national journals covered it all: BRITISH LINK BOMB TO RUSHDIE; IRAN HINTS AT DEATH REPRIEVE IF 'VERSES' AUTHOR APOLOGIZES; CAT STEVENS GIVES SUPPORT TO CALL FOR DEATH OF RUSHDIE; DAUGHTER DESCRIBES KHOMEINI AS STERN PATRIARCH; PUBLISHERS BEMOAN BRASH STYLE, BIG BUCKS OF RUSHDIE'S AGENT; and RUSHDIE ANSWERS HIS CRITICS IN A POEM. This last, "6 March 1989," Rushdie's first known creative work since he went into hiding, published in *Granta 28*, proved to be a clumsy, rhymed clinker of a poem (which, luckily for him, cannot be quoted, in any part or form) of a man obviously confused and distressed.

There were moments of high and low silliness all around: Gay Talese leading a large crowd in the Lord's Prayer; the *New York Times Book Review* of 12 March sending limp "greetings" from twenty-eight writers of twenty-one countries to Rushdie; Ted Koppel and Phil Donahue cranking out talk shows on the subject; Howard Fast comparing the Ayatollah Khomeini to J. Edgar Hoover; columnist Richard Cohen of the *Washington Post* (in "Needed: More Iron," 17 February 1989) apparently calling for war with Iran–"As for England, the steel it displayed in the Falklands has been sorely missing on this issue." There were showers and blizzards of letters, resolutions, statements, readings, and appeals. A lengthy and somewhat pompous *New Republic* editorial (13 March), "Two Cheers For Blasphemy," denounced spineless Americans of all kinds while appealing to patriotic motives: "If you are for the banning and burning of books, if you deny the right of a writer to write and the right of a publisher to publish, if you believe that an opinion may be refuted by a bullet, you are anti-American." Also on 13 March, in the *Nation*, John Leonard reviewed *The Satanic Verses*, calling it "infinitely more interesting than those hundreds of neat little novels we have to read between Rushdies." Neal Kozodoy published a

sharp response (the lines drawn in America were soon enough and clearly enough political) to Leonard entitled "John Leonard in the Satanic Mess" (*Contentions*, April 1989). A story published in the *Authors Guild Bulletin* (Summer 1989), "Miller, Styron Discuss Rushdie and Censorship," recounts an 18 June fund-raiser for the Roxbury, Connecticut, Library at which Arthur Miller and William Styron spoke. Styron was described as somewhat ambiguous about the whole thing, saying: "No one in his right mind could condone this incident, yet . . ." The article continues: "The *yet* led Mr. Styron to try to imagine a similar event in the U.S. Borrowing a suggestion from a Harvard professor, he asked what would happen if a book were to appear here entitled *The Secret and Sensational Life of Martin Luther Coon*. 'There would be an extraordinary uproar,' he said."

In all the Rushdie excitement many people missed the quieter news that Mitchell Levitas had moved on from his post as editor of the *New York Times Book Review*, being replaced by staff member Rebecca Sinkler.

Of course censorship and book banning are perennial subjects of literary journalism, and 1989 was witness to a flurry of activity in response to Senator Jesse Helms (R-N.C.) and his attempt to restrict the funding of "objectionable" art by the National Endowment for the Arts. This, together with other more subtle and more successful ways and means of control, was the subject of two articles in the *Authors Guild Bulletin* (Fall/Winter 1989): "Censors Planning End Runs Around First Amendment," by Christopher M. Finan and "New Obscenity Provisions Put Arts Grants at Risk," by Katherine Rowe. Less pressing in its impact, but steady year after year, and, evidently, implacable, is the problem of the banning of books in local schools and libraries in America. In an article in the *New York Times* (3 September 1989), "In a Small Town, a Battle Over a Book," People For the American Way, a lobbying group, was quoted as listing, up to that date, the year's total of banning incidents–172 incidents in forty-two states. The particular *Times* story concerned Boron High School in Boron, California, where (what else is new?) *The Catcher in the Rye* (1951) by J. D. Salinger had been banned from the classroom once again.

The year that began with all the excitement of the Rushdie affair staggered to its end with another kind of controversy, artificially induced and aroused, and essentially far less dangerous, though probably not much less acrimonious. This began with the publication in *Harper's* (November 1989) of Tom Wolfe's "Stalking the Billion-Footed Beast: A literary manifesto for the new social novel." Wolfe is one of the most intelligent, amusing, clever, and satirical writers of our time, a rhetorician able to arouse and manipulate emotional response from all kinds of readers. This piece, airbrushed with ironies, purports to hold up his own hugely successful first novel, *The Bonfire of the Vanities* (1987), as an example of what the American novel ought to be doing . . . if it knew what was good for it. To make this point he is required to present conjunctively a little personal history—his own career and his arrival at full understanding, the history of the times as it has been relevant, and his view of the trends and fashions of the American novel in his time, these times. This latter allows him to have a good deal of good fun at the expense of many highly regarded American fiction writers who gave up the grand traditions of "the realistic novel" (Balzac and Zola, Dickens and Thackeray) and "keeping with the cosmopolitan yearnings of the native intelligentsia," tried to create different forms of fiction—"Absurdist novels, Magical Realist novels, and novels of Radical Disjunction . . . in which plausible events and plausible characters were combined in fantastic or outlandish ways, often resulting in dreadful catastrophes that were played for laughs in the ironic mode." This descriptive literary history allowed Wolfe to use the ironic mode and play for some laughs at the expense of certain of his contemporaries, Ronald Sukenick, Frederick Barthelme, John Hawkes, John Barth, and Robert Coover, for example. He makes a good, strong gadfly case while presenting sound arguments for more factual knowledge and practical experience ("reporting") to create the realistic fiction worthy of late-twentieth-century America. Behind it all, and mostly missed by his opponents, who were so bedazzled and annoyed by his aesthetic sleight of hand and soft shoe that they missed the deeper cause of their unease, is Wolfe's revisionist picture of America from the 1960s until now, a laudable triumph of "overt racial conflict" and "the American century," even enduring such aberrant things as "the so-called sexual revolution, which I always thought was a rather prim term for the lurid carnival that actually took place."

Opponents? *Harper's* asked several writers to respond to Wolfe's essay and in the February 1990 issue published letters in reply by Philip Roth, Walker Percy, Scott Spencer, Alison Lurie,

Madison Smartt Bell, Mary Gordon, Jim Harrison, T. Coraghessian Boyle, and John Hawkes. Of these only two seem to have understood Wolfe's argument—Madison Smartt Bell, who uses Wolfe's own criteria to argue Jimmy Breslin got there before him, and Walker Percy, who understands the aesthetic problems as well as Wolfe does (tending, in fact, to agree with him), but is far less interested in those than in their spiritual implications. Less sympathetic all around, and saying so at much greater length, is Robert Towers, whose "The Flap Over Tom Wolfe: How Real Is the Retreat From Realism?," published in the *New York Times Book Review* (28 January 1990), differs in its view of the history of American fiction during the last thirty years, arguing that Wolfe missed many outstanding writers who meet his requirements (and Towers's) for "large-audience" fiction and more, people such as Don DeLillo, Anne Tyler, Russell Banks, Richard Ford, and Mary Gordon. He says Wolfe doesn't do justice to the late Raymond Carver and, finally, returns to an old hobbyhorse of his own—"the novel of radical disjunction"—among whose favored practitioners he cites as Joseph Heller, E. L. Doctorow, Gunter Grass, Robert Coover, and (to round off things) Salman Rushdie. Except for one little political kidney punch—"Probably the books I have mentioned are too left-leaning for Mr. Wolfe's conservative tastes, but there is no inherent reason why a sufficiently witty, imaginative, verbally inventive, angry and playful Tory novelist couldn't write one as well"—Towers's piece serves to confirm and merely modify Wolfe's thesis.

Between Rushdie at the outset and Wolfe at the finale of the year, there were all kinds of other topics for literary attention, some of them directly concerned with the business of book reviewing, others not so, but in their focus and direction telling us some things about the critical enterprise in this country as we enter the century's final decade.

Among the variety of subjects dealt with by the literary journalists during this year were such highly serious matters as the ongoing battle of canon and core curriculum, much written about and discussed, perhaps nowhere more clearly or fully than in a forum in the September issue of *Harper's*—"Who Needs the Great Works?"—and, earlier, in Benjamin McArthur's "The War of the Great Books," *American Heritage* (February 1989). McArthur is solidly for the new and improved at the expense of the tried and true, but nevertheless, in summation, tries to be fair to the conservatives: "The party of the Future maintains the loyalty of most Americans at most times. That is why the ancients must struggle just to hold their ground. Yet we will not call for their surrender." Equally lofty were the arguments concerning authorial ethics, though the examples, the practical applications from which the abstract considerations arose, were sufficiently sordid to be entertaining. Two of these stories were related. Author Joe McGinniss was sued for breach of contract by the subject of his nonfiction book, *Fatal Vision* (1983), convicted murderer Jeffrey MacDonald. This suit, ending in 1987, resulted in an out-of-court settlement whereby McGinnis paid MacDonald $325,000. Another much-publicized suit involving *New Yorker* writer Janet Malcolm (who had, separately, written a piece for that magazine intensely critical of McGinniss in particular and the habits and mind-set of journalism in general) was won by her. *Time* (21 August 1989) described the outcome of the suit in "The Right to Fake Quotes": "U.S. appeals court held that a writer may misquote a subject–even deliberately–so long as the sense is not substantially changed." All this resulted in several interesting and informative critical pieces, the best of which included "Dangerous Liaisons" (*Columbia Journalism Review*, July-August 1989), in which twenty leading "media figures" commented on the ethical problems involved; which, in turn, was criticized by Naomi Munson in "The Columbia Journalism Review Takes Up A High Moral Issue" (*Contentions*, September 1989). More comprehensive and challenging in its rigorous examination of the implications was "The McGinniss Case: A Travesty of Libel," by attorney Martin Garbus (*Authors Guild Bulletin*, Summer 1989). Garbus pointed out a problem that is already a matter of serious concern: "The free speech concern is the extent to which libel suits, disguised as breach of contract and fraud suits by book subjects, can stop the writing, sale, and reading of books."

The nuts and bolts, that is, the dollars and cents, of the publishing business continued throughout the year to be a matter of fascination to literary journalists and, presumably, to readers. Certainly dollars-and-cents stories are of great (and apparently increasing) interest to people at all levels of the business. Thus, as might be expected, *Publishers Weekly* regularly pays attention to advances and earnings; and such things merit stories in the large newspapers. Perhaps less predictably, more specialized publications such as the *Authors Guild Bulletin* and even *Poets*

and Writers devote considerable space and attention to commercial news. From all these sources and others, including a feature article in the "Business" section of *Time* (12 June 1989), "Big Books, Big Bucks," it was easy to learn not only such news as the huge advances accruing to the blockbuster writers–$30 million to $40 million for Stephen King; $10 million from Harper and Row to Len Deighton; $10.5 million to Mary Higgins Clark; $9 million to Barbara Taylor Bradford; $7.5 million to Colleen McCullough; $5 million to $7 million to Tom Wolfe; $3 million to Scott Turow; $4.9 million to Alexandra Ripley for her assigned sequel to *Gone With the Wind*; $4.5 million to Elmore Leonard; $1.2 million to Philip Roth; but also the extraordinary first novel success of Amy Tan with *The Joy Luck Club* (Putnam's), paperback rights alone going for $1.2 million; $300,000 to Layne Heath for his unfinished first novel *CW2*; and the unusual $150,000 advance paid by Doubleday for Marti Leimbach's debut, *Dying Young*. You could find the same thing, the attitude at least, in such an unlikely place as *Modern Maturity*, where Simon & Schuster's Michael Korda was quoted in explanation of the case for the inflated advance: "I'd rather pay $10 million, $15 million, $20 million, whatever, for a bunch of books by a proven best selling author than endlessly pay $5,000 for an author whose books do not sell."

Emphasis on all this, however, tends to misrepresent the facts and the actual trends, as "Adam Smith" persuasively argued in "A Literary Illusion" (*Esquire*, February 1989): "The public may think most authors are rich because Tom Clancy and Judith Krantz get a lot of publicity, but the economic rewards of mainstream literary activity have been eroding for many years." No surprise, then, for any but the utterly uninitiated that at the year's end there was much talk, in popular and recondite publications alike, about the necessity of a new austerity in the publishing business (to begin, of course, with reducing outrageous advances to authors). No surprise, either, though a certain awkward embarrassment, in the attention paid to publisher Saul Stein's *A Feast For Lawyers: Inside Chapter 11: An Expose* (M. Evans), an account of how his publishing company, Stein and Day, in spite of a solid backlist, collapsed and went under in very short order in the present scene where the cash flow is glacially slow and everyone is in debt to everyone else, a situation described by another publishing executive, Gerald Howard of Norton, in an important article ("Mistah Perkins–He Dead: Publishing Today," *American Scholar*, Summer 1989) as "a combination hall of mirrors, MTV video, commodities pit, cocktail party, soap opera, circus, fun house, and three-card monte game." Elsewhere Kurt Vonnegut, in the context of an article about his old friend, novelist Richard Yates ("The Great Unknown," *Fame*, Summer 1989), put it more succinctly: "It's a one-shot economy now. Winner take all. Old books never come back." As if to give the lie to Vonnegut, Andrew Wylie, the superagent, was widely reported to have sold the rights to the late Italo Calvino's published and unpublished works to Mondadori for something in excess of $12 million.

Two sides of the same thing like a coin. This can be easily seen in two pieces written during the year about Steven Schragis, part owner of *Spy* magazine, who bought out Lyle Stuart Inc. in 1989 and founded Carol Publishing and its "quality" imprint, Birch Lane Press. *Inside Books* (August 1989), in "Steven Schragis: Publishing's New Blockbuster Baron," by Ray Bennett, is upbeat and complimentary. Robert S. Boynton's earlier piece, "Publishing's Dennis the Menace" (*Manhattan Inc.*, April 1989) is basically uncomplimentary and unconvinced.

Even more than the confusing business of American publishing, it is the *people*–publishers and writers–who seem most to fascinate our literary journalists. In part this is doubtless a result of the *People* magazine syndrome; though in fairness a case can be made that *People* is simply a symptom of the larger condition (call it malaise, if you choose) whereby there is a large public feeding off the briefly incandescent lives of celebrities of all kinds, not excluding literary celebrities. I cannot recall seeing so many and various published profiles, exposés, memoirs, interviews, and confessions involving writers. The relevance of this journalistic fashion is simple and direct. Except for the very limited number of publications that restrict themselves exclusively to book reviewing (and not even the *New York Times Book Review* or *Washington Post Book World* are all that rigorous), a very significant part of the book reviewing that is done in America at this time comes wrapped and packaged in the form of a piece about the author. The new book is an excuse and occasion for–and, in the best cases, stands at the center of–a piece focused on the author.

This sort of approach has become almost habitual in the popular magazines. It starts fairly high, however, with such models as the *New York Times Magazine*, where, for example, novelist Wesley Brown in "Who To Blame, Who To Forgive" (10 September 1989) managed to work an appreciative account of Russell Banks's brand-new novel, *Affliction* (Harper and Row), into a biographical profile of the author. This is the standard. And so a book critic and reviewer such as Philadelphia's Carlin Romano, in "Art D'Eco" (*Fame*, October 1989), manages to get his licks in concerning Umberto Eco and his work, old and new, a piece described with revealing emphasis in the table of contents: "Umberto Eco has written another best-seller from his palatial home atop Monte Cerignone in Italy. Carlin Romano drops in on the Renaissance Man at home." Also in the same issue, on a smaller scale, critic David Streitfeld manages to put together a few brief reviews in an article that seems to point in another direction–"Crackerjacks: A new generation of Southern Writers finds refuge at Algonquin Books."

In a sense this form of article represents a gain, more space in more places for book reviewing, and the proliferation of and competition among the top slick magazines led this year to a surprising number of essentially literary articles. *Vanity Fair*, for example, had full-scale pieces on Thomas Sanchez (October 1989), author of *Mile Zero* (Knopf); John Le Carré (June 1989); and Kingsley Amis (April 1989). These were appreciations, but there was at least an occasional example of negative criticism of both an author and his work, as in James Wolcott's article "Guns and Poses: A revisionist view of Richard Ford, the lauded novelist" (August). There were pieces on publishers, high- and lowbrow, as in Leslie Bennett's "Talent–To Amuse: Why power couple Susan and Howard Kaminsky (Morrow) write 'trashy' fiction" (August) and Michael Van Meulen's "Publishing: Belles Lettres' Bad Boy" (November), a profile of "Buffalo Bill" Buford, editor of *Granta*. (Another chic magazine, *Taxi*, dealt with *Granta* and two other examples of trendy little magazines–*Conjunctions* and the *Quarterly*–in Will Nixon's April article "Big Words in a Small Package: The Little Magazine"). And Evelyn Hofer's "Mondo Mondadori" (April), a profile of Italian publisher Leonardo Mondadori. Others were more personal in form, as in William Styron's "The Distant Shaw" (August), a remembrance of his friend Irwin Shaw. (Styron also contributed a similar recollection to *Esquire* in April–"A Literary Friendship: William Styron Remembers James Jones"; likewise, in September

Esquire published a lengthy memoir in Tobias Wolff's "Raymond Carver Had His Cake And Ate It Too.") There was also a place for the confessional piece, as for example Styron's moving account of his own struggles with depression in "Darkness Visible" (December).

Mirabella works with shorter takes, but nevertheless found space for pieces on, among others, Australian novelist Robyn Davidson, Truman Capote, Janet Flanner, and in Cathleen Medwick's "Pop Goes the Novel" (November), consideration of Danielle Steele, Stephen King, and Larry McMurtry. Someone with a campy sense of humor hired prolific author Joyce Carol Oates to write about Gloria Vanderbilt's first novel, *Never Say Good-Bye* (Knopf), in "Love and Gloria" (October).

Fame, as might be expected, does its full share of literary gossip and personality pieces, as in John Tytell's article about Henry Miller and Anaïs Nin–"Past Perfect: Two Spies in the House of Love" (February). And there were like-minded pieces on Jack Kerouac's estate (January), on the fate of Hemingway's three sons–John, Patrick, and Gregory–(September), on a personal tragedy in the family of William Wharton (November). (Probably the most moving, certainly the most devastating account of personal tragedy in the life of a literary celebrity was Chip Brown's "Blood Circle," a profile of the troubled life of African-American writer John Edgar Wideman, in the August issue of *Esquire*.) But *Fame* managed to sandwich at least fragmentary reviews into some of its personal profiles as, notably, in David Streitfeld's "Gargantuan Gurganus: The man who excited John Cheever's deepest love writes an epic first novel" (August), which is a good deal less about Gurganus's relationship with Cheever than an account of his book–*Oldest Living Confederate Widow Tells All* (Knopf).

Smart magazine, which boasts three prominent book editors on its staff–Gary Fisketjon, Morgan Entrekin, and George Plimpton–was alone among the magazines in publishing lengthy excerpts from new books, letting the writers' words speak for themselves. Among those published this year were Larry McMurtry, Thomas McGuane, Alan Gurganus, John Gregory Dunne, Bruce Jay Friedman, and a chunk of the Raymond Chandler/Robert B. Parker *Poodle Springs* (Putnam's). There were, to be sure, more usual pieces: the October 1989 issue featured an article on the late Edward Abbey (1927-1989) by Michael Moore and Carole Mallory's "Checking in with Norman Mailer," an interview.

In last year's preliminary summary of magazine book reviewing we singled out *Elle* for special praise both for the scope and high quality of its reviews. Here we reiterate that praise with a difference. No less than the others, *Elle* seems to have moved more and more to the personality piece as an occasion for reviews and criticism. But the interesting thing is the people whose lives and works they choose to deal with. Here are some of this year's stars in *Elle*: Oliver Sacks, Tahar Ban Jelloun, Bruce Chatwin, Jorge Amado, E. M. Cioran, Kazuo Ishiguro, Danilo Kis, Clinua Achebe, J. R. Ackerley, J. G. Ballard, Patrick McGrath, Graham Swift, David Leavitt, and Ronald Firbank. *Elle* also deserves credit for publishing one of the best reviews of Rushdie's controversial novel in Andrew Harvey's "Hellish 'Satanic Verses' " (February 1989), wherein Harvey concludes that the failure of the novel, measured against Rushdie's other work, is "a failure of spiritual vision."

Inevitably some standing and moving targets were fired on (or saluted) in the popular press. The story of "the baby novelists," aka The Brat Pack, continued with a remarkable critical document produced by *Spy* magazine and published by Doubleday. In a parodic copy of the form and format of *Cliff's Notes* came *Spy Notes on McInerney's "Bright Lights, Big City," Janowitz's "Slaves of New York," Ellis' "Less Than Zero" . . . And All Those Other Hip Urban Novels of the 1980's*. The editors of *Spy* do an admirable job analyzing and satirizing the novels of the title together with seventeen other novels by fifteen young writers, a thorough study guide replete with charts and graphs and including a remarkable device, "The Spy Novel-O-Matic," a kind of slide rule which, if well used, promises to lead to literary success: "Your masterpiece will seem to write itself."

One inevitable source of copy and occasion for articles these days seems to be writer-teacher-editor Gordon Lish, who found himself photographed, interviewed, and praised or blamed in three separate major articles during the year: Lisa Grunwald's "Captain Fiction Rides Again: The further adventures of Gordon Lish" (*Esquire*, March 1989), more or less neutral in that it is in the form of a question-and-answer dialogue, though primarily positive, perhaps in view of the fact that Lish served for some years as an editor of *Esquire*. In the May issue of *Gentlemen's Quarterly* came Neal Karlen's strongly satirical, less-than-enthusiastic endorsement, "For $2,400, Gordon Lish Will Tell You How To Reach God," a report on a session in Lish's paid master class in creative writing. Regina Weinreich's "A Lish Called Gordon" (*Fame*, August 1989) combines a personal account of another twelve-week master class and interviews with former students with a review of his new novel–*Extravaganza* (Putnam's). Although Weinreich makes no bones about her own supportive appreciation of Lish, she presents a reasonable see-for-yourself picture, complete with quotations of the subject that may be judged and taken by the reader as he or she pleases: "I make no secret of my delight in having a big stick but hope to exercise its use for the glory of the god of fiction."

Another example of the importance of authors as recognizable people, more or less public figures like any others, to be known as much for themselves as for their words and works, came with the beginning, in January 1989, of the television program "Bookmark," hosted by Lewis Lapham of *Harper's* (who announced his aim to be "the Louis Rukeyser of letters"–*Washington Post*, 31 January 1989). Lapham put together twenty-six talk shows featuring writers such as Robertson Davies, Alison Lurie, Margaret Atwood, Robert Coles, Robert Stone, Edna O'Brien, E. L. Doctorow, Louis Auchincloss, and *Playboy's* fiction editor–Alice Turner. The only problem with the show at the outset, in television terms, was the level of public civility. "They're tigers in the locker room," Lapham said, "but when they come on to the set, they're tabby cats."

Perhaps, if it has no other value, the very existence of such a show can indicate the problems arising from book reviewing by name and personality more than subject and achievement, the chief problem clearly being the absolute necessity of creating and maintaining a literary establishment, one composed of recognizable, predictable purveyors of what might as well be breakfast cereal or toothpaste. This, in turn, creates huge problems for the new, the undiscovered and unrecognized, the genuinely innovative and original writers (in both form and content), who, without being labeled, cannot be marketed. "Bookmark" may or may not "work" as a television program, but the idea of book reviewing and criticism taking place in the context of a talk show demonstrates the limits and limited goals of contemporary criticism.

Some recognition of the problem (at least that it *is* a problem), the rather surprising assimila-

tion of literary people and business into the ineluctable celebrity culture of the times, was clearly evident in a PEN panel held on 11 January 1989, "Book Reviewing: The Good, the Bad, and the Overlooked" (published in *PEN Newsletter*, August 1989), when critic James Wolcott responded to a question that predicated a difference between celebrity and literature: "Celebrity is intertwined with literature–look at Lord Byron. It can be taken too far: If you turn into Tama Janowitz and begin to believe your own act, you're in trouble. Despite the fact that he says 'his fame will be posthumous,' Harold Brodky's output as a writer is entwined with his sense of being a celebrity. You have to deal with that . . . . As I said, you can take it too far; it can get to the point that people are reviewed because they are celebrities rather than because their books are particularly good. I mean, if Jerzy Kosinski weren't famous, his books would not get any reviews: he hasn't written a good book for a long time."

Beyond all this, however, the trenches and brutal no-man's-land of book reviewing, there were more serious consideration and discussion (including the PEN panel), on what might be called the strategic level, about the state of book reviewing in America. Writing for the newspaper trade magazine *Presstime* (November 1989), Rolf Rykken wrote a major article, "Book Reviews," interviewing widely, checking his sources far and wide (including the *Dictionary of Literary Biography Yearbook*), and offering a variety of useful statistics that, taken together, prove at best that book pages are more or less the same as a decade ago. Some gains–the 1986 introduction of a twelve-to-sixteen-page weekly tabloid, *Tribune Books*, published by the *Chicago Tribune*, the expansion of the book tab of the *Los Angeles Times* from twelve to sixteen pages–have been offset by lost space elsewhere, most notably the end of the book tab in the *Philadelphia Inquirer* in 1987. An equally important article, though more focused on qualitative than quantitative concerns, was "Book Reviewing in America: A Forum," published in the Spring 1989 issue of the *Review of Contemporary Fiction*. Here twenty-one editors and reviewers were asked to respond to a quoted critique by French writer Patrice Roussel, the central point of which was this: "The whole system is made up of self-fulfilling economic and cultural prophecies that result in keeping serious literature from Americans." These editors and reviewers, ranging from people such as Sybil Steinberg of *Publishers Weekly* through several high-circulation newspaper book editors to Alan Cheuse of National Public Radio, are not entirely in agreement on anything, yet seem unlikely to find much fault with this comment by Mark Feeny of the *Boston Globe*: "Only a very foolish editor—of an unusually worthless section—would limit his reviews to books by Judith Krantz, Robert Ludlum and, say, Herman Wouk. Yet only an equally foolish review editor (at a mass-market newspaper, anyway) would restrict his section to reviews of, let us say, Kathy Acker, John Hawkes, and Georges Perec."

The PEN panel, which involved critics Sven Birkerts (*New Republic*), Rebecca Sinkler (*New York Times Book Review*), Nina King (*Washington Post*), and James Wolcott (*Vanity Fair*) and was moderated by novelist Hilma Wolitzer, was concerned mainly with bread-and-butter issues such as how books are chosen for review and how reviewers are chosen to review them. This soon led to intense discussion of ethics and integrity, insoluble, since, after all is said and done, book reviewing works by a kind of honor system. More interesting was the fact (and discovery of same by many listeners and readers) that only the *New York Times Book Review* has anything like the staff (ten) to enjoy the luxury of "previewing" most of the books before sending them out for review. A few others have the aid and comfort of some staff. But, by and large, most reviewing publications, even major and influential papers and magazines, have only whatever information they can glean from the trade publications and press releases to guide them. All of which adds up to yet another force for orderly simplification, for choosing on the basis of the established and predictable (author or publishing house) and therefore, innocently or not, becoming a servant of the status quo. This panel of important reviewers agreed that book reviews must justify themselves as news and as "entertainment." Only Birkerts, who regularly reviews for little magazines and quarterlies, insisted of journalistic book reviewing that "it's tied in very closely with the mechanics of the book-publishing industry."

Wearing her official hat as president of the National Book Critics Circle, Nina King also participated in a special panel program at the Modern Language Association's annual convention, "The National Book Critics Circle Looks at the Novelist as Critic" (29 December 1989), which also included Jack Sullivan of Rider College as moderator and Charles Simmons, novelist and former staff member of the *New York Times Book Review*, writer Joyce Carol Oates, and novelist and critic

Alan Cheuse. The special nature of the topic might have been strictly limiting had the panelists dealt exclusively with it. But the discussion (as yet unpublished) was more embracing. Again, problems of ethics and critical integrity arose, leading an observer to conclude that this may be one of the most troubling unexamined issues in the American literary scene. Behind the questioning lay some serious doubts not yet understood or addressed by the professionals. Simmons discussed the difficulty of finding good reviewers for "first novelists and relatively unknown people," emphasizing the need for "imaginative and inventive" reviewers to treat sensitive or slightly unusual material. Cheuse's comments were entertainingly anecdotal, but he also offered a serious definition of the value of book reviewing to the practicing writer: "It helps you to visualize your own practice as a writer and to catch a glimmer of your own aesthetic by putting into words on a review your measured impressions of another novelist." Similarly, "it helps you to keep in contact also with the contemporary field of action." He added that "now and then you can have some effect on the success, if not the aesthetic progress of good writers and can contribute to the decline in reputation of some bad ones." Arguing that book reviewing is an almost "unexplored and unexamined genre, defined more by opposition and disgruntlement than by any coherent sort of criteria," Joyce Carol Oates presented a series of large questions: "Is there any sort of shared literary or cultural background? Is there any longer, or was there ever, an absolute set of literary values against which the present work could reasonably be measured?" In the sequence of questions she paused long enough to point out that literary criticism "has often been a strategy in which those who doubt their own worth can express doubt of others' work, in which the morally reprehensible can pass judgment on the 'morals' of a book, in which the slovenly can masquerade as lovers of the orderly, the classic, and the pure." Going on to add: "Most of all, criticism has, as we all know, provided an arena for the discharge of resentment; those who have failed in their own enterprises may there strike out at those they imagine to be more successful."

Strong words and strongly needed, though not, on this occasion, seriously addressed by either the panel or the audience.

Another significant public discussion of book reviewing, with a somewhat different focus, took place on 10 November 1989 in Atlanta at the convention of the South Atlantic Modern Languages Association. "Book Reviewing: The Art and the Agony" was moderated by Staige Blackford, editor of the *Virginia Quarterly Review*; and included a publisher–Edwin Barber, vice-president and editor at W. W. Norton; another quarterly editor–George Core of the *Sewanee Review*; and two writers, Samuel Pickering and George Garrett. Some of the basic things were reiterated here; however, this discussion offered many things that others did not. First, there was some specific, if brief, talk about the fate at the hands of reviewers, and at the same time the relationship of reviews and sales figures, of two 1989 novels–Mary Lee Settle's *Charley Bland* (Farrar, Straus & Giroux) and Ward Just's *Jack Gance* (Houghton Mifflin). No firm or serious conclusions were arrived at except that a lot of timely and favorable and well-positioned reviews, while helpful, do not necessarily translate into huge sales figures. In the case of Settle, it was noted that, while certain of her reviews were exceptional as criticism in a journalistic context (especially those of Monroe Spears in the *Washington Post Book World*, 15 September 1989; Richard Dyer in the *Boston Globe*, 12 October; and Marion Montgomery in the *Washington Times*, 16 October), other reviewers, such as David Leavitt in the *New York Times Book Review*, seemed to have read another book or, more exactly, to have missed the chief and stated theme of the novel. Editor Barber presented a clear outline of the place of reviews in the publishing process: "Sometimes there comes a sort of desperate moment, a kind of dark night of the soul in publishing, when you realize that no reviews are going to come, or at least no more, or none that are good enough. And that is about as bleak as it can get."

Perhaps the most important point of view expressed on this occasion, not a surprising one since two editors of major quarterlies were participating and since the two writers publish as much or more in the quarterlies as anywhere else, was that of the quarterly reviews. Predicating his talk on a basic assumption–"Book reviewing is one of the most essential activities of the literary magazine and the scholarly journal. A good many people who follow academic periodicals, including some editors, do not understand this simple fact"–Core described the ways and means of the *Sewanee Review* (essay reviews of forty to fifty books per issue and "briefer" notice of many more) and praised the somewhat similar practices of the *American Scholar*, the *Hudson Review*, the

Georgia Review, and the *New England Review*. "As I see the reviewing transaction," Core said in summary, "what we are chiefly trying to accomplish, other than having as many books reviewed as fairly and intelligently as possible, is to make reviewing a department of criticism. . . . It is our duty as editors to make sure that the reviews we publish are exceptions to the dismal run of journalistic reviewing." Core continued and amplified his discussion of the place and purpose of the quarterly in a short piece, "American Quarterlies and Robert Penn Warren," in the Fall 1989 issue of the *Sewanee Review*, criticizing such quarterlies as the *Kenyon Review, Grand Street*, the *Southern Review*, and the *Gettysburg Review* for their failure to develop "a critical program": "The major quarterly, as Monroe Spears has written, features a critical program carried out in reviews as well as essays and at once publishes new fiction and poetry." As for the forms of criticism to be found in more specialized journals, Core cites Irving Howe's piece in the 12 June issue of the *New Republic*, "The Treason of the Critics," which argues that "critics might learn once more to speak to the common reader, as if he still matters, as if she will still respond; and to speak in English, a language that for some time served criticism well."

Just at the year's turning appeared an article that seems likely, for a variety of reasons, to be argued about for some time to come. In "The New American Assembly-Line Fiction: An Empty Blue Center" (*American Scholar*, Winter 1990), John W. Aldridge deals with many complex issues, including the proliferation and influence of creative writing programs; but at heart his essay argues much the same thing that Core does–namely, that with serious criticism losing ground on the one hand to highly specialized and uninfluential academic criticism–"mostly theoretical and analytical rather than evaluative in approach (and thus unbearably jargon-laden)," and, on the other, to the literary journalists ("the people whose function it is to report regularly on newly published books, but who, because of limitations of time and space, are nearly always forced to treat them superficially"), contemporary writers find themselves "in an extremely bizarre position," victims of "publicity overkill" and therefore eminent (if at all) as "familiar names known mostly for being familiar names." Measured against earlier masters of the century, Aldridge finds the work of the new breed of writers seriously flawed: "These books have so far not created new circuits in the public imagination or provided the charged symbols for a new vision of the human condition in our time, nor has their language enlarged the vocabulary with which we describe the most urgent problems and preoccupations that concern us."

Aldridge's essay is, in itself, challenging criticism, but if the terms of it are true and if the movement is, as we argue here, more and more toward assimilation in the culture of celebrity, fame, and notoriety (ill fame), then things appear to be getting distinctly worse as we enter the century's final decade. This gloomy prognosis would seem to be strongly witnessed by a questionnaire sent out by *Esquire* to "sexy, well-known authors" for its July 1990 "literary" issue, a questionnaire that asks writers fifteen personal questions, including such relevant examples as these: "How do the pleasures of sex compare to those of writing and reading?"; "What fellow writer do you find the sexiest, either in person or in his or her work?"; "Do you feel most sexually aroused before, during, or after writing?"; and "How does your sexual activity affect your productivity as a writer?"

Perhaps our next report will contain a review of the sex lives of American writers in 1990. (Matter of fact, the next addition will offer an examination of book reviewing in the major and minor quarterlies, together with some other conventional and more or less respectable topics.)

Meantime, our nomination for the funniest review of 1989 is Christopher Schemering's "Vanderbilt's Wacky Debut" (*Washington Post*, 7 November), a review of Gloria Vanderbilt's *Never Say Good-Bye* (Knopf). And for the emphatically negative review of the year, consider Thomas M. Disch on poet Michael Ryan's *God Hunger* (Viking) in "The Rhyming Scheme" (*Nation*, 27 November). Disch honorably chooses to defend the values of negative criticism, offering reasons for panning *God Hunger*: "Because sometimes, as one watches the emperor's latest fashion show or reads reports of it in the press, it is reassuring to hear someone else echo one's own sense of the event ... I also feel that every critic is obligated to give his or her aversions at least a regular airing, if not equal time with the enthusiasms, for to do otherwise is to take part in a conspiracy of silence."

Which seems to me a natural and proper place to segue into Henry Taylor's examination of poetry reviewing in our time.

II: Looking for the Golden Mountain: Poetry Reviewing, by Henry Taylor

Several times in the last few months, thinking about the state of poetry reviewing in America has led me to a jumbled fullness of mind too much like blankness, and I have gone to the phone, called people up, and mystified them by asking what they think about it. R. H. W. Dillard, when he realized I was serious, said, "That's like being asked to discuss the Golden Mountain: it might exist, but it's hard to know where to look for it."

Peter Stitt, also a distinguished reviewer, finds "literary criticism, broadly considered, in a badly fragmented and ineffective state. Theorists in universities are spinning webs that have little or nothing to do with addressing individual works, and they end up talking exclusively among themselves. The New Critics, at least, applied themselves to literary works, and so they could help sustain a dialogue between critics and practitioners. There doesn't seem to be any such dialogue going on now; poetry reviewers seem unable to be useful and educational, either to readers of poetry or to poets. It's hard to know why this is; part of it may be the quality of the reviewing, but part of it may be that the gulf between theoretical critics and reviewers has encouraged poets not to take reviewers seriously."

For centuries, there have been two ways of reviewing poetry. There is the traditional reading, description, and evaluation of books of poems; that still goes on, if less extensively than most poets would like. There is also a body of literary journalism that reviews poetry in general—its place in contemporary civilization, its dependence on universities, its health, its death.

This second class of poetry reviewing is always with us, but periodically it comes in more concentrated bursts. The years 1988 and 1989 have been ones of unusual activity in this genre, though its practitioners have performed with unequal diligence as readers of poetry.

There is no way to know exactly where the present troubles started, but a benchmark was established in the September 1986 issue of *Poetry*, in which Greg Kuzma bewails the deficiencies of a single volume of poems, *The Catastrophe of Rainbows*, by Martha Collins. And by occasion foretells the ruin of our corrupted writing programs, then in their height. "Within five years," he writes, "there will be a creative-writing program available for anyone in America within safe driving distance of his home."

Kuzma thinks this is bad news. Like most writers who worry about the proliferation of writing programs, he believes that only a small percentage of graduate writing students will write anything durable. Unfortunately, in his view, many graduates of such programs may go to their graves believing that they have written durably and well, because their former mentors will say in public that they have. Kuzma indicates that these mentors do this in order to maintain their own programs' credibility: the more published and praised writers there are from a given program, the more talented applicants will seek to become part of it. Furthermore, now that creative writers are fully accredited colleagues of the professors of literature in their departments, saddled with various distracting administrative duties, the question of whether their writing is any good becomes less and less significant: their job is to run programs, recruit students and faculty, and to adjust standards and expectations to the facts of the marketplace. Kuzma finds the situation circular, self-deceptive, self-serving, and disgusting.

Martha Collins and her book are little more than the occasion for Kuzma's rant. He recognizes this, and from time to time expresses his regret that chance has thrown her his way. "There is, probably, no acceptable way to apologize to her," he writes, "for using her work as I have. And yet I mean to apologize, and to wish only the best for her and her poetry." Ironically enough, Collins has reason to wonder when she or her work will again be the occasion for so extended a piece in so prestigious a journal.

A couple of years later, in August 1988, Joseph Epstein created a greater furor with a blander exercise. "Who Killed Poetry?" was the arresting title of an essay he first published in *Commentary*; he permitted its reprinting in the May 1989 issue of the *AWP Chronicle* (the official organ of the Associated Writing Programs) whose editors thought the remarks deserved response from their readership. Large portions of two issues of the *AWP Chronicle* were given over to thirty-three responses (one of which, I confess, was mine). A few were favorable, but most bring into focus the many respects in which Epstein wrote with insufficient consideration. For one thing, he fails to establish, or even assert, that poetry is dead; so it is hard to draw from his remarks many clear inferences concerning the identity of the killer or killers. His problem, as expressed in the essay, is that no living poets can elicit from him the reactions he had to the poets he encountered when he was considerably younger. Contemporary poetry "flourishes in a vacuum" for many possible reasons; Epstein devotes considerable space to the possibility that the recent proliferation of writing programs has contributed heavily to this state of affairs and quotes from Kuzma's review of Collins the first of the quoted sentences above. He makes it clear, perhaps unintentionally, that he does not read widely in the work of living poets and that his reading of poetry generally is somewhat restricted as to race, class, and gender. For example, in support of his impression that "Poets have not altogether given up" the narrative element in poetry, he cites the work of five white male poets, four of whom are dead: Robert Frost, T. S. Eliot, Wallace Stevens, Robert Lowell, and Herbert Morris.

But Epstein came closest to dishonesty when he mentioned attending a poetry reading. He puts it thus: "I not long ago had occasion to hear two poets read and talk about their craft. Both were men, both in their thirties, both had regular teaching jobs at large universities, both had published two books and had had their share of grants and awards. One of the two was a Hawaiian of Japanese ancestry, the other was middle-class Jewish. . . . In their discussions after they read, both poets were full of quotations from Pound and Eliot and Kant and Rilke, giving off a strong whiff of the classroom."

Epstein snidely summarizes three of the poems presented during the reading, and says, "I bring them up only because they seemed so characteristic, so much like a great deal of contemporary poetry: slightly political, heavily preening, and not distinguished enough in language or subtlety of thought to be memorable." So his not quoting or naming the two poets has the look of patronizing charity.

In the spring of 1988, it turns out, Stephen Goodwin, then the director of the literature program of the National Endowment for the Arts, asked two poets to appear before the annual review of NEA programs by the National Council on the Arts, of which Epstein was then the sole member representing literature. The two poets were Garrett Hongo and Edward Hirsch. During the question period, Hongo says, Epstein engaged both poets in exchanges that had acrimonious moments.

The responses in the *AWP Chronicle* were remarkable for their variety. A few briefly dismissed Epstein's essay as useless or foolish; a few agreed with it almost wholly; several noted that Epstein's experience of poetry seems somewhat narrow; and several respondents found some points worth elaborating and some deserving of rebuttal.

Perhaps the most intelligent response to Epstein's essay came from Donald Hall, whose "Death to the Death of Poetry" appeared not among the responses published in the *AWP Chronicle* but in *Harper's*, in September 1989. Hall subsequently made some additions to the piece and used it as the introduction to *The Best American Poetry 1989*, which he edited.

Hall is quite right to remind us, as some other respondents did, that at any time in literary history, there are apparently responsible voices crying that things are worse than ever. But he is much more interesting and useful when he offers evidence that poets need to complain about their lot, because "we love the romance of alienation and insult."

As part of his evidence, Hall provides a brief account of the *Los Angeles Times* "Flap." A couple of years ago, Jack Miles, book editor at the *Los Angeles Times*, decided to do something about the extraordinary difficulty of deciding which books of poetry ought to be reviewed. He ran an announcement to the effect that henceforth, the *Los Angeles Times Book Review* would print a poem in a box every week, with a note on the poet and the book from which the poem had been reprinted. At that time, Miles thought it possible that this policy would reduce the number of poetry books getting full-length reviews in his pages.

This announcement, as Hall points out, outraged many poets, who picketed the newspaper. In fact, since Miles's announcement, the *Los Angeles Times* has paid "more attention to poetry than any other newspaper in the country." Hall wants us to understand this, but he also wants us to understand that most poets are unwilling to believe it, because they believe only that evidence that casts them as victims. This cast of mind is familiar enough, alas; when poets picketed the *Los Angeles Times*, some of them were probably aware that they were protesting increased coverage of poetry, which would make them feel even more neglected than they had been feeling, since it might continue to ignore them. Epstein writes that "the happy few are rarely happier than when they are

even fewer"; a corollary is that the neglected many are rarely more miserable than when their numbers are diminished by notice.

Similarly, most people refuse to believe Hall when he quotes some of his favorite figures. There are living poets whose books have sold in the tens of thousands; Lawrence Ferlinghetti and Allen Ginsberg have sold over a million copies of their most famous works. Louis Harris and Associates, conducting a poll in 1988, found that forty-two million adult Americans write poems or stories. In connection with the task of choosing the poems for *Best American Poetry 1989*, Hall cites an important effect of this plenitude:

> Forty-two million writers—or two hundred thousand, or three hundred—make judgment difficult. The Lottery Effect takes over—for prizes, for fellowships, for book publication, and for reprinting in anthologies. The Lottery Effect occurs when numbers diminish the possibilities of judgment, allowing too much weight to chance: On what day, or at what time of day, did the editor or judge approach this book or that poem? Most critics avoid the Lottery Effect by denial, as when Edmund Wilson claimed that Robert Lowell alone was worth reading. It saves time, but it's a lie. I have no suggestions for overcoming the Lottery Effect, except to propose more lotteries.

The important role of chance in these matters is emphasized in a review by John Ash in the 31 December 1989 issue of the *Washington Post Book World*. In a brief mention of Hall's anthology and its "cheerfully combative introduction," he misattributes the essay on the death of poetry to *Jason* Epstein and goes on to say that he particularly enjoyed work by six of the seventy-five poets in the anthology. Five of the six poets' names are correctly spelled. The remainder of the review takes up Robert Hass's *Human Wishes* (unfavorably) and Charles North's *The Year of the Olive Oil* (favorably). The editors of *Book World*, in an apparent belief that reviewing poetry matters no more than which Epstein is the right one, give the title "Going Metric" to this review, which does not directly mention metrical writing, though Andrew Marvell's name comes up.

*   *   *

Four to six collections of poetry arrive in my mail every week; in a year, I receive about three hundred. I glance at all of them, read a handful of poems from most of them, keep several, and review a few. It would be impossible to review all of them, though hope of a review is what induces publishers to send them either to me, or to the *Washington Times*, where my reviews of poetry appear with more regularity than frequency. And yet, according to recent figures, the books I receive account for considerably less than one-third of the annual production of poetry collections. Of course most of them are undistinguished. But a few of them are wonderful, and a few are egregious to a point that requires comment.

Clearly, I am not "keeping up." On the other hand, I read enough good poetry these days to convince me that the days are gone when I would with confidence devote a semester or a year to a course in contemporary American poetry. There are too many poets whose work I would be sorry not to take up, and there are even more for whose work other poets and reviewers would lobby.

Who are these reviewers? Where do they hold forth? Their opinions are widely distributed, from newspapers of national significance to magazines that specialize not just in poetry, but in poetry of one or another kind. In 1988 the *New York Times* reviewed thirty-five books of poems, and the *Washington Post* reviewed twenty. *Poetry*, one of the oldest and most prestigious poetry magazines in the country, reviewed forty books between April 1988 and March 1989. Inevitably, there is some duplication. Ten books were reviewed in two of those journals; most were the work of poets accustomed to relatively widespread notice: John Ashbery, Joseph Brodsky, Josephine Jacobsen, William Stafford, May Swenson, and Richard Wilbur. Perhaps less inevitably, W. S. Merwin's *The Rain in the Trees* was not only reviewed in all three journals but was also reviewed twice in the *New York Times*, along with his *Selected Poems*: once by Michiko Kakutani in the daily "Books of the Times" column, and once by Edward Hirsch in the *Book Review*.

If you ask a close student of current poetry to name some prominent reviewers of poetry, he or she will doubtless mention some few of the people who helped cover the scene for these three journals. But in this particular sample of twenty-nine reviews, only Edward Hirsch and Michiko Kakutani have written more than one. (Five other people–Paul Breslin, Alfred Corn, William Logan, Robert B. Shaw, and Leslie Ullman–turn

up both as reviewers and as authors of books reviewed, but there is no auto-reviewing, or even direct reciprocity.)

Liam Rector, executive director of the Associated Writing Programs, finds this variety of points of view bewildering. He recently had this to say in response to my question about the state of poetry reviewing:

> It's probably in as deplorable a state as it's ever been. One of the most glaring deficiencies is that of consistency among the editors of reviewing journals. Instead of having one person, in the stable or on the staff, whose responsibility is poetry, they assign poetry reviews haphazardly, probably in a serious effort to get a variety of opinions. But the regular reader of one newspaper and a few magazines hasn't the opportunity, as we did a few years ago with Louise Bogan and the *New Yorker* or Randall Jarrell in the *Nation*, to become accustomed to one voice, one set of opinions, and thereby to have some basis for judging the reviewer's opinions in a given instance.

It's an interesting point. On the other hand, readers in search of diversity might fairly ask about the preponderance of white males among the reviewers (twenty-two of twenty-six), and among the reviewed (fifty-five of eighty-three). This is the sort of statistic that makes some people whine about a powerful Literary Establishment.

There may be such an entity, though "powerful" is a relative term. Certainly there are poets whose names alone will all but guarantee that they will be reviewed in journals of national importance, but it takes a fairly radical reader to claim that Richard Wilbur, for example, gets more notice than he deserves. And there may be a few people in the poetry racket who possess what they think is power, and who like to exercise it by insuring that an enemy gets creamed in a review, or that a friend gets praised. But thinking in Establishment terms requires a belief that everything important gets said in established, large-circulation journals. That, like Edmund Wilson's remark about Lowell, is a lie, but there are people who prefer not to know that here and there, in relative obscurity, more interesting work than theirs is regularly being done.

No one knows how many magazines there are, all over the country, that are hospitable to poetry and to reviews of poetry, but it is generally agreed that they may be numbered in the hundreds. The same may be said of the circulation of many of these magazines; even *Poetry* has a circulation below 7,000. But one magazine's circulation is no more indicative of poetry's health than the sales figures on a single book. Even major libraries are unable to subscribe to more than a fraction of the available poetry magazines. Yet they continue to thrive; over the past twenty years, the mass of small poetry magazines has developed a life cycle in which 1.1 will be born for every one that dies.

Among the luxuries these publications make available is space for a reviewer to do a decent job on a book. Consider again the figures cited above. Twenty-six reviewers, twenty-eight reviews, eighty-three separate treatments. The results would be acceptable if most reviews covered the average three books, but book-review editors have become accustomed to chucking a batch of books into a bag with some reviewer and seeing what sort of commentary emerges. The *Washington Post* reviews cover between four and six poets each; six reviewers covered forty books in *Poetry*; a seventh reviewer devoted his space to one critical book. It could be argued, then, that the total number of poets reviewed in the *New Republic*, for example, is less important than its willingness to let Anthony Hecht devote an elegant, medium-length essay to Richard Wilbur's *Collected Poems*.

*   *   *

It is hard, because of the Lottery Effect, to fasten on good examples with which to conclude this survey; fine reviews, many of which reach small or specialized audiences, are more plentiful than many readers, especially poets, realize. Some of these reviewers, it must be admitted, are more fun to read from the security of having so far failed to come under their scrutiny.

William Harmon is at his best when given plenty of room. It is not that he is a wasteful writer; his style is direct and epigrammatic, free of automatic poetry-reviewing language. What requires space is his knowledge of poetic technique and of past poetries. It is likely that he knows no more than any of us in the profession ought to know, but poets are as good as anybody at making the Knowledge Explosion seem to have been a rubble-making disaster, and Harmon is better than most at reminding us of this.

It has been several years since his thorough and hilarious dismantling of Christopher Clau-

sen's *The Place of Poetry: Two Centuries of an Art in Crisis* (1981) appeared in *Poetry*, but his remarks are still making the rounds, being brought to the attention of readers who need them–including Joseph Epstein, who wrote his essay while under the impression that Professor Clausen's book was "excellent."

Harmon's work has also appeared in *Parnassus*, a weighty journal devoted to poetry in review. Unfortunately, *Parnassus* appears infrequently and expensively, so it is usually among the last publications to review a given book. In this circumstance, Harmon's extended essay reviews, which are always entertaining, take on even more of the character of autonomous literature than his skill has already given them. In the second of two issues published in 1988, for example, Harmon considers two anthologies published in 1986: *Strong Measures: An Anthology of Contemporary American Poetry in Traditional Forms*, edited by Philip Dacey and David Jauss; and *In the American Tree: Language, Realism, Poetry*, edited by Ron Silliman. As the second of these is chiefly concerned with the products of "people called Language poets," this essay might at first be taken as a study in polarities–raw and cooked, shaggy and well-groomed, and so on. Instead, it is a patient and witty comparison between the place of knowledge in the poetic tradition and its place in these two books. Neither of them, in Harmon's opinion, exhibits much appreciation of the complexities suggested by their titles. Large portions of this essay are devoted to deft exposition of matters most poets ought to have in mind but which many poets have not considered. His metrical analyses, especially, are immensely valuable, coming as they do at a time when metrical writing rarely amounts to much more than counting syllables and stresses.

Kelly Cherry's response to my phone call was a provocative observation concerning the reviewer's duty: "Reviewing fiction or poetry means learning how the book becomes itself. When you review, you ought to transform yourself in the way that the book transforms or completes itself; that is the only way to place yourself in a position of authority with respect to it." This is a delicate expression of a high ideal, and some would argue that, rather than transforming oneself, the reviewer should hold to whatever identity and character he or she brings to the book. But a steady sympathy, and an openness to possibility and to the risks of inescapable prejudice, allow some reviewers to approach Cherry's ideal of wide-ranging, sympathetic authority.

One's generally perceived place in the literary firmament may have something to do with it. Thomas M. Disch, also known in print as Tom Disch, comes to poetry reviewing with an unusual set of credentials, including some fine science fiction, one of the earliest interactive computer novels, a couple of very successful children's books, and several books of poems. His independence has made him seem something of an outsider, a rebel, a neglected figure. (There are problems with this perception. In a *Newsweek* profile, Walter Clemons said that "Disch may be the most formidably gifted unfamous American writer.")

Disch's engaging irreverence, and his respect for excellence, seem at their best when, like most poetry reviewers, he must deal with several books in one review. He can do a series of individual miniatures, or something more unified, such as "The Rhyme Scheme" (*Nation*, 27 November 1989), in which, anent J. D. McClatchy's *White Paper*, he corrects the widespread notion that "the purpose of creative writing programs is to train armies of accomplished poets and novelists." He points out that writing with eloquence should be part of everyone's education, and then puts the industry in an interesting, and maybe its rightful, place:

> Creative writing courses serve many of the same educational purposes as athletic programs. They channel excess energies to harmless, healthful purposes, promote a sense of well-being and develop real skills. They also encourage a portion of the students to suppose they can be contenders; inevitably, those who don't make it into the major leagues often stay on at the universities to conduct the athletic departments and the writing workshops.
>
> The difference is that in poetry the process of elimination and ranking is less decisive than in sports. It has become the kind of noncompetitive contest in which every child goes home with a prize.

There are so many forms of recognition and notice that many of them are not valued as highly as they should be. One example is selection for review in *Magill's Literary Annual*, a sturdy two-volume compendium that includes reviews of two hundred of the preceding year's best books. Roughly twenty of these are collections of poetry. Each review is about two thousand words in length; the quality is uneven, but over the years the *Annual* has had some distinguished contributors.

Like most of the publications produced by the Salem Press, the *Annual* is designed for use in libraries. Its reputation among literary people suffered at first because Frank Magill, the founder of Salem Press, invented *Masterplots*, a useful collection of plot summaries. It was some time before people began to catch on that the essay reviews in the *Annual* were no more useful to lazy or dishonest students than any other essay reviews. Furthermore, until very recently, it was not the policy of the Salem Press to provide publishers with tear sheets, so even the author of a book covered in its pages could be unaware of the review for several years.

The fragmentation that Peter Stitt described is partly a result of plenitude. *Magill's Literary Annual* produces some sound and extensive criticism of contemporary literature, along with a few hasty treatments by people who don't know what they are talking about. It gives these reviews a kind of accessible permanence in the reference shelves of libraries. It is not a Golden Mountain, but if more poets and readers of poetry were aware of it, there might be a bit less complaint.

III: An Interview With Paxton Davis, by George Garrett

Paxton Davis, author of seven novels, two books of nonfiction, former Washington and Lee professor and head of the Department of Journalism there, and, pertinently, book editor, for a little more than twenty years, of the *Roanoke Times & World News*, has retired from the paper now (except for a feisty and irregular column, on all subjects that interest him, that he continues to write), and he lives in the historic Virginia town of Fincastle, deep in the Shenandoah Valley. He still writes book reviews for various papers, including the *Baltimore Sun*, the *New York Times Book Review*, and the *Washington Post Book World* ("I still review but I don't have to any more"). And he has just finished *A Boy's War*, a memoir of his time as a sergeant in Merrill's Marauders in Burma from 1943 to 1946. Davis's earlier books, beginning in the 1950s, were published by Simon and Schuster; Little, Brown; Morrow; and Atheneum. But this one will be published by Blair of Winston-Salem, North Carolina, which earlier published his memoir *Being a Boy* (1988) with considerable success by any standard. This somewhat surpris-

Paxton Davis

ing thing is occasion for us to talk a little about the rise of small presses in recent years, what they can do and what they can't. "They can focus on a book's special appeal," Davis says, "if it has one, in a way that the big publishers neither think about nor attempt. They are just as good these days at getting a book out to the book pages and sections and at getting a little special push behind it. They are every bit as good as the major publishers in this way, though they may not be as widespread." Using this example of Blair's handling of *Being a Boy*, he says: "They were very focused on the big southern papers, where I got reviewed everywhere and almost everywhere favorably." He describes as "the most bizarre thing" the fact that roughly six months after publication *Southern Living* reviewed the book on its lone book page, which consists of four five-hundred-word reviews and a color shot of the book jackets. Within three days after the issue was published, hundreds of orders for the book came in. The small presses these days—he specifically cites Algonquin, North Point, Peach-

tree, and the university presses—can be successful because "they have modest expectations and they can concentrate their efforts." And, of course, reviews, especially regional and local reviews, can be very influential in the success or failure of a small-press book.

We turn to his personal history as a long-time book editor. He came to his job in 1961, with not only experience as a writer and book reviewer behind him but also a record as a reporter for several southern papers and many years of teaching journalism at Washington and Lee.

"Louis D. Rubin, Jr. (now of Algonquin Books) is really the one who talked the Roanoke paper into creating a book page. Then after a couple of years he quit. They had this thing going, and it was going very successfully. He had a wide open page, no ads of any kind on it, except maybe at Christmas. He had created something they never had before—a genuine, once-a-week Sunday book page that was serious, that attempted to do in a smaller daily the sort of thing that serious book review media had done before and elsewhere. They asked me to do it. I had to clear it with Washington and Lee, which could be very stuffy about those things. To my surprise, they said sure, go ahead. I would finish teaching class at W & L around ten o'clock on Friday morning. Then I drove over to Roanoke—and this was before the interstate I-81 was completed, and it took a little more than an hour and a half. I would work there many hours and then go back home. I was paid twenty-five dollars a week in those days, and I worked hard. . . .

"Most of the time I was there I wrote a column on the book page. And I did not write a book news column; I wrote a review column. I reviewed a great many serious general trade books in that time in that column. It was double columned and boxed always. That was a way of giving particular prominence to a book.

"I wanted absolute authority over every detail. That may be foolish, but I could put out precisely the page I wanted. And I think the results justified that."

He goes on to tell me something about his boss, Barton W. Morris, publisher of the Roanoke papers, and how much the book page owed to him.

"Barton was just an outstanding news executive. He picked people and then, unless they did something grievously wrong, he let them alone. And he gave me the most complete free hand

and the most complete backing. So that if the advertising department or somebody else got troublesome, he always backed me up. Every time I had any problem with either the news side or the advertising side, he always backed me up. And I can't speak enough for that. Because one of the problems book editors traditionally have had on papers everywhere is they never have the final say. Often they are outsiders, as I was. Or else they are insiders who are bossed by a managing editor who doesn't give a damn about books anyway. Or maybe they decide to give the book page to some hack who's been sitting on the copy desk for twenty or thirty years, and they don't know what else to do with him. Then they'll get exactly what you would expect."

But, as Davis is quick to point out, fascinating as the old days inside the newspaper business in America were, and difficult as it was, in all but a few places, for book pages to thrive or even survive, it came down to the quality of reviews and reviewers, always, and to the ability of a book editor to endure other sorts of pressure. It was basically a no-win situation. As Davis puts it: "I was always accused, I thought very unfairly, by academic people of putting out too commercial a book page. I was accused by people at the paper, constantly, of having too highbrow a book page. I have to hope that means there was some kind of happy medium. This is a traditional problem, today as well, for book pages. They are certainly not part of the academic literary journal world. They're not seeking to do that. On the other hand they're not part of the book business, either." The pressure from the book business, from publishers, was less at the beginning of his stint than it is now.

"I don't think in those days they ever thought we [regional and local newspaper book reviewers] were a very important element in selling their books. They *couldn't* have!" But the times have changed. "Now there is a tremendous pressure to review pop books to an extent not present thirty years ago."

In any case, the key to a worthwhile book page or section lies in the quality of the reviews and the people who write them. Davis considers himself lucky. "Louis Rubin had left me a considerable number of reviewers. And I added to them or replaced them as they dropped out." He recruited from the college faculties all over the Commonwealth of Virginia. He sent them books and asked them for guidance as well: "I encouraged them, that if they knew about a book coming

out, they would call me or write me, and I would get it for them. The result was that we reviewed a lot of university-press books over the years, more than other papers. And that added to my bad reputation with my newspaper people. Meanwhile my more academic readers—the faculty people at nearby Hollins College, for example, it did nothing to pacify them."

He grins in recollection of old battlefields.

Davis adds another comment about book reviewers, one that few working editors will openly admit to or discuss. "As time goes on," he says, "I think there is clearly a principle of diminishing returns in reviewing. The quality may go up for a while, as the person learns to write six hundred words effectively. But then either they become so mechanical that they're not any good in the long haul. These are the old whores, whose bylines we all see, who review year in and year out. That happens. And I saw it happen to some people who had reviewed regularly for me. Their boredom showed. . . .

"To keep a book section or book page you have to have a constant infusion of new reviewers. Because they get tired, they get bored, they get uninterested. They begin to slip not only in the quality of what they do, but also they become less dependable about returning copy. That's a routine problem that affects the quality of book reviewing in an invisible way. The other side is what happens to the person who is making the decisions. Which in most cases is a one-person decision process. They had better be very good, or the results will show almost at once. They also have to have intuition; they have to have some kind of gestalt in their heads about what's coming out and what's ahead and what is this in the total picture.

"Book editors get tired. I am not going to pretend that I kept my level of sharpness. I kept my conscious level of commitment up to the last page I put out, but I think I got jaded. I think, finally, I saw too many books. You know how I knew this was true? When I stopped wanting to take them home every week. I realized I didn't want most of those books. Then it began to dawn on me—I was worn out with it.

"I wish I had quit five years sooner. Twenty years is too long. . . ."

It is an easy move to begin to talk about how things have changed in the world of book reviewing in America. What does he perceive as happening now? Are we doing better or worse?

"I think I'm reasonably objective about what they are doing and how they are doing it. For example, the *New York Times Book Review* is very good-looking. It is mechanically much more orderly than it was thirty years ago. But the quantity of books reviewed has declined. The new type systems take up much more space, and then they have added so many more pictures. They have also added essays and charts and a lot of art. And the result is that they don't review as many books as they once did.

"And the *Los Angeles Times* is pretty good. But I don't have the feeling there's any consensus across the country in newspaper journalism that book reviewing is very good. It's all spotty. It's all dependent on strong local bookstores providing some kind of constituency or else an editor who doesn't give a damn whether this is popular or not. Someone who believes that one of the functions of journalism is to do this. You can't predict what you are going to see these days. It all depends on the support of the paper's management and on the type of person who takes on the job of being book editor."

Asked to be a little more specific, albeit in a general way, as to what he has noticed over the last few years, he speaks first of the book pages and sections of some of the area newspapers. He feels that the quality at the *Charlotte Observer* has declined and concludes that the Richmond papers "don't do very well." On the other hand, both Greensboro and Raleigh are doing well and getting better. "Raleigh has two facing pages, and they pay their reviewers well–as well as the *New York Times Book Review*."

What about the magazines?

"I think the whole magazine reviewing thing has gone to pot, with the possible exception of the *New Yorker*. Magazine reviewing is certainly not as important as it was in the late nineteenth century or even the 1920s and 1930s. They just don't have the weight they once had.

"Some of the best reviews are in the quarter-lies these days, and they are reviewing more popular books than they once did. He cites for particular praise the *Sewanee Review* and the *Virginia Quarterly Review*, adding that the *Sewanee* gave his most recent book an excellent and favorable review.

"Did it help the book?" I ask.

He laughs. "It helped my ego."

"You know," he continues, "I think one of the things we are overlooking here is something that has happened in the time I have been paying systematic attention to book reviewing. And that is the rise of the sort of celebrity author. We had Hemingway before that, yes. But this has all happened in the past few years because of television. But it is, of course, fed back to the book publishing industry. And it is fed back to the book pages, which often want to reflect this. I don't think this was anywhere near as serious a factor when I was still working. Publishers did not put the hype on books that they now do routinely. They send out elaborate press kits and so forth. The only writer I remember from the 1960s for whom they did anything like this was James Michener.... They have gotten better about things like that. But none of it seems to mean anything. Does it prove they take book reviewing seriously? The publishers evidently regard book-page space as having some kind of value."

Is it, I ask him, that the publishers have become better organized and efficient about promoting their books, getting them out to the appropriate places? He is not so sure about that. "When I quit the book page and passed it on to the present editor, Mike Mayo," Davis tells me, "I sent out a letter to all the publishers informing them of this change. About half a dozen major publishers still regularly send me review copies of their books. I get fifty or sixty books a month this way, after all this time, in Fincastle. Does this prove they are so indifferent they can't even clean up their mailing lists?"

The Profession of Authorship: *Scribblers for Bread*

George Greenfield

George Greenfield is the author of three novels and has recently retired as managing director of the John Farquharson literary agency in London. His Scribblers for Bread: Aspects of the English Novel Since 1945 *(New York: Norton, 1989) is one of the few key current books on the profession of fiction writing—and the only one by a publishing insider. In* Scribblers for Bread *he examines the ways in which novelists' work is influenced by the conditions of publishing and marketing. Publication is the essential act of authorship: a writer's career and his words are inevitably shaped by the ways his books reach readers—or do not reach them. The following excerpt is taken from the chapter "Once upon a future time."*

In the calendar year 1986, 6,002 novels were published, of which 2,806 were reprints or new editions and 288 were translations of foreign novels. In other words, that year 2,908 new novels were published in Britain, several hundred of which were of American origin. Probably 150—at the most 350—were first novels by British authors. Yet I have estimated . . . that at any given time the typescripts of up to 6,000 unpublished British novels may be circulating on a doomed path between one London publishing house and another.

At least half of that multitude—and I write from sad and prolonged experience—are wholly unpublishable. A bricklayer learns his trade before he begins to lay the bricks that will become the wall of a house. An accountant, a doctor or a lawyer has to study and pass professional exams before he can earn his living. But many people who have not really mastered the rudiments of English grammar, let alone the subtleties of dialogue or even the formation of a paragraph, believe that because English is their native language, they are qualified to compete with the master story-tellers of their generation.

Even so, when one has discounted the unpublishable and the derivative and the banal, though competently written, there could well be several hundred unpublished novels in any one year that in happier circumstances could have been published—and with at least modest success. Yet what can happen to all those 'regretful rejections', to use Tom Rosenthal's words, apart from leaving them to moulder in a bottom drawer? One answer is a form of *samizdat* publication. As Q. D. Leavis said in an essay, published in 1980, 'We may well see a return to the primitive circulation of manuscripts among a select company'. There are several photocopying bureaus in London and other main centres—one of the most important being Legastat off Chancery Lane in London—which have sophisticated Xerox and collating machines, 'perfect' binding and jacketing facilities. Such a firm can produce a few hundred or more copies of a book (from a cleanly typed script) at prices well below normal printing charges. Publishers always say—and with reason—that it does not pay them to print fewer than 1,500 copies and their preferred first printing would be twice that number. By the time orthodox printing machines have been made ready and the setting process carried out, the costs are indeed considerable. (In the future, authors using word processors compatible with computer-typesetting will cut costs through eliminating the setting process.) The author whose novel has been narrowly rejected by perhaps half a dozen publishers but who is determined to give his work a wider circulation would do well to investigate the photocopying bureaus; as indeed would publishers, who often let a book go out of print because there are only a few 'dues' on the order book. The novelist who becomes his own publisher still has to cope with the problems of storage, subscribing, selling, packing and distributing copies of his book—but at least he can always give it away to his family and friends or supply copies to the local bookshop on a sale or return basis. After all, as George Bernard Shaw said in 1895:

> All that is necessary in the production of a book is an author and a bookseller, without any intermediate parasite.

The advent of reasonably cheap photocopying and binding has, nearly a century later, brought his words that much closer to reality.

There has been a great change in the status of authors since the war. Successful writers have always been in demand and held in respect by their publishers but, particularly in the past twenty-five years authors of any potential are liable to be treated more favourably by publishers than ever before. This is partly thanks to the efforts of professional bodies like the Society of Authors and the Writers' Guild, partly due to the pressure of agents and perhaps largely due to the rise of conglomerates with greater funds that lead to greater demand and an inadequate supply of the very talented and successful writers—talent and success are not necessarily synonymous. One can hardly imagine a publisher today repeating, even as a joke, Michael Joseph's 1950s remark, 'Authors are easy to get on with if you are fond of children'. In the future, we are bound to see greater efforts made by publishers to make their authors feel part of 'the family'. It is good business as well as good sense.

Bloomsbury has already made a start through its Authors' Trust, whereby five per cent of the issued share capital has been set aside; the trust's shares are likely to be sold when the institutional investors realise their shareholdings and the resulting cash will be shared out between qualified authors on a title by title basis. This appears to be a once-and-for-all payout but it is an important step which shows that one publishing house at least recognises that its success depends on authors who deserve to share financially, if modestly, in the company's fortunes.

It may be possible for publicly quoted publishing houses to move a step further. For a very established author, an advance of £250,000 on his next book—or £350,000 or even £500,000—is often just a status symbol; he doesn't actually *need* the money and, if he pays United Kingdom taxes, will still lose a large chunk of it to the Revenue. An author takes a large advance for one (or more) of four main reasons: because his agent thinks it will keep the publisher 'on his toes'; because he has heard on the grapevine that his rivals A and B get somewhat less and he wants to feel one up on them; because it gives him a feeling of power and gratification that his publisher thinks his new book is worth that immense sum; and because he may happen to need the money.

It would make considerable sense for the publisher, instead of his paying out, say,

£300,000 in instalments, to offer that author an advance of £150,000 plus a shareholding in the company of the same amount. The shares would rank for dividends and, if the publishing house prospers, could eventually be sold on the market for a capital gain. If the book earns out its actual advance and the initial value of the shareholding, royalties and other payments in excess would be paid out in the normal way.

The scheme would require to be approved by the Inland Revenue and the author might have to pay earned income tax on his shareholding even though he had not had access to the funds. There is also the argument that, if ten or more very successful authors took part in the scheme and each over a period produced six or more books, the company might find itself with a substantial minority shareholding in the hands of a few powerful authors. That would present no great problem to a group like Reed International or Pearson or Collins—and it is very unlikely that top authors would ever band together for some power ploy over the company. The great advantage, both actual and psychological, is that the method would tie the author far more closely to the publishing house than any contractual option could achieve and it would save the house a considerable sum through paying out smaller advances.

One other ingenious plan, which is already under way and which may produce revolutionary results in the future shape and scope of the larger publishing companies, is the creation of Tim Hill of Hill & Company, Publishers, in Boston.* Having observed how the growth of television in the United States and the consequent drop in cinema attendances broke up the old Hollywood studio monopoly and gave rise to the independent producer, whose overheads were low and who assembled a new 'creative' team for each picture he made, Tim Hill decided to apply the same techniques to the top end of book publishing—initially in the USA. In his own analysis,

From an author's viewpoint, the constancy of working relationships is threatened by editors changing houses, managements changing policies, or companies changing ownership. The objectives of publishing house and author may no longer coincide. In many respects each book com-

*I must register an interest by declaring that I act as a part-time consultant in the United Kingdom to Hill & Company.

petes for attention and resources with every other book on a publisher's list. While the major author is unlikely to be subordinated to other authors, inevitably he is in the position of subsidising losses. More importantly, he may involuntarily underwrite the institution's excessive overhead or growth objectives.

. . . Major authors represent a far higher percentage of total sales than in the past. Publishers pay large royalty advances because they need the disproportionate contributions to overhead and/or profit represented by bestselling books.

The Hill answer is to have on call a freelance team of experienced editors, designers, typographers, advertising and publicity experts and marketing executives. An individual programme is worked out with each author and every step is subject to the author's approval. If, for example, the author has a long-standing association with an editor he respects and that editor is able to undertake freelance work, he will be brought on to the team. The author is shown all the costings related to his book including a *fixed* percentage of sales to cover Hill & Company's overheads. So the quality of paper, the typeface, the design, the binding, the dust-jacket and the published price are all agreed by the author before the book appears. The distribution, warehousing and invoicing can either be carried out by arrangement with the author's previous regular publisher or by a major house suggested by Hill & Company.

The plan strikes at the soft underbelly of the current publishing structure. The present practice is to set a published price which, allowing for production costs and the author's advance/royalties at one end and sales discounts at the other, will ideally leave a gross profit margin of about 50-55 per cent on every copy sold. Out of this must come a share of the publisher's overheads–rent, rates (soon to be a poll tax), heat, light, salaries etc, leaving something like 10 to 15 per cent pretax profit on the turnover achieved. But, as I demonstrated in the earlier chapter, 'The Crunch',–and as Mr. Hill shows in his analysis–the big-selling author is making a surplus that goes not to him, but to defray the publisher's overheads and to support unsuccessful authors on the same list. Hill & Company, along with most major authors, would agree that profits from bestselling books should help support less commercial publishing–to a *reasonable* extent. As so often with publishing contracts, the word 'reasonable' is susceptible to opposing interpreta-

tions, depending on whether one is wearing the publisher's or the successful author's hat.

In order to maintain his profit margin, the publisher has to ensure that the big author does not receive too high a royalty, although the usual excuse is the impact of inflation. Up to the mid-1950s, a royalty of 25 per cent of the published price was paid to the few top sellers, while 20 per cent was fairly common. Today, 15 per cent would be considered the bestseller's rate, while 171/2 per cent would be exceptional.

Thus, if one takes a major novel, published in New York at $18.95 and selling 300,000 copies, under the normal publishing procedure with a flat 15 per cent royalty, the author would earn $852,750. Under the Hill plan, he would get all the earnings after the fixed editorial fee, the production costs, a modest percentage profit and overhead figure for the publisher and promotion costs had first been deducted. His 'take' would then amount to $1,550,391–the equivalent of a 27 per cent royalty. The marketing of subsidiary rights, book club and paperback, in the main would not be affected and the author would receive his normal share of proceeds.

One important 'plank' in the Hill programme is that after ten years from first publication, all rights automatically revert to the author. This allows a paperback house, publishing one year after the initial hardcover edition, a nine-year licence, which is usually adequate. It avoids that perennial problem and complaint for writers that a publisher who undertakes a licence for the duration of copyright, provided he keeps the book minimally in print in one form or another, can retain the rights and make little effort to exploit them except through a Micawberish aspiration that something may come along–a film, a television series, sudden notoriety for the author–to reawaken the public interest. For some years now, the Writers' Guild has been pressing hard on this point in their Minimum Terms Agreement; it is significant that a new publisher, far from resisting, is in fact strongly advocating that same point in his publishing plan.

Significantly, it is named the Hill & Company Author Partnership Program. The key word is 'partnership'. Even the most considerate and author-favouring houses do often, perhaps subconsciously, treat their authors as not quite grown up enough to be told the inner secrets. Royalty statements show the numbers of copies sold at home and abroad but only a very few reveal the initial printings and almost none show discounts to the trade. Often, such details would rebound to the publisher's credit; if, for example, the royalty statement revealed that the publisher had printed 10,000 copies but had only sold 4,000, he would at least get marks from the author for having had initial, if misplaced, confidence in the book's sale appeal.

What of other aspects of the trade between now and the end of the century? When–it is not really a case of *if*–the Hill (or some similar) plan comes into being, the effect on major publishing houses, both in New York and London, will be immense. Publishers, liable to lose their 'milch cows' except for distribution, will need to take rearguard actions or advance their own attractive substitute plans for those fairly rare bestselling authors. They will argue that they cannot afford to seek out and sustain new writing talent unless they have access to the additional gross profit accruing from their top authors. But behind the plaintive cries, they will have to adapt. Faced with the choice of half a loaf or no bread at all, most big publishers will take the half-loaf and feed their lesser authors on crusts.

Bibliographical and Textual Scholarship Since World War II

Joel Myerson
University of South Carolina

The era of bibliographical and textual scholarship since World War II is the Age of Fredson Bowers: nearly all textual and bibliographical work during this period either takes issue with Bowers's findings or builds upon or refines Bowers's studies, as in G. Thomas Tanselle's series of informative essays. The brief, general overview that follows will focus upon the areas of descriptive and enumerative bibliography, the history of the book, and textual editing, discussing some of the major advances made in each field, and the importance of these researches for all scholars.

Some benighted people labor under the misunderstanding that bibliographers are mere list makers. The bibliographies done before World War II have unfortunately reinforced that view, as do some modern bibliographies. Early primary or descriptive bibliographies were, for the most part, very unsophisticated. Full bibliographical description consisted of entries such as "8 vo., brown cloth, 136 pages." These early bibliographers were usually book dealers or book collectors, and to them, stating that they had the work in their catalog or their possession was more important than fully describing it. Manuscripts, incunables, and Renaissance texts were described in a more sophisticated manner than were nineteenth-century texts, which were, after all, merely the books of the previous generation. The publication of Bowers's *Principles of Bibliographical Description* in 1949 changed all that. Bowers's great contribution was to bring order to chaos, to provide a terminology and a taxonomy for describing all the parts of the physical object we call a book. Inherent in Bowers's study was the assumption that books consist of more than paper and binding; that is, they also contain, through letterform reproduction, the text of a work of art. Descriptive bibliography, then, helped to establish variant forms of the text, and made it possible for a generation of textual editors to do their work.

Descriptive bibliography also helps us to understand the history of printing, from stop-press corrections in Renaissance printing shops to such modern concepts as desk-top publishing. Examinations of individual cases provide evidence for large-scale assumptions. For example, the discovery of single copies of books composed of American sheets with a British cancel title leaf, serving as deposit copies in British libraries, led to new information about how the copyright laws worked in the early part of this century, and how American publishers tried to secure protection for their works in Britain. Similarly, the examination of works by American authors that consisted of American sheets with a cancel Canadian title leaf showed another way in which British copyright was established–namely, by the author being on Commonwealth soil on the day a book was officially published–and helped to explain why authors such as Mark Twain took frequent short trips into Canada.

As descriptive bibliographies became more sophisticated, they became a type of biography of their subject. Series such as the Soho Bibliographies, the Pittsburgh Series in Bibliography, and the Bibliographical Society of the University of Virginia bibliographies all present comprehensive histories of authors' publishing careers. In these works readers may find information about authors' literary reputations, as measured by the sales of their books; authors' incomes from their books, or, to use William Charvat's phrase, their contributions to the profession of authorship; the popularity of individual works, as measured by separate publications and reprintings of them; the popularity of authors' works outside of their native countries; and the textual histories of authors' works. Descriptive bibliographies, then, provide not only information about individual books but also large-scale biblio-biographies of their subjects.

Enumerative or secondary bibliographies have also emerged as valuable scholarly tools. Even bad bibliographies–those that merely Xerox sources and conflate the results–save us the time and expense of doing it ourselves. But good secondary bibliographies do much more. A comprehensive, annotated, chronologically arranged secondary bibliography is another type of biblio-biography. In it, we can see the peaks and valleys of authors' literary reputations; the reaction of their contemporaries to them; the development of scholarship on them; and their relative importance, as measured by the number of critical articles and books written about them. Good bibliographies point us to what studies are significant, and–just as important–to those works we should avoid. Another version of the secondary bibliography, the bibliographical essay, provides a similar evaluative service, and the success of this genre can be seen in the MLA series on Reviews of Research and Criticism, as well as in the long-

running and essential, *American Literary Scholarship*. The days when an individual scholar could keep up with the scholarship in his or her field by subscribing to a few journals and reading the annual MLA bibliography are long gone. Secondary bibliographies are essential, and we should all thank their compilers; not only have they done our legwork for us, the best of them contribute original works of scholarship.

The sophistication shown in recent bibliographical scholarship has had an impact upon the history of the book. To give a simple example, the study of seventeenth- and eighteenth-century watermarks has made it possible to say where the paper used in printing a particular book came from, and this information makes possible new conclusions about commercial trading patterns between England and the Continent during this period.

Historians of the book are interdisciplinary in nature, combining the best of literary, historical, bibliographical, and cultural scholarship. They recognize that a book is more than a physical object, that it is also a cultural artifact that may be used for broader purposes. The introduction of moveable type served not only to put many manuscript copyists out of work, it made possible the distribution of books to a wider audience. The printed word–and all that it embodied for the potential of political and cultural change–was now available to the masses. Knowledge was power, and literacy became a means of sharing that power.

With the spread of literacy came a dramatic change in the profession of authorship. Through as late a period as the early nineteenth century, authors as a rule were gentlemen who wrote for each other. For example, a gentleman wishing to publish his epic poem written upon the occasion of the death of his favorite hunting dog would approach his gentlemen friends to subscribe for the edition–in effect, getting them to pay in advance for a copy of the book. With these monies, the author paid the printer and the book was published and distributed to the author's friends. As literacy spread, the audience for literature became more varied. What was once a small audience of friends from the same social class who shared similar concerns and beliefs turned into a large and multifaceted audience, which became known as the marketplace. Writing became a commercial venture, and success was measured by the number of copies that a work sold. All this research has resulted in exciting new studies of American writers, such as David Reynolds's *Beneath the American Renaissance* (1988) and Cathy Davidson's *Revolution and the Word* (1986). Authors can no longer be viewed as writing in isolation, but, rather, their works must be judged as products of an interaction between the creative process and the economic necessities of making a living.

The advances made by descriptive bibliographers soon helped to revolutionize the field of textual editing. Before World War II, a good deal of work had been done on Renaissance literary texts, but practically none on American ones. Typical of statements of textual policy was this one, from F. B. Sanborn's 1917 life of Henry David Thoreau: "Mr. Sanborn was not a slavish quoter, and . . . he used the privilege of an editor who is thoroughly familiar with his author's subjects and habits of thought to rearrange paragraphs, to omit here, [and] to make slight interpolations there." If, therefore, the reader finds occasional discrepancies between Sanborn's texts and earlier ones, "he is not to set them down to carelessness, but is rather to thank Mr. Sanborn for making these passages more orderly and more readable."

The lines of debate over editorial policies and procedures were drawn early in the century, between those who wanted all-encompassing rules and those who wished for each case to be treated on its own merits within a general conceptual framework. The best spokesman for the latter position was A. E. Housman, who compared the editor to a dog chasing fleas: "If a dog hunted for fleas on mathematical principles, basing his researches on statistics of area and population, he would never catch a flea except by accident. They require to be treated as individuals. . . . If a dog is to hunt for fleas successfully he must be quick and he must be sensitive. It is no good for a rhinoceros to hunt for fleas; he does not know where they are, and could not catch them if he did." On the other side were critics such as R. B. McKerrow, who argued in his 1939 *Prologomena to the Oxford Shakespeare* that whatever form of the text seems to embody the author's last intentions should be chosen *as a whole* as the base or copy-text. In other words, the latest edition in an author's lifetime over which he or she had control was to be used as the basis for any modern edition.

In his landmark 1949 paper, "The Rationale of Copy-Text," Sir W. W. Greg opposed what he called "the tyranny of copy-text," caused by McKerrow's insistence on using a single form of the text in its entirety. Greg argued, as a "practi-cal" rather than "philosophical" matter, that we need to "draw a distinction between the significant, or as I shall call them 'substantive,' readings of the text, those namely that affect the author's meaning or the essence of his expression, and others, such in general as spelling, punctuation, word-division, and the like, affecting mainly its formal presentation, which may be regarded as the accidents, or as I shall call them 'accidentals,' of the text." Accordingly, Greg proposed that the earliest form of a text, being closest to the author's manuscript, should be used as copy-text. Moreover, since printers imposed a publisher's house styling on the manuscript when preparing it for publication, the authority for accidentals (usually punctuation) would be, in the lack of a manuscript, the copy-text readings, since later editions invariably introduce even more changes in house styling. But in the case of substantive variants (usually changes in wording), emendations to the copy-text could be made if the editor could demonstrate that such changes were done by the author.

In essence, Greg's rationale provided editors with a general rule for choosing among variants: for accidentals, the copy-text reading would nearly always be followed, on the ground that authors rarely paid as much attention to publishers' styling of their punctuation as they did to changes in their wording, especially in later, revised editions; for substantives, variants that were indifferent, or unprovable as being by the author, would be rejected in favor of the copy-text readings, while changes that could be shown to be the author's were adopted. The result of applying Greg's rationale was that editors produced an eclectic text. Such a text, based on a copy-text or form of the text closest to the manuscript, was one that had never existed before, since it introduced substantive readings from later printings or editions, as well as corrected obvious typographical errors in the copy-text.

The main proponent of Greg's theory has been Fredson Bowers, in his editions of Renaissance and American texts, in numerous published works of his own, and in his editorship of *Studies in Bibliography*. Later, G. Thomas Tanselle would extend Bowers's arguments into other areas, as well as proposing editorial procedures of his own.

Greg's rationale appeared at a propitious historical moment. The rise of New Criticism (that is, the "old" New Criticism), with its emphasis upon the text itself, rather than any biographical or historical influences that may have been exerted upon it, caused a new emphasis to be placed upon the importance of having accurate texts. In 1963 the Center for Editions of American Authors (CEAA) was formed, and in 1967 it published a series of guidelines called *Statement of Editorial Principles*, which clearly reflected the influence of the Greg-Bowers school of copy-text editing. The CEAA received NEH funding from 1966 to 1976, during which period it approved over 140 volumes. In 1976 the MLA created the Committee on Scholarly Editions (CSE), which replaced the CEAA.

Greg's rationale was so simple in its statement of goals, and so nonprescriptive in its setting forth of them, that it soon came under attack. Some felt that Greg's rationale was applied in a monolithic fashion by the CEAA and the CSE, which were seen as purveyors of the only "correct" way to edit. In point of fact, this perception was incorrect, since both groups have approved editions prepared according to non-Gregian principles that were appropriate to that particular work.

There are two other major areas of textual debate since World War II that have produced interesting discussions: editions of unpublished manuscripts and the question of authorial intention.

Because Greg's rationale dealt only with editions of printed texts, there were few guides for the editors of unpublished manuscript texts—such as letters, journals, and diaries—to follow. Clearly, a different policy would need to be employed for materials never intended for publication. One procedure—quickly rejected—was that employed by historical editors, who presented clear texts that were modernized for the convenience of readers. These editions did not use editorial symbols in their texts, and they expanded abbreviations, corrected misspellings, and changed earlier punctuation practices to conform with twentieth-century usages. Most literary editors felt that all these changes resulted in unreliable texts, and they searched for ways to reproduce exactly what the author wrote. Type-facsimiles were one solution, but a little-used one due to the high costs of printing them. Photo-facsimiles were also expensive to produce and often failed to show all the features of the manuscript, such as erasures or faint pencil writing. What evolved was the so-called genetic-text transcription, modeled upon the Hayford-Sealts edition of Herman Melville's *Billy Budd*. Most notably practiced in the edition of

Ralph Waldo Emerson's *Journals and Miscellaneous Notebooks*, it used editorial symbols within the text to convey how that text was inscribed; for example, angle brackets surrounded canceled material and up-and-down arrows surrounded inserted material.

This mode of editing received a deathblow when Lewis Mumford reviewed the Emerson edition in the January 1968 *New York Review of Books* under the title "Emerson Behind Barbed Wire" and complained that the edition was unreadable because of what he felt were intrusive editorial symbols. The image Mumford presented of poor Waldo cringing behind a barbed-wire fence, which separated him from his readers, while goon squads of editors hovered above in helicopters to keep him imprisoned, stuck permanently in scholars' minds. Even though the CEAA published a response to Mumford, few editors were willing to produce editions using genetic-text transcriptions. Nearly all editions of letters and journals today employ a clear text with information about cancellations, insertions, and other revisions described separately in editorial apparatus.

The question of authorial intention is currently uppermost in most scholarly discussions of textual editing. Greg's rationale developed from a study of Renaissance printing techniques, when the author's manuscript had nearly always been lost. But nineteenth- and twentieth-century authors' working and printer's copy manuscripts are often extant, giving editors many more forms of the text to choose among as their copy-text. The question to be answered is: At what point does the author consider his text to be finished? The answer is important, since that form of the text would usually be chosen as copy-text. Most editors, following Greg's rationale, have chosen the finished form of the manuscript as copy-text, and rejected house styling of accidentals. Indeed, if the printer's copy manuscript is lost, and only working drafts exist, these editors would usually choose the first printed edition as copy-text and emend back to the working draft manuscripts for accidentals.

The concept of authorial intention has come under attack from editors such as Jerome McGann, who argue that, since texts are produced within a social environment, the concept of authorial intention (and its attendant emphasis upon the manuscript as copy-text) is murky at best. To these editors, the work of art is produced by the author in concert with his friends, publisher, editor, copy editor, compositor, and printer. To simplify a complicated argument, McGann feels that any changes not specifically rejected by the author were implicitly accepted. Thus, house styling, rejected by Greg's rationale, would be accepted by McGann as something which the author expected to happen in the normal course of producing a printed text. This view has been opposed by Tanselle, who, in his recent *A Rationale of Textual Criticism*, has written: "If we grant that authors have intentions and therefore that the intentions of past authors are historical facts, we require no further justification for the attempt to recover those intentions and to reconstruct texts reflecting them, whatever our chances of success may be. . . . Any so-called intention that is actually an expectation about what will be done to the text by others can have no bearing on the reconstruction of an authorially intended text." The debate continues.

Another critic of Greg's, Hershel Parker, has argued that authors often revise in such a way as to produce less satisfactory works of art than were present in the text's original readings; therefore, the editor should ignore those later revisions that are aesthetically inferior to the earlier readings rejected by the author. Again, Tanselle disagrees: "As long as our concern is with au-

thors and their intentions, we cannot reject revisions made by authors simply because we consider them misguided, for we are then placing ourselves, not the authors, at the center of attention." Here, too, the debate continues.

When I began preparing this survey, I was struck by how puzzling it would be to a now-deceased pre–World War II scholar if he or she could read it. After all, bibliographical and textual scholarship *was* scholarship before World War II. I am sure that if any of these scholars were alive today, they would applaud the new critical approaches that extend our knowledge of authors and their times. I am equally sure that their response to the recently imported continental critics and the newfound indeterminacy of texts would be to quote from Luke: "Heaven and earth shall pass away; but my words shall not pass away."

An earlier version of this essay was presented at the general American Literature session at the Modern Language Association convention in Washington, 28 December 1989.

The Bicentennial of James Fenimore Cooper: An International Celebration

George A. Test
State University of New York College at Oneonta

From Moscow to Scarsdale, from Zurich to Cooperstown, scholars, journalists, James Fenimore Cooper enthusiasts, and schoolchildren of all ages celebrated the birth of the creator of Leatherstocking with lectures, concerts, displays, commemorative stamps, contests, newspaper articles, radio and television broadcasts, books, and other publications. The various observances suggest that America's first internationally recognized writer (1789-1851) is still admired and indeed popular around the world.

The most striking celebration of the bicentennial was sponsored by the Soviet Union, which issued commemorative stamps. In August a fifteen-kopeck stamp bearing the John Neagle portrait of Cooper appeared, followed in November by five different twenty-kopeck stamps, each with a scene from one of the Leatherstocking tales.

In the German-speaking world Cooper's bicentennial was celebrated with newspaper articles, radio broadcasts, and television features. On Cooper's birthday, 15 September, the *Neue Zurcher Zeitung* of Zurich, Switzerland, ran an article by Romeo Giger under the heading "Founder of the American Myth" that characterized Cooper as "the philosopher of the wilderness" and the creator of a myth that is an integral part of the culture of the United States. In Austria a week earlier, the *Vienna Neues Tageblatt* ran an illustrated two-page article headed "Is Leatherstocking Dead?," which noted that Cooper's novels are disappearing from the shelves of literature for the young.

West German newspapers did their share for the bicentennial as well. Under the headline "Immortal Leatherstocking," the *Main Echo*, a Frankfurt-area regional newspaper, included a short biography of Cooper and a discussion of Cooper's style and the quality of German translations, which date mainly from the 1930s (the bicentennial prompted Diogenes Verlag to publish new translations in time for the Christmas holiday trade). *Allgemeinen Zeitung*, also of Frankfurt,

ran a lengthy article by Thomas Steinfeld that had originated as a thirty-minute broadcast on Radio Bremen (10 September). The newspaper version was headlined with a paraphrase of Goethe's quotation "Noble be the Trapper, Helpful and Good"; the radio broadcast was entitled "James Fenimore Cooper: The Well-Disliked Critic of his Country." Steinfeld noted that the bicentennial of Cooper was overshadowed by the fiftieth anniversary of the National Baseball Hall of Fame in Cooperstown and suggested that Cooper may be more widely read in Germany, Russia, and China than in his native country. Steinfeld also emphasized Cooper's efforts to mediate between the cultures of America and Europe and between the diverse cultures of America itself.

The most thorough analysis of Cooper's life and works appeared in the weekend edition preceding Cooper's birthday in the Hannover *Allgemeinen Zeitung* under the headline "A Pathfinder with a Pen." Citing the enthusiasm of Balzac and Goethe for Cooper, Heiko Postma also discussed the American reaction to the Chainbearer trilogy and Cooper's troubles with the press and libel suits. The article stressed Cooper's masterly painting of scenery, the thoroughness of his research in geographical details, and his realistic depiction of Indians. The article included a large portrait of Cooper and drawings from the well-known edition of Cooper's works illustrated by Felix Darley. A series of television presentations also appeared in West Germany in August and September, ranging from fifteen-minute features (one by Westdeutcher Rundfunk on 13 September) to a forty-five-minute feature by Hessischer Rundfunk that included material shot in Cooperstown by a West German TV crew.

Elsewhere outside the United States a special issue of the *Canadian Review of American Studies* was devoted to Cooper. Edited by Ernest Redekop of the University of Western Ontario, it includes articles by Donald Ringe, Thomas Philbrick, and Kay House, as well as several by Ca-

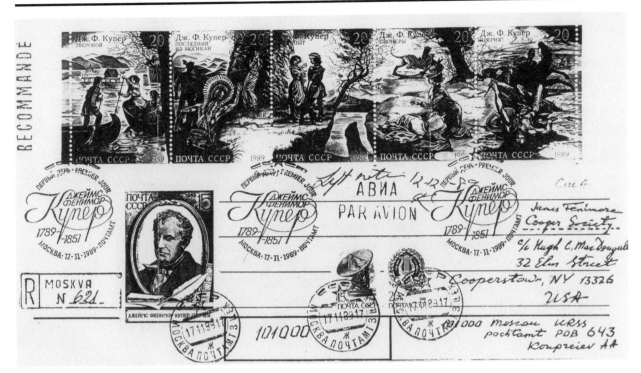

First day cover for stamps issued by the Soviet postal service to commemorate the bicentennial of Cooper's birth

nadian contributors, including Geoffry Rans and Ian Steele, a historian whose expertise is *The Last of the Mohicans* (1826).

In the United States the most extensive celebration of the bicentennial outside of New York State was sponsored by the Burlington County (New Jersey) Historical Society, which is housed in the Cooper birthplace. Beginning in March the society held an essay contest for junior and senior high school students on the topic "Why May James Fenimore Cooper be Considered the First American Writer?" In June, Robert Thompson, secretary of the Burlington Historical Commission, delivered a slide program on Cooper's Burlington. Also beginning in June there was an exhibit of an edition of Cooper's works illustrated by T. Chalkley Matlack, a Burlington County artist.

The week of Cooper's birth date was a busy one for the Burlington society. On the fifteenth there was a reception for charter members of the James Fenimore Cooper Fellows, special contributors to the historical society. The following day was dedicated to Cooper himself, including talks on his life and times. In addition Michael Rockland, chairman of the Department of American Studies at Rutgers University, spoke on "Palefaces and Indians: James Fenimore Cooper's Ideas about Civilization and Barbarism," and

Jane Brown, professor of English at Trenton State College, spoke on the European influence of Cooper's works. Carl Prince, professor of English at New York University, also spoke. On the seventeenth the Powhatan Renape Nation erected teepees and provided Iroquois Indian dancers for an open house in the afternoon.

Beginning with the school year in September Lynne Sloane, a professional storyteller, visited grade-school classrooms to relate one of the Leatherstocking tales and tell children about Cooper. In October the society sponsored a three-day bus trip to Cooperstown. Burlington Historical Society activities were supported and assisted by various state and local historical societies, state and local government agencies, the local newspaper, and the Powhatan Renape Nation.

One further celebration outside New York State was held at Westminster College in New Wilmington, Pennsylvania. Cooper scholar George Bleasby, emeritus professor of English, set up an extensive display in the McGill Library devoted to maps, photographs, portraits, and clippings of articles on Cooper, his Otsego Lake novels, and Cooperstown.

Of course, the greatest concentration of ceremonies was in New York State. The Scarsdale Historical Society capitalized on Cooper's stay in Scarsdale after he married native resident Susan

Delancey, as well as on the fact that *The Spy* (1821) is set in Westchester County. The society mounted an exhibition that ran from April through October and consisted of portraits, memorabilia, and photographs all related to Cooper and his connections with the area. Cooper's birthday was observed with a celebration on the grounds of the society near a monument devoted to *The Spy* as well as a talk on Cooper by C. Edwin Linville, a trustee of the society and a former history teacher.

Cooperstown was of course the center of a great deal of activity during the bicentennial year. The 1989 "I Love New York" Summer Festival tourism campaign sponsored by New York State was devoted in part to the bicentennial. (It was linked with the fiftieth anniversary of the National Baseball Hall of Fame.)

The New York State Historical Association (NYSHA), whose headquarters is in Cooperstown, sponsored a variety of activities aimed at everyone from grade-school children to Elderhostel participants. A centerpiece of NYSHA's efforts on behalf of the bicentennial was a display in its main building, the Fenimore House, of paintings from its excellent collection of nineteenth-century art. Among the works on display were Thomas Cole's *Last of the Mohicans* (1827), Tompkins H. Matteson's *The Turkey Shoot* (1857), John Wesley Jarvis's famous portrait of Cooper (c. 1822), and P. J. David d'Angers's marble bust commissioned by Cooper in 1828. The NYSHA library presented three displays, two in the main lobby prepared by Adele Johnson of the library staff and a third prepared by Robert Engel, a student in the graduate program in history of museum studies of the State University of New York College at Oneonta. The displays in the lobby were devoted to Cooper as a writer, one featuring copies of nearly all his works, fiction and nonfiction, the other dealing with Cooper as author-publisher and as foreign author, with manuscripts and foreign editions on display. The third display dealt with the Leatherstocking novels.

Numerous functions sponsored by NYSHA involved children. Wayne Wright, technical services librarian, pursued his hobby of storyteller, especially of *The Pioneers* (1823), speaking to schoolchildren and teachers in the guise of Natty Bumppo. Also active with similar groups were Helen Beckwith, librarian, and Tina Morris, art teacher, at the Greater Plains Elementary School in Oneonta, New York. Beckwith and Morris

served as guides for a boat tour of Lake Otsego sites associated with Cooper's novels. The tour was arranged for high-school students who are junior members of NYSHA and their teachers at their annual conference. Beckwith and Morris also conducted a walking tour of Cooperstown and presented a program entitled "James Fenimore Cooper: Visionary York Stater." In December they produced a pamphlet, based on their program, for elementary school students. (The pamphlet was published by NYSHA.) At a meeting of librarians of the Otsego-Northern Catskills BOCES (Boards of Cooperative Educational Services) School Library System in March, Beckwith impersonated Cooper as part of a presentation of a successful educational unit for elementary school students.

In addition to the pamphlet mentioned above, NYSHA published several other items. A leaflet by Kenneth Chandler and Randall Schon, students in the museum studies program, is called "James Fenimore Cooper, Pioneer Conservationist" and is directed at seventh and eighth grade social studies teachers across New York State. The most ambitious publication was Hugh Cooke MacDougall's *Cooper's Otsego County*, a 114-page illustrated guide to sites associated with Cooper's life and writings. MacDougall also conducted two Elderhostel sessions in October under the title "The Coopers and Cooperstown." These consisted of three days of lectures, a walking tour of Cooperstown, and visits to the displays in the NYSHA Library. MacDougall also spoke to various groups in the area during the fall and winter regarding the bicentennial.

NYSHA also sponsored an organ recital on 10 September in observance of the bicentennial. The recital was performed on a Howe barrel organ owned at one time by James Fenimore Cooper. His father, Judge William Cooper, the founder of Cooperstown, had purchased it around 1802. The organ has remained in the Cooper family and was restored to playing condition for the bicentennial. A thirty-minute professionally recorded cassette of the organ music has been produced. An article about the organ appeared in the September-October issue of *Heritage*, the NYSHA magazine.

The bicentennial celebration of an important author would not be complete without proclamations by officials and their agencies. The governor of New York, Mario M. Cuomo, declared 15 September James Fenimore Cooper Day. The New York state legislature passed a resolution to

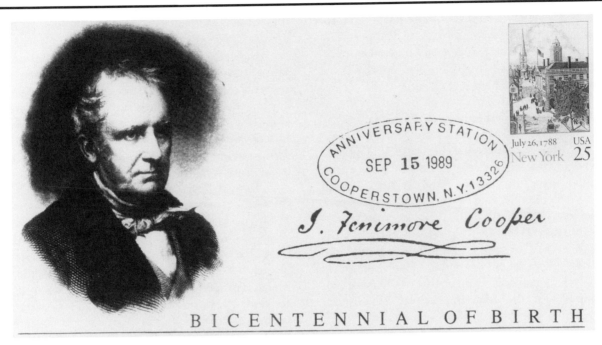

July 26, 1788
New York
USA
25

ANNIVERSARY STATION
SEP 15 1989
COOPERSTOWN, N.Y. 13326

J. Fenimore Cooper

BICENTENNIAL OF BIRTH

Commemorative envelope bearing the well-known portrait of Cooper by John Neagle

the same effect sponsored by James L. Seward, senator from the 50th District. The board of trustees of the Village of Cooperstown went further and declared September James Fenimore Cooper Month. Documents to support these proclamations were presented to Henry S. F. Cooper, great-great-grandson of the writer, at a special ceremony in Christ's Church, Cooperstown, which James Fenimore Cooper had helped remodel in the 1840s. The proclamations by Governor Cuomo and the state legislature were presented by Senator Seward, and the village proclamation was presented by Harold Hollis, the mayor.

Henry Cooper was also presented with a poster of Three-Mile Point Park made by Janet Munru, a local primitive folk artist. The presentation was made by Jane Patrick, chair of Friends of the Park, a local environmental group, who recounted the controversy surrounding the Three-Mile Point Park, Cooper, and the village in the 1830s. In receiving the proclamations and the post, Henry Cooper emphasized the importance of his ancestor as the first American writer to be associated with the environmental movement and recounted how passages of Cooper's novels had been used in a legal brief by opponents of a power line that was to have passed close by Otsego Lake. The line was routed elsewhere. The program in Christ Church, which was attended by more than four hundred people, also included remarks by Daniel Porter, director of

NYSHA; Alan Donovan, president of the State University of New York College at Oneonta, which with NYSHA cosponsored the program; and George A. Test, professor emeritus of the College at Oneonta, who surveyed Cooper's literary output and current reputation.

The ceremony was also the occasion for the announcement of the founding of a James Fenimore Cooper Society to promote the study and appreciation of the writer and his works. Henry Cooper is Honorary Chairman of the group, as was James Franklin Beard (1918-1989), editor of Cooper's journals and until his death in charge of the ongoing republication of Cooper's works by the State University of New York Press. Impetus for the founding of the organization came from Hugh C. MacDougall, who serves as its secretary-treasurer. A newsletter is planned.

Elsewhere on the local scene the United States Post Office in Cooperstown issued a James Fenimore Cooper souvenir cover with a special postal service cancellation dated 15 September bearing Cooper's signature, a 1940 two-cent Cooper commemorative stamp, and a twenty-three-cent Mary Cassett commemorative stamp. The Smithy Pioneer Gallery mounted a summer exhibition of paintings and photographs under the title "Lake Otsego, or the Glimmerglass: James Fenimore Cooper and the Power of Literary Imagery." The display included paintings, nineteenth-century photographs from a collection at NYSHA, as well as contemporary photographs of the lake made famous by Cooper. The Smithy Gallery is in the oldest building in Cooperstown, built in 1786 by Judge Cooper and later owned by the writer for a short time.

The major scholarly recognition of the bicentennial occurred 9-14 July in Oneonta at the State University of New York College with the seventh Cooper conference. Attracting scholars, teachers, students, and readers of the author, the five-day program consisted of lectures, small group discussions, and a tour of Cooperstown and Lake Otsego, the latter conducted by Hugh MacDougall. The following lectures covered various aspects of Cooper's works: "Cooper and the Literary Discovery of the Sea" (Thomas Philbrick, emeritus, University of Pittsburgh); "Cooper and the Idea of History" (Ernest H. Redekop, University of Western Ontario); "Cooper's Presence in Australian Culture" (Richard Pascal, Australian National University); "The Two Chronologies of Leatherstocking" (Richard Morton, McMaster University); *"The Crater"* (John Hales, Fresno State University); "Cooper's 'Course of Empire': Mountains and the Rise and Fall of American Civilization in *The Last of the Mohicans, The Spy* and *The Pioneers*" (Ian Marshall, Penn State University at Altoona); and "Cooper's Problematic Pilot: 'Unrighteous Ambition' in a Patriotic Cause" (Donald Darnell, University of North Carolina at Greensboro).

Two lectures assessed Cooper at two hundred: "Cooper's Status and Stature Now" (Kay Seymour House, emeritus, University of San Francisco) and "Cooper Today: A Partisan View" (Donald A. Ringe, University of Kentucky). As to Cooper's critical status, especially in the United States, House concluded that Cooper is still "very visible on the literary scene, but his work is being mined largely for examples to prove one thesis or another. . . . His fiction seems to be provocative, even indispensable, to people who are writ-

ing about American cultural history, literary history, or the development of the American vernacular style." House further concluded that Cooper's status "involves an accompanying insistence on his works as possessions belonging to our past, . . . that he has nothing to say to us here–at present." But abroad, House said, Cooper still seems to have stature as an American and world writer, citing current scholarly interest in Japan, Germany, Russia, and Italy.

Donald Ringe called for a new approach to Cooper, charging that much contemporary scholarship is open to challenge because of its "tendency to follow well-trodden paths and leave large areas of [Cooper's] work relatively unexplored." The well-trodden paths, according to Ringe, are Cooper as social critic, Cooper as a spokesman of American beliefs, and Cooper as subject for psychological analysis. "It is time," Ringe said, "for Cooper scholars to address the problem: to engage the entire corpus of Cooper's writings and see his works, not as material to support some modern theory, but as historical documents that have meaning in their own right and give us access to the complex mind that created them." To this end, Ringe argued, scholars must come to grips with Cooper's preoccupation, late in life, with religion. Such an approach would tie together "the social criticism and the romances of the frontier, [bring] forward the maritime novels as a significant part of his accomplishments, and [provide] the means for examining his development as both artist and thinker throughout his career."

The author thanks George Bleasby, Godehard Czernik, Victoria Smith, Marie Devlin, Thomas Steinfeld, Wayne Wright, and the Burlington County Historical Society for their help in compiling information for this report.

Ardis Publishers

Ronald Meyer
Senior Editor, Ardis

Ardis Publishers is the largest publisher of Russian literature in the original and in English translation outside the Soviet Union. Joseph Brodsky, the winner of the Nobel Prize in Literature in 1987 and an Ardis author, has said that "from the point of view of Russian literature, the existence of this house is the second great event in literature, after the invention of the press."

Denounced in the Brezhnev years as "an anti-Soviet bakery" by the influential newspaper *Literaturnaya Gazeta*, the role of Ardis as caretaker and ambassador of Russian literature is now officially recognized in the USSR under the new policies of glasnost and perestroika instituted by Mikhail Gorbachev. Vladimir Vigilyansky, writing in the popular weekly *Ogonyok* (4 November 1989), states that "Ardis is one of the best-known foreign publishers of Russian literature. For almost twenty years now it has been performing the noble role of 'ambassador' of that part of our Russian literature which only now is receiving 'a residency permit' in Soviet journals and publishing houses. The novels of V. Nabokov and A. Platonov, the plays of N. Erdman and M. Bulgakov, the poetry of J. Brodsky and V. Khodasevich, the songs of B. Okudzhava and the memoirs of L. Kopelev. Because of the impossibility of publishing at home, the following published their works with Ardis: A. Bitov, V. Aksyonov, F. Iskander, E. Popov, V. Voinovich, A. Gladilin, A. and B. Strugatsky, S. Lipkin, V. Sosnora, I. Lisnyanskaya, Yu. Kublanovsky, A. Tsvetkov, and many, many others. Ardis discovered such writers as Yuz Aleshkovsky, Vladimir Maramzin, Yury Miloslavsky, Sergei Dovlatov, Sasha Sokolov. . . ."

The other side of Ardis, the publication of English translations and English-language scholarly studies of Russian literature, rivals the contributions of any single press in the United States. Though often identified with such twentieth-century authors as Osip Mandelstam, Marina Tsvetaeva, and Anna Akhmatova, as well as more contemporary writers (Vassily Aksyonov, Andrei Bitov, and Yury Trifonov), the Ardis catalog includes the nineteenth-century masters Alexander Pushkin, Mikhail Lermontov, Fyodor Dostoevsky, and Ivan Turgenev, not to mention a host of lesser-known writers.

Founded in Ann Arbor in 1971 by Carl R. and Ellendea Proffer, Ardis remains an independent enterprise. It has no academic affiliation and receives no institutional support. Carl Proffer (1938-1984), who earned his Ph.D. in Russian literature at the University of Michigan, had returned to Ann Arbor, after teaching at Reed College and Indiana University, to assume a professorship in the Department of Slavic Languages and Literatures. Already an established scholar, his book publications included *The Simile and Gogol's "Dead Souls"* (1967), *The Letters of Nikolai Gogol* (1967), *Keys to "Lolita"* (1968), and *The Critical Prose of Alexander Pushkin* (1969). Ellendea Proffer (born 1943), a graduate student at Indiana University, had recently completed her dissertation on the Soviet writer Mikhail Bulgakov, a figure who would figure prominently in the Ardis catalog. Formerly on the faculty of Wayne State University and the University of Michigan—Dearborn, she abandoned academia to pursue her work with Ardis and her own scholarship and writing.

Academic credentials aside, the Proffers possessed keen intelligence, youth, apparently unfathomable energy, and a reckless daring that enabled them to turn their initial capital investment of three thousand dollars into a major publishing force. The Proffers' partnership came to an end with Carl's death in 1984, after dozens of collaborations under the Ardis imprint and elsewhere. Ellendea Proffer continues directorship of Ardis as sole proprietor. In 1989 she was awarded a MacArthur Fellowship for her work as "author, translator and co-founder and director of Ardis Publishers, which has helped sustain the publication of Russian literature."

Ardis came into being out of the Proffers' desire to publish a new, independent journal of translation and criticism, *Russian Literature Triquarterly*. The first issue carried the following edi-

Carl and Ellendea Proffer

torial statement: "We see the journal as a 'post-horse of enlightenment.' Whether it will be a thoroughbred or a nag remains to be seen. We will not publish articles on literary politics or similar cold-war criticism of either the American or Soviet variety. This is a literary journal, not a political one. . . . The contents reflect the tastes of the editors, the needs of English-speaking readers, and chance." Twenty-two issues of *Russian Literature Triquarterly* have been published in the years 1971-1989. Often organized thematically, the characteristically wide-ranging journal has included issues devoted to Symbolism, the Golden Age, Futurism, Mikhail Bulgakov, Alexei Remizov, and women in Russian literature. A special Vladimir Nabokov issue, with the first publication in Russian of *The Enchanter* (1986), is scheduled for publication in 1990.

Nadezhda Mandelstam, widow of the poet Osip Mandelstam, proved a major influence on the Proffers and Ardis, to which Carl Proffer makes eloquent tribute in his posthumously pub-

lished *The Widows of Russia and Other Writings* (Ardis, 1987). The Proffers first met Nadezhda Mandelstam in 1969, when the couple was on a research trip in Moscow. The 1969 trip provided the Proffers with the materials and contacts to begin Ardis, but Mandelstam remained their single most important source of inspiration. A facsimile edition of Osip Mandelstam's first book of poetry, *Kamen'* (Stone, 1913), marked the debut of Ardis with the signature carriage logo, designed by Vladimir Favorsky. The Proffers had purchased the rare edition of Mandelstam's book as a present for Nadezhda Mandelstam, who in turn made a gift of it to the Proffers, saying that though she had not seen the actual book for some years, she knew all the poems by heart. That first Ardis edition of *Kamen'* (five hundred copies, not counting subsequent reprintings) was an attempt to return the gift to Mandelstam and to acknowledge the Proffers' love and admiration for her. Mandelstam had passed on to the Proffers not only her knowledge and experience, but she had also served as a historical conduit to Russia's past.

Ardis's early years (1971-1973) saw the publication of the first English translations of Andrei Bely's *Kotik Letaev, The Unpublished Dostoevsky* (edited by Carl Proffer), Mikhail Bakhtin's *The Problems of Dostoevsky's Poetics*, and Anna Akhmatova's *A Poem without a Hero*, while the first publication in Russian of Mikhail Bulgakov's *Zoya's Apartment* was followed by facsimile editions of Vladimir Mayakovsky's *About That* (with the original Rodchenko montage published for the first time as the cover), Marina Tsvetaeva's *Versts*, and Osip Mandelstam's *Tristia*. The addition, however, of Vladimir Nabokov to the Ardis list in 1974 defined to a great extent the young company's profile.

Nabokov and Ardis were destined for each other. Ardis takes its name, which means "the point of an arrow" as well as "passion," from the family estate in Nabokov's novel *Ada or Ardor* (1969). The Proffers first met Vladimir and Véra Nabokov in 1969 in Montreux, Switzerland, though Vladimir Nabokov had written to Carl Proffer earlier regarding the latter's *Keys to "Lolita."* (Some of Nabokov's letters to the Proffers are included in his *Selected Letters 1940-1977*, published by Harcourt Brace Jovanovich/Bruccoli Clark Layman in 1989.) The Proffers were able to give the Nabokovs news of Nabokov's Russian readers, little suspecting at the time that they would become the publisher of Vladimir Nabokov's works in Russian. The initial reprints in 1974 of *Mashen'ka* (1926; translated as *Mary*, 1970) and *Podvig* (1932; translated as *Glory*, 1971), both long out of print, were soon joined by the complete catalog of Nabokov's Russian books; the first edition of his collected verse (*Stikhi*, 1979); and a volume of his correspondence with his sister, Helene Sikorskaya (*Perepiska s sestroi*, 1985)–a total of fifteen volumes. In 1983 Russian translations of two of Nabokov's novels– *Pale Fire* (1962) and *Pnin* (1957)–inaugurated the publication of Nabokov's English works in Russian. (*Pale Fire* was translated by Véra Nabokov.) At present Ardis is in the process of publishing the first edition of Nabokov's collected works (*Sobranie sochinenii*, 1987-), a projected fifteen-volume set that will include prose, poetry, and drama.

The Proffers' interests and contacts, however, led them to complement their role as temporary guardians with a search for new talent. The case of Sasha Sokolov and his novel *A School for Fools* deserves special mention. Sokolov's unsolicited manuscript arrived in Ann Arbor with a Vienna postmark, though the author still resided in the USSR. The Proffers mounted an energetic publicity campaign for the unknown author, whose novel Nabokov termed "an enchanting, tragic and touching work." *A School for Fools* was published in Russian in 1976 and in Carl Proffer's English translation in 1977, and has remained in print ever since. The poet Alexei Tsvetkov and the prose writers Sergei Dovlatov, Vladimir Maramzin, and Sergei Yuryenen are other examples of Ardis's commitment to new writers.

Primarily a literary publishing house, Ardis released the first volume of Lev Kopelev's autobiographical trilogy, *To Be Preserved Forever* (Ardis Russian edition, 1975; English translation, 1977), forcing the company into the political arena and catapulting its author to international fame. Kopelev, who is portrayed by Alexander Solzhenitsyn in *First Circle* (1968), and his wife Raisa Orlova, both literary scholars, met the Proffers in Moscow in 1969, and they became fast friends. Reasoning that they were not going to submit to self-censorship to curry favor with the Soviet regime, the Proffers published Kopelev's account of the end of World War II and his first arrest, fully aware that this might end their annual trips to Moscow. Though there were repercussions, Ardis was officially permitted to attend the Moscow Book Fair in 1977.

Ironically, the book that closed the doors to Moscow for the Proffers was not an explicitly political work but a literary one. In 1979 the editors of the literary almanac *Metropol* petitioned to publish their collective work without the interference of censorship. The permission was denied, and the almanac was published by Ardis. The authors and publishers were severely criticized in the Soviet press, and the event made headlines worldwide. The twenty-three contributors met different fates. Some, such as Vassily Aksyonov, Yuz Aleshkovsky, and Yury Kublanovsky, immigrated to the West; Semyon Lipkin and his wife Inna Lisnyanskaya resigned from the Union of Writers in protest; others suffered their fates in silence in the USSR, rarely able to publish their work (for example, Andrei Bitov and Fazil Iskander). The Proffers were repeatedly denied visas to attend the Moscow book fairs and were frequently attacked in the Soviet press–a situation that did not change until 1987, when Ardis was again permitted to visit Moscow. The 1987 Book Fair, however, did not pass without scandal. Some twenty books were banned from display, and Ellendea Proffer, who had recently edited the first volumes of the only Russian edition of Mikhail Bulgakov's collected works, was attacked in the press and falsely accused of stealing documents from the Bulgakov archive, to which she had never been granted entry. She was nonetheless visited by numerous people at the book fair who came to express their gratitude that she, a non-Russian, had undertaken this important task.

The last half of the 1980s has seen a remarkable shift in the literary politics of the USSR. The following titles, all published by Ardis in Russian, have appeared or are scheduled to appear in the Soviet Union: Andrei Bitov, *Pushkin House* (1978), Fazil Iskander, *Sandro from Chegem* (1979), Vassily Aksyonov, *The Island of Crimea* (1981), Vladimir Voinovich, *The Life and Extraordinary Adventures of Private Ivan Chonkin* (1985-1987), and the poetry of Joseph Brodsky, who has published all of his Russian books with Ardis since his immigration to the United States in 1972.

The Ardis catalog of Russian literature in English spans the period from Old Russian literature with Vladimir Nabokov's translation of *The Song of Igor's Campaign* (1989) to the present: Andrei Bitov, *Life in Windy Weather* (1986), Yury Trifonov, *The Long Goodbye* (1978), and Vassily

Aksyonov, *The Steel Bird and Other Stories* (1978). Other works that should be mentioned are Osip Mandelstam's *Complete Critical Prose and Letters* (1979), Marina Tsvetaeva's *A Captive Spirit* (1980), Mikhail Lermontov's *A Hero of Our Time* (1988; again in Nabokov's translation), Alexander Pushkin's *Collected Narrative and Lyrical Poetry* (1983), and the anthology *Contemporary Russian Prose* (1982). Critical studies of Russian literature and culture include Konstantin Rudnitsky's *Meyerhold the Director* (1981), Ellendea Proffer's *Bulgakov: Life and Work* (1984), and William Edward Brown's four-volume *History of Russian Literature of the Romantic Period* (1986), which was awarded the Wayne S. Vucinich Prize by the American Association for the Advancement of Slavic Studies. Anna Akhmatova's *Selected Prose*, Bulgakov's *Notes on the Cuff*, and a photobiography of Nabokov are scheduled for publication in 1990.

During the years 1971-1989 Ardis published 200 titles in the Russian language and 251 in English. The current backlist includes more than 200 titles. In 1990 Ardis will begin publication of its Contemporary Russian Prose series with Vintage Press. The first two titles to be announced for publication are Andrei Bitov's *Pushkin House* and an anthology of Russian writings of the late 1980s, *Glasnost: The New Soviet Prose*.

The G. Ross Roy Scottish Poetry Collection at the University of South Carolina

G. Ross Roy
University of South Carolina

There are few instances in the literary history of the English-speaking world to approach the phenomenon of the instant and sustained popularity of Robert Burns. Almost overnight he became famous after the publication of *Poems, Chiefly in the Scottish Dialect* (Kilmarnock, 1786), and his public has never flagged since. In the decade after copyright expired there were almost seventy editions of Burns's poems, without counting chapbooks, periodicals, and books that included selections of his work. His songs are sung throughout the world—"Auld Lang Syne" is probably the best-known convivial song ever written. It is said that if there were only two books in the baggage of a nineteenth-century Scottish emigrant these would be the Bible and an edition of Burns. So it was with my great-grandfather; while I don't know the extent of his library when he left Scotland, these two books were certainly represented. He died fairly young, leaving these two books to my grandfather, W. Ormiston Roy. I cannot identify the Burns volume in the collection, so I date the collection from 1892 when my grandmother inscribed an edition of Burns to "her friend" whom she was to marry a couple of years later. From this modest beginning the Roy Collection is now one of the greatest assemblages of printed material by and about Burns in the world.

My association with Scottish poetry began in earnest in 1951 when I moved into my grandfather's house. A widower for some years, he was glad of the company, and I was happy to be in a house that boasted a separate room as a library. We often ate dinner together at night, and the meals were punctuated by his disappearance to search out a volume containing a poem that was particularly appropriate to the moment. We agreed that it would save time if I were to put a fifty-years' accumulation of books into some order. As an already confirmed book collector, this "hands-on" contact with a large collection of

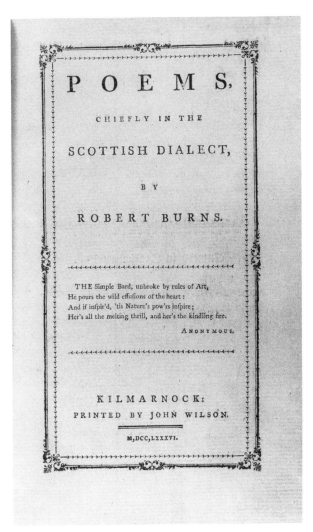

Title page for the cornerstone volume in the Roy Collection. Of this edition, some forty-five copies are extant (G. Ross Roy Collection, Thomas Cooper Library, University of South Carolina).

the works of Burns has served me in good stead ever since.

Our paths parted, and I was in France when my grandfather died, leaving me his books. After taking stock I decided that the first thing I must do was to dispose of the duplicates–I didn't have a separate room for a library. The duplicates were so numerous that I was able to put together a collection of over two hundred editions of Burns and Burnsiana. With the proceeds of the sale of these books I went after the "keystone" volume, which was not in my grandfather's collection–the Kilmarnock edition. It took just over three years to find a suitable one. I say "suitable" because there are some made-up copies floating around, most with title page and various other leaves wanting, sometimes supplied in facsimile and bound in. In those days there was usually one or more of these available because no library or serious collector wanted them, so they changed hands between dealers and "dabblers" quite a bit. The wait was worthwhile, because in December 1961 Ian Grant was able to offer me a splendid tall copy of the Kilmarnock edition, bound in early twentieth-century red polished morocco, with green polished morocco doublures. I probably still have Mr. Grant's letter describing the book he was offering me, but no words could have prepared me for what I saw when the book arrived. When I showed it to a specialist in Riviere bindings he said that it was one of the finest examples of the firm's work he had ever seen.

From my undergraduate days I had been a dedicated collector of Canadian poetry, but by about this time I realized that neither my space nor my financial resources would permit me to continue to collect Canadian poetry as well as Burns and other Scottish poets. The collection of Canadian poetry was one of the better ones in existence, with some really nice association copies, such as an author's presentation copy to Sir Wilfred Laurier when he was Prime Minister of Canada, another author's presentation copy to Henry Wadsworth Longfellow, and another from the author to the dedicatee of the volume. Reluctantly, I decided that the Canadian poetry must go, and so the collection was offered to and purchased by the University of Montreal. I cannot say, "I never looked back," because thirty years later I still see books that I should have liked to have added to my collection, but to quote Wordsworth completely out of context, "other gifts / Have followed, for such loss, I would believe / Abundant recompense. . . ."

It was at this time that two of my activities added weight to my decision to concentrate on collecting Scottish poetry: I was occupied in Burns scholarship, which meant that I required copies of all the important Burns editions, as well as an-

thologies and works by and about the poet's predecessors; and I had founded *Studies in Scottish Literature*, the editing of which encouraged me to collect as many editions of Scottish poetry as possible, particularly the works of twentieth-century writers. (To collect prose would have necessitated not just a separate room for a library, which I now have, but a separate building!) Chief among these poets of the Scottish Renaissance was Hugh MacDiarmid (the nom de plume of Christopher Murray Grieve), with whom I had made contact, and who had enthusiastically agreed to serve on the editorial board of *Studies in Scottish Literature*.

Both my research and my editing of *SSL* took me to Great Britain each summer, and so I was able to browse in a good number of bookshops at a time when prices were very modest by today's standards, a time when one hesitated before parting with a five-pound note for most books. This was when I acquired a fine set of James Johnson's *Scots Musical Museum* (6 volumes, Edinburgh, 1787-1803) the well-known collection of six hundred Scottish songs, with music, of which Burns was the unnamed editor, and to which he contributed almost one-third of the contents. My copy is in the second state, but it came with an ALS from Charles Kirkpatrick Sharpe, the antiquarian, about one of the leaves of music in the set. (I have since added a complete set in the first state, as well as five separate volumes with title-page variations.)

For my research it was necessary to have the first collected edition of Burns's works, James Currie's monumental *Works of Robert Burns; With an Account of his Life, and a Criticism of his Writings* (4 volumes, Liverpool, 1800), and I was able to purchase a five-volume set that included the volume of additional collected material edited by R. H. Cromek (London, 1808), all in original boards in pristine condition. My research on Burns had alerted me to the fact that in subsequent editions published during his lifetime (he died in 1805) Currie had made changes. There were editions in 1801, 1802, 1803, and five further "editions" after his death, including three so-called eighth editions, one published in 1814, one in 1820 completely reset and in a different format, and a reprinting of this with added plates dated 1823. The Roy Collection contains all ten of these "editions," apparently the only collection in the United States to have them all. Currie has been much maligned by modern scholars, but by the standards of the early nineteenth century he was a competent editor. Like all scholars of his age he did not hesitate to alter and delete material which he considered inappropriate. It is interesting to note that in the 1800 edition, which was printed by J. McCreery of Liverpool for Cadell and Davis of London, words have the *o* form rather than the *ou* (*honor* rather than *honour*), whereas in the 1801 edition, printed in London by R. Noble, the *ou* form becomes the norm. It was at about this time that the *ou* form was generally adopted, but as this edition shows, provincial printers were slower to follow this practice.

Needless to say Currie, who undertook the edition of Burns to raise money for the support of the poet's widow and children, omitted anything which might give offense to those who could afford to purchase a set (he turned over all the profits from the edition to Jean Burns, and she was able to live somewhat comfortably for the remainder of her life), so there were discreet alterations to letters (and some left out altogether) as well as omitted poems and songs. There are no bawdy poems or songs in the edition, although we know that Burns both wrote and collected them. For over a century these were known to scholars under the title *The Merry Muses of Caledonia; A Collection of Favourite Scots Songs, Ancient and Modern; Selected for the Use of the Crochallan Fencibles*, but the only known copy of this work was mutilated–the title page of this "mean-looking volume," as a later editor, Duncan M'Naught, called it, was torn and the date wanting, although following the law of the period the date was included in the watermark. In the case of *The Merry Muses*, however, watermarks of 1799 and 1800 appear in the paper. In 1965 I was fortunate enough to obtain a copy with mounted half-title (wanting in the other copy) and a complete title page that reads "Printed in the Year / 1799." The volume is, obviously, the crown jewel of the Roy Collection. I have written elsewhere about the details of this book and also about the likelihood that its existence was known to James Currie. Further publication of Burns's erotic poetry followed. The earliest, *The Fornicator's Court*, was published about 1810, apparently in a printing of ten copies, and republished in 1823; there is a copy of the 1823 edition in my collection.

Victorian Britain was not, officially, receptive to racy works so, as might have been expected, there developed a flourishing market in such books sold sub rosa. One of the texts to find its way into "private" collections was an edition of *The Merry Muses* dated 1827. G. Legman discusses this edition in his *Horn Book: Studies in Erotic Folklore and Bibliography* (1963), suggesting that the book was the work of John Camden Hotten, a publisher and bookseller who dabbled in this sort of material, and that the actual date of publication was 1872; by switching around the last two digits Hotten could sell copies of the work as antiquarian books and thus avoid the possibility of prosecution for publishing pornography. What is assumed to be the first edition of the "1827" *Merry Muses* was not acquired by the British Museum until 1881 and is limited to ninety-nine copies–or so the limitation claims. Since no one was admitting to having published these copies, and most owners were probably not publicly admitting to ownership, the possibility of fraud was limitless. Without copyright protection, numerous piracies appeared during the next thirty years. Collecting information on these has been made difficult by the refusal or reluctance of libraries to purchase copies of them or to catalog those copies they did possess. After nearly thirty years of gathering information about variants of this "1827" *Merry Muses*, I published an annotated checklist of them in the *Burns Chronicle*. All of the significant collections in Great Britain and the United States were worked through, and I came up with a total of nineteen variants of this work. By assiduously collecting all variants I was able to list thirteen of these in my own collection, more than in any other collection I have examined. Within a year, however, serendipity led me to acquire a variant which was previously unknown to me.

By noting supposed oddities attributed to scarce editions, one is sometimes able to score a lucky stroke. I had long thought it was strange that the 1801 Oliver edition of Burns (2 volumes, Edinburgh) should have been published (as it was claimed) wanting six pages of text (C^4-C^6), particularly when the missing pages left one poem unfinished and omitted the beginning of another. I was even more suspicious because the only known copy had been rebound. I was thus prepared when I was offered a copy of the set, untrimmed in contemporary or near-contemporary boards–and as I hoped, the "wanting" leaves were present!

As every serious collector knows, the trick is to get into that part of a dealer's shop where most clients are not admitted. Before much of the center of Glasgow was redeveloped there were several secondhand bookshops in the area. One of these, down a small lane, seemed particularly unlikely, but I determined to wade through

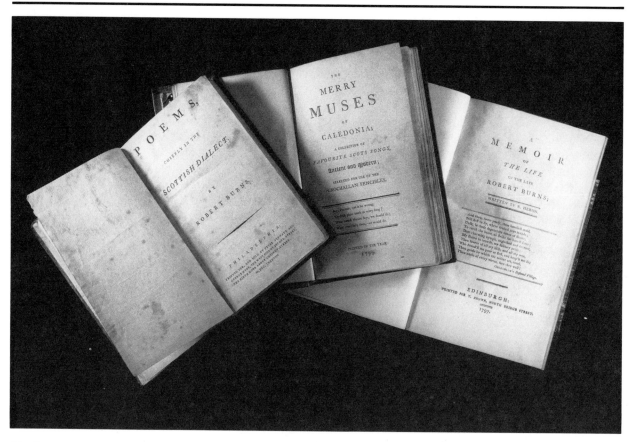

The first American printing of Poems, Chiefly in the Scottish Dialect *(1788); one of only two extant copies of* The Merry Muses of Caledonia *(1799), a collection of erotic verse; and the first biography of Burns (1797); from the G. Ross Roy Collection, Thomas Cooper Library, University of South Carolina*

the rows of dank shelves and was rewarded with quite a few nice items. Finally, there remained only a small room where the owner kept books that had not yet been priced, including unusual items for which he did not know how much he could ask. I got his permission to have a look, and there, beside a cracked teapot and an unwashed cup, I found a book sewn in late nineteenth-century cardboard that was an extremely rare Burns item, the two-volume Paisley collection of 1801-1802. I knew this was something good and tried to appear just mildly interested when the dealer came to it, judiciously placed in the middle of the stack of books I was buying. I asked him what he wanted for it (it was unpriced), and he looked me up and down, doubtless wondering how much this foreigner would be willing to lay out for such a scruffy-looking item. "I paid a high price for it," he said, "and I have to make a return on my investment." My heart sank as I thought that he must indeed know what he had; I was also convinced that he had gauged his customer aright, that he knew I would pay him just about any price he named. I wondered what gesture or comment I could have made that had given me away. "Yes," he continued, "I've got to get . . . " and he named a price that was about one hundredth of what I had expected to pay him. I tried to look as though the price was high but acceptable as I wrote him a check. When I got to the Mitchell Library (which has one of only two other recorded copies of the edition) I discovered that my prize was even better than I had thought; my crudely sewn copy had several parts sewn in complete with their original wrappers, proof of serial issue that is not to be found in the other copies.

One must occasionally be willing to purchase an expensive unneeded book in a collection in order to obtain a much-wanted lesser work. I may be the only collector who has ever simultaneously owned two copies of the Kilmarnock Burns. The second one was the principal attraction in a small collection of early Burns editions that was offered as a lot. What I wanted was the copy of the second edition of Burns (Edinburgh, 1787) in original boards in pristine condition, as well as a copy of the London edition of the same year, also in original boards, not as clean as the Edinburgh copy but still the finest copy of this work I have seen. The dealer was un-budging, the collection must be sold intact, so for a few months I owned two Kilmarnocks, and the Roy Collection still has the "secondary" editions for which I had purchased the collection.

For fifty or more years after his death many chapbooks were published that were entirely or partially devoted to Burns poems. These had be-come scarce by the beginning of the century and are now very difficult to find. I had from my early collecting days tried to get as many of these chapbook publications as possible. I have man-aged to put together a complete set of the ninety-nine eight-page chapbooks that make up *Poetry; Original and Selected*, published by the Glasgow firm of Brash and Reid between 1795 and 1798 or 1799, and I also have a set of the twenty num-bers of *The Polyhymnia; being a Collection of Poetry, Original and Selected* (Glasgow, 1799). Both of these collections include work by Burns, and the Brash and Reid set also has memorial poems writ-ten for Burns. Chapbooks such as these are impor-tant because they detail what humble people read at that time. Sir Walter Scott realized this and put together a good collection of them, still housed in the library at Abbotsford. Another chap-book of this period includes Burns's "Elegy on the Year Eighty-Eight" and two other poems by him; this collection was published by George Gray of Edinburgh in 1799 and is, according to J. W. Egerer's *Bibliography of Robert Burns*, "one of the rarest of Burnsian . . . items." I was able to find a copy of it along with the second of these "Gray's Tracts," as they were called. This other chapbook also contains three poems by Burns, in-cluding "Bruce's Address" ("Scots, wha hae"). It was known only by the copy listed by W. Craibe Angus, but this copy had disappeared by the time Egerer compiled his bibliography. It seems probable that the copy in my collection is the Angus copy.

One does not need to collect very early Burns in order to make interesting discoveries. Until superseded by the James Kinsley edition of 1968, the four-volume *Poetry of Robert Burns* (1896-1897), edited by William Ernest Henley and Thomas F. Henderson, was the standard scholarly edition of the poet's works. Although the text is identical in all sets of this edition, there were variants of this publication, including large paper, extra-illustrated, and library edi-tions, so I attempted to obtain a copy of each.

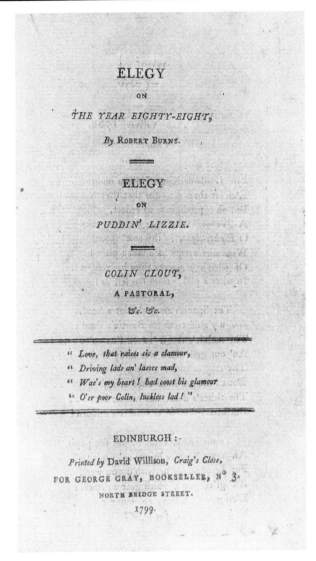

Title page for one of the popular chapbooks known as "Gray's Tracts." Only two copies of this work are extant. (G. Ross Roy Collection, Thomas Cooper Library, University of South Carolina).

After many years of collecting and collating at li-braries, I published an annotated checklist of these editions. In all I know of nineteen varia-tions of the Henley and Henderson *Poetry of Rob-ert Burns;* there are eleven in the Roy Collection, and the University of South Carolina has two addi-tional variants; this total of thirteen appears to be more than any other library possesses.

In order to study Burns, I realized that I must familiarize myself with the earlier Scottish poets who had influenced his work. Over the years I managed to pick up most of the separate editions of Robert Fergusson, including the first, second, and third collected editions. Allan Ram-say, whose work Burns used extensively in collecting and refurbishing material for Johnson's *Scots Musical Museum* and George Thomson's *Select Collection of Original Scotish Airs* (1793-1818), is a more difficult subject for the collector. The bibliography of Ramsay runs to over four hundred entries (an updated bibliography on which I am working will add about a hundred more) so that the Ramsay collector can never expect to come even close to completion. For instance, the first two editions of the first volume of *The Tea-Table Miscellany* (1723 and 1724) are known in only one copy each; this is true also of early editions of the succeeding three volumes. I have managed, though, to obtain a copy of the first collected *Tea-Table* (London, 1740). Ramsay's play *The Gentle Shepherd* was an eighteenth-century bestseller; so far the first edition (Edinburgh, 1725) of this work has eluded me. There is a copy in the collection of the 1729 edition, with notation by Ramsay as to where the songs that have been added to the play may be found in Ramsay's *Tea-Table Miscellany*. This is the first edition to show that Ramsay, following the success of John Gay's *Beggar's Opera* in 1728, had converted his own play to a ballad-opera. I have managed to assemble over sixty eighteenth-century editions of Ramsay, one of them with an invitation to attend the poet's funeral tipped in.

Another area of strength in the collection is anthologies of Scottish poetry. These were added because of the useful critical notes that they frequently contain. Almost every anthology since Arthur Johnston's *Delitiae poetarum Scotorum* (2 volumes, Amsterdam, 1637) is to be found in the Roy Collection; several are of considerable scarcity. One of the most interesting is a single volume made up of parts 1, 2, and 3 of James Watson's *Choice Collection of Comic and Serious Scots Poems* (Edinburgh, 1706, 1709, 1711), together with a second edition of part 1 (Edinburgh, 1713). The volume has been made up with the addition of several early engravings of poets represented in the book. It also been interleaved and is copiously annotated by the antiquarian book dealer Joseph Ritson.

The need to trace the influence of Burns on nineteenth-century Scottish poets led to the gathering of a strong collection of these minor writers. Many of their books were produced in small printings for a local market, and it is not surprising to find that there is no deposit copy in the British Library, nor one listed in the *National Union Catalogue*. And yet they are important scholarly tools for the study of the development of Scottish poetry in addition to giving the reader insights into the society that nurtured these writers.

Given the span of the collection I was building, it seemed natural to add twentieth-century poetry. Through my editing work I have met many of the poets active in the post-World-War II period, and there are inscribed copies of many of their books in the collection. To name a few, I have strong holdings of George Bruce, Maurice Lindsay, Norman MacCaig, Hugh MacDiarmid, Alexander and Tom Scott, Iain Crichton Smith, as well as Sydney Goodsir Smith and William Soutar (whom I did not know).

Over the past quarter-century I have also encouraged the University of South Carolina Library to acquire its own very respectable collection of Scottish literature. We purchased, for example, the Douglas Gifford Collection of post-World-War II Scottish fiction, probably the most complete in the United States. Through coordination, duplication with my own collection has been small. Now that the Roy Collection is in the process of becoming the property of the University of South Carolina, a budget has been established to keep it growing. In the past few months we have acquired the Roger L. Tarr Collection of Thomas Carlyle (one of the best in the country). Not long ago an almost complete collection of first editions of Robert Louis Stevenson was acquired. Recently we added a copy of the 1802 *Letters Addressed to Clarinda, By Robert Burns* in hitherto unknown paper wrappers, as published. In the area of chapbooks, *The Cottager's Saturday Night* (Lancaster, [1810?]) has been purchased, as well as a volume of turn-of-the-nineteenth-century Scottish poetry chapbooks, several including selections from Burns. There appears to be no copy of several of these listed in the *NUC*, the British Library, or the National Library of Scotland. We all expect the holdings of Scottish poetry at this university library to go from strength to strength.

In order to make the Burns portion of the Roy Collection known to the scholarly world it is planned to publish a catalog of this material. Furthermore, the W. Ormiston Roy Memorial Fellowship has been established to subsidize short periods of research in the collection.

The Agee Legacy: A Conference at the University of Tennessee at Knoxville

Jack Armistead
University of Tennessee at Knoxville

From 27 March through 1 April 1989 James Agee's life and works were celebrated in Knoxville, Tennessee. The conference was occasioned by the fiftieth anniversary of Agee's collaboration with the photographer Walker Evans on a study of southeastern sharecroppers, *Let Us Now Praise Famous Men*. Lectures, films, exhibits, a teleconference, dramatic readings, a walking tour, the acquisition of important Agee manuscripts, and the placement of a historical marker made this not only a rich tribute to the author but also a stimulating and instructive series of experiences for anyone interested in or curious about Knoxville's best-known writer.

The week began with a conference overview by Wilma Dykeman, Tennessee historian, journalist, and novelist, and with the announcement by Dean of Libraries Paula Kaufmann that the University of Tennessee had just acquired a valuable collection of Agee manuscripts, including journals, letters, and unpublished sections of his unfinished novel, *A Death in the Family* (1957). The lecture series was then initiated by George Brown Tindall, distinguished historian from the University of North Carolina at Chapel Hill, who spoke about what he called "The Lost World of James Agee," specifically the world of southern sharecropping and its economic and political background.

The following day several other papers were read. Another eminent professor from the University of North Carolina at Chapel Hill, Linda Wagner-Martin, investigated Agee's narrative strategies in *Let Us Now Praise Famous Men*, focusing on his techniques of presenting women and children. Professor Michael Lofaro of the University of Tennessee discussed a previously unknown journal in which Agee reveals key motives for taking on the *Fortune* magazine assignment that led to *Let Us Now Praise Famous Men*: the need to explore his own alienated "Southernness" and his interest in southern labor move-

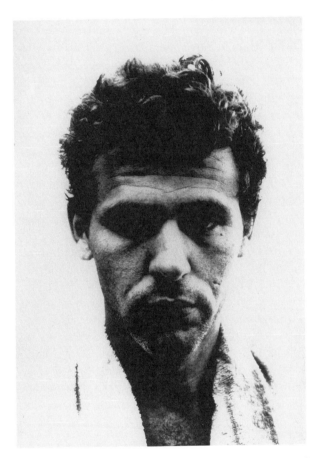

Photograph of James Agee by Walker Evans (by permission of the Fogg Museum, Harvard University, and the estate of Walker Evans)

ments. David Madden, writer-in-residence at Louisiana State University, spoke of Agee's personal dialogue with the reader of *Let Us Now Praise Famous Men*, a dialogue that draws the reader into the process of creation while Agee writes his own story into that of the sharecroppers. Later in the week Madden read aloud a short story that he had written while attending the conference; it recounted experiences related to his effort to reconstruct a piece of Agee's past. Jack Agricola, chairman of the Millsaps College art department, lectured on how both Agee and Evans drew upon the lexicon of the painter to create symbolic collages within their respective art forms.

Agee's contribution to film studies was honored not through discussions or demonstrations of his own film criticism and screenplays but rather through films about him and his work. A showing of *All the Way Home* (1962), the film version of *A Death in the Family*, was followed by a panel discussion featuring professors Charles Maland, a film specialist; Paul Ashdown, compiler of a collection of Agee's journalism; and Phillip Hamlin, an expert on Agee's Knoxville—all from the University of Tennessee. The next evening offered a showing of *Agee* (1985), a film biography by Ross Spears, current director of the James Agee Film Project, and at the end of the week Spears talked about his new documentary, *To Render a Life*, which deals with the composition of *Let Us Now Praise Famous Men*.

The lectures and films were complemented by presentations in other media. One afternoon was devoted to a teleconference in which experts discussed the importance of Agee's writings and received questions and comments from telephone callers at broadcast reception sites around the region. The panel, moderated by Dykeman, consisted of Spears, Ashdown, and Madden. Throughout the week conferees used free time to visit two exhibits at the Ewing Gallery in the Art and Architecture Building: a set of images from Agee's life and environment, and a selection of Walker Evans's photographs. The exhibits, commentaries on them, and an opening lecture were all presented by Professor Baldwin Lee of the University of Tennessee art department, who is a former student and colleague of Evans. To make the second exhibit more widely accessible, it has been loaned for "99 years" to the new Knoxville Museum of Art, where it will be displayed intermittently, in rotation with other holdings of the museum.

The conference closed with three somewhat unusual activities. First, Professor Charles Aiken, a University of Tennessee geographer and author of "The Transformation of Agee's Knoxville," led a walking tour of the Knoxville preserved in the pages of *A Death in the Family*. This was followed by the dedication of a historical marker, newly placed by the state of Tennessee, that points visitors to the neighborhood where Agee spent his boyhood. Finally, Professor Faye Julian of the University of Tennessee Department of Speech Communications directed a sequence of dramatic readings of passages from Agee's works.

Three publications have emerged from the conference thus far. First, the official program guide includes, in addition to the daily schedule, several photographs, a map of Agee's Knoxville, and "An Annotated Bibliography of Agee Criticism" compiled by Mary Moss, an advanced graduate student in the University of Tennessee English department. Second, the walking tour of Agee's Knoxville has been transcribed by Professor Aiken and published by the College of Liberal Arts at the University of Tennessee. Finally, Professor Lofaro has combined several of the conference papers with additional essays by Agee experts in a volume to be published by the University of Tennessee Press.

New Literary Periodicals: A Report For 1989

Richard R. Centing
Ohio State University

The following report on new literary periodicals, the third in a series of annual surveys scheduled to appear in the *Dictionary of Literary Biography Yearbook*, documents scholarly journals, annuals, newsletters, and reviews launched in 1989, along with some 1988 titles that had not come to our attention by press time last year. Any 1989 titles that we missed will be covered in the 1990 *Yearbook*. These descriptions are not meant to be evaluative, although we do stress the importance of a few titles. By highlighting outstanding facets of each serial, our intention is to bring them to the attention of librarians and scholars for purposes of collection development, scholarly submission, and to alert indexing services of the need for the inclusion of new titles in their core lists. Please contact the author with any comments on the report for 1989 or suggestions for inclusion in the 1990 report.

Exemplaria: A Journal of Theory in Medieval and Renaissance Studies (Medieval & Renaissance Texts & Studies, State University of New York, Binghamton, New York 13901) is a substantial, multidisciplinary journal jointly sponsored by the English departments of Loyola University (New Orleans) and the University of Florida (Gainesville). Concerned with theoretical and experimental approaches to medieval and Renaissance culture, each semiannual issue runs over two hundred pages. The first issue (Spring 1989) includes studies of three of Geoffrey Chaucer's *Canterbury Tales*, an article on Dante and Frederick II, and Rosemarie P. McGerr (Yale University) on "Medieval Concepts of Literary Closure: Theory and Practice." Jacques Le Goff (Ecole des Hautes Etudes en Sciences Sociales) contributes an analysis of historical biography based on his in-progress life of Saint Louis (1214-1270). The articles conclude with detailed endnotes, some running half a page. The editor, R. A. Shoaf (University of Florida), has his Ph.D. from Cornell University. He is on the editorial board of the *Chaucer Review* and has published extensively on Dante, Chaucer, and Milton. Three associate editors and a twenty-five-member advisory board as-

A Journal of Theory in Medieval and Renaissance Studies

Cover for the first issue of the journal edited by R. A. Shoaf

sist Professor Shoaf in editing this important refereed journal.

Marguerite Duras, the French novelist, dramatist, and screenwriter, was born 4 April 1914 in what was then French Indochina (Vietnam). She is often ranked as one of the most important women writers in France and certainly deserves the critical scrutiny of the *Journal of Durassian Studies* (Duras Society, George Mason University, Foreign Languages & Literatures, Fairfax, VA 22030). The first annual (Fall 1989) includes 142 pages of critical discussion covering such subjects as the concept of "feminine writing" in Duras and Hélène Cixous, Peter Handke's film adaptation of a prose poem by Duras, *The Malady of*

Death (1982), and the use of voice-over in Duras's film *Indian Song* (1974). The editor, Janine Ricouart, has her Ph.D. from the University of California-Davis, although she took her masters degree in France, where she was born. A specialist in French twentieth-century literature, she now teaches at George Mason University. Her contribution to the *Journal of Durassian Studies* is a twenty-seven-page primary and secondary bibliography that includes French editions, English translations, and in the secondary list, articles and books in both French and English.

Emily Dickinson (1830-1886) has been the focus of the *Emily Dickinson Bulletin* (1968-1978) and its successor, *Dickinson Studies* (1978-). A less substantial competitor is the new semiannual the *Single Hound: The Poetry and Image of Emily Dickinson* (Single Hound, Box 598, Newmarket, NH 03857), named after a collection of Dickinson's poems edited by her niece Martha Dickinson Bianchi in 1914. The first issue (May 1989) consists of twenty-four pages and includes an interview with Dickinson biographer Richard B. Sewall; an article on Dickinson in Japan by Japanese authority Masako Takeda; a stylistic study; a brief look at Dickinson's poem numbered 1333 ("A little Madness in the Spring"); and a report on a poetry reading by Robert Bly that included two Dickinson poems. The editor, Andrew Leibs, is a journalist and free-lance writer who lives in Newmarket, New Hampshire. He holds an M.A. in writing from the University of New Hampshire.

Eugene O'Neill (1888-1953) has been tracked for years by the triquarterly *Eugene O'Neill Newsletter* (1977-1988), now expanded into the *Eugene O'Neill Review* (Suffolk University, Department of English, Boston, MA 02114), a semiannual with an improved appearance that continues the volume numbering of the newsletter. The first issue of the review is dated Spring 1989 (v. 13, no. 1). It includes six substantial essays, three conference reports, four performance reviews, and seven book reviews. Documents of the Eugene O'Neill Society are also published here. The review is illustrated. Frederick C. Wilkins remains as editor.

The *Merton Annual: Studies in Thomas Merton, Religion, Culture, Literature & Social Concerns* (AMS Press, Inc., 56 E. 13th Street, New York, NY 10003) is a hardbound scholarly survey. Thomas Merton (1915-1968) was a Trappist monk whose quest for solitude ended with secular fame and a growing amount of scholarship on his work and influence. The first annual

(1988) acknowledges this growth by entitling its annual bibliographic survey "The Merton Phenomenon." Listed are film biographies of Merton, oral history tapes concerning him, tapes of Merton's lectures, numerous full-length biographies, critical monographs, theses, and hundreds of articles on his life and writings that appear in specialized religious journals and national publications. Merton was a poet, letter writer, spiritual essayist, and journal keeper. He produced one best-seller, *The Seven Storey Mountain* (1948), and several other popular religious books. The annual publishes articles on these works, and on general topics such as Zen and peace studies. The second volume (1989) includes interviews, more than a dozen long articles, and in-depth book reviews. Merton's major papers are in the Thomas Merton Studies Center, Bellarmine College, Louisville, Kentucky, and mention should be made of that center's quarterly *Merton Seasonal of Bellarmine College*, a more informal periodical published since 1976. The editor of the *Merton Seasonal*, Robert E. Daggy, serves as a coeditor of the *Merton Annual*, along with Patrick Hart (Abbey of Gethsemani), Dewey Weiss Kramer (DeKalb College), and Victor A. Kramer (Georgia State University).

The *Tennessee Williams Literary Journal* (Clare B. Pierson, Managing Editor, Tennessee Williams Literary Journal, 4517 Cleary Avenue, Metairie, LA 70002) began with an eighty-four-page issue dated Spring 1989. The semiannual plans to publish criticism and bibliographic updates on the work of Tennessee Williams (1911-1983), covering his plays, poems, novels, short stories, and essays. It also covers events related to the annual Tennessee Williams/New Orleans Literary Festival. The first article, "Tennessee Travels to Taos," is a memoir by Jim Parrott, a friend of Williams since the late 1930s. Milly S. Barranger, chairperson of the Department of Dramatic Arts at the University of North Carolina-Chapel Hill, examines the role of Blanche DuBois in *A Streetcar Named Desire* (1947) as portrayed by Jessica Tandy, Uta Hagen, and Vivien Leigh. Five other articles provide criticism on Williams. A "Checklist of Tennessee Williams Scholarship: 1980-87" cites other bibliographies, books, interviews, and production reviews. Some of the references are to the defunct *Tennessee Williams Newsletter* (1979-1980) and the *Tennessee Williams Review* (1981-1983). The journal concludes with news about forthcoming productions, conferences, and in-progress biographies. The editor is W. Kenneth Holditch.

Brasil/Brazil (Brown University, Center for Portuguese and Brazilian Studies, Providence, RI 02912) is a semiannual edited by Nelson H. Vieira (Brown University) and Regina Zilberman (Editora Mercado Aberto, Porto Alegre, Brazil). The first issue is dated Fall 1988. An international group of scholars, critics, and translators serves on the editorial and advisory boards. Dedicated principally to Brazilian literature from all periods, it will publish scholarship as well as fiction and poetry. The journal is bilingual, in English and Portuguese. Each essay is preceded by a useful abstract in the other language. Peggy Sharpe Valadares (University of Illinois) offers an English-language article that resurrects the neglected poet and novelist Nisia Floresta Brasileira Augusta (1809-1885). One of the Portuguese articles is on the contemporary novelist Antônio Callado. There are also translations into English of two short pieces of fiction. The journal concludes with some book reviews, announcements of conferences, and other news.

The first issue of the semiannual *Journal of Interdisciplinary Literary Studies/Cuadernos Interdisciplinarios De Estudios Literarios* (University of Nebraska-Lincoln, Department of Modern Languages and Literatures, 1110 Oldfather Hall, Lincoln, NE 68588) is dated Spring 1989. Devoted to Hispanic studies, it will accept manuscripts in Spanish, English, Catalan, or any language of the Iberian Peninsula. An English-language article by Teun A. van Dijk (Universiteit van Amsterdam) examines developments in discourse analysis from 1978 to 1988, a growing discipline that relates discourse, social cognition, and social structures. This article is of use to scholars in many fields, including communication. Another English article is on translation studies. An article in Catalan discusses the repression of the Catalan language in Spain. Spanish-language articles discuss the Spanish "Generation of 1927," an important cultural journal that began in 1963 during the Franco regime, and censorship of books under Franco. The editors are Manuel L. Abellán (Universiteit van Amsterdam) and Catherine Nickel (University of Nebraska).

Letras Peninsulares (Michigan State University, Department of Romance and Classical Languages, East Lansing, MI 48824) publishes articles, interviews, and book reviews pertinent to the study of Peninsular Spanish literature from the eighteenth century to the present. Published three times a year, it is bilingual, in Spanish and English. The first issue (Spring 1988) includes an interview in Spanish with the contemporary writer Esther Tusquets. An article in English notes the paucity of women dramatists in Spain and the lack of "an audible feminist voice prior to the death of Franco in 1975." Gonzalo Navajas (University of California, Irvine) offers a Spanish-language article on the nineteenth-century novelist Juan Valera. The editor, Mary S. Vásquez, has a Ph.D. in Romance Languages from the University of Washington and currently is a professor of Spanish at Arizona State University. She is also a poet and the author of several books and articles on contemporary Spanish literature.

The quarterly *American Literary History* (Oxford University Press, Journals Department, 16-00 Pollitt Drive, Fair Lawn, NJ 07410) is one of the most important literary journals launched in 1989. The first number (Spring 1989) is 250 pages long, raising the specter of an annual bound volume of 1,000 pages. In a literary field already well served by numerous journals, the publicity release for *ALH* claims that it will "extend and challenge the terms of recent literary inquiry" and "define new ground." Its brief editorial charge says that it will publish "essays, commentaries, critical exchanges, and reviews on American literature from the colonial period through the present. The journal welcomes articles on historical and theoretical problems as well as writers and their works. *ALH* also invites interdisciplinary studies and papers from related fields." A note at the end of its "Notes on Contributors" section offers additional information on the goals of *ALH*: "Along with our general commitment to the diversified study of American literature and theory, *American Literary History* is especially interested in soliciting essays on American literature and culture after World War II; religion in America; class in twentieth-century American fiction; the Jacksonian period; gender and capitalism; pragmatism; the Civil War and Reconstruction literature; settlement and immigration; redefinition of modernism; the means of literary production. We also continue to welcome interdisciplinary approaches." These statements introduce a journal whose first issue includes five long articles, a theoretical statement, a response to that statement, six long critiques of recent books, and a response to one of the critiques. The first article is a reappraisal of American pastoral ideology by a leading scholar in the field, Lawrence Buell, author of *New England Literary Culture From Revolution Through Renaissance* (Cambridge University Press, 1986). Following are articles on

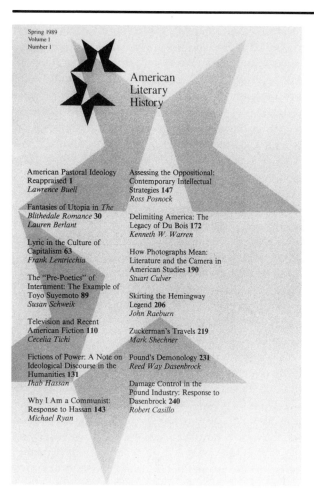

*Table of contents for the first issue of the journal edited by
Gordon Hutner*

Nathaniel Hawthorne's *The Blithedale Romance*
(1852), the poetry of Ezra Pound and Robert
Frost in the culture of capitalism, and the relationship of television and American fiction. Ihab
Hassan, Vilas Research Professor of English and
Comparative Literature at the University of
Wisconsin-Milwaukee, submits a statement on the
underlying ideologies in discourse on the humanities that is responded to by Michael Ryan in
"Why I Am a Communist." One of the long articles is a ground-breaking investigation by Susan
Schweik (University of California-Berkeley) on
the Nisei poet Toyo Suyemoto, who was interned
with other Japanese Americans during World
War II. Two of Suyemoto's poems, sent from the
Topaz camp, were published in the *Yale Review* in
1946. Schweik's bibliography includes references
to an internment-camp literary magazine of
1943, *Trek,* and to other specialized documents
on Asian-American writers. (Suyemoto now resides in Columbus, Ohio, where she still writes po-

etry. Suyemoto is her maiden name; her married
name is Toyo Kawakami.) Some of the subjects of
the book pieces are W. E. B. Du Bois, Ernest Hemingway, Philip Roth, and Ezra Pound. The journal, which is printed on acid-free paper, includes
a few advertisements and no illustrations. The editor, Gordon Hutner, received his doctorate at the
University of Virginia. He has taught English at
the University of Wisconsin since 1982 and is
best known for his study of Hawthorne's novels,
*Secrets and Sympathy: Hawthorne's Forms of Disclo-
sure* (University of Georgia Press, 1988).

The *Stanford Humanities Review* (Stanford Humanities Center, Mariposa House, Stanford, CA
94305) is the latest in the line of periodicals from
Stanford University that includes the highly regarded *Stanford French Review, Stanford Italian Review* and *Stanford Literature Review.* Published
triannually, the journal intends to include work
from "a wide variety of disciplines, including an-
thropology, classics, history of science, literary criticism and theory, law and philosophy." The first
issue is dated Spring 1989. The creative side of literary endeavor is represented by three poems by
Adrienne Rich, an excerpt from Gilbert Sorrentino's forthcoming novel, *Misterioso,* and an excerpt from Arturo Islas's work-in-progress, "Mi-
grant Souls" (all three writers are on the Stanford faculty). There are several translations,
including eight sections of Rainer Maria Rilke's
Sonnets to Orpheus (1923) translated by Leslie Nor-
ris (a Welsh poet teaching at Brigham Young University). The book-review section is devoted to
five scholarly reviews of advanced works on
chaos theory, Jacques Derrida, Umberto Eco's second novel, *Il Pendolo di Foucault* (1988), translations of the Spanish prose of Nellie Campobello,
and an anthology of fiction from Latin America.
The editor is Eden Quainton.

Dan De Quille Journal (Falcon Hill Press, Box
1431, Sparks, NV 89432) is a single-author, irregular periodical first published in April 1989. Dan
De Quille was the nom de plume of William
Wright (1829-1898). De Quille achieved fame as
a journalist and editor, writing for Iowa newspapers as well as the well-known *Territorial Enterprise* in Virginia City, Nevada, where he became
an early influence on Mark Twain, who worked
on the newspaper's staff from 1862 to 1864. He
is also known for his western stories and writings
on Nevada's Comstock Lode. The *Dan De Quille
Journal* is a handsomely designed tribute that includes reprints of De Quille's political satires, an
annotated bibliography of literary criticism from

1944 to 1988, and a review of *Dives and Lazarus*, a novella by De Quille that has only recently been published, with an introduction by Lawrence I. Berkove, director of the American Studies Program at the University of Michigan-Dearborn. The editor and publisher, Dave Basso, was born in Lovelock, Nevada, and graduated from the University of Nevada-Reno with a degree in journalism. Besides publishing the journal, his company, Falcon Hill Press, specializes' in limited edition Nevadiana.

Also concerned with western culture, *Comstock Quarterly* (Comstock Chronicle, Inc., P.O. Box 436, Virginia City, NV 89440) publishes poetry, fiction, essays, and artwork that deal with the traditions "of the land around and between the Rockies and the Sierra." Many of the authors invoke a plea for the perpetuation of the western spirit, and most of the presentations are in a popular vein. The first issue is dated Spring 1989. A humorous piece by Dan De Quille, "A Search for Solitude," is reprinted from the *Salt Lake Tribune* (22 August 1891). Ray Gonzalez, the editor of the *Midnight Lamp* (also covered in this report), contributes a poem entitled "The Seduction of Loneliness." The visual arts are represented by reproductions of Jim McCormick's "Comstock Suite," a series of lithographs. The quarterly is edited by Gary Elam.

The *Southern Reader* (Guild Bindery Press, 2071 Lakeway Station, Paris, Tennessee 38242) is a quarterly previewing service providing long excerpts from new nonfiction books on the South. Additionally, it features signed book reviews on other recent publications, including novels. The first number (Summer 1989) includes six excerpts, with an emphasis on Civil War books. Also included is a 1978 interview with the distinguished literary critic Cleanth Brooks, conducted by William Ferris, director of the Center for the Study of Southern Culture at the University of Mississippi. The interview, which is illustrated with photographs from Ferris's personal collection, is announced as forthcoming in an untitled collection of interviews on the South. R. J. Bedwell, the editor, is the owner of the Guild Bindery Press, a journalist, and a teaching assistant in history at Murray State University.

An independent annual journal, *Notes on Modern Irish Literature* (Edward A. Kopper, Jr., Editor, Notes on Modern Irish Literature, R. D. 1, Box 370, Fenelton, PA 16034), publishes "notes of up to 2000 words dealing with Anglo-Irish writers from about 1900 to the present." The first

forty-page issue (Fall 1989) has eight notes: three on James Joyce, two on John Millington Synge, one on Samuel Beckett, and one each on Flann O'Brien and Edna O'Brien. The lead note of two pages is by Joyce scholar Fritz Senn and concerns the phrase "a rump and dozen" in *Ulysses* (1922): a note that may have been more strategically placed in any of the numerous Joyce periodicals. The same could be said of the excellent note on Beckett's use of the "Belacqua" theme from Dante. Irish literature scholars will need access to every issue of *Notes On Modern Irish Literature*, despite its brevity and infrequency. Professor Kopper has his Ph.D. from Temple University. His dissertation was on the subject of Catholic allusions in Joyce's *Finnegans Wake* (1939), and he has published monographs and articles on Irish literature.

The premiere issue of *i: The First Person* (Zeugma Press, P.O. Box 663, Graton, CA 95444) is dated Fall 1989. The eccentric quarterly specializes in "writings and art in the first person point of view." The informal thirty-six-page issue contains short poems and articles on a variety of life experiences. There are no notes on contributors, although a few recognizable small-press poets such as Laurel Speer and Ruth Daigon are represented. It is edited by John Labovitz and Paul Schwartz.

"Miz Martha Say She Quittin' " is the theme of the Autumn 1989 *Thema* (Bothomos Enterprises, Box 74109, Metairie, LA 70033), a quarterly that began with the Autumn 1988 issue, in which the unique concept of asking writers to submit stories and poems that "must relate to a specified unusual topic" was first developed. Previous themes included "Fortune Cookies" and "A Train Wreck Involving a Circus." *Thema* sounds like a lark, and many contributors play up the humorous, even resorting to dialect in their response to the "Miz Martha" theme. The editor/publisher, Virginia Howard, works in the Louisiana State University Medical Center.

Devoted to poetry, fiction, and essays, *Gulf Stream Magazine* (Florida International University, North Miami Campus, North Miami, FL 33181) is bibliographically designated "no. 1" (1989) without an indicator of frequency. It is edited by short-story writer Lynne Barrett, who is an associate professor at FIU, and staffed by graduate students in the university's M.F.A. program. The single issue is priced, but there is no announcement about subscription rates, nor any editorial credo. The contributors' credentials include an impressive array of book-length and periodical publications. Some contributors practice law, some teach, and some are merely identified by their cities of residence, which range from Brooklyn to San Francisco. There are some contributors who are known as small-press regulars, such as Arthur Winfield Knight and Lyn Lifshin, and some received their first publication here. An essay by Kat Meads, "Shall We Gather," provides an incisive portrait of a North Carolina Baptist childhood that leads to a rejection of fundamentalism; and "The Love of Whiskey," by Laurie Kirk, is an honest poem about the attractions of addiction.

Alcohol and drug addiction in literature is actually the specialty of a thirty-two-page journal, *Dionysos: The Literature and Intoxication Triquarterly* (University of Wisconsin-Superior, 1800 Grand Avenue, Superior, WI 54880). It publishes articles, reviews, and news "on any aspect of the relation between intoxication and the cultural/aesthetic scene." The first issue (Spring 1989) includes an article on the drunken wife in Daniel Defoe's *Colonel Jack* (1722) and a comparative study of alcohol in the family context in the works of Tennessee Williams, Eugene O'Neill, and William Inge. Book reviews are included, and also short excerpts from popular press comments by authors on their drinking, such as Athol Fugard on his recent sobriety. The editor, Professor Roger Daniels Forseth, has his Ph.D. from Northwestern University. He joined the faculty of the University of Wisconsin-Superior in 1964. His extensive list of publications includes articles on alcohol and literature and an in-progress critical biography of Sinclair Lewis.

The *Key West Review* (Key West Review, Inc., P.O. Box 2082, Key West, FL 33045) is an ambitious quarterly that has an impressive roster of contributors including Peter Taylor, Richard Eberhart, Richard Wilbur, and James Merrill. Many of the writers have connections with Key West and the other Florida Keys, although the review accepts work from outside the region. The first issue (Spring 1988) has an interview with Alison Lurie, and the second issue (Fall 1988) one with Lawrence Durrell. The editor, William Schlicht, has a Ph.D. in clinical psychology. He had a long professional career as a psychotherapist and is now on a second career as a writer of fiction and critical essays. His essay "Exciting and Comforting Prospects in the Contemporary Novel" (Spring 1988) speculates on trends in modern novels by authors such as John Barth and

Kurt Vonnegut that question the relationship between reality (fact) and imagined worlds ("alternate realities").

The annual *Tampa Review* (University of Tampa, Tampa, FL 33600) began in 1988. The first issue includes a short story by Lee K. Abbott entitled "1963." Abbott is published by major houses and is one indicator of the quality of the contributors. Poets such as William Stafford and Denise Levertov are included, along with newcomers Meg Files and Penelope Laurans. Distinguished artwork graces many pages, as do interviews with artists and filmmakers. The editors decided to "reflect the international flavor of the city of Tampa" and have included significant work by Dmitri Prigov (Russia), Silvia Curbelo (Cuba), Jerzy Jarmiewicz (Poland), and Derek Walcott (Caribbean). The editor, Richard Mathews, holds a Ph.D. in English from the University of Virginia. His dissertation was on the late prose romances of William Morris. An associate professor at the University of Tampa since 1986, he is a poet and also a scholar of science fiction and fantasy. A cadre of faculty editors assist him in editing the departments of poetry, fiction, and nonfiction.

The premier issue of the *Paper Bag* (Michael and Deborah Brownstein, 1839 W. Touhy, Chicago, IL 60626) is dated Winter 1988-89; the next two issues are dated Spring and Summer 1989. A yearly subscription promises "four or more issues." It is a typical little magazine featuring mostly poetry, short fiction (five hundred words or less), and black-and-white artwork. Veterans of the small-press circuit and local beginners are the contributors. One poet, Debbie Rittner, is identified as the "co-founder of the Beth El Arts Chevrah, a synagogue-based group for artists." The widely published Arthur Winfield Knight also contributed a poem. Michael Brownstein is an inner-city science teacher, and Deborah Brownstein is "an artist, photographer, mother, interior decorator, mathematician, wife, student of bioengineering, and the art editor for *The Paper Bag*."

The Appalachian Chain from Alabama to Quebec is the regional focus of a small, semiannual market for poetry, fiction, artwork, and book reviews called *Potato Eyes* (Nightshade Press, P.O. Box 76, Troy, ME 04987). The first issue is dated Spring/Summer 1989; the founding editors are Roy Zarucchi and Carolyn Page. Although creativity originating from Appalachian-related states is their first priority, writers from elsewhere are also considered. John Ditsky, a widely published Canadian poet on the faculty of the University of Western Ontario, is published here, along with the ubiquitous Lyn Lifshin (her biographical note rightly claims that she "has appeared practically everywhere"). A story about rural Maine by Carl Perrin is a humorous look at a town fighting the encroachment of the "summer people." Other country themes include weather vanes, roosters, chickens, and potatoes. Nightshade Press also publishes books, such as Walt Franklin's chapbook of poems, *The Wild Trout* (1989).

Santa Monica Review (Santa Monica College, Center for the Humanities, 1900 Pico Boulevard, Santa Monica, CA 90405) is a semiannual dedicated to publishing original poetry and prose that shuns traditional book reviews and graphics. The editor, Jim Krusoe, has assembled a who's who of contributors for the first two issues (Fall 1988 and Spring 1989), including Joyce Carol Oates, Stuart Friebert, Ann Beattie, Tom Clark, Alice Notley, and Norman Dubie. The style ranges from the traditional to the experimental.

Sycamore Review (Purdue University, Department of English, Heavilon Hall, West Lafayette, IN 47907) is another academically housed semiannual. The first issue (Spring 1989) is ninety pages long and features the work of nineteen poets, including William Stafford, and four fiction writers. There are also two poems translated from Polish and an essay by David Hopes, "Roosevelt Ditch," a meditation on the Northern Ohio landscape near Akron. All of the contributors seem to have been published in other literary reviews, and many have books to their credit. Boyd White, an associate editor of *Iowa Review*, contributes a poem entitled "A Photograph of Cologne, 1945." The editor, Henry Hughes, is a graduate student in the Purdue English Department, host of a local poetry series on radio, and a published poet.

The first number of the annual *Blue Mesa Review* (University of New Mexico, Department of English, Humanities 217, Albuquerque, NM 87131), dated Spring 1989, is a hefty 208 pages. The attractively printed journal will focus on the Southwest but will publish writers from any area. It has attracted some contributors of international prominence such as Robert Creeley. Short stories, novel excerpts, and poems make up the contents, along with three book reviews that evaluate works relating to the Southwest. There is no artwork except for the cover illustration by a Chi-

nese artist. The editor is Rudolfo A. Anaya, a Chicano novelist best known for *Bless Me, Ultima* (1972). The journal was founded to coincide with the centennial of the University of New Mexico (1889-1989).

The Fall 1989 double issue of *Mānoa: A Pacific Journal of International Writing* (University of Hawaii Press, 2840 Kolowalu Street, Honolulu, HI 96822) launches this exquisite semiannual that is comparable to established periodicals such as the *Georgia Review*. It is named after the valley where the University of Hawaii is situated and means in the Hawaiian language, "vast and deep." Poetry and fiction are the main elements, along with a couple of essays, book reviews, and a symposium on the self in contemporary American short fiction. Frederick Busch is represented by an excellent short story, "Pix TK," the title of which hinges on the printer's term meaning pictures to come. Busch is also one of the respondents in the symposium on fiction, along with John Updike and Joyce Carol Oates. The poet Gene Frumkin is given nine pages for a sequence called "Dostoevsky & Other Nature Poems." The varied typography and layout of this sequence are exceptional, with appropriate white space between the broken lines. Since the pages in *Mānoa* measure 7 x 10 inches, there is enough space margin-to-margin to display extra-long lines. These superior production values suggest that the University of Hawaii Press has committed itself to long-term support for *Mānoa*. Photography by Wayne Levin illustrates the journal. The editor is Robert Shapard.

The revived *Story* (F & W Publications, Inc., 1507 Dana Avenue, Cincinnati, OH 45207) continues the short-story outlet founded by Whit Burnett and Martha Foley in 1931. After surviving periods of cessation, *Story* ended its run in 1963. Reintroduced as a quarterly, the first 128-page issue (Autumn 1989) includes an excerpt from Norman Mailer's latest novel, *Harlot's Ghost* (Mailer was launched in the original *Story* in 1941). There is also a reprint of Erskine Caldwell's "Indian Summer," which was published in *Story* in 1932. The editor calls this reprint "A Story Classic," and each issue will include "a story that ignited the career of a famous writer who was first published in *Story*." Emerging writers such as Melissa Pritchard, Wayne Johnson, and Sharon Sheehe Stark are published in the new *Story*, professionally printed on acid-free paper in Baskerville typeface. Each story is preceded by an informal biographical assessment.

MĀNOA

A Pacific Journal of International Writing
Volume 1 · Numbers 1 and 2
Double Issue · Fall 1989

Cover for the semiannual journal edited by Robert Shapard

The editor is Lois Rosenthal, wife of the publisher, Richard Rosenthal, the fourth-generation owner of F & W Publications. The firm was founded in 1868 and is well known for its line of writer's resources such as the magazine *Writer's Digest.*

The *Midnight Lamp* (Mesilla Press, 5719 Allison, Arvada, CO 80002) is an independent poetry/prose journal edited and published by Ray Gonzalez. Gonzalez, who graduated from the writing program at the University of Texas, is a published poet. He has edited an anthology, *Crossing the River: Poets of the Western U.S.* (Permanent Press, 1987); a collection of craft essays, *Tracks in the Snow: Essays by Colorado Poets* (Mesilla Press, 1989); and is also poetry editor of the *Bloomsbury Review* (1028 Bannock Street, Denver, CO 80204). The first issue of the *Midnight Lamp* (Spring 1989) includes poetry, translations, and essays. It presents excerpts from Pablo Neruda's recently translated prose poems, an article on Kenneth Rexroth, poetry by Gary Soto, and a review of Bruce Weigl's Vietnam poems, *Song of Napalm* (Atlantic Monthly Press, 1988).

Onthebus (Bombshelter Press, 6421 1/2 Orange Street, Los Angeles, CA 90048) is a high-quality literary review that publishes poetry, stories, essays, interviews, artwork, translations, and book reviews. It is a solid addition to the growing list of California-based journals that seem destined to overshadow their ancestors out in the Midwest and along the Atlantic seaboard. Jack Grapes, the editor, is a poet and a publisher. His Bombshelter Press has published several volumes of verse, including his own *Trees, Coffee, and the Eyes of Deer* (1987). The roster of names in *Onthebus* includes Stephen Dobyns, Diane Di Prima, Richard Kostelanetz, and Laurel Speer, along with numerous newcomers. Most of the contributors reside in the Los Angeles area. The first issue is dated Winter 1989.

Published abroad in English since 1988, the annual *Tel Aviv Review* (Ah'shav Publishers, 3 Smolenskin Street, 63415, Tel Aviv, Israel) is distributed in the United States by Duke University Press. The review's "Statement of Aims" says it will be devoted to "translations from ancient and modern Hebrew literature; to poetry, fiction and drama of non-Israeli Jewish writers; and to essays on aspects of Judaism, Israel, the Middle East, and other issues bearing on these." The journal's political position is defined as "liberal." Each book-length issue is a rich compendium of fiction and nonfiction, including recognized writers such as Dannie Abse, Yehuda Amichai, John Hollander, Irving Howe, Naguib Mahfouz, and Jon Silkin. Interviews with Isaac Bashevis Singer and Allen Ginsberg appeared in the first two annuals. Much of the material included in the review was written originally in Hebrew (some also in French and Russian) and is translated into English for the first time. Political questions covered thus far include the Holocaust and the Palestinian situation. Gabriel Moked, a literary critic who received his Ph.D. in philosophy from Hertford College, Oxford, is the editor.

Theatre Insight (Theatre Insight Associates, Winship Drama Building, Austin, Texas 78712) was created as a publishing outlet for emerging scholars and graduate students. The first issue is dated Autumn 1988. Three twenty-eight-page issues are promised each year. Group-edited by graduate students in the drama department at the University of Texas at Austin, the theme of the inaugural number is "The Female Protagonist." Articles cover such topics as the feminist/

socialist rhetoric in Caryl Churchill's play *Vinegar Tom* (1976) and the use of Marilyn Monroe's persona in plays written since her death in 1962. The journal also includes book reviews and notes on important theater archives.

Editor/publisher Ruben Sosa Villegas has launched the *Blood Review: The Journal of Horror Criticism* (Blood Review, P.O. Box 4394, Denver, CO 80204) as a serious quarterly devoted to research and news on the horror genre. The first seventy-two-page issue (October 1989) is attractively printed and benefits from a professional layout (Villegas is layout editor of the *Rocky Mountain News*). The first article, written by Villegas, is entitled "Magazine Madness." It is a useful survey of recently defunct and existing magazines of horror that must be the best checklist of the field. A section called "Bookmarks" has detailed information on new books, awards, and conventions. The "People" section profiles John Skipp and Craig Spector, labeled as "splatterpunk" writers, that is, writers who use an overabundance of gore in their fiction. The first issue of the *Blood Review* also includes book reviews, an essay on genre definitions in science fiction, interviews, artwork, original fiction and poetry, and a discussion of horror films. Stephen King's books, and movies based on them, are heavily covered.

The *Science Fiction & Fantasy Book Review Annual* (Meckler Corporation, 11 Ferry Lane West, Westport, CT 06880) began in 1988 as "a comprehensive critical overview of the genres of science fiction, fantasy and horror in 1987." Coedited by Robert A. Collins and Robert Latham, the first 486-page hardbound annual is an ambitious qualitative bibliography that includes roughly six hundred reviews of fiction and nonfiction. Each review is signed and discusses such things as plot, genre, literary value, and comparisons to similar books. In addition, four essays by noted experts survey the year's work in fantasy, horror, science fiction, and research and criticism. Each essay has a best-of-the-year list that should assist collection development in libraries. A section entitled "Writer of the Year" profiles Orson Scott Card and includes primary responses from Card to the profiler, Mark L. Van Name. The volume concludes with a title index.

According to the editor's preface, *War, Literature, and the Arts* (United States Air Force Academy, Department of English, USAF Academy, CO 80840) is "a forum in which scholars can exchange ideas and examine intellectual perspectives on war as depicted in fiction, film, painting, or other art forms produced within any culture or cultures, past or present." The first semiannual issue is dated Spring 1989 and includes articles on the literature of Vietnam, the Vietnam Veterans Memorial, Thomas Pynchon's *Gravity's Rainbow* (1973), Thomas Mann's wartime memoirs, Homer's *Iliad*, and *The Song of Roland* (illustrated with scenes from *The Bayeux Tapestry*). The editor of the first issue, Lieut. Col. James R. Aubrey, has left the USAF Academy and is now teaching eighteenth-century English literature at Metropolitan State College in Denver. The new editor, Lieut. Col. Donald C. Anderson, USAF Academy, has his MFA in creative writing from Cornell University.

Published twice a year, *Cardozo Studies in Law and Literature* (Cardozo School of Law, Jacob Burns Institute for Advanced Legal Studies, Yeshiva University, 55 Fifth Avenue, New York, NY 10003) began publication with the Spring 1989 issue. The editor, Richard H. Weisberg, is supported by eight coeditors and an editorial board boasting names such as Stanley Fish. The journal hopes to encourage interdisciplinary work on the relationship between law and literature, recognizing that judges and lawyers rely on language as much as writers. Legal themes in fiction are the focus of the first number, which includes ten articles on Herman Melville's story "Billy Budd" that were presented at a symposium in October 1987. The credentials of the authors are split between English and law. Forthcoming are studies of the late deconstructionist Paul de Man and the novelist Salman Rushdie.

Humor: International Journal of Humor Research (Walter de Gruyter, Inc., 200 Saw Mill River Road, Hawthorn, NY 10532) is a refereed academic quarterly devoted to the interdisciplinary study of humor. Published in English by Mouton de Gruyter in Berlin and edited by Victor Raskin (Purdue University Department of English), the first issue (1988) includes essays on the classification of puns, laughter and blood pressure, laughing as a defensive process, the application of the semantic theory of humor to advertising, and a definition of the discipline of "humorology." Book reviews cover two books on Jewish humor and one on the films of Woody Allen. Deficiencies in the books are acutely revealed. A back section called "Newsletter" publishes short notes, letters, and conference announcements.

Scholarship addressed to feminist concerns is the backbone of the *NWSA Journal: A Publication of the National Women's Studies Association*

(Ablex Publishing Corporation, 355 Chestnut Street, Norwood, NJ 07648). A mixture of sociology, cultural criticism, and literary analysis, the quarterly includes a variety of subjects: teaching American women's literature in China, lesbian sexuality, texts for teaching an introduction to women's studies, African-American women's literary history, and the problem of integrating Jewish women's history into feminist studies. The book reviews are numerous and long, some running four or five pages and comparing related titles. There is a special section on research-in-progress, and a listing of books received. More than fifty editors and advisers are listed as supporting the primary editor, Mary Jo Wagner, who is headquartered at the Center for Women's Studies, Ohio State University. She has her Ph.D. in Women's History and American History from the University of Oregon. The journal began with the Autumn 1988 issue.

Critical Studies: A Journal of Critical Theory, Literature & Cultural Studies (Editions Rodopi, 233 Peachtree Street, N.E., Suite 404, Atlanta, GA 30303) is an English-language semiannual forum of "contemporary theory, poetics, and cultural history with emphasis on areas of scholarship committed to critical interrogations within disciplines or systems, and through the range of cross-disciplinary inquiry." It is open to scholars worldwide interested in such fields as "literary theory, philosophy, and history, as well as gender, ethnic, media and cultural studies." The first issue (Spring 1989) includes an article on the definition of Hispanic modernism by Iris M. Zavala (University of Utrecht); Jerome J. McGann (University of Virginia) on William Blake, with respect to the issue of truth in poetry; and a summary by Teun A. van Dijk (University of Amsterdam) of his recent study of news discourse in the press. All correspondence related to editorial matters should be sent to the editor, Myriam Diaz-Diocaretz, University of Amsterdam, Department of Literary Studies, Section of Discourse Studies, 210 Spuistraat, 1012 VT Amsterdam, Netherlands. Diaz-Diocaretz is a published poet who has also written monographs on Adrienne Rich, poetic discourse, and feminist identity.

Stephen Crane: A Revaluation
Virginia Tech Conference, 1989

J. D. Stahl
Virginia Polytechnic Institute and State University

The conference "Stephen Crane: A Revaluation," organized by Paul Sorrentino and held at Virginia Polytechnic Institute and State University on 28-30 September 1989, offered new insights and interpretations of Stephen Crane's life, as well as his poetry, fiction, and journalism. Attended by about forty scholars from across the United States and by the leading Japanese Crane scholar, Zenichiro Oshitani of Kyoto Prefectural University, the conference was particularly noteworthy for the exposure of forgery and fraud in the influential biography of Crane by Thomas Beer and for the vigorous incursion of postmodern critical methods into Crane scholarship in papers by various participants, particularly by Lee Clark Mitchell of Princeton University and Donald Pease of Dartmouth College. The conference was distinguished by lively and open-minded dialogue between representatives of traditional scholarship and several Young Turks of postmodernist theory. As such, it represents a turning point in Stephen Crane studies.

James D. McComas, the new, internationally minded president of Virginia Polytechnic Institute and State University, welcomed the group, especially honoring the presence of Professor Oshitani, the pioneer of Japanese Crane scholarship. In the first session, Walter Sutton of Syracuse University and Donald Vanouse of SUNY–Oswego each placed Crane's poetry in somewhat different relations to the Modernist movement. Sutton, in "Stephen Crane and Modern Poetics," analyzed the affinities to and differences between Crane's writing, both poetry and prose, and the principles and practices of the Imagists. He found in Crane's uses of irony and paradox an effort that has its place in the modern. Taking a different approach, Vanouse, in "A Man Spoke to the Universe: Fantasy in the Poetry of Stephen Crane," examined the ambition of the poetry, an ambition declared but not defined by Crane himself. It is an effort which through the "fantastic imposes alternative possibilities [to realism] in the

structuring of the world." Vanouse interpreted the poems as Crane's effort to suggest meanings that arise from doubt and indirection, linking them in purpose to the koan rather than to the "sensory precisions" of haiku or imagist poetry. By analyzing the fantasy poems that deal with writing itself, Vanouse concluded that "the ambition of Stephen Crane's poems appears to be the liberation of the issues of perception and expression from the narrow parameters of individual psychology and cultural environment which circumscribe them in his prose writing."

In a superb introduction to the session on biography, John Clendenning of California State University, Northridge, quoted Sigmund Freud's caustic observation about the problems of biography: "Whoever turns biographer commits himself to lies, to concealment, to hypocrisy, to embellishments, and even to dissembling his own lack of understanding, for biographical truth is not to be had, and even if one had it, one could not use it," a statement particularly appropriate to the revelations Stanley Wertheim was about to make. Clendenning noted, without condemnation, that each of the three best-known biographies of Stephen Crane, by Beer, John Berryman, and R. W. Stallman, is an expression of the personality of its author "inscribed between the lines in invisible ink." He also drew attention to the function of the recently published *Correspondence of Stephen Crane*, edited by Wertheim and Paul Sorrentino, as an "*ur*-biography" that can aid in the crucial process of separating myth, error, and subjectivity from the verifiable facts of Crane's life.

Wertheim, of William Paterson College, produced a major highlight of the conference with his paper "Thomas Beer: The Clay Feet of Stephen Crane Biography," (coauthored with Sorrentino) in which he proved that Beer's 1923 biography *Stephen Crane: A Study in American Letters*, which has widely influenced Crane scholarship, is fraudulent and to a significant degree fictional. Wertheim, in August 1988, discovered in

STEPHEN CRANE

A Revaluation

September 28-30, 1989

LOCATION: Donaldson Brown Center for Continuing Education, Virginia Tech, Blacksburg, Virginia

SPONSOR: Department of English, College of Arts and Sciences, Virginia Tech

FOR MORE INFORMATION: Contact Paul Sorrentino, Department of English, Virginia Tech, Blacksburg, VA 24061-0112, phone 703-231-6501

PARTICIPANTS

John Clendenning, California State University, Northridge • James B. Colvert, The University of Georgia • William Crisman, The Pennsylvania State University, Altoona • Elizabeth Friedmann, Jacksonville, Florida • Ronald K. Giles, East Tennessee State University • Miriam Gogol, Fashion Institute of Technology • Patricia I. Heilman, Indiana University of Pennsylvania • W. Milne Holton, The University of Maryland • J. C. Levenson, University of Virginia • Amy Kaplan, Mount Holyoke College • Sally McWilliams, University of Washington • Elaine Marshall, Atlantic Christian College • Michael J. Mendelsohn, The University of Tampa • Lee Clark Mitchell, Princeton University • George Monteiro, Brown University • Zenichiro Oshitani, Kyoto Prefectural University • Hershel Parker, University of Delaware • Donald Pease, Dartmouth College • Kevin M. Plunkett, Merrimack College • Michael Robertson, Lafayette College • David Roessel, Shaker Heights, Ohio • Joyce Caldwell Smith, University of Tennessee, Chattanooga • Walter Sutton, Syracuse University • Donald Vanouse, State University of New York, Oswego • Stanley Wertheim, The William Paterson College of New Jersey • Chester L. Wolford, The Pennsylvania State University, Behrend College

Poster announcing the conference intended to bring together traditional and postmodern approaches to Crane's works

the Thomas Beer Papers at Yale the early and middle drafts of most of Beer's biography. By careful comparison of the differing versions of Crane's letters as they appeared in subsequent drafts (none of the "original" letters are extant, a fact that is in itself suspicious), Wertheim showed how Beer embellished, altered, and edited the letters which he, it appears now, almost certainly fabricated. Beer's alterations in the chronology of Crane's life, his advocacy of a myth of "Saint Stephen the Martyr," and his obfuscation of Crane's character led Wertheim to assert that "letters, accounts of incidents and persons and chronology which cannot be verified from sources outside of Beer's writing should be extirpated from Crane biography and criticism. . . . The proverbially elusive Stephen Crane will seem more elusive than ever."

Beer appears to have fashioned his version of Crane's life less out of a motive to deceive than out of a passionate admiration that could not, in its idolatrous love, distinguish between his imagined version and reality. There is a Cranean irony in the fact that one of his most influential biographers invented a vivid Stephen Crane who has long been accepted as the real one.

Free-lance journalist Elizabeth Friedmann (who was featured in *Newsweek* in 1987 for her efforts as a scuba diver in finding the sunken wreck of the *Commodore* and who is writing a biography of Cora Crane) skillfully presented evidence that demolishes R. W. Stallman's characterization of Cora Howorth's life as "banal" and John Berryman's view of Crane's attraction to Cora as a "manifestation of an Oedipal fixation which compelled Crane to seek out and try to rescue 'fallen women.' " Friedmann, in "Cora Before Crane: The Prologue," assembled much more detailed evidence concerning Cora's early life than Lillian Gilkes did for her 1960 biography, *Cora Crane.* Friedmann demonstrated the social prominence of Cora's previous two marriages, the first to Vinton Murphy, son of the controversial, politically important former collector of the port of New York, Thomas Murphy; the second to Donald Stewart, a highly decorated British military officer "with a weakness for drink, horse-racing, and American women." Gambling and racehorses were interests that connected the men in Cora's life, beginning with Jerome Stiver, the son of the leading carriage manufacturer of New York, with whom she lived for four years before she married Vinton Murphy. Her second marriage ended after she began an affair with Ferris Thompson, a Princeton alumnus and inheritor of his father Samuel C. Thompson's banking millions. Friedmann established that the travel notes that Gilkes assumed were from Cora's journey to Greece with Crane are probably notes from one of Cora's journeys with Ferris Thompson (whom Gilkes inexplicably identified as a young theological student), thus undercutting Gilkes's position in the long-standing argument between her and Stallman about the likeliest route of Crane's journey to Greece. Cora's wide-ranging interests and her managerial skills furthermore contradict the image of her as an undereducated opportunist who "discovered" her literary calling when she met Crane. As Friedmann argued, if Cora's memorandum book, the source of her travel notes, predates 1896, it "establishes Cora as a thoughtful reader and aspiring writer, with a craving for adventure and disdain for conventionality that would find their match in the person of Stephen Crane." Friedmann also offered a display of artifacts she recovered from the *Commodore.*

In the following session on fiction, Milne Holton of the University of Maryland analyzed the indebtedness of Crane's story "Death and the Child," written in the fall of 1897, to the experiences he described in battlefront dispatches sent to the *Westminster Gazette* and the *New York Journal* that spring. The confrontation with the "upturned face," a symbol of death and of the indifference of the universe made notorious by Michael Fried in his interpretive study *Realism, Writing, Disfiguration: On Thomas Eakins and Stephen Crane* (1987), is perhaps best represented in "Death

and the Child," Holton suggested. Drawing on the similarities between Crane's "The Open Boat" (1897) and James Dickey's *Deliverance,* (1970), Chester Wolford of Pennsylvania State University–Erie gave a close reading of both works that crystallized the character of each writer's naturalism. While both writers are intensely concerned with personal honesty, though well aware of necessary self-deceptions, Dickey "wrests from [a strictly materialistic universe] a celebration lacking in [Jack] London's mythology and Crane's bitter irony." Patrick Dooley, professor of philosophy at St. Bonaventure University, argued that Crane paid attention to "marginal ethical matters"–responsibilities to animals, on the one hand, extraordinary situations calling forth heroic actions on the other. Dooley selected "The Monster" (1898) as the crucial test case for the middle range of ordinary moral questions and proposed through his interpretation of Dr. Trescott's actions that it was dubiously heroic of the doctor not to seek to preserve Johnson's life, but to put Johnson's care above his family's welfare in the long run. Dooley argued that Crane was remarkably nonjudgmental about the responses of the residents of Whilomville. Ultimately, as the story "A Mystery of Heroism" (1895) confirms, "Crane's central moral position firmly rests on two norms: an unselfish response to genuine human need and a tolerant respect for others . . . Crane's maxim of tolerance requires patience, openness and sensitivity to the meaning and context required for a correct ethical judgment."

Lee Clark Mitchell of Princeton University, in his talk, "Face, Race, and Disfiguration in Stephen Crane's 'The Monster,' " presented a theoretically sophisticated interpretation of the concept of disfigurement in order to suggest answers to the question "Is 'the monster' the disfigured black man or is it the town that comes to disfigure him?" Mitchell focused upon verbal figures, prosopopoeia in particular, casting in doubt Fried's "visualizing interpretation" of *The Monster and Other Stories* (1899). In Mitchell's words, Fried argues "that Crane was obsessed with the primal 'scene of writing,' and that the ubiquitous image of disfigured faces in the work reenacts the moment of putting words on a page." By contrast, Mitchell examined the "disfiguration" of language that the story enacts through Henry Johnson's loss of facial features and through racist narrative strategies. Mitchell concluded that the story "that so obsessively figures forth characters as upturned countenances, and that at the same time so explicitly confronts the implications of facelessness, moves through an artfully repetitive structure that seems to promise a coherent moral, and yet ends by defying a reader's projective assumptions." Mitchell's talk was one of several at this conference that sought to confront the implications of Fried's controversial book, a work that was much honored by the intensity of the criticism leveled at it.

One of the highlights of the conference was the showing, in conjunction with a literature and film course, of the feature-length film adaptation of "The Monster," *The Face of Fire* (1959), directed by Albert Band and starring Cameron Mitchell and James Whitmore. The film, in which Henry Johnson is a white man, was introduced by Professor Shoshana Knapp of Virginia Polytechnic Institute and State University, who also led the discussion afterwards, noting how issues of race, society, and narrative form were altered through the process of cinematic adaptation.

Professor Zenichiro Oshitani of Kyoto Prefectural University, in "The Theory of Complementary Colors in *The Red Badge of Courage* and Henry's Mental Development," established that Crane, through Hamlin Garland, was familiar with theories of color from Goethe's *Zur Farbenlehre* (1810; translated as *Goethe's Theory of Colours*, 1840). Oshitani argued that the use of complementary colors, in particular red and green, and purple and gold, combinations that when mixed on a palette produce gray, not only suggests emotional states but comments on the degree of Henry's maturity in the novel as well. Oshitani, the author of the only three books on Crane to appear so far in Japan, also surveyed the reception of Crane in Japan. From 1965 to 1985, 137 articles on Crane appeared in Japan, compared to 565 on Ernest Hemingway, 300 on Mark Twain, and 640 on Henry James.

Through a close examination of the draft of *The Red Badge of Courage* (1895) compared to the final manuscript, Professor Kevin J. Hayes of the University of Delaware showed that Crane learned about the nature of his protagonist as he composed and revised and that Crane increasingly emphasized Fleming's alienation and confusion. The changes Crane made as he revised his draft intensify the ironic treatment of Fleming, increase his isolation, and contradict the possibility of his maturation. Hayes made the case that Crane's creative process in composing the novel was effectively concluded in the summer of 1893

and that the revisions he made immediately before the novel was published by Appleton in 1895 "seem more and more like simple publishing house expurgations rather than coherent, purposeful changes made by an author during the creation of a novel."

How did Crane arrive at the style of "realism" that marked *A Red Badge of Courage*, a style that caused some early readers to marvel at the authenticity of the novel? George Monteiro of Brown University, in his paper "Man in the Open Air: Crane, Rimbaud, and Some Others," compared Crane's descriptions of a soldier's battlefield behavior with Oliver Wendell Holmes's account of his own experience of battle and injury in a letter of 23 October 1861 to his mother, as well as to images of battlefront emotions, based on direct experience or imagined, in writings by Crane's contemporaries Thomas Wentworth Higginson and Henry Adams. Monteiro pointed to the convention of the "corpse among the flowers" as one possible source for the style of description Crane employed and noted that Crane's wide reading of war stories no doubt influenced his imagination in writing *The Red Badge of Courage*. However, Monteiro also presented a more surprising source of imagery for Crane's descriptions of Henry Fleming's encounters with death: temperance literature. Monteiro convincingly demonstrated parallels between the horrors of delirium tremens as described in temperance texts and the horrors of dead and dying bodies as seen by Henry Fleming. The symbolism of blue in the Blue Button Temperance Brigades entered into Crane's work directly and indirectly, and Monteiro suggested that it was an ironic and oblique but fitting tribute to Crane that Temperance Crusader Col. Henry H. Hadley entitled his memoirs, published in 1902, *The Blue Badge of Courage*.

A judicious and perceptively discriminating survey of the impact on Crane studies of recent critical theory was offered by University of Georgia Professor James B. Colvert in "Stephen Crane in Some Postmodern Perspectives." Skewering Michael Fried's book and a 1981 article by Charles Swann as "examples of empty critical extravagance," Colvert praised recent essays by Amy Kaplan, Andrew Delbanco, Christine Brooke-Rose, and Lee Clark Mitchell (in a volume edited by Mitchell, *New Essays on The Red Badge of Courage*, 1986) for applying postmodern critical ideas to practical criticism in fruitful and stimulating ways.

Donald Pease of Dartmouth College presented one of the most challenging papers of the conference, "*The Red Badge of Courage* as the Domestication of Urban Life." Pease argued that *The Red Badge of Courage* examines protosocial forces: emotions that human beings regress to in extreme situations such as war. Crane recognized the connection between the mass forces operating in the Civil War and the mass movement of urban industrialization, and henceforth used war as a metaphor to describe industrialization. For Crane, existence in society was a state of permanent war, Pease asserted. Crane revealed the "endlessly provisional *ad hoc* negotiations of the subject in relation to shifting forces" in his fiction.

J. C. Levenson of the University of Virginia, in "Crane's Modernity," argued against reductive categorizations of Stephen Crane. "Complexity is the historic condition," he stated. "When a pigeonhole becomes as big as an aerie, it still won't do." Something like William James's "faculty psychology," which states that bodily responses precede and evoke emotions, rather than the reverse, is visible in Crane's writing, and Crane explores the "relation of consciousness and event" through disjunction and irony. Yet, beneath the irony, Levenson asserted, lies a faith in real values. "The moral center reminds us that Crane held tight to the old-fashioned virtues–courage, loyalty, grace under pressure–in a world of flux so inhospitable that his commitment could seem absurd."

Finally, in a panel session on Crane's journalism, William Crisman of Pennsylvania State University–Altoona defended the newspaper sketch "The Revenge of the Adolphus" (1899), not as a masterpiece, but as a piece of writing that explores, in remarkably complex ways, the problems of journalistic observation and reporting. Patricia Heilman of the journalism department of Indiana University of Pennsylvania traced "The Influence of Stephen Crane's Seaside, Western, and War Journalism on His Re-

lated Fiction," noting Crane's reluctance to judge customs and values in Mexico and his ability to transmute the materials of reportorial experience into art in his short stories. Michael Robertson of the Department of English at Lafayette College classified the critical modes of approach to Crane's journalism as hierarchical, egalitarian, and contextual. He explored the virtues and possibilities of the third methodology in particular, citing Peter Conrad's chapter on Crane in *The Art of the City* as an excellent example. He pointed out, however, that Crane's assumption of the role of a tramp in "An Experiment in Misery" (1894) owed less to a "streak of posturing knight errantry in the young man," as Conrad claims, than to the fact that "each week during early 1894, when [the sketch] appeared in the *New York Press*, Joseph Pulitzer's *New York World* published an article by a reporter who assumed a temporary identity as a member of some exotic or marginalized social group: a firefighter, a lion tamer, or a member of Coxey's Army of tramps, to take three examples." Robertson drew attention to the fact that excellent editions of Crane's journalism can have the unintended effect of encouraging scholars to read the work out of its original journalistic context. David Roessel of Shaker Heights, Ohio, brought to light the professional rivalry between Crane and Richard Harding Davis. Crane's novel *Active Service* (1899), set in the Greco-Turkish War, parodies Davis, and Davis's romantic farce, the play *The Galloper* (1906), borrows its plot and characters from Crane's novel but turns its satiric edge against the character who represents Crane–showing "that Davis still considered the dead Crane a rival."

"Stephen Crane: A Revaluation" lived up to its name. It provided a forum for close readings and reinterpretations of Crane's texts, the dramatic disclosure of Thomas Beer's falsification of Crane's life, and the revolutionary integration of postmodernist discourse and methodology into the dialogue and practice of Stephen Crane scholarship.

Donald Barthelme
(7 April 1931 - 23 July 1989)

Stanley Trachtenberg
Texas Christian University

See also the Barthelme entries in *DLB 2: American Novelists Since World War II* and *DLB Yearbook: 1980.*

BOOKS: *Come Back, Dr. Caligari* (Boston: Little, Brown, 1964; London: Eyre & Spottiswoode, 1966);

Snow White (New York: Atheneum, 1967; London: Cape, 1968);

Unspeakable Practices, Unnatural Acts (New York: Farrar, Straus & Giroux, 1968; London: Cape, 1969);

City Life (New York: Farrar, Straus & Giroux, 1970; London: Cape, 1971);

The Slightly Irregular Fire Engine; or, The Hithering Thithering Djinn (New York: Farrar, Straus & Giroux, 1971);

Sadness (New York: Farrar, Straus & Giroux, 1972; London: Cape, 1973);

Guilty Pleasures (New York: Farrar, Straus & Giroux, 1974);

The Dead Father (New York: Farrar, Straus & Giroux, 1975; London: Routledge & Kegan Paul, 1977);

Amateurs (New York: Farrar, Straus & Giroux, 1976; London: Routledge & Kegan Paul, 1977);

Here in the Village (Northridge, Cal.: Lord John Press, 1978);

Great Days (New York: Farrar, Straus & Giroux, 1979; London: Routledge, 1979);

Presents (Dallas: Pressworks, 1980);

Sixty Stories (New York: Putnam's, 1981);

Overnight to Many Distant Cities (New York: Putnam's, 1983);

Paradise (New York: Putnam's, 1986);

Sam's Bar: An American Landscape, with Seymour Chwast (Garden City, N.Y.: Doubleday, 1987);

Forty Stories (New York: Putnam's, 1987);

The King (New York: Harper & Row, forthcoming 1990).

Donald Barthelme (photograph by Jerry Bauer)

PLAY PRODUCTION: *Great Days,* New York, American Place Theater, 15 June 1983.

SELECTED PERIODICAL PUBLICATIONS UNCOLLECTED:

FICTION

"Basil From Her Garden," *New Yorker,* 61 (21 October 1985): 36-39;

"Tickets," *New Yorker,* 65 (6 March 1989): 32-34.

NONFICTION

"Not-Knowing," *Georgia Review,* 39 (Fall 1985): 509-522.

When, in the early 1960s, Donald Barthelme first submitted a story to the *New Yorker* magazine, agented, as he later noted, probably by a nine-cent stamp, his innovative fiction at once broke new ground and continued a tradition brought into prominence by such humorists as Robert Benchley, James Thurber, E. B. White, and S. J. Perelman, among others who addressed the complexities of modern urban experience by adopting a posture of reassuring helplessness, or better, of mildly bewildered incompetence. This pose of democratic if knowing elegance was, at least in part, a reaction against the burlesque anti-intellectualism of cracker-barrel wisdom uttered by the shrewd New England Yankee as well as by the literary comedian, whose distortions of language opposed a regional provinciality to a more cosmopolitan pretentiousness. The *New Yorker*, in contrast, was noted for the somewhat elitist taste it championed against a common vulgarity and, perhaps most notably, for the value it placed on precision and clarity of expression. What Barthelme brought to this tradition was a linguistic experimentalism that blended the exaggerations of the Southwest, where he grew up, with the more sophisticated linguistic play of the East Coast, where he lived part of each year. Barthelme's stories do not explore depth of motives or psychological states and do not, in fact, present characters in the usual sense at all. What they dramatize is the play of ideas, or rather of words, which he combines or transforms or invents or displaces or echoes or isolates so that the structure of the narrative seems to hang on surprising and comically disjointed or discontinuous observations. The dilemma encountered in Barthelme's stories, then, is not psychological or social or even spiritual; it is the menace of language not out of control but too sharply reined in.

Early in his career, Barthelme objected to the inarticulateness of the Group Theatre of Lee Strasberg, Marlon Brando, and Elia Kazan that, along with influences such as the neorealism of postwar Italian movies, substituted an inflated poetic rhetoric for genuine feeling, and that finally accepted silence as the only response to what it took to be the inescapably repetitive pattern of history. In contrast, Barthelme's fiction attempts to liberate language and so liberate the figures out of which it is constructed. There is, accordingly, in his stories, a freedom that appears in the unlikely combinations of words, the digressive structure, the freewheeling play with genre and mode, the mixture of social commentary, literary criticism, and the expression of personal anxiety, and the rejection of marginality, all of which affirm

the concrete reality out of which the imagination can be made to speak.

What seems to hold these disparate elements in suspension is a principle of association, often described as collage, that is explicit in Barthelme's earliest stories. In "Florence Green is 81" (collected in *Come Back, Dr. Caligari*, 1964), for example, the self-conscious narrator boasts, "I am free associating, brilliantly, brilliantly, to put you into the problem. Or for fear of boring you: which?" Salted with puns, word games, allusions, unlikely pairings, and with clichés and jargon drawn from a wide variety of social levels including advertising, jazz, Freudian psychology, the military, computer technology, and corporate management, language in Barthelme's stories, as Anatole Broyard noted, "crunches underfoot like broken glass." The result was a unique prose form that appeared distinctly referential, often parodic, even at times autobiographical, but that seemed as well to take place against a background impossible to place, to incorporate elements of fantasy along with readily recognizable aspects of contemporary culture, and even to make language into a world all of its own.

The oldest of five children, Donald Barthelme was born to Donald and Helen Bechtold Barthelme on 7 April 1931 in Philadelphia but soon moved with his family to Houston, Texas, where his father, a noted architect, established his practice. Barthelme attended the University of Houston and worked for a time on the *Houston Post*. In 1953 he was drafted and served in Korea and Japan before returning to Houston where he worked in the public relations department of the university. In "See the Moon?," arguably one of Barthelme's more autobiographical stories, the narrator is hired to work in a university as a "poppycock man, to write the admiral's speeches."

While at the university, Barthelme founded the University of Houston *Forum* and subsequently served for two years as director of Houston's Contemporary Arts Museum. The association led him to accept an invitation to edit the magazine *Location* in New York for Harold Rosenberg and Thomas Hess. The journal lasted only two issues, however, and though he maintained his residence in New York's Greenwich Village, Barthelme returned to Texas, where he continued to teach part of the year at the University of Houston. After three unsuccessful marriages, Barthelme, in 1978, married the former Marion Knox. Though alternating between Houston and

New York, Barthelme was exhilarated by the variety and excitement of his Greenwich Village neighborhood. New York, he once said, reminded him of a Kurt Schwitters collage. He celebrated the city in many of the short pieces he wrote for the "Notes and Comment" section of the *New Yorker* and collected in a volume entitled *Here in the Village* (1978).

Barthelme was uncomfortable with the identification he believed critics made of his work with that of pop artists and sensitive to the charge that it did not offer enough emotion. Although he is known primarily as a writer of short fiction, he was challenged by the sustained involvement that working on a novel offered. His first novel, *Snow White* (1967), a parody of the traditional fairy tale, depicted a heroine whose restlessness accurately reflected the period of the 1960s. Snow White allows herself to engage in sexual relations with all of the dwarfs while waiting both for her prince and for some new words with which she can express her longing. In what may be taken as a comment on the then-widespread cultural attitude that refused to place limits on individual expression, the dwarfs, who do not have the distinctive characteristics that marked the Disney version, are successful businessmen (selling Chinese baby food) while Snow White's sensuality does not interfere with her eventual re-virginization. Including such self-conscious typographical devices as interchapters set in bold-faced, meaningless lists, and even a questionnaire that asks the reader to assess its progress, the novel clearly signaled a break with the assumptions of belief conventional narrative demanded of the reader. Still, Barthelme later acknowledged, the book was not his favorite.

His second novel, *The Dead Father* (1975), equally played with mythic themes, treating the Oedipal struggle between father and son. The action centers on the drawn-out attempt by his children to bury a dominant figure whose influence continues to make itself felt. *Paradise* (1986) Barthelme's third novel, describes the experience of a modern-day architect who seemingly has his fantasies realized when three lingerie models come to live with him only to find the situation yields at least as many domestic pleasures (and irritations) as erotic ones. Barthelme's last novel, a reimagining of the Arthurian legend called *The King* (forthcoming 1990), confirms the mellower, more ruminative posture that informed his later work. Written all in dialogue, the novel projects the mythic characters as part of current events. Ar-

thur not only struggles with his son, Mordred, to rule the kingdom but, against the background commentary of Ezra Pound and a gossipy Lord Haw Haw, he battles against the Nazis during World War II. The comic displacement through which these mythic figures confront contemporary anxieties as part of the ordinary events of their lives both reduces its threatening mystery to the compass of the every day and at the same time invests that dailiness with the qualities of the marvelous that mark Arthurian legend.

Like Barthelme's other novels, there is, in *The King*, little sense of narrative development. It is structured in short chapters (none more than three or four pages) that serve chiefly as the occasions for conversations ranging over a wide variety of topics including aging, taxes, nuclear war, adultery, and the process of fiction. Talking to a reporter, Arthur expresses what might be Barthelme's own view of the role of psychology, not to say autobiography, in fiction. Though a public figure, the King explains, he cannot speak about his inner life, for then "it would be outer not inner and keeping the inner *in* is the very essence of kingship."

At its deepest level, the battle that Arthur fights is what Launcelot, quoting Tennyson, calls "The war of Time against the soul of man," and though like the Court itself, Arthur and, in particular, the promiscuous Guinevere rely on myth-making as a weapon, it is finally to domesticity that the royal couple turns for contentment. As the novel ends, even Launcelot comes to suspect that the dream of Paradise they have imagined is only a fantasy prompted by the knowledge of the apple tree, under whose earthy presence it must eventually come to rest if it is to begin again.

Barthelme died of cancer in Houston on 23 July 1989. He was fifty-eight years old. In a moving tribute by John Barth, Barthelme was described as a rigorous literary craftsman, whose writing was informed by the particulars of "post-Eisenhower American life and a late-modern conviction, felt to the bone, that less is more." Barthelme's work will be remembered and valued, Barth concluded, "for its wonderful humor and wry pathos, for the cultural-historical interest its rich specificity will duly acquire, and—most of all, I hope and trust—for its superb verbal art."

Formal recognition of Barthelme's achievement includes a Guggenheim Fellowship, a PEN/Faulkner Award for his 1981 collection *Sixty Stories*, and a National Book Award in the juvenile literary category for *The Slightly Irregular Fire En-*

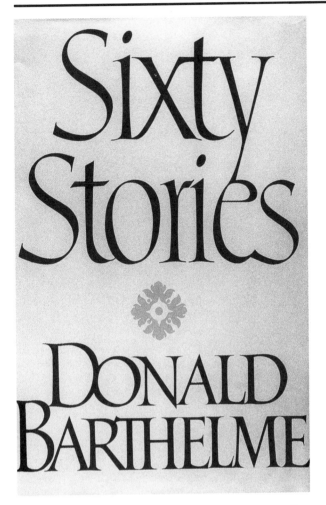

Dust jacket for Barthelme's 1981 retrospective short-story collection, which won a PEN/Faulkner Award for Fiction

gine; or, the Hithering Thithering Djinn (1971), which he also illustrated. In 1974-1975 he served as distinguished visiting professor of English at the City College of the City University of New York. That Barthelme's appeal extends beyond an exclusively academic audience is surprising in the light of the difficulties his innovative style presents. "I was trying to make fiction that was like certain kinds of modern painting," he told one interviewer, explaining that his stories tended toward the abstract. Labeled variously minimal, surreal, experimental, metafictional, Barthelme's stories do not, in fact, resemble the traditional linear narrative that begins with an imbalance–a problem faced or a desire expressed by a central figure–confronts that figure with a person or force that opposes his or her purpose, traces the development or complication of the struggle between them, and finally shows what changes have occurred and what difference they have made in

the reader's understanding of or feelings about things. In *Snow White*, one of the dwarfs sums up what might be taken as the philosophy that informs Barthelme's fiction: "We like books that have a lot of *dreck* in them, matter which presents itself as not wholly relevant (or indeed, at all relevant) but which, carefully attended to, can supply a kind of 'sense' of what is going on. This 'sense' is not to be obtained by reading between the lines (for there is nothing there, in those white spaces), but by reading the lines themselves–looking at them, and so arriving at a feeling not of satisfaction exactly, that is too much to expect, but of having read them; or having 'completed' them."

Barthelme provides a metaphor for his own fictive practice in "The Balloon," which deals with a balloon that mysteriously appears over forty-five blocks of midtown Manhattan but which, the narrator takes care to point out, should not be regarded as a situation. "It is wrong to speak of 'situations,' " he insists, "implying sets of circumstances leading to some resolution, some escape of tension, there were no situations, simply the balloon hanging there." Attempts at interpretation are similarly discouraged. "We have learned not to insist on meanings," he reveals, "and they are rarely even looked for now, except in cases involving the simplest safest phenomena." Though the narrator finally reveals the balloon to be a "spontaneous autobiographical expression" resulting from his unhappiness at the absence of his lover, little of his life is, in fact, revealed, and all of it seems under control. The story rather concerns itself with the acceptance of the various ways in which people in the city respond to his creation (and, not incidentally, with the lack of response from the absent lover). What is perhaps most revealing is that no element either of the balloon or its reception–frequently indicated in lists composed of seemingly gratuitous items–appears to be marginal, and though they do indicate human scale none is accorded the attributes that would provide human dimension.

That this shift from the specific does not prohibit a corresponding emphasis on the concrete is one of the defining elements of Barthelme's style. Backgrounds are seldom identified in more than general terms or as part of an invented landscape. In fact, although references to familiar objects and figures are frequently drawn from popular culture, they are placed in an unfamiliar landscape, characteristically more linguistic than social or even psychological. In its more extreme form this reductive tendency emerges in stories consisting of dialogue alone, unencumbered even by tags that indicate who the speakers are, so that, as Barthelme has said, he does not have to get people in or out of doors or even describe them but just deal with their voices.

Barthelme acknowledged wide-ranging influences on his elliptical style from Franz Kafka and Heinrich von Kleist to Rafael Sabatini. He also expressed admiration for the concise prose of Samuel Beckett and Ernest Hemingway, one suggesting a resolve to continue despite the absence of meaningful purpose, the other a sense of rhythm and precision. In addition to writers, Barthelme has acknowledged debts in his work to the filmmaker Luis Buñuel and to musicians such as the drummer Big Sid Catlett, the piano player Peck Kelly, as well as to the country music of Bob Wills and the Texas Playboys. Most important, perhaps, is the influence of modern American artists such as Ad Reinhardt, Barnett Newman, and Frank Stella, whose formal experimentation Barthelme termed a laboratory for everybody.

It is to movies, however, that Barthelme consistently turned for instantly recognizable images against which his stories attempt to establish a reality while pointing to our collective imagination about it. His first collection of stories, *Come Back, Dr. Caligari*, draws its title from a celebrated film of German Expressionism, *The Cabinet of Dr. Caligari* (1919), whose irony lies in the fact that the central figure's anxieties about a mad scientist prove to be the imaginings of an inmate confined in a lunatic asylum. Perhaps the most celebrated of the fourteen stories in the collection is "A Shower of Gold," which views ironically the pose of existential philosophy fashionable during the 1960s. In the story an artist named Peterson appears on a television program called "Who Am I," which explores the condition of absurdity that defines everyone's existence. "Do you encounter your own existence as gratuitous?" Peterson is asked by a woman named Miss Arbor, who interviews him for the program, "Do you feel *de trop*? Is there nausea?" "I have an enlarged liver," Peterson confesses and is immediately accepted as a contestant. Once on the program, however, Peterson adopts an optimistic view of the bizarre occurrences out of which the everyday quality of his life seems shaped. In an ecstatic affirmation of possibility he describes his identity in mythic terms. "My mother was a royal virgin," he ex-

claims, "and my father a shower of gold," to which the story lends its assent with the concluding statement that "although he was, in a sense, lying, in a sense he was not."

Barthelme's second collection of stories, *Unspeakable Practices, Unnatural Acts* (1968), marked a broadening of fictive interests and an increasingly assured mastery of technique, both of which were evident in stories such as "The Indian Uprising," "The Balloon," "Robert Kennedy Saved from Drowning," "The Dolt," and "See the Moon." In "The Indian Uprising," the unlikely attack on a modern city plagued by "baldness, errors, infidelity" by marauding Comanche Indians, is given no logical basis in the narrative but seems to suggest both the war between the sexes and the struggle of the artist to create his art out of a barricade of disparate objects in the face of a more instinctive impulse. Confronted by the unorthodox teacher Miss R., whose relation to him is one of both affection and betrayal, the narrator learns that the only approved form of discourse is the litany. "I hold to the hard, brown, nutlike word," Miss R. declares, pointing out that "there is enough aesthetic excitement here to satisfy anyone but a damned fool."

The barricade of art against the meaninglessness, even the difficulty of getting a grip on experience, is further explored in "Robert Kennedy Saved from Drowning," where the title character is pulled onto firm ground by a narrator who saves him from drowning in a sea of interpretation, and in "See the Moon," where the narrator's attempt to organize the fragmentary nature of his experience into a more coherent progression is both obstructed and made meaningful by the ordinary events of which it consists. Alan Wilde, in his essay "Barthelme Unfair to Kierkegaard," observed that what may be most distinctive about Barthelme's work is "the articulation not of the larger, more dramatic emotions to which modernist fiction is keyed but of an extraordinary range of minor, banal dissatisfactions."

In his essay "Not-Knowing" (1985), Barthelme indicated the relation between imagination and reality in his work by describing the world as a horizon that bounds the efforts of art. That limiting awareness of the world rather than a mimetic attempt to reproduce it remains part of even the most extravagant inventions of his subsequent collections. Focusing on the domestic and personal anxieties that texture the surface of urban living, *City Life* (1970) confirmed Barthelme's reaction against the psychological interiority that defined modernist fiction. In the title story, two young women launching their careers in New York struggle against the exaggerated images often drawn from movie versions of irresponsible wealth and privilege. The struggle takes in both the necessity of immersing themselves in the urban "dance of fear and suggestion" and the distortions to which consciousness subjects them and leaves them with a reluctant acceptance of the compromises such a confrontation demands.

Committed, as a character in "The Glass Mountain" is described, to a "libidinous commitment to reality," Barthelme approaches it through an often contradictory mixture of the figurative and the literal and through a comic treatment of popular myth. In stories such as "Paraguay," "The Falling Dog," "The Policemen's Ball," and "The Phantom of the Opera's Friend," he additionally raises the alternative possibilities of reality often presented through the mocking account art gives of it and the confusion finally of not knowing which is which. Irony is not, however, the controlling mode of Barthelme's fiction; in "Kierkegaard Unfair to Schlegel," two disembodied voices labeled only Q and A conduct a discussion of it which ironically concludes with the admission that the ironic posture, largely defensive in nature, is inadequate. What is wanted, Kierkegaard argues for the story, is not the victory over the world that irony through its distancing provided but a reconciliation with the world.

Such a reconciliation, as the story suggests, must go beyond anecdote. Extending to the opposition of art to reality as well, it becomes the focus of the domestic crises around which Barthelme's subsequent fiction seems to revolve. Though in "Critique de la Vie Quotidienne," the initial story of *Sadness* (1972), the narrator is convinced that "the world in the evening seems fraught with the absence of promise if you are a married man," that urgency itself receives comic treatment in subsequent stories in the collection, whether leading to the flight of pigeons that constitutes one of many exhibits in what may be taken as a palace of art, the troubling sexual dreams that threaten an otherwise perfect city of churches, the equation of drawings and chocolate that qualifies an otherwise triumphant encounter Engineer-Private Paul Klee has with the critics or to the writer Daumier's involvement with his own characters. In "The Sandman," though the narrator shares his girlfriend's view of the world as less satisfactory than art and though he resists her psychiatrist's attempt to reconcile her to it,

he is prepared, on the whole, to accept her at least "as is," while in "The Temptations of St. Anthony," the saint's idealistic withdrawal from the marital and social arrangements of the world is qualified by the narrator's recognition that "you have to keep the ordinary motors of life running in the meantime."

Critics found much less variety and color in *Amateurs* (1976), whose partial truths, sometimes flat humor, and often strained inventions led Richard Locke to question the value of pop art's cool avoidance of narrative. Speaking of Barthelme's facile "fragments of conversation, monologues, historical and literary snapshots, glimpses of domestic strife, the burdens and groans of urban child-raising, and sexual activity," Locke complained that "It's as if Beckett's ashcans had been rounded up to serve as ornamental vases or cocktail party favors." Perhaps the most successful stories were "Porcupines at the University," in which a university administration is confronted with the prospect of a more open and prickly enrollment than it is prepared for and "The Great Hug," which projects the opposition of invention and reality in terms of the always-impending conflict between the imaginative constructs of a Balloon Man and the threatening encounter with a Pin Lady. As in so many of Barthelme's stories, "The Great Hug" turns on the situation of the writer, who attempts to compensate for the absence from or unhappiness of a companion. In "I Bought a Little City," for example, the narrator, whose wealth seems inexhaustible, still finds it inadequate to solve either arbitrary and often contradictory civic demands or his own amorous longings. The distinction between fiction and nonfiction seems more indistinct than ever in *Guilty Pleasures* (1974), a collection of occasional pieces Barthelme labeled as parodies, satires, "brokeback fables," and "bastard reportage." Some originally appeared under the "Notes and Comment" heading of the *New Yorker*. Others are constructed in the form of collage, in which period-style engravings are tagged with humorous captions. The tension generated by these pieces arises more from the self-conscious awareness of their own fictive and typographical strategies than from any internal conflicts the characters experience. At their best more meditations than stories, they are nonetheless frequently cast in the form of narrative or in dramatic situations, where the direct commentary on the absurdities of the culture seems burdened by the attempt to express attitudes or make value judgments.

Virtuosity for its own sake or cleverness (the exposure of superficial similarities in unlikely objects) easily lapses into mannerism and arguably constitutes the greatest threat to Barthelme's experimental style in that the effort seems to show through the spontaneity of his surprising juxtapositions, deadpan reworkings of cliché, anachronisms, or pop images. Such effort seems less apparent in *Great Days* (1979), which, as in the title story, returns from the more oppressive sense of the cultural, professional, and personal situation described in *Amateurs* to if not contentment with then at least appreciation of the ordinary conditions of life.

Nearly half of the sixteen stories in this collection take the form of dialogues that, as in the exchanges between two women in *The Dead Father*, are presented without attribution. The conversations are antiphonal but nonresponsive, often at cross purposes or seemingly without reference to what each speaker is saying. Not surprisingly, they are called upon to repeat what they have said, suggesting something of the mystery with which Henry James's characters often play with speech. Though still somewhat solemn, as in the awareness of aging and loss that troubles two brothers' attempt to comfort themselves in "Morning," or as in the attempt by a woman in "On the Steps of the Conservatory" to deal with rejection, and despite the acknowledgment by one of the speakers in "The Leap" that he is incorrigibly double-minded, they reafffirm the resolve to keep on trying to make a leap of faith. In part that effort is made through the elliptical rhythms and jazz improvisations of the prose itself that marks "The King of Jazz," one of Barthelme's most successful stories and one of his own favorites, as well as the somewhat more plaintive but equally musical "The Abduction from the Seraglio," in which the artist-narrator's description of his work as "the art of the possible plus two" along with his pursuit of someone who exists "in delicate relation to the real" suggest Barthelme's relation to his own fiction. However, in this story, and in "Cortes and Montezuma" as well, Barthelme allows the personal voice to triumph over what history obscures no less than what art invents to take its place.

In *Overnight to Many Distant Cities* (1983), that voice emerges in a series of brief interchapters, the first of which deals with the construction of a utopian city and begins with the statement "They called for more structure." The appeal seems wryly apposite to Barthelme's own

fiction, but despite some skepticism the narrator expresses for part of the loosely designed plan, the "passionate construction" continues along the arbitrary lines that dictate its component parts. Similarly, the dialogue story "Wrack" confirms the principle of arbitrary selection and the reluctance to effect closure while in "The Mothball Fleet" the narrator and the mysterious admiral of a ghost navy proceed at full speed despite the absence of a conventional crew manning the ships.

While Barthelme continued to resist convention both in his social commentary and in his aesthetic criticism no less than in his fictive style (at one point a character makes the case for adultery as almost an obligation of awareness), in these later stories he seems increasingly optimistic about the possibilities for felicity, particularly as they appear in the always transient and scrambled accidents that enliven an urban environment. That transience is suggested even by the title of "Visitors," a story which describes a divorced father's relation with his visiting teenaged daughter and the equal fragility of an affair he has had with a younger woman. The story concludes with Bishop, the father, looking across his garden in the early morning, after a restless night. He sees two old ladies having breakfast by candlelight and wonders whether they are being romantic or just trying to save money on electricity. Balanced between the pragmatic and romantic, the look across the garden leaves things open; yet in the face of uncertainty it is Bishop's insistence on these encounters with the world and his refusal to close out their possibilities that make his awareness at once poignant and necessary.

Confronted with the pointlessness of behavior (each of the many women with whom he is involved has a different obsession) and the variety of forms desire takes, the narrator of "The Sea of Hesitation" nonetheless resists the notion that some people have forgotten how to want, while in "Terminus" even the impending end of an affair (which had been marked by the luminously quirky behavior of the woman) and the self-questioning that accompanies it is welcomed by her reminder that "That which exists is more perfect than that which does not. . . ." The appeal of that which exists is confirmed in the title story, "Overnight to Many Distant Cities," which takes the form of a disconnected series of accounts the narrator gives of his travels. As in "The Sandman," the story concludes with the narrator's only slightly ironic "ecstasy of admiration for what is" and the optimistic prediction, framed in terms of a weather report, for what is about to come.

This appreciation for what is, which becomes increasingly evident in Barthelme's later fiction, finds its most confident expression in "Basil From Her Garden," which was selected for inclusion both in the O. Henry Prize Stories of 1987 and by Raymond Carver for the 1986 edition of the Best American Short Stories. (With some modification the story was incorporated by Barthelme into his novel *Paradise*). In the story, which once more takes the form of exchanges between two figures identified only as Q and A, the spice which adultery adds to Q's life is reduced to the innocence of a literal gift of herbs from his neighbor. The reassurance that transcendence is possible, with which the story concludes, leaves somewhat ambiguous whether what is meant is the getting beyond the limiting discipline of conformity or the painfully uncertain outcome of desire. The surprising, even contradictory, form such desire takes is suggested in Q's fondness for frozen dinners, a product associated more with self-denial than self-indulgence. As in most of his fiction, Barthelme does not afford the reader a distancing perspective from which judgments can comfortably be made. What these fictions do provide is a sense of the variousness and immediacy, ultimately of the concrete quality, which give our lives substance, and therefore meaning, and of equal urgency with which art struggles to express those qualities. Speaking of Samuel Beckett's work, Barthelme called it "an embarrassment to the void." The same might accurately serve to describe the legacy of his own fiction.

Interviews:

J. D. O'Hara, "Donald Barthelme: The Art of Fiction LXVI," *Paris Review*, 80 (1981): 180-210;

Larry McCaffery, "An Interview with Donald Barthelme," in *Anything Can Happen: Interviews with Contemporary American Novelists*, edited by Thomas LeClair and Larry McCaffery (Urbana: University of Illinois Press, 1982).

References:

John Barth, "Thinking Man's Minimalist: Honoring Barthelme," *New York Times Book Review*, 3 September 1989, p. 9;

Anatole Broyard, "Metaphors for Madness" [review of *Unspeakable Practices, Unnatural Acts*],

New York Times Book Review, 12 May 1968, p. 7;

Lois Gordon, *Donald Barthelme* (Boston: G. K. Hall, 1981);

Jerome Klinkowitz, *The Self-Apparent Word: Fiction as Language, Language as Fiction* (Carbondale: Southern Illinois University Press, 1984), pp. 14-15, 30-32, 71-75, and passim;

Richard Locke, Review of *Amateurs*, *New York Times Book Review*, 19 December 1976, pp. 17-18;

Charles Molesworth, *Donald Barthelme's Fiction: The Ironist Saved from Drowning* (Columbia: University of Missouri Press, 1982);

Wayne B. Stengel, *The Shape of Art in the Short Stories of Donald Barthelme* (Baton Rouge: Louisiana State University Press, 1985);

Philip Stevick, *Alternative Pleasures: Postrealist Fiction and the Tradition* (Urbana: University of Illinois Press, 1981), pp. 19-26, 31-40, and passim;

Lee Upton, "Failed Artists in Donald Barthelme's *Sixty Stories*," *Critique*, 26 (Fall 1984): 11-17;

Alan Wilde, "Barthelme his garden," in his *Middle Grounds: Studies in Contemporary American Fiction* (Philadelphia: University of Pennsylvania Press, 1987), pp. 161-172;

Wilde, "Barthelme Unfair to Kierkegaard," in his *Horizons of Assent: Modernism, Postmodernism, and the Ironic Imagination* (Baltimore: Johns Hopkins University Press, 1981), pp. 166-188.

A TRIBUTE

from ROBERT COOVER

The power of Donald Barthelme's originality is evidenced by his name having become an adjective. "Barthelmesque" refers to a style–precise, urbane, ironic, rivetingly succinct, and accumulative in its comical and often surreal juxtapositions– and to a worldview: bleakly comic, paradoxical, and grounded in the beautiful absurdities of language.

Shortly before Donald's death, I received a set of questions from an interviewer who opened his inquiry with a provocative quote from Donald having to do with barnacles on a wreck. I sent him my reply, but the letter got drenched in the mails somehow and arrived completely illegible. The interviewer asked me to send another copy, but in the interim, Donald had died, forcing me to change my verb tenses in the answers, an extraordinarily disturbing but peculiarly

"Barthelmesque" experience, especially juxtaposed as it was, in multiple ways, with the wedding of metaphor and what we call reality in those "underwater wrecks."

There will be many "Barthelmesque" writers and "Barthelmesque" fictions to come, but, as always, none will match the original master, as much tall-tale telling Texan as megalopolitan wit, who so named and (under water we go again) spawned them. One of the great citizens of contemporary world letters.

A TRIBUTE
from JOHN HAWKES

Strength, clarity—even terseness—are perhaps the first words prompted by the memory of Donald Barthelme, a man who was as paradoxical as his work. If he was generally quiet he was also outspoken, a quick and ready demolisher of illusion and mere sentiment. His formidable wit and taciturnity, his impatience with careless thinking and living, this fiercely quiet presence of his was inseparable, paradoxically, from his great gentleness and generosity. He was large, powerful, a Texan (physically and in manner too) who lived both in Houston and New York City—the places suggest the extremes of his personality—who was in fact as intellectual as were many of his friends. He was serious, he could be extremely funny with no more than a word or two, he was loyal, he had no use for pretension, he was quick to help other writers. Once, at a party, when I was complaining about a novel of mine unfairly treated in a review, Don turned and said, "Hell, it's not a cavalry charge." That one typical deflating and supporting sentence helped me then and thereafter. But the single memory that means most to me and that best suggests his extraordinary character, is of Don and Marion at a dinner party they gave in January, 1989, only months before his death. Don had lost weight since I had last seen him, yet his voice was as strong and as much his own as ever. A young couple at that dinner had brought along their new baby which was smaller and even more rarely beautiful than most babies are. While the parents ate, Don, who

sat at the head of the table, held the baby, cradling it against his shoulder. No baby ever looked more protected or more content. For me that's the essential image of Don Barthelme, the ever-gentle and life-giving satirist and visionary writer who was like no other.

A TRIBUTE
from GORDON LISH

It was the early sixties. I lived in San Francisco, had a literary magazine out there, *Genesis West* it was called, wherein Barthelme's "To London and Rome" had appeared. Was putting together an anthology of short stories; Barthelme's "The Piano Player" was an entry. Traveled to New York to accomplish an interview with Barthelme, this for the recordings that were to accompany the anthology. Had three interviews to do in New York—Barthelme, Paley (her story "The Subject of Childhood"), and Purdy ("Daddy Wolf"). No trouble doing Paley and Purdy. But nope, Barthelme said no dice, nothing doing, he's not going to talk into anybody's microphone. So I crossed the street from Paley's to Barthelme's, buzzed his buzzer, and was received by ditto, him with bottle of beer in hand—imported, the beer, not the hand. Did he offer me a beer once he had me in the door? Don't remember. Expect he did. But when I exhibited my recording equipment, no, no, no, no, there was nothing like welcome in his bearing, no. But in due course we made our way into his living room and matters began evolving as I had wished they would. Yes, the interview—on recording tape—did occur, and was produced, this as one of twelve such in the book and audio adjunct *New Sounds in American Fiction*. But here is the substance of my recollection of Barthelme (the Barthelme of that context, that time): he was willing to talk, all right, but he was entirely unwilling to come close enough to the microphone for his talk to be accurately—let us say *amply*—recorded. What other direct contacts I had with Barthelme, over the course of my years at *Esquire* and at Knopf, seem to me not at all as telling as the first one, though certainly not at odds with it.

Malcolm Cowley

(24 August 1898 - 28 March 1989)

Hans Bak
Catholic University of Nijmegen

See also the Cowley entries in *DLB 4: American Writers in Paris, 1920-1939*; *DLB 48: American Poets, 1880-1945*; and *DLB Yearbook: 1981*.

BOOKS: *Racine* (Paris: Privately printed, 1923);
Blue Juniata: Poems (New York: Cape & Smith, 1929; London: Cape, 1929); revised and expanded as *Blue Juniata: Collected Poems* (New York: Viking, 1968); revised and expanded again as *Blue Juniata: A Life* (New York: Viking, 1985);
Exile's Return: A Narrative of Ideas (New York: Norton, 1934; London: Cape, 1935); revised as *Exile's Return: A Literary Odyssey of the 1920s* (New York: Viking, 1951; London: Bodley Head, 1961);
The Dry Season (Norfolk, Conn.: New Directions, 1941);
The Literary Situation (New York: Viking, 1954; London: Deutsch, 1955);
Black Cargoes: A History of the Atlantic Slave Trade, 1518-1865, by Cowley and Daniel P. Mannix (New York: Viking, 1962; London: Longman, 1963);
Van Wyck Brooks, by Cowley and R. D. Oakes (N.p., 1963);
The Faulkner-Cowley File: Letters and Memoirs, 1944-1962 (New York: Viking, 1966; London: Chatto & Windus, 1966);
Think Back on Us . . . A Contemporary Chronicle of the 1930s, edited by Henry Dan Piper (Carbondale & Edwardsville: Southern Illinois University Press, 1967);
A Many-Windowed House: Collected Essays on American Writers and American Writing, edited by Piper (Carbondale & Edwardsville: Southern Illinois University Press, 1970);
A Second Flowering: Works and Days of the Lost Generation (New York: Viking, 1973; London: Deutsch, 1973);
—And I Worked At the Writer's Trade: Chapters of Literary History, 1918-1978 (New York: Viking, 1978);

Malcolm Cowley (photograph by Nancy Crampton)

The Dream of the Golden Mountains: Remembering the 1930s (New York: Viking, 1980);
The View from 80 (New York: Viking, 1980);
Unshaken Friend: A Profile of Maxwell Perkins (Boulder, Colo.: Rinehart, 1985);
The Flower and the Leaf: A Contemporary Record of American Writing Since 1941, edited by Donald W. Faulkner (New York: Viking, 1985);
Conversations with Malcolm Cowley, edited by Thomas Daniel Young (Jackson & London: University of Mississippi Press, 1986);

179

The Selected Correspondence of Kenneth Burke and Malcolm Cowley, 1915-1981, edited by Paul Jay (New York: Viking, 1988);

The Portable Malcolm Cowley, edited by Faulkner (New York: Viking, 1990).

TRANSLATIONS: Pierre MacOrlan, *On Board the Morning Star,* translated by Cowley (New York: A. & C. Boni, 1924);

Joseph Delteil, *Joan of Arc,* translated by Cowley (New York: Minton, Balch, 1926; London: Allen & Unwin, 1927);

Paul Valéry, *Variety,* translated, with an introduction, by Cowley (New York: Harcourt, Brace, 1927);

Marthe Lucie Bibesco, *Catherine-Paris,* translated, with an introduction, by Cowley (New York: Harcourt, Brace, 1928);

Raymond Radiquet, *The Count's Ball,* translated by Cowley (New York: Norton, 1929);

Bibesco, *The Green Parrot,* translated by Cowley (New York: Harcourt, Brace, 1929; London: Selwyn & Blount, 1929);

Maurice Barrès, *The Sacred Hill,* translated, with an introduction, by Cowley (New York: Macaulay, 1929);

André Gide, *Imaginary Interviews,* translated, with an introduction, by Cowley (New York: Knopf, 1944);

Paul Valéry, *Leonardo Poe Mallarmé,* translated by Cowley and James R. Lawler (Princeton: Princeton University Press, 1972; London: Routledge & Kegan Paul, 1972).

OTHER: S. Foster Damon and Robert Hillyer, eds., *Eight More Harvard Poets,* includes poems by Cowley (New York: Brentano's, 1923);

Adventures of an African Slaver, Being a True Account of the Life of Captain Theodore Canot, Trader in Gold, Ivory & Slaves on the Coast of Guinea: His Own Story as Told in the Year 1854 to Brantz Mayer . . . , edited, with an introduction, by Cowley (New York: A. & C. Boni, 1928; London: Routledge, 1928);

After the Genteel Tradition, edited, with contributions, by Cowley (New York: Norton, 1937; revised edition, Carbondale: Southern Illinois University Press, 1964);

Books That Changed Our Minds, edited by Cowley and Bernard Smith (New York: Doubleday, Doran, 1939);

The Viking Portable Library Hemingway, edited, with an introduction, by Cowley (New York: Viking, 1944);

Aragon, Poet of the French Resistance, edited by Cowley and Hannah Josephson, with translations by Cowley and others (New York: Duell, Sloan & Pearce, 1945); republished as *Aragon, Poet of Resurgent France* (London: Pilot, 1946);

The Portable Faulkner, edited, with an introduction, by Cowley (New York: Viking, 1946; London: Macmillan, 1961; revised and enlarged edition, New York: Viking, 1967); republished as *The Essential Faulkner* (London: Chatto & Windus, 1967);

The Portable Hawthorne, edited, with an introduction and notes, by Cowley (New York: Viking, 1948; revised and enlarged, 1969); republished as *Nathaniel Hawthorne: The Selected Works* (London: Chatto & Windus, 1971);

The Complete Poetry and Prose of Walt Whitman, 2 volumes, introduction by Cowley (New York: Pellegrini, 1948); republished as *The Works of Walt Whitman,* 2 volumes, with a new introduction in volume 1 and a new prefatory note in volume 2 by Cowley (New York: Funk & Wagnalls, 1968);

"To a Girl I Dislike," "An Old Fellow to His Friends," and "To a Dilettante Killed at Vimy," in *The Harvard Advocate Anthology,* edited by Donald Hall (New York: Twayne, 1950), pp. 151-153;

The Stories of F. Scott Fitzgerald, edited, with an introduction, by Cowley (New York: Scribners, 1951);

F. Scott Fitzgerald, *Tender Is the Night: A Romance . . . with the Author's Final Revisions,* edited, with a preface, by Cowley (New York: Scribners, 1951);

Three Novels of F. Scott Fitzgerald: The Great Gatsby, Tender Is the Night (With the Author's Final Revisions), The Last Tycoon, edited, with introductions, by Cowley and Edmund Wilson (New York: Scribners, 1953);

Writers at Work: The Paris Review Interviews, first series, introduction by Cowley (New York: Viking, 1958; London: Secker & Warburg, 1958);

Walt Whitman, *Leaves of Grass, The First (1855) Edition,* edited, with an introduction, by Cowley (New York: Viking, 1959; London: Secker & Warburg, 1960);

Sherwood Anderson, *Winesburg, Ohio*, introduction by Cowley (New York: Viking, 1960);

The Bodley Head F. Scott Fitzgerald . . . Short Stories, volumes 5 and 6, selected, with an introduction, by Cowley (London: Bodley Head, 1963);

"A Theme with Variations," "To a Dilettante Killed at Vimy," and "Nantasket," in *Harvard Advocate Centennial Anthology*, edited by Jonathan D. Culler (Cambridge: Schenkman, 1966), pp. 109, 111, 113;

Fitzgerald and the Jazz Age, compiled by Cowley and Robert Cowley (New York: Scribners, 1966);

The Lessons of the Masters: An Anthology of the Novel from Cervantes to Hemingway, edited by Cowley and Howard Hugo (New York: Scribners, 1971);

The Portable Emerson, edited by Carl Bode in collaboration with Cowley (New York: Viking, 1981).

Although his services to American letters were many and diverse, Malcolm Cowley remains best known as the literary historian of the "lost generation." An alert and sensitive witness to the interplay of cultural and historical forces from which emerged, between 1915 and 1930, a distinctly modern American literature, Cowley registered the impact of European modernism on the writers of his age group, writing their collective literary history as he watched it unfold. That literary generation produced a body of creative work complex and challenging enough to require a sustained effort at interpretation and elucidation, and Cowley, in response to the "second flowering" of American literature, helped to develop the set of critical instruments and the historical perspective necessary for an evaluation of its place in the context of international modernism. In the process he helped, in his own fashion, to make American criticism come of age.

The writers of his generation were fortunate in having Cowley as a conscientious chronicler and historian as well as a devoted apologist and loving curator. He first predicted the arrival of a new age group on the literary scene, then aimed to define its achievement at an early stage. Later, he sought to establish its connection with the traditions of the past, while he continued to review its attainments in the light of the shifting present and to judge the present in the light of his changing perceptions of the past. Still later, speaking up as "the Ishmael of his generation," he per-

sistently, with affection as well as critical detachment, defended its achievements against the "jackals" and "parricides" of various critical and political persuasions. At the end of a long career spanning seven active decades he could himself bask in the glow of the classic stature of many of the writers he championed.

Cowley was born on 24 August 1898 in his family's farmhouse near Belsano, Cambria County, Pennsylvania, on the western slope of the Alleghenies, some seventy miles east of Pittsburgh, where his father practiced as a homeopathic physician. Though he received most of his early education in big-town schools, the long summers he spent in the country gave Cowley a deep-seated attachment to rural living: he always thought of himself as a countryman at heart. A lifelong conservationist, he shared William Faulkner's love of the land (as well as his anxiety about its destruction) and empathized with Ernest Hemingway's nostalgia for the lost natural world of the past. For Cowley the landscape of childhood was a magical realm, a country (to quote from "Boy in Sunlight," the opening poem of *Blue Juniata: A Life* [1985]) absorbed and "stamped in the bone" as a way of judgment and perception. The memory of a boyhood rooted in the land reverberated through Cowley's writings; nostalgia remained his strongest poetic incentive, yielding his finest pastoral lyrics, such as "The Chestnut Woods" and "The Urn." The latter expressed most lucidly the feeling of severance and alienation—what Lewis Simpson, in "Malcolm Cowley and the American Writer," has called a "poetics of exile"–at the heart of Cowley's work. To be, as the poem says, a wanderer outside the gates, sustained by memories of home, not only was a leitmotif in Cowley's literary life, it also formed the cornerstone to his interpretation of the writers of his "lost" generation. Though he spent a large part of his professional life in the company of urban writers and intellectuals, in personal life he always sought to root himself in rural environs. Likewise, his conception of culture as an organic outgrowth of the writer's background and experience, his humanistic insistence on the correlation between life and art, and his manifold endeavors to establish a sustaining sense of literary milieu and community are all part of Cowley's attempt to assuage what Alfred Kazin has called the American writer's "alienation on native grounds."

Cowley's parents were hardworking, unpretentious middle-class people. His mother, Josephine Hutmacher, was the daughter of German Catholic immigrants who had settled in Quincy, Illinois. She had little or no interest in books but was supremely skillful in practical matters. His father, William Cowley, descended from a family of Scotch-Irish Presbyterians who around 1840 had settled in Pittsburgh. Like his father before him, he had exchanged the family's protestantism for the mystical writings of Emanuel Swedenborg. Though every day his father would read to him from Swedenborg's writings, as well as from the Bible, Cowley was never formally instructed in religious doctrine. From early youth his pragmatic temperament clashed with his father's predilection for the mystical and transcendental; he had begun to reject Swedenborgianism well before he was fifteen, and in 1912 he refused to stay at a Swedenborgian school near Philadelphia.

Instead, Cowley attended Peabody High School in Pittsburgh. He regularly contributed poems and stories to the school literary paper, the *Peabody*, became president of the debating club, won a medal for essay writing, and was elected class poet in 1915. His most intimate companion at Peabody—they had known each other as toddlers and attended eighth grade together—was Kenneth Burke, the future critic and philosopher of language. The two often met at night at the Carnegie Library, where they were fond of reading technical books on poetry and drama and took a special interest in the modern authors on the librarian's list of "restricted" literature. Their early views on art and life were developed in close communion; they aided each other in their intellectual development and strengthened each other's inclination toward a literary vocation. Their correspondence, extending over seven decades, testifies to their lifelong rivalry and friendship, and constitutes a unique chapter in American literary history.

By the time of his graduation in 1915 Cowley had come to question most of the values of his upbringing. At seventeen he was "converted to indifferentism." Prevailing morality he repudiated as the cloak of a prudish puritanism. To want to be a poet was in itself an act of filial disloyalty; he was, to quote from the confessional "Prayer on All Saints' Day," "a bad son, but a poet"—" 'My world has deeper colors than yours,' / I boasted, 'and the words will come / to match the colors.' " The intensity of Cowley's literary ambition was unmistakable; uncertain were its form and direction. As he observed in *Exile's Return*

(1934; revised and expanded, 1951), his high-school instruction in literature had implied that only foreign authors were worthy of admiration and that America was "beneath the level of great fiction." For a young apprentice writer only Carl Sandburg and Edgar Lee Masters seemed to prove that art could be made out of midwestern provincialism, and Cowley wrote his earliest poetry under their influence. The *Smart Set* first taught him the names of modern European writers—Arthur Schnitzler, James Joyce, D. H. Lawrence, Frank Wedekind, Gabriele D'Annunzio—and set him on a course of reading that continued through his college years and worked a revolution in his literary taste. Cowley's earliest exposure to the sensibility of modernism— "ironical, introspective and self-questioning"—set in motion a process of discovery and adjustment that was by no means easy or unambiguous; it continued through the 1920s and beyond.

In the fall of 1915 Cowley entered Harvard, at the time a veritable mecca for the young, ambitious writer, but one where American literature was held in low critical and scholarly esteem. Nor was there any way to obtain training in the principles of formalist, aesthetic criticism, except outside of academe, either by following one's own critical bent or the example of such poet-critics as T. S. Eliot and Ezra Pound. It would be part of Cowley's achievement to help raise America's understanding of the nature and merit of its literature and to assist in the forging of a critical language and approach for dealing seriously with the formal properties and historical context of modern American writing.

Determined to cultivate literary friendships and make an impact on Harvard's literary scene, Cowley for a while moved on the fringes of the so-called Harvard Aesthetes and allowed his verse to be tainted by their spirit of languishing decadence. He wrote mostly for the *Harvard Advocate*, which published over thirty of his early pieces of prose and verse. Inclined to observe and record as much as to participate, Cowley regularly attended meetings of the Harvard Poetry Society, where he heard Robert Hillyer, S. Foster Damon, and John Brooks Wheelwright (his closest friends at college) recite their unorthodox poetry. Though the aesthetic direction of his poetry was as yet uncertain—he made regular excursions into free verse but had a predilection for such stricter forms as the sonnet and the ballad—critically and temperamentally Cowley was already entrenched on the side of the "moderns." In March 1917 he was elected to the *Advocate* editorial board. As a scholarship student from a midwestern public high school, Cowley was somewhat intimidated by Harvard students from privileged and exclusive prep schools. Neither an "in" nor a complete outsider, he was insecure about his social status and allowed some of the snobbishness and ethnic prejudice of the social elite to rub off on himself. There was, indeed, much in his Harvard experience to foster a sense of culture, not as something organic or endemic to his native background but as "a veneer, a badge of, class distinction."

Cowley's undergraduate studies were interrupted when, in April 1917, he enlisted as a volunteer in the American Ambulance Field Service. Like many of his consorts at the Harvard Poetry Society, he was prepared to don a military uniform without giving much conscious thought to the larger purposes of the war. In France, Cowley was relegated to driving a munitions truck for the military transport service rather than, as he had romantically hoped, an ambulance. Eager to witness history in the making, he jotted down his impromptu observations in a war diary, hoping to rework them into publishable reports. Cowley's "Camion Service Notes" (which are among his papers at the Newberry Library in Chicago) hold the germs of the interpretation he would put on his wartime service in *Exile's Return*; many of them imply the "spectatorial attitude" he later posited as the essence of his and his coevals' war (and postwar) experience. In his diary entries and war reportages, Cowley first developed a sense of himself as the recording instrument of a generational experience. His wartime writings not only made him, in the estimate of Charles Fenton, "the most prolific and polished of the truck-driver writers," they also evinced a dawning capacity for intuiting the historical importance of the present.

Cowley returned to America in late 1917, and over the next three and a half years he regularly resorted to Greenwich Village, alternating his last two semesters at Harvard with forays into New York bohemia. In Cambridge it was the exhilarating presence of such "moderns" as Conrad Aiken and Amy Lowell that made life intellectually exciting. Aiken, a lifelong friend, impressed the young Cowley by his complete dedication to the life of letters, while Amy Lowell, to whom he was introduced by Damon and Wheelwright, helped to place his poems with American magazines. With Ezra Pound, she fanned Cowley's en-

thusiasm for French poetry and further encouraged him in the direction of a "modern" art. In the spring of 1918 Cowley was elected president of the *Harvard Advocate*. Editing the *Advocate* suited him perfectly: it fitted his pragmatic bent, gave him an opportunity to develop his talents for organization and critical selectiveness, and, early, taught him the habit of watching out for new and exciting poets. Demobilized in the fall of 1918, Cowley spent his next ten months in New York before returning to Cambridge to complete his college education. His time in the Village, away from the sheltered literary milieu of Harvard, confronted him for the first time with a problem that would remain a professional preoccupation: how to accommodate his ideals of the literary life with the practical realities of living in American society.

In August 1919 Cowley married Marguerite Frances (Peggy) Baird, recently divorced and much at home in Greenwich Village bohemia. From the first Peggy's freewheeling habits collided with the discipline required to fulfill Cowley's writing ambitions. Cowley entered upon marriage with a strong belief in "conjugal love" derived from his Swedenborgian upbringing; it was only after twelve years that he could bring himself to divorce and remarry. She was content to share the financial insecurities attending Cowley's struggles to live as a free lance on Grub Street and helped him gain a wide acquaintanceship among the writers and editors in the Village. An occasional review, however, was barely sufficient to subsist on, and Cowley was prosaically forced to find work as a copywriter for various commercial magazines. His correspondence shows his time in the Village to have been one of uneasy accommodation to the debilitating conditions of the writing life, a period of discouragement when the possibility of failure loomed large.

By 1919 Cowley had assumed a cynical and disillusioned stance of social disengagement and political noncommitment. Hoping to preserve a personal integrity in the realm of art, he was drawn strongly toward French symbolism, with its emphasis on conscious craftsmanship, its disdain for the world, and its ideal of art as a sacred vocation. Feeling at odds with his native culture, he sought in art the emotional and psychological sustenance others found in tradition or religion. Besides an aesthetic ideal, the creed of symbolism represented for him a literary ethics and a guide to conduct. The spirit and technique of symbolist poetry seemed perfectly attuned to the tone of life in Greenwich Village. The verse of Jules Laforgue, in particular, suggested that one way of dealing poetically with a mood of disenchantment and a squalid urban environment was to cloak one's feelings in irony, "a sort of crooked sentiment, a self-protective smirk." Cowley's early frustrations as a struggling apprentice writer helped persuade him of the need to create, in America, a cultural milieu in which writers, unhampered by practical difficulties and sustained by a sense of literary community, might work in freedom and responsibility to their art.

When he returned to Harvard in the fall of 1919, Cowley found that merely to have lived among the artists and Bohemians in the Village was enough to have him branded a radical revolutionary by the conservative student elite. His last semester at Harvard was a time of social humiliations, which left him with ambivalent feelings about his alma mater. In February 1920 Cowley was graduated from Harvard "as of 1919." He earned his B.A. degree as well as a Phi Beta Kappa key, having finished his college education in a little less than six semesters scattered over five calendar years. Cowley's departure from Harvard coincided with the beginning of his connection with the *Dial*, newly refurbished under the editorial direction of James Sibley Watson and Scofield Thayer. In its pages Cowley and Burke represented a younger generation with an outspoken, if not unambiguous, interest in modern, avant-garde writing. Writing for the *Dial* helped to establish Cowley's position as a poet and critic in the 1920s; he gave it his best and most substantial early reviews and essays, as well as some of his better poems. For Cowley, indeed, the literary tone and ambience of the *Dial* seemed not so far removed from the spirit of his Harvard days; over the years he continued to think of the magazine as a more cosmopolitan reincarnation of the *Harvard Monthly*.

The seventeen months Cowley spent in Greenwich Village in 1920-1921 were marked by alternate exhilaration and discouragement. Though as a free lance he was assured of a modest income, he felt increasingly skeptical about the role and position of the writer in America. While he reserved his more respectable work for the *New Republic* and the *Dial*, he was occasionally prepared to engage in hackwork, provided it did not compromise his standards of honest workmanship. Clinging to his old dream of living as an independent writer in the country, surrounded by a community of kindred spirits and maintaining his commercial and professional contacts with the city from a distance, Cowley found himself still mired in New York, struggling to eke out a meager living by writing book reviews. In June 1920 he accepted a job as copywriter at Sweet's Catalogue Service. In his reviews, meanwhile, he expressed his ambivalence about the tendency of modern art toward willful obscurity and the overcultivation of the private sensibility, attacked the influence of Freudianism on contemporary fiction, and, typically, combined an openness to modern experiment with a respect for traditional craftsmanship. By the spring of 1921 Cowley had become convinced that the New York ambience offered inadequate opportunities for serious writing, while France, beckoning seductively as the center of modernism, held out the promise of congenial working conditions and the freedom to pursue his literary education.

In 1921 Cowley was awarded an American Field Service Fellowship for a year of graduate study at the University of Montpellier in southern France. The two years he spent in France were a time of literary fermentation and intellectual ripening, which crystallized his attitudes and sharpened the ambiguity of his response to modernism. Paradoxically, but not uncommonly, his foreign venture prompted him to revaluate the aesthetic potential of his native culture and to redefine his role as an American writer. Eventually, his time in France left permanent traces on his literary and intellectual outlook.

In "This Youngest Generation" (*Literary Review of the New York Evening Post*, 15 October 1921), written during his first few weeks in France, Cowley made his earliest concerted effort to define the aesthetic contours of a generation destined to go far but as yet largely unpublished. At Montpellier he observed the advance of avant-garde aesthetics from a skeptical distance, devoting much of his time to the study of French history and literature, which in 1922 yielded him a diploma of French studies. In the conventions of French classicism—Nicolas Boileau-Despréaux, Jean Racine, Molière—he found a congenial critical perspective from which to judge modernity. Against the Rosicrucianism and introverted aestheticism of modern writing Cowley posited his "classical" demand of clarity and communicability. He early struggled to reconcile a formalist belief in the autonomy of art with his humanist persuasion that art existed in a context of history, society, and tradition, and that a major function of criticism was to mediate between artist, art, and audience. Such beliefs became the axioms of an eclectic, nontheoretical, pluralistic approach to criticism as "a many-windowed house." Cowley's attraction to French classicism culminated in his first "book," *Racine,* a critical essay privately published in Paris in 1923.

When his fellowship was extended for a second year, Cowley left Montpellier to confront the flood tides of European modernism in full force. After a summer of travel past the centers of the international avant-garde, the Cowleys settled down in rural Giverny, fifty miles west of Paris. There, despite his ambivalence about the modern, he helped edit two of the more notorious avant-garde little magazines, *Broom* and *Secession.* Through his friend Matthew Josephson he fell under the spell of the French Dadaists–Louis Aragon, André Breton, Philippe Soupault, Tristan Tzara–and participated in their pranks and manifestations. Partly attracted to Dada for its exuberant, ironic celebration of an ultramodern American culture, Cowley for a time absorbed its moral fervor and provocative excitement. Aragon, in particular, impressed him by the moral intensity of his literary commitment. Ultimately, Cowley's respect for form, intelligence, and clarity made him skeptical of Dada's extreme romanticism, its deliberate obscurity, its abolition of logic, and its veneration of the subconscious–he never followed Dada into surrealism. Conversely, its effervescent commitment to the present pointed up the tepid dignity of classicism. Typically, he remained open to the diversity of literary life in Paris, regarded Dada as merely one of its multifarious manifestations, and made a point of meeting many writers of various persuasions. He wrote a series of "penportraits" for the *Bookman* about, among others, Henri Barbusse, André Salmon, and Georges Duhamel, and met Pound, Joyce, and Paul Valéry. A serious student of French letters, Cowley did much, through criticism and translation, to introduce French writers to an American audience, while continuing to explore the impact of European modernist aesthetics on the American writers of his age group.

Cowley's years in France laid the groundwork for the "little bundle of beliefs" he carried with him through his long career. On the eve of his departure he had evolved a broad and eclectic ideal of the man of letters as one "whose province is all of literature," who possessed an almost religious dedication to the life of letters, and who concerned himself, as he wrote in *Exile's Return,* "with every department of human activity, including science, sociology and revolution." With modifications, the ideal would stick.

Even in Europe the justification for Cowley's expatriation more and more lay in the creation of a supportive cultural milieu in the United States. His mounting literary nationalism strengthened his commitment to *Broom* and *Secession,* which he hoped might be instrumental in transplanting to New York the intellectual climate of defiance and exuberance he had relished in Paris. However, back in America in late 1923, his efforts (with Matthew Josephson) to arouse a lethargic literary scene into an appreciation of the artistic potential of "machine-age" America foundered on the petty bickerings and dissensions among the editors of *Broom* and *Secession,* as much as on the moral conservatism of the Coolidge era. In early 1924 *Broom* was suppressed.

Discouraged, Cowley resumed work as an advertising copywriter for Sweet's, slowly but painfully reaccommodating himself to Manhattan. In 1925 he resigned from Sweet's to become a full-time free-lance writer and moved to Staten Island, struggling through the second half of the 1920s to maintain the relative purity of a rural literary life against the compromises of an urban culture of consumerism. With his friends Kenneth Burke, Matthew Josephson, William Slater Brown, Robert Coates, Hart Crane, and Allen Tate he regularly reconvened, either in the Village, or on Tory Hill, some seventy miles upstate, near Sherman, Connecticut. Feeling subtly at odds with a dominant business ethos, together they issued *Aesthete 1925*–in the verdict of one critic "the last Dada fling in America"–and published group manifestos in the *Little Review* and *transition.* Between 1925 and 1929 Cowley's output steadily increased: he wrote more than 125 essays and reviews, translated seven books from the French (among them works by Paul Valéry, Maurice Barrès, and Raymond Radiquet) and published twenty-five poems in such magazines as *Poetry,* the *Dial,* the *Little Review* and the *Hound & Horn.* His rising reputation as poet and reviewer, however, could not obviate a feeling of despondency about his struggles to maintain his independence and integrity against the practical necessity of hackwriting. Only Valéry, who managed to preserve the "essential unity" of his thought amidst his various assignments, seemed able to make a virtue out of "the instrumentality of his mind," thus offering Cowley an intellectual methodology that promised to put an end to a lack of coherence and direction in his life and writings.

Cowley and Robert Penn Warren (Estate of Malcolm Cowley)

In 1927 he received a one-hundred-dollar prize from *Poetry* magazine, which he used as the down payment on a farm near Sherman. Two years later, with the help and encouragement of Hart Crane, he published his first book of poetry, *Blue Juniata*. It was, in the words of Louis Untermeyer, an "auspicious debut," which received wide and responsible critical notice and clinched Cowley's reputation as one of the serious poets of his generation. Like Baudelaire, Cowley was essentially a one-book poet; he continued to perfect, adapt, and add to the original fifty-four poems, hoping to make the book into "the integrated record of a life." A much expanded edition, which incorporated his second volume, *The Dry Season* (1941), and included seventeen new poems, appeared in 1968, but it was only with *Blue Juniata: A Life* (1985), including another six new poems, that the book received its proper subtitle.

In early 1928 Cowley began reviewing regularly for the *New Republic* under Edmund Wilson.

As the decade neared its close, Cowley's critical horizons were broadening to include the public issues of his time, especially as they affected the fate of American writing. In 1929, at the invitation of Irita Van Doren, he wrote a series of essay-reviews for the *Herald-Tribune* book section that demonstrated, even before the imminent depression could have an impact on his thought, that Cowley had come to think of literary culture as inextricably embedded in a social and economic context. By 1929, also, Cowley's claim about the future stature of "Our Own Generation" no longer sounded as preposterous as it had in 1921. Though he was critical of the thwarting effects of mass consumerism and cultural standardization, and convinced that the American writer must leave his symbolist hermitage and actively strive to affect the quality of life and culture in his native land, he continued to see possibilities for a creative individualism within the limits of the social system. On the threshold of the socially responsible 1930s he articulated most fully his belief in the "humanizing function" of art, which, reiterated in the original epilogue to *Exile's Return*, remained a cornerstone conviction.

Three weeks before the stock market crash Cowley was appointed a junior editor on the *New Republic* staff. When, not long after, Edmund Wilson left the magazine, Cowley succeeded him, becoming the publication's last independent literary editor, an influential position he held until 1940. The *New Republic* provided Cowley with an authoritative platform from which to comment on the intellectual, literary, and political crosscurrents of a turbulent era in American history. In the verdict of Alfred Kazin, Cowley's weekly lead review "represented the most dramatically satisfying confrontation of a new book by a gifted, uncompromising critical intelligence." For a time, also, under Cowley's direction the "back of the book" became the magazine's most radical section.

Faced with the social and human sufferings of economic collapse, Cowley came to feel (as he put it to Burke) that "a whole scheme of life" had simultaneously given in. In early 1931 he decided to separate from his wife. Peggy Cowley left for Mexico, where she was joined by Hart Crane. (On their return trip to the United States Crane committed suicide by jumping off their ship.) In June 1932 Cowley married Muriel Maurer. During that same time Cowley's political radicalization peaked in a series of public acts of commitment. He joined the National Committee for the Defense of Political Prisoners and, with fellow writers Waldo Frank, Mary Heaton Vorse, and Edmund Wilson, distributed food to striking miners in Kentucky. He marched in that year's May Day parade and reported for the *New Republic* on the flight of the Bonus Army and the National Hunger March on Washington. In the summer of 1932 he joined the League of Professional Groups for Foster and Ford and supported the Communist party presidential candidate by helping to write the campaign pamphlet *Culture and the Crisis*. In private correspondence, meanwhile, he struck a more ambiguous note, explaining to Burke that he was "not plunging blindly ahead" into communism, but "trying to evolve a theory, a hypothesis, that will fit what I see happening." Rather than political caution, it was a mixture of literary reservations and a wish to preserve his independence of judgment that prevented Cowley from joining the party. "I would never be more than a fellow traveler," he wrote in *The Dream of the Golden Mountains* (1980), "and yet I was an ardent one at the time, full of humility, the desire to serve, and immense hopes for the future."

Much of the early 1930s was given over to the writing of *Exile's Return: A Narrative of Ideas*. The book began as a group manifesto by Cowley and friends at the Yaddo writer's colony in the spring of 1931; it was finished in May 1934, with an epilogue that Cowley remembered as "the high summit of my revolutionary enthusiasm." Its various parts were published as a series of articles in the *New Republic*. In 1933, discouraged by his slow progress on the book, Cowley spent ten weeks at Cloverlands in Tennessee with Caroline Gordon and Allen Tate, where, between fishing expeditions and discussions with the southern Agrarians, he filled out his revaluations of the 1920s. Though politically he objected to the conservative implications of the Agrarian solution to the crisis in industrial capitalism, his rural background gave him a sense of kinship with many of its advocates. In the long run, that affinity with southern writers–Tate, Robert Penn Warren, and Hamilton Basso were friends for life–would be literary as much as "agrarian." Still, for Cowley, regionalism remained the moral touchstone in matters literary and political. Even at the peak of his radicalism he was inclined to judge the social and political well-being of the nation by its capacity to provide a decent life for its marginal or small farmers, just as he measured the feasibility of plans for social change by its effects on the literary profession and the lives of American writers.

The writing of *Exile's Return* was partly inspired by Cowley's feeling that in the 1920s his life–personal, literary, and political–had been set in self-defeating directions. Cowley's critique of the literary past centered in a repudiatory analysis of the symbolist ethics and aesthetics at the heart of modern literature: in its dissociation of art from life, in its pursuit of a pure and purposeless poetry, in its hermetic and narcissistic subjectivism, the religion of art, Cowley believed, had proved "essentially anti-human" and "anti-social," the equivalent in literary art of a bankrupt individualism in the economic and political sphere. Only involvement in the movement for revolutionary change, he now felt, could put an end to the "real exile" of American writers and redeem an artistic isolation by offering "a sense of comradeship and participation in a historical process vastly bigger than the individual." Cowley's repudiation of symbolism was less the result of his conversion to radicalism than a natural outgrowth of his earlier skepticism about the aesthetics of modernism. In effect, his earlier humanism was now given the pragmatic coloration of a radical vision of history and politics; it remained fundamental.

In 1934 *Exile's Return* met with a barrage of negative reviews. Not only did Cowley's political opinions come under heavy fire; the brunt of the excoriations concerned the book's claim that the achievements and vicissitudes of the 1920s exiles deserved serious critical attention at all. When it was republished in 1951, in a much revised and expanded edition entitled *Exile's Return: A Literary Odyssey of the 1920s*, the book was as lyrically acclaimed as it had been abusively condemned. The critical somersault was partly due to the revisions, which served to divest the book of its radical politics; it was also the result of a broader critical rehabilitation of the 1920s in the years after World War II. *Exile's Return* exemplified a sui generis form of literary history. The first book of its kind to give an authoritative design of interpretation to the social, historical, and literary forces shaping the "lost generation," it was informed with a novelistic understanding that abstractions and ideas do not live unless embodied in character, action, and situation. Infused with touches of poetic lyricism, it survives as a literary work that derives much of its effectiveness from the orchestration of interpretative metaphors, the building of narrative line, and the intensity of Cowley's personal involvement with its subject. It is partly for such literary reasons that the book can be seen, not merely as a milestone in American literary history but as part of the legacy of the "lost generation."

In the many reviews Cowley wrote in the 1930s under the aegis of a radical literary criticism—as he told Burke, he was "driven toward" Marxian criticism because it considered "art as organically related with its social background, and functionally affecting it"—the glowing fervor of his often naive political sentiments does not entirely obfuscate his ethical and aesthetic standards, which show a surprising continuity from the 1920s. Tendentious as some of his literary judgments may have been, he rarely confused political correctness with literary achievement. Undue emphasis on Cowley's political mistakes (real enough though they were) obscures the basic soundness of his literary intuitions and fails to register the many and repeated reservations he expressed about the crudity of revolutionary writing, the dogmatism of leftist literary thought, and the limitations of Marxist criticism. If Cowley's lack of political prescience made him cling to a Stalinist line long after more perceptive literary fellow travelers had seen through its fallacies, in the domain of letters he mostly retained his independence of judgment. To elevate the personal qualities of Stalin was ultimately, as Edmund Wilson saw, less "real" to Cowley than to explore the humanizing impact on Baudelaire's art of his revolutionist engagement, or to write about Karl Marx as a man of letters.

Through the 1930s Cowley remained concerned with the creation of a sustaining literary climate in America. Persuaded of the benefits of the revolutionary movement for the writer, he gave it his seemingly unambiguous allegiance as long as he could believe it the best possible practical instrument for realizing art's "humanizing function." His efforts as vice-president of the League of American Writers, which he helped found at the First American Writers' Congress in 1935, were a natural exfoliation of earlier, nonpolitical efforts to foster a sense of literary community among his fellow writers; they take on a wider resonance when placed in the context of Cowley's ongoing endeavors on behalf of the "commonwealth of letters," both at Yaddo and at the National Institute and American Academy of Arts and Letters.

In 1936 the Cowleys, who now had a two-year-old son, Robert, moved to a remodeled barn in Sherman, which over the years Cowley transformed into a comfortable farmhouse, while planting his own pine forest and maintaining his professional links with New York. During the second half of the 1930s Cowley's hopes for a united endeavor on the left—he actively endorsed the cultural policies of the Popular Front—were thwarted by vicious factional bickerings, notably between Trotskyites and Stalinists. Nor was he himself always able to preserve the above-the-battle impartiality befitting his position as a *New Republic* editor. He allowed his name to be used in public support of radical organizations affiliated with the Communist party (many of them relief committees for victims of the civil war in Spain), chaired meetings with party speakers, once or twice wrote for the *Daily Worker*, took a stand against the American Committee for the Defense of Leon Trotsky, controversially defended the official version of the Moscow Trials, and quarreled with the editors of *Partisan Review*. Though often his position was more subtle than it was made out to be by overly zealous opponents, in a climate of political polarization Cowley was easily identified with the Party line in politics. He was publicly attacked as a Stalinist stooge by such Trotskyist sympathizers as Felix Morrow, Eugene Lyons, and James T. Farrell, and privately berated by his trusted friends Basso, Burke, Tate, and Wilson. Cowley's public stance fails to suggest what his memoirs, letters, and unpublished journals indicate: that after 1936 much of his earlier political idealism had begun to seep away, and he had come to feel a sense of disillusionment and moral fatigue. A "man of good will," trying to maintain "a shopkeeper's honesty" about his beliefs, Cowley was nonetheless led into false positions because he failed to voice clearly enough in public the doubts and reservations about the U.S.S.R. and communism that he confided to his notebooks. As his memoirs suggest, in their cumulative impact his self-confessed "sins of silence, self-protectiveness, inadequacy, and something close to moral cowardice" left Cowley with a feeling of guilt about the second half of the decade.

Always, literature came first. *After the Genteel Tradition* (1937), edited and partly written by Cowley, was a compilation of essays on American literature between 1910 and 1930 that began as a series of "Revaluations" in the *New Republic*. Though not conceived as such, it fitted in with the Popular Front emphasis on the "defense of culture" and with the nascent mood of literary nationalism in the late 1930s. Its counterpart in intellectual and cultural history, *Books That Changed Our*

Minds (1939), edited by Cowley and Bernard Smith, likewise ran in the *New Republic*.

In the summer of 1937 Cowley traveled to Europe, where he renewed his friendship with Louis Aragon, now a leading literary and Communist figure in France, and personally witnessed the havoc caused by the war in Spain. Later he dated the beginning of his disenchantment with communism from attending the Second International Writers' Congress in Madrid that summer. His reservations were fanned by "the big sellout" in Munich in 1938 and by the Nazi-Soviet pact of August 1939. A long letter to Wilson, written in early February 1940 and published in –*And I Worked at the Writer's Trade* (1978), evinced his troubled state as a mixture of frustrated hopes, a harassing uncertainty about the future, an angry disillusionment with communism, and a persistent loyalty to the idealism and self-sacrifice of the best of the radicals. In May 1940, later than most, he resigned from the League of American Writers and publicly broke with radical politics.

His defection from radicalism and his early interventionist sentiments exposed Cowley to fierce attacks in the leftist press–he was caricatured as a renegade in the *New Masses* and lambasted in the *Daily Worker*–while, privately, he was engaged in a painful process of self-examination, marked by a "double drive" of guilt and self-justification. Typically, his disaffection from radicalism was motivated by his persuasion that the movement no longer seemed beneficial to writers but had succumbed to, as he wrote in "The Michael Legend" (1941), an "academic and inhibited" doctrinalism that precluded "the capacity for fresh observation or independent thinking" indispensable for a living and human art. When, in a 1941 essay entitled "Faith and the Future" (included in *Whose Revolution?*, edited by Irving Dewitt Talmadge, and reprinted in slightly revised form in *The Flower and the Leaf* [1985] as "Communism and Christianism"), he came to settle his intellectual accounts in a sober investigation of communism as a "religion," he rejected it essentially because it had come to violate his deepest humanist beliefs.

In late 1940 an internal reorganization at the *New Republic* relieved Cowley of editorial responsibility, but he continued to write a weekly book page through the war years, in which he reviewed books on the international situation, considered the effects of the war on American writing, remained sensitive to new directions in poetry, and defended the writers of his genera-

tion against attacks by Archibald MacLeish and Bernard De Voto. As early as 1940 he projected a book on "the writers' crusade" of the 1930s, but the subject was fraught with too many painful and conflicting feelings for early summation and responsible digestion; the first part of his memoirs of the 1930s, *The Dream of the Golden Mountains*, did not appear until 1980. Further pain was caused by his experiences in Washington in 1942, when attacks in *Time* magazine and on the floor of Congress (by the Dies Committee on Un-American Activities) made Cowley decide to resign as chief information analyst for the federal Office of Facts and Figures, where he had hoped to make a constructive contribution to the war effort.

After what he remembered as "the worst two years" of his life, Cowley avoided political controversy, though not always successfully. With a "sense of release and opportunity" he now returned to his "proper" field of interest: the history of American letters, of the present and the past. As his letters to Burke and others indicate, Cowley's political concerns in the McCarthy years did not so much disappear as become subterraneous. He felt sharply the paralyzing effect of "the need to keep silent" in public, but in private correspondence showed himself intensely worried about the atrophy of liberty, the emasculation of the liberals, and the lack of effective resistance. His political past cast a long shadow over his subsequent career. Thus, he had to fight the forces of political reaction that tried to prevent his appointment as Walker-Ames lecturer at the University of Washington in Seattle in 1949, was called up twice to testify at the Alger Hiss trials, and was denied a teaching assignment at the University of Minnesota in 1950. As late as 1980 the publication of *The Dream of the Golden Mountains* engendered attacks by neoconservative reviewers.

From a literary perspective, the period between 1944 and 1954, when he published *The Literary Situation*, were "high years" for Cowley. Released from his weekly obligations to the *New Republic* and supported by a generous five-year grant from the Mellon Foundation, he now joined in the large-scale critical-historical endeavor of those years to recover "a usable past" for American literature. Helping to define the contours of a national literary tradition, Cowley wrote many of his best and most influential essays in this period, among them sensitive revaluations of Nathaniel Hawthorne, Walt Whitman, Henry James, and the naturalists, as well as of

Hemingway, Faulkner, and F. Scott Fitzgerald. He explored the modified continuance of the naturalist tradition in postwar American writing (Nelson Algren, Saul Bellow, and Ralph Ellison) and became persuaded of the restricted validity, for the writers of his own generation, of the symbolist aesthetics he had once so fiercely repudiated. By reconnecting the literature of his own times to that of the past Cowley did much to "clear away misconceptions" and to redeem his generation's supposed dissociation from a native tradition.

In the 1940s, besides translating André Gide's *Imaginary Interviews* and bringing out, in impeccable English renderings, the war poems of Louis Aragon, Cowley helped to initiate the Viking Portable Library series by editing (and writing influential introductions to) interpretative collections of Hemingway (1944), Faulkner (1946), and Hawthorne (1948). *The Portable Faulkner*, published at a time when most of Faulkner's works were out of print, helped to bring a great writer's reputation in line with his achievement. Cowley has told the story of Faulkner's reclamation and published the pertinent correspondence in *The Faulkner-Cowley File* (1966). In 1949, when the Mellon subvention expired, he went to work as publisher's adviser for Viking Press, a mutually profitable association that lasted far into Cowley's old age. That same year he wrote, for *Life*, the first extended biographical essay on Hemingway. In the early 1950s, riding the wave of a "boom" of interest in the 1920s, Cowley republished *Exile's Return*, edited *The Stories of F. Scott Fitzgerald* for Scribners, and prepared what he felt was the "final version" of Fitzgerald's *Tender Is the Night*, an edition today rejected by most scholars in favor of the original 1934 version.

In the practice of his criticism Cowley remained loyal to the values and beliefs he had developed in his early years. Through the postwar decades he argued against the separation of literature from contemporary life, urging writers to negotiate—emotionally, intellectually, and artistically—the social and historical realities of the present, rather than withdraw into subjectivist isolation. When, in "Criticism: A Many-Windowed House" (1961; collected in *A Many-Windowed House*, 1970), he explicitly formulated the assumptions underlying a lifetime of writing about literature, his critical credo gave testimony of his persistent humanism, pluralism, and eclecticism. The essay was partly written in response to what Cowley viewed as the excesses of the dominant New Criticism in the 1940s and 1950s, a period when

the "career open to talent" was preeminently the critical consolidation of the modernist achievement, rather than vigorous experimentation in the creative arts. In this "new age of the rhetoricians" Cowley's approach fell into critical disfavor. The case against his historical and contextual criticism was made most sharply in 1954 by a one-time critical disciple, John W. Aldridge, who, in search of modes of critical "heresy," thought he found a perfect specimen in *The Literary Situation*, which, as Cowley had intended, was less a book of criticism than "a social history of literature in our times." With the highbrow New Criticism at the peak of its prestige, Cowley was sometimes condescendingly dismissed as a "middlebrow" or "sociological" critic. At the same time he enjoyed a high respect in academic circles on the basis of his reclamation of Faulkner, his studies of Hemingway and Fitzgerald, and his authoritative claim on behalf of the first (1855) edition of Whitman's *Leaves of Grass*. Founding fathers of the New Criticism such as Tate, Warren, Burke, Cleanth Brooks, and R. P. Blackmur, unlike more dogmatic followers, continued to recognize the literary soundness of Cowley's criticism.

Impervious to the critical and literary fashions of a later day and age, Cowley avoided "critical endogamy" and rejected any single point of view—be it textualist, historicist, psychoanalytical, moral, or political—as inevitably narrow and reductive. He resisted the tendency to make criticism into a separate and autonomous genre, insisted on its dependency on the primary literary arts, and remained antagonistic to any critical method that extricated the human element from art. Always alive to the diversity of American writing and skeptical of the exclusivism of literary canon-making, he deemed it an essential task of the critic to discover new or explore underestimated writers (though he did not often write on women) and did not shirk voicing "dissenting opinions" on such canonized authors as Robert Frost or Pound. Above all else loomed his aversion to unwarranted obscurity and his defense of honest and lucid expression against the advance of bureaucratic, academic, or commercial jargon.

Through his long career Cowley remained faithful to an ideal of the man of letters he early recovered from the "classical" tradition of the Renaissance and the Enlightenment. Like the French Encyclopedists, he aimed to create, for his own times, *une société de gens des lettres* and to act as a sensitive mediator between "high" art and the "common reader." As Lewis Simpson has suggested, Cowley's approach to the literary profession, like that of William Dean Howells and Van Wyck Brooks, was infused with "a poetics of literary community" combined with a pragmatic understanding of the interrelatedness of the various aspects of the "writer's trade." From his earliest experiences in the Village, Cowley was concerned with the living and working conditions of American writers and with their opportunities to pursue a fruitful career. In this context he wrote knowledgeably about literature as a business and an institution, about the economics of book production, the sociology of the writing profession, and the changing conditions in publishing. He was the first to alert a larger audience to the importance of editors in a profile of Maxwell Perkins that was republished as a booklet in 1985, forty-one years after its first appearance in the *New Yorker*. "A Natural History of the American Writer," a near-book-length study of the writing profession in America incorporated into *The Literary Situation*, perhaps best illustrated Cowley's characteristic perception of the literary artist as *also* the member of a living human community, and, as such, subject to regular domestic, marital, social, economic, and psychological pressures.

True to his conception of the "man of letters," Cowley wrote in many genres and combined an astounding multiplicity of functions: he was poet, critic, literary chronicler and historian, memoirist, editor of books and magazines, literary consultant to publishers and writers, and, in general, "middleman" of letters. Recurrently, he spoke out against the various "dangers" he saw threatening the literary profession in America. In 1949 he took his own firm stand in defense of the "little American republic of letters" in the controversy over the Bollingen Award to Ezra Pound, reminding writers of their "double duty, to the public and to the values of their own profession." In the dystopian 1950s he feared that growing collectivization and commercialization might transform writers from "independent craftsmen" into members of a "specialized bureaucracy," while he was disturbed by the pervasive anti-intellectualism of the McCarthy years, the impact of mass culture, the decline of the reading habit, and the effect of the appropriation of creative and critical writing by the universities. "Today," he observed presciently in 1954, "for the first time we have to admit the possibility of a situation in which American writing would be confined to an elite of scholars, in which it would become as elaborate and dead as late-Roman writ-

ing, and in which the public would find its aesthetic satisfactions in bang-bang gunsmoke on the television screen."

Such critique notwithstanding, Cowley himself worked successfully within academe as a teacher, writer-in-residence, and lecturer at writers' conferences. He held guest professorships at various American schools, including Stanford, Michigan, Minnesota, Hollins College, and Cornell, and taught at the University of Warwick in Great Britain. Always, however, he felt slightly out of place among academic scholars and was most at ease consorting with writers, artists, publishers, and editors. It was as characteristic of Cowley to devote his Hopwood lecture at the University of Michigan in 1957 to "The Beginning Writer in the University" as it was to edit the first in a series of literary conversations on the practical and technical problems of the "craft" of fiction in *Writers at Work: The Paris Review Interviews* (1958).

Few have had Cowley's capacity for friendship or the geniality of temperament to associate on terms of equality (and often intimacy) with a wide and varied circle of literary friends and acquaintances, from Faulkner, Hemingway, Crane, and Tate, to such younger writers as John Cheever, Tillie Olsen, and Ken Kesey, or visual and sculptural artists such as Peter Blume, Arshile Gorky, and Alexander Calder. In his dealings with writers Cowley often showed (in the words of George Core) "an uncommonly even disposition, a remarkable ability to forgive, and a wise but not uncritical acceptance of human fallibility" (*American Writers*, 1981). As critic, teacher, and roving scout of new talent for Viking Press, Cowley tirelessly exhorted and advised young writers, urging them to meet the challenges of their own world and time and to search for new and authentic forms of expression. His early discovery of Cheever, his efforts on behalf of Jack Kerouac, and his encouragements of Kesey and Larry McMurtry (members of his creative writing class at Stanford in 1961) are only the better-known examples of a long list of services rendered to numerous writers.

Toward the end of the 1950s Cowley's barometric sensitivity to changes in the literary situation began to lose its former acumen, as he felt himself slowly growing out of touch with the literary temper of the times. "A deaf man gardening in the country and writing about books," he was a bemused but detached observer of "the unbelievable 1960s." Cowley's account of the "love generation" (included in *—And I Worked At the Writer's Trade*) revealed the troubled perplexity of a man of letters confronted with a generation desirous of social change but impervious to the order of literary ethics and aesthetics in which he himself breathed most naturally. It also showed that Cowley's own best writings depended on a degree of personal and imaginative connection with his subject matter. Though he continued to look at contemporary writing with an open mind, he did not always like what he saw. He could muster little appreciation for most of the postmodernist experimental fiction of the 1960s and early 1970s, preferred writers who intuitively grasped the shaping force of social or historical reality in human life—one thinks of his essays on John P. Marquand, James Gould Cozzens, Willa Cather, and Cheever, but also of his encouragement of such writers as Mary Lee Settle and Tillie Olsen—and wrote a flamboyant defense of the ancient art of storytelling. He also found himself sharply at odds with newer developments in criticism: such approaches as structuralism, poststructuralism, and deconstructionism were regarded as modes of critical heresy by "a humanist by instinct," one who by 1978 had come to feel "increasingly alone and beleaguered."

The 1960s were for Cowley a time of critical consolidation and of revaluations of his radical past. The latter were given a new impetus by the emergence of the New Left and the concomitant revival of interest in the "old" left. Cowley participated in symposia on the 1930s, wrote "remembrances" of his "red romance" as well as much of what later became *The Dream of the Golden Mountains*, and, with the help of Henry Dan Piper, collected his *New Republic* articles of the 1930s in book form as *Think Back on Us . . . A Contemporary Chronicle of the 1930s* (1967). He also gathered the best of his other past writings into what he tried to make into unified collections. He revisited and revalued his efforts on behalf of Faulkner, assembled and revised his collected poems, and, once again with the help of Piper, compiled *A Many-Windowed House*, a key volume containing some of his best essays on classical and modern American writers. Later compilations are *—And I Worked At the Writer's Trade: Chapters of Literary History, 1918-1978* and (both edited by Donald Faulkner) *The Flower and the Leaf: A Contemporary Record of American Writing Since 1941* (1985) and *The Portable Malcolm Cowley* (1990).

In literary criticism, too, Cowley's career became increasingly dominated by restrospection

and the ongoing revaluation of the high years of American literary modernism. *A Second Flowering* (1973), the culmination of a lifetime of thought about the literature of his age group, pictured the writers of his "lost" generation as, on the one hand, isolated artists incorruptibly committed to the production of high and autonomous art and, on the other, true and honest "historians . . . of a living community in a process of continual and irreversible change." Like many of his later writings, Cowley's "swansong" to his generation was infused with his conception of writing as "a priestly vocation with its own strict ethical code." Indeed, insofar as *A Second Flowering* signaled a modified return to the ethical premises of the "religion of art," it completed the curve of Cowley's literary development from the 1920s to the 1970s.

By the mid 1960s Cowley had become an official member of the literary establishment. He had been elected to the National Institute of Arts and Letters in 1949, served as its president from 1956 to 1959 and again from 1962 to 1965, and in 1964 had been "elevated" to the American Academy of Arts and Letters, serving as its chancellor from 1967 to 1976. Though, with advancing years, he found himself increasingly besieged by ailments and infirmities, he almost naturally became a wise and genial chronicler of the experience of old age in the beautifully written *The View from Eighty* (1980). As far as age permitted, he also remained an active force within the "commonwealth of letters," a timeless and placeless "republic" that he defined, in typical pluralistic fashion, as a "loose federation composed of many dukedoms and principalities." As its "roving diplomat" Cowley moved with ease, tact, and generosity between the realm of serious criticism, literary history, and academic scholarship and the pragmatic world of publishing, editing, writers' conferences, and artists' colonies—mediating, as few have been capable of doing, between a disinterested pursuit of letters and the literary marketplace. Outliving most of his coevals, as well as many literary friends born after him, in old age Cowley naturally, if sadly, became the elegiac celebrant and obituarist of the community of letters.

In his last decade Cowley's stature and influence were confirmed by many literary awards and honorary academic degrees. Among the literary honors were the Gold Medal for Belles Lettres and Criticism of the American Academy and Institute of Arts and Letters, the Hubbell Medal of the Modern Language Association for service to the study of American literature, and *Who's Who in America*'s 1983-1984 Achievement Award for Arts and Communication. "That's the way we ought to structure our lives," Cowley wrote to Burke in 1981, "with the best coming last, in a graded series." At the end of his life, after a "second flowering" in his own career that saw the publication of nine books since his eighty-sixth year, Cowley could look back upon a literary life in which, in his own fashion, he had fulfilled the ideal of the man of letters he had first developed as a young man. Though he did not live to complete his book of memoirs of the late 1930s, he left behind a rich and lasting literary heritage. Malcolm Cowley died of heart failure in New Milford, Connecticut, on 28 March 1989.

Bibliography:

Diane U. Eisenberg, *Malcolm Cowley: A Checklist of His Writings, 1916-1973* (Carbondale & Edwardsville: Southern Illinois University Press, 1975);

Ruth M. Alvarez and Eisenberg, "Malcolm Cowley: A Checklist Updated. A Preliminary Version," *Visionary Company*, 2, no. 2/3, no. 1 (Summer 1987): 203-230.

References:

Daniel Aaron, *Writers on the Left* (New York: Harcourt Brace & World, 1961), pp. 334-344, and passim;

John W. Aldridge, *In Search of Heresy* (New York: McGraw-Hill, 1954), pp. 166-176;

Aldridge, "Malcolm Cowley at Eighty," *Michigan Quarterly Review*, 18 (Summer 1979): 481-490;

Hans Bak, " 'Contest in Vilification': The Literary Friendship of Kenneth Burke and Malcolm Cowley," *Southern Review*, 26 (January 1990): 226-235;

Bak, "The Fabulous Ostrich of Art: Malcolm Cowley's Notebooks of the Twenties," *Visionary Company*, 2, no. 2/3, no. 1 (Summer 1987): 131-161;

Bak, "Malcolm Cowley and the Rehumanization of Art," *Georgia Review*, 39 (Fall 1985): 649-654;

Bak, "Malcolm Cowley: The Critic and His Generation," *Dutch Quarterly Review of Anglo-American Letters,* 9 (1979): 261-283;

Bak, "Malcolm Cowley: The Formative Years, 1898-1930," Ph.D. dissertation, Catholic University of Nijmegen, the Netherlands, 1988;

Susan Jenkins Brown, *Robber Rocks: Letters and Memories of Hart Crane, 1923-1932* (Middletown, Conn.: Wesleyan University Press, 1969);

Eleanor Bulkin, "Malcolm Cowley: A Study of His Literary, Social and Political Thought to 1940," Ph.D. dissertation, New York University, 1973;

George Core, "Malcolm Cowley, 1898- " in *American Writers*, supplement 2, part 1, edited by A. Walton Litz (New York: Scribners, 1981), pp. 135-156;

Core, "Malcolm Cowley and the Literary Imperium," *Visionary Company*, 2, no. 2/3, no. 1 (Summer 1987): 16-28;

David C. Duke, *Distant Obligations: Modern American Writers and Foreign Causes* (New York & Oxford: Oxford University Press, 1983), pp. 81-88, 96-100;

Charles A. Fenton, "Ambulance Drivers in France and Italy, 1914-1918," *American Quarterly*, 3 (Winter 1951): 326-343;

Adam Gussow, "Bohemia Revisited: Malcolm Cowley, Jack Kerouac, and *On the Road*," *Georgia Review*, 38 (Summer 1984): 291-311;

Gussow, " 'Whatever Roots We Had in the Soil': Malcolm Cowley and the American Scholar," *Horns of Plenty*, 1 (Spring 1988): 5-15; 19-24;

Horns of Plenty: Malcolm Cowley and His Generation, edited by William and Yolanda Butts, 1 (Spring 1988-);

Alfred Kazin, *On Native Grounds* (New York: Harcourt, Brace, 1942);

Kazin, *Starting Out in the Thirties* (Boston: Little, Brown, 1965), pp. 15-20;

James M. Kempf, "Cowley's 'Middle Career': In Defense of the 1920s at the American Mid-Century," *Visionary Company*, 2, no.2/3, no. 1 (Summer 1987): 121-130;

Kempf, *The Early Career of Malcolm Cowley: A Humanist Among the Moderns* (Baton Rouge & London: Louisiana State University Press, 1985);

Kenneth S. Lynn, *The Air-Line to Seattle: Studies in Literary and Historical Writing About America* (Chicago & London: University of Chicago Press, 1983), pp. 93-96, 163-171;

Lawrence Schwartz, "Malcolm Cowley's Path to William Faulkner," *Journal of American Studies*, 16 (August 1982): 229-242;

David E. Shi, "Malcolm Cowley and Literary New York," *Virginia Quarterly Review*, 58 (Autumn 1982): 575-593;

Lewis P. Simpson, "Cowley's Odyssey: Literature and Faith in the Thirties," *Sewanee Review*, 89 (Fall 1981): 520-539;

Simpson, "The Decorum of the Writer," *Sewanee Review*, 86 (Fall 1978): 566-571;

Simpson, "Malcolm Cowley and the American Writer," *Sewanee Review*, 84 (Spring 1976): 221-247;

Robert E. Spiller, *Milestones in American Literary History* (Westport, Conn.: Greenwood, 1977), pp. 39-41;

Dickran Tashjian, *Skyscraper Primitives: Dada and the American Avant-Garde, 1910-1925* (Middletown, Conn.: Wesleyan University Press, 1975), pp. 116-142;

Louis Untermeyer, "Auspicious Debut," *Saturday Review of Literature*, 6 (28 September 1929): 178;

Visionary Company: A Magazine of the Twenties, special issue on Cowley, 2, no. 2/3, no. 1 (Summer 1987);

Edmund Wilson, *Letters on Literature and Politics, 1912-1972*, edited by Elena Wilson (New York: Farrar, Straus & Giroux, 1977);

Philip Young, "For Malcolm Cowley: Critic, Poet, 1898- ," *Southern Review*, new series 9 (Autumn 1973): 778-795.

Papers:

The largest collection of Cowley's papers is in the Newberry Library, Chicago.

A TRIBUTE

from JAMES DICKEY

There are certain solidly set presences in the history of a time whose removal seems an affront as well as a numbing loss. Malcolm Cowley was one of these. The world may think of him as perhaps the foremost chronicler of the most important period of our literary history, for he knew the Great—Hemingway, Fitzgerald, Faulkner, Hart Crane—and moved among them as one of their own, which he certainly was, and his accounts of the lives and careers of these writers, and many others, are not only perceptive and intensely personal; they are just. From Cowley more than from any other such interpreter, not excluding Edmund Wilson or Van Wyck Brooks, one comes away with the feeling of satisfaction, of the essential thing having been said.

Yet despite all this, I think of Malcolm Cowley most valuably of all as a poet, and regret very much the comparatively limited number of poems he saw fit to give us. But among these are some remarkable bequeathals: particularly the great—or certainly near-great—"Stone Horse Shoals." Perhaps the fact that he wrote so few poems is in a way an advantage, for you can read all of them in a single night, and before you have gone very far you know that it will be a good night, and that when you rise from where you are, or sleep in the same place, it is quite possible that "you shall ride / eastward on a rain wind, wrapped in thunder, / your white bones drifting like herons across the moon."

A TRIBUTE

from JAMES LAUGHLIN

Malcolm Cowley's *Exile's Return* influenced my life. I read it just when I was getting bored with Harvard and concluded that Europe was the place to be. From a summer working for Gertrude Stein at her place in the Ain I moved on to Rapallo and enrollment in Pound's "Ezuversity." It was he who persuaded me to become a publisher, his publisher, and from that came New Directions, which has occupied me now for over fifty years. And it all goes back to Malcolm. *Exile's Return* is still, I think, the best book on the expatriates. There have been several more exhaustive studies but none of them have the color and feeling of Malcolm's book. I was able to make some slight return for the direction he had given me when ND published his chapbook of poems *The Dry Season* in 1941 in our Poets of the Year Series. And very good poems they were. He was a true man of letters.

A TRIBUTE

from LEWIS P. SIMPSON

Malcolm Cowley earned his living by writing and talked about the "writer's trade." But this was a special way of saying the writer's vocation, a vocation which, for all his pragmatic grasp of the nature of the literary marketplace, was a spiritual vocation. He had a strong faith that the serious pursuit of writing is a redemptive act, and even compared some of the great moderns to saints. He would liked to have been a poet—indeed insisted on referring to himself as poet, though his collected poems make up only a small volume and have won no acclaim. But as a critic and literary historian he was indeed a poet, whose portrayal of twentieth-century American lit-

erary history in a series of books beginning with *Exile's Return* essentially constitutes a poetics of our literary history.

Georges Simenon

(13 February 1903 - 4 September 1989)

Stanley G. Eskin

See also the Simenon entry in *DLB 72: French Novelists, 1930-1960.*

SELECTED BOOKS: *Au rendez-vous des terre-neuvas* (Paris: Fayard, 1931); translated as *The Sailor's Rendezvous* in *Maigret Keeps a Rendezvous* (1940);

Le Charretier de la "Providence" (Paris: Fayard, 1931); translated as *The Crime at Lock 14* in *The Triumph of Inspector Maigret* (1934); published with *The Shadow in the Courtyard* (New York: Covici, Friede, 1934);

Le Chien jaune (Paris: Fayard, 1931); translated as *A Face for a Clue* in *The Patience of Maigret* (1939);

Un Crime en Hollande (Paris: Fayard, 1931); translated as *A Crime in Holland* in *Maigret Abroad* (1940);

La Danseuse du Gai-Moulin (Paris: Fayard, 1931); translated as *At the "Gai-Moulin"* in *Maigret Abroad* (1940);

M. Gallet décédé (Paris: Fayard, 1931); translated as *The Death of Monsieur Gallet* (New York: Covici, Friede, 1932); translated as *The Death of M. Gallet* in *Introducing Inspector Maigret* (1933);

La Nuit du carrefour (Paris: Fayard, 1931); translated as *The Crossroad Murders* in *Inspector Maigret Investigates* (1933); translation published separately (New York: Covici, Friede, 1933);

Note: Stanley G. Eskin is the author of *Simenon: A Critical Biography* (McFarland, 1987), from which he has drawn for this essay. All translations are by the author.

Georges Simenon (copyright Horst Tappe)

Le Pendu de Saint-Pholien (Paris: Fayard, 1931); translated as *The Crime of Inspector Maigret* in *Introducing Inspector Maigret* (1933); translation published separately (New York: Covici, Friede, 1933);

Pietr-le-Letton (Paris: Fayard, 1931); translated as *The Case of Peter the Lett* in *Inspector Maigret Investigates* (1933); translated as *The Strange*

Case of Peter the Lett (New York: Covici, Friede, 1933);

Le Relais d'Alsace (Paris: Fayard, 1931); translated as *The Man from Everywhere* in *Maigret and M. l'Abbé* (1941);

La Tête d'un homme (Paris: Fayard, 1931); translated as *A Battle of Nerves* in *Patience of Maigret* (1939);

L'Affaire Saint-Fiacre (Paris: Fayard, 1932); translated as *The Saint-Fiacre Affair* in *Maigret Keeps a Rendezvous* (1940);

Chez les Flamands (Paris: Fayard, 1932); translated as *The Flemish Shop* in *Maigret to the Rescue* (1940);

Le Fou de Bergerac (Paris: Fayard, 1932); translated as *The Madman of Bergerac* in *Maigret Travels South* (1940);

La Guinguette à deux sous (Paris: Fayard, 1932); translated as *Guinguette by the Seine* in *Maigret to the Rescue* (1940);

"Liberty Bar" (Paris: Fayard, 1932); translated in *Maigret Travels South* (1940);

L'Ombre chinoise (Paris: Fayard, 1932); translated as *The Shadow on the Courtyard* in *The Triumph of Inspector Maigret* (1934); published as *The Shadow in the Courtyard* with *The Crime at Lock 14* (1934);

Le Passager du "Polarlys" (Paris: Fayard, 1932); translated as *The Mystery of the "Polarlys"* in *Two Latitudes* (1942); translated as *Danger at Sea* in *On Land and Sea* (1954);

Le Port des brumes (Paris: Fayard, 1932); translated as *Death of a Harbour Master* in *Maigret and M. l'Abbé* (1941);

Les Treize Coupables (Paris: Fayard, 1932);

Les Treize Enigmes (Paris: Fayard, 1932);

Les Treize Mystères (Paris: Fayard, 1932);

L'Âne rouge (Paris: Fayard, 1933); translated by Jean Stewart as *The Nightclub* (New York: Harcourt Brace Jovanovich, 1979);

Le Coup de lune (Paris: Fayard, 1933); translated as *Tropic Moon* in *Two Latitudes* (1942); translation published separately (New York: Harcourt, Brace, 1943);

L'Ecluse no. 1 (Paris: Fayard, 1933); translated as *The Lock at Charenton* in *Maigret Sits It Out* (1941);

Les Fiançailles de M. Hire (Paris: Fayard, 1933); translated as *Mr. Hire's Engagement* in *The Sacrifice* (1956);

Les Gens d'en face (Paris: Fayard, 1933); translated as *The Window Over the Way* in *The Window Over the Way* (1951);

Le Haut-mal (Paris: Fayard, 1933); translated as *The Woman in the Grey House* in *Affairs of Destiny* (1942);

Inspector Maigret Investigates, translated by Anthony Abbott (London: Hurst & Blackett, 1933)—comprises *La Nuit du carrefour* and *Pietr-le-Letton;*

Introducing Inspector Maigret, translated by Abbott (London: Hurst & Blackett, 1933)—comprises *M. Gallet décédé* and *Le Pendu de Saint-Pholien;*

La Maison du canal (Paris: Fayard, 1933); translated as *The House by the Canal* in *The House by the Canal* (1952);

L'Homme de Londres (Paris: Fayard, 1934); translated as *Newhaven-Dieppe* in *Affairs of Destiny* (1942);

Le Locataire (Paris: Gallimard, 1934); translated as *The Lodger* in *Escape in Vain* (1943);

Maigret (Paris: Fayard, 1934); translated as *Maigret Returns* in *Maigret Sits It Out* (1941);

Les Suicidés (Paris: Gallimard, 1934); translated as *One Way Out* in *Escape in Vain* (1943);

The Triumph of Inspector Maigret (London: Hurst & Blackett, 1934)—comprises *Le Charretier de la "Providence"* and *L'Ombre chinoise;* republished as *The Shadow in the Courtyard* [and] *The Crime at Lock 14* (New York: Covici, Friede, 1934);

Les Clients d'Avrenos (Paris: Gallimard, 1935);

Les Pitard (Paris: Gallimard, 1935); translated as *A Wife at Sea* in *A Wife at Sea* (1949);

Quartier nègre (Paris: Gallimard, 1935);

Les Demoiselles de Concarneau (Paris: Gallimard, 1936); translated as *The Breton Sisters* in *Havoc by Accident* (1943);

L'Evadé (Paris: Gallimard, 1936); translated by Geoffrey Sainsbury as *The Disintegration of J. P. G.* (London: Routledge, 1937);

Long cours (Paris: Gallimard, 1936); translated by Eileen Ellenbogen as *The Long Exile* (San Diego: Harcourt Brace Jovanovich, 1983);

45° à l'ombre (Paris: Gallimard, 1936);

L'Assassin (Paris: Gallimard, 1937); translated as *The Murderer* in *A Wife at Sea* (1949);

Le Blanc à lunettes (Paris: Gallimard, 1937); translated as *Talata* in *Havoc by Accident* (1943);

Faubourg (Paris: Gallimard, 1937); translated as *Home Town* in *On the Danger Line* (1944);

Le Testament Donadieu (Paris: Gallimard, 1937); translated by Stuart Gilbert as *The Shadow Falls* (London: Routledge / Toronto: Musson, 1945; New York: Harcourt, Brace, 1945);

Ceux de la soif (Paris: Gallimard, 1938);

Chemin sans issue (Paris: Gallimard, 1938); translated as *Blind Path* in *Lost Moorings* (1946); translation republished separately as *Blind Alley* (New York: Reynal & Hitchcock, 1946);

Le Cheval blanc (Paris: Gallimard, 1938); translated by Norman Denny as *The White Horse Inn* (New York: Harcourt Brace Jovanovich, 1980);

L'Homme qui regardait passer les trains (Paris: Gallimard, 1938); translated by Gilbert as *The Man Who Watched the Trains Go By* (London: Pan, 1945; New York: Reynal & Hitchcock, 1946);

La Marie du port (Paris: Gallimard, 1938); translated as *A Chit of a Girl* in *Chit of a Girl* (1949);

La Mauvaise Etoile (Paris: Gallimard, 1938);

Monsieur La Souris (Paris: Gallimard, 1938); translated in *Poisoned Relations* (1950);

Les Rescapés du "Télémaque" (Paris: Gallimard, 1938); translated as *The Survivors* in *Black Rain* (1949); published separately (San Diego: Harcourt Brace Jovanovich, 1985);

Les Sept Minutes (Paris: Gallimard, 1938)—comprises *Le Grand Langoustier, La Nuit des sept minutes,* and *L'Enigme de la "Marie Gallante";*

Les Sœurs Lacroix (Paris: Gallimard, 1938); translated as *Poisoned Relations* in *Poisoned Relations* (1950);

Le Suspect (Paris: Gallimard, 1938); translated as *The Green Thermos* in *On the Danger Line* (1944);

Touriste de bananes (Paris: Gallimard, 1938); translated as *Banana Tourist* in *Lost Moorings* (1946);

Les Trois Crimes de mes amis (Paris: Gallimard, 1938);

Le Bourgmestre de Furnes (Paris: Gallimard, 1939); translated by Sainsbury as *The Bourgomaster of Furnes* (London: Routledge & Kegan Paul, 1952);

Chez Krull (Paris: Gallimard, 1939); translated in *A Sense of Guilt* (1955);

Le Coup de vague (Paris: Gallimard, 1939);

The Patience of Maigret, translated by Sainsbury (London: Routledge/Toronto: Musson, 1939; New York: Harcourt, Brace, 1940)—comprises *Le Chien jaune* and *La Tête d'un homme;*

Les Inconnus dans la maison (Paris: Gallimard, 1940); translated by Sainsbury as *Strangers in the House* (London: Routledge & Kegan Paul, 1951; New York: Doubleday, 1954);

Malempin (Paris: Gallimard, 1940); translated by Isabel Quigly as *The Family Lie* (London: Hamilton, 1978);

Maigret Abroad, translated by Sainsbury (London: Routledge / Toronto: Musson, 1940; New York: Harcourt, Brace, 1940)—comprises *Un Crime en Hollande* and *La Danseuse du Gai-Moulin;*

Maigret Keeps a Rendezvous, translated by Margret Ludwig (London: Routledge, 1940; New York: Harcourt, Brace & World, 1941)—comprises *Au rendez-vous des terre-neuvas* and *L'Affaire Saint-Fiacre;*

Maigret to the Rescue, translated by Sainsbury (London: Routledge / Toronto: Musson, 1940; New York: Harcourt, Brace, 1941)—comprises *Chez les Flamands* and *La Guinguette à deux sous;*

Maigret Travels South, translated by Sainsbury (London: Routledge, 1940; New York: Harcourt, Brace, 1940)—comprises *Le Fou de Bergerac* and *"Liberty Bar";*

Bergelon (Paris: Gallimard, 1941); translated by Ellenbogen as *The Delivery* (New York: Harcourt Brace Jovanovich, 1981);

Cour d'assises (Paris: Gallimard, 1941); translated as *Justice* in *Chit of a Girl* (1949);

Il pleut bergère (Paris: Gallimard, 1941); translated as *Black Rain* in *Black Rain* (1949);

Maigret and M. l'Abbé, translated by Gilbert (London: Routledge, 1941; New York: Harcourt, Brace, 1942)—comprises *Le Relais d'Alsace* and *Le Port des brumes;*

Maigret Sits It Out, translated by Ludwig (London: Routledge / Toronto: Musson, 1941; New York: Harcourt, Brace, 1941)—comprises *L'Ecluse no. 1* and *Maigret;*

La Maison des sept jeunes filles (Paris: Gallimard, 1941);

L'Outlaw (Paris: Gallimard, 1941); translated by Howard Curtis as *The Outlaw* (San Diego: Harcourt Brace Jovanovich, 1986);

Le Voyageur de la Toussaint (Paris: Gallimard, 1941); translated by Sainsbury as *Strange Inheritance* (London: Routledge & Kegan Paul, 1950);

Affairs of Destiny, translated by Gilbert (London: Routledge / Toronto: Musson, 1942; New York: Harcourt, Brace, 1944)—comprises *Le Haut-mal* and *L'Homme de Londres;*

Le Fils Cardinaud (Paris: Gallimard, 1942); translated as *Young Cardinaud* in *The Sacrifice* (1956);

Maigret revient (Paris: Gallimard, 1942)–comprises *Cécile est morte*, translated by Ellenbogen as *Maigret and the Spinster* (London: Hamilton, 1977; New York: Harcourt Brace Jovanovich, 1977), *Les Caves du Majestic*, translated by Carolyn Hillier as *Maigret and the Hotel Majestic* (London: Hamilton, 1977; New York: Harcourt Brace Jovanovich, 1978), and *La Maison du juge*, translated by Ellenbogen as *Maigret in Exile* (London: Hamilton, 1978; New York: Harcourt Brace Jovanovich, 1979);

Oncle Charles s'est enfermé (Paris: Gallimard, 1942); translated as *Uncle Charles Has Locked Himself In* (San Diego: Harcourt Brace Jovanovich, 1987);

Two Latitudes, translated by Gilbert (London: Routledge / Toronto: Musson, 1942)–comprises *Le Passager du "Polarlys"* and *Le Coup de lune;*

La Vérité sur Bébé Donge (Paris: Gallimard, 1942); translated by Sainsbury as *The Trial of Bebe Donge* (London: Routledge & Kegan Paul, 1952); translated as *I Take this Woman* in *Satan's Children* (1953);

La Veuve Couderc (Paris: Gallimard, 1942); translated by John Petrie as *Ticket of Leave* (London: Routledge & Kegan Paul / New York: British Book Service, 1954);

Les Dossiers de l'agence O. (Paris: Gallimard, 1943);

Escape in Vain, translated by Gilbert (London: Routledge / Toronto: Musson, 1943; New York: Harcourt, Brace, 1943)–comprises *Le Locataire* and *Les Suicidés;*

Havoc by Accident, translated by Gilbert (London: Routledge, 1943; New York: Harcourt, Brace, 1943)–comprises *Les Demoiselles de Concarneau* and *Le Blanc à lunettes;*

Le Petit Docteur (Paris: Gallimard, 1943); translated by Stewart as *The Little Doctor* (London: Hamilton, 1978; New York: Harcourt Brace Jovanovich, 1978);

Les Nouvelles Enquêtes de Maigret (Paris: Gallimard, 1944);

On the Danger Line, translated by Gilbert (London: Routledge, 1944; New York: Harcourt, Brace, 1944)–comprises *Faubourg* and *Le Suspect;*

Le Rapport du gendarme (Paris: Gallimard, 1944); translated as *The Gendarme's Report* in *The Window over the Way* (1951);

Signé Picpus (Paris: Gallimard, 1944)–comprises *Signé Picpus,* translated by Sainsbury as *To Any Lengths* in *Maigret on Holiday* (1950), *L'Inspec-*

teur Cadavre, translated by Helen Thomson as *Maigret's Rival* (London: Hamilton, 1978; New York: Harcourt Brace Jovanovich, 1980), *Félicie est là,* translated by Ellenbogen as *Maigret and the Toy Village* (London: Hamilton, 1978; New York: Harcourt Brace Jovanovich, 1979), and *Nouvelles exotiques;*

L'Aîné des Ferchaux (Paris: Gallimard, 1945); translated by Sainsbury as *Magnet of Doom* (London: Routledge / Toronto: Musson, 1948); translated as *The First Born* (New York: Reynal & Hitchcock, 1949);

La Fenêtre des Rouet (Paris: Editions de la Jeune Parque, 1945); translated by Petrie as *Across the Street* (London: Routledge & Kegan Paul, 1954);

La Fuite de Monsieur Monde (Paris: Editions de la Jeune Parque, 1945); translated by Stewart as *Monsieur Monde Vanishes* (London: Hamilton, 1967; New York: Harcourt Brace Jovanovich, 1977);

Je me souviens (Paris: Presses de la Cité, 1945);

Le Cercle des Mahé (Paris: Gallimard, 1946);

Lost Moorings, translated by Gilbert (London: Routledge, 1946)–comprises *Chemin sans issue* and *Touriste de bananes;*

Les Noces de Poitiers (Paris: Gallimard, 1946); translated by Ellenbogen as *The Couple from Poitiers* (San Diego: Harcourt Brace Jovanovich, 1985);

Trois Chambres à Manhattan (Paris: Presses de la Cité, 1946); translated by Lawrence G. Blochman as *Three Beds in Manhattan* (Garden City: Doubleday, 1964; London: Hamilton, 1976);

Au bout du Rouleau (Paris: Presses de la Cité, 1947);

Le Clan des Ostendais (Paris: Gallimard, 1947);

Maigret et l'inspecteur malchanceux (Paris: Presses de la Cité, 1947)–comprises *Le Client le plus obstiné du monde,* translated as *The Most Obstinate Man in Paris* in *The Short Cases of Inspector Maigret* (1959), *Maigret et l'inspecteur malchanceux, On ne tue pas les pauvres types,* and *Le Témoignage de l'enfant de chœur;*

Lettre à mon juge (Paris: Presses de la Cité, 1947); translated by Louise Varèse as *Act of Passion* (New York: Prentice-Hall, 1952; London: Routledge & Kegan Paul, 1953);

Maigret à New York (Paris: Presses de la Cité, 1947); translated by Adrienne Foulke as *Maigret in New York's Underworld* (Garden City: Doubleday, 1955);

Maigret se fâche (Paris: Presses de la Cité, 1947);

Le Passager clandestin (Paris: Editions de la Jeune Parque, 1947); translated by Nigel Ryan as *The Stowaway* (London: Hamilton, 1957);

La Pipe de Maigret (Paris: Presses de la Cité, 1947);

Le Bilan Malétras (Paris: Gallimard, 1948); translated by Emily Read as *The Reckoning* (London: Hamilton, 1984; San Diego: Harcourt Brace Jovanovich, 1984);

Le Destin des Malou (Paris: Presses de la Cité, 1948); translated by Denis George as *The Fate of the Malous* (London: Hamilton, 1962);

La Jument perdue (Paris: Presses de la Cité, 1948);

Maigret et son mort (Paris: Presses de la Cité, 1948); translated by Stewart as *Maigret's Special Murder* (London: Hamilton, 1964); republished as *Maigret's Dead Man* (Garden City: Doubleday, 1954);

La Neige était sale (Paris: Presses de la Cité, 1948); translated by Varèse as *The Snow Was Black* (New York: Prentice-Hall, 1950); translated by Petrie as *The Stain on the Snow* (London: Routledge & Kegan Paul, 1953);

Pedigree (Paris: Presses de la Cité, 1948); translated by Robert Baldick (London: Hamilton, 1962);

Les Vacances de Maigret (Paris: Presses de la Cité, 1948); translated as *Maigret on Holiday* in *Maigret on Holiday* (1950); republished separately as *No Vacation for Maigret* (Garden City: Doubleday, 1953);

Black Rain, translated by Sainsbury (London: Routledge & Kegan Paul, 1949)–comprises *Les Rescapés du "Télémaque"* and *Il pleut bergère;*

Chit of a Girl, translated by Sainsbury (London: Routledge & Kegan Paul, 1949)–comprises *La Marie du port* and *Cour d'assises;*

Les Fantômes du chapelier (Paris: Presses de la Cité, 1949); translated as *The Hatter's Ghost* in *The Judge and the Hatter* (1956); translated by Willard R. Trask as *The Hatter's Phantom* (New York: Harcourt Brace Jovanovich, 1976);

Le Fond de la bouteille (Paris: Presses de la Cité, 1949); translated as *The Bottom of the Bottle* in *Tidal Waves* (1954);

Maigret chez le coroner (Paris: Presses de la Cité, 1949); translated by Francis Keene as *Maigret and the Coroner* (London: Hamilton, 1980); republished as *Maigret at the Coroner's* (New York: Harcourt Brace Jovanovich, 1980);

Maigret et la vieille dame (Paris: Presses de la Cité, 1949); translated by Robert Brain as *Maigret and the Old Lady* (London: Hamilton, 1958); published in *Maigret Cinq* (1965);

Mon Ami Maigret (Paris: Presses de la Cité, 1949); translated by Ryan as *My Friend Maigret* (London: Hamilton, 1956); republished as *The Methods of Maigret* (Garden City: Doubleday, 1957);

La Première Enquête de Maigret, 1913 (Paris: Presses de la Cité, 1949); translated by Brain as *Maigret's First Case* (London: Hamilton, 1958); published in *Maigret Cinq* (1965);

Les Quatre Jours du pauvre homme (Paris: Presses de la Cité, 1949); translated as *Four Days in a Lifetime* in *Satan's Children* (1953);

A Wife at Sea, translated by Sainsbury (London: Routledge & Kegan Paul, 1949)–comprises *Les Pitard* and *L'Assassin;*

L'Amie de Madame Maigret (Paris: Presses de la Cité, 1950); translated by Helen Sebba as *Madame Maigret's Own Case* (New York: Doubleday, 1959); republished as *Madame Maigret's Friend* (London: Hamilton, 1960);

L'Enterrement de Monsieur Bouvet (Paris: Presses de la Cité, 1950); translated by Eugene MacCown as *The Burial of Monsieur Bouvet* (Garden City: Doubleday, 1955); republished as *Inquest on Bouvet* (London: Hamilton, 1958);

Maigret on Holiday, translated by Sainsbury (London: Routledge & Kegan Paul, 1950)–comprises *Signé Picpus* and *Les Vacances de Maigret;*

Un Nouveau dans la ville (Paris: Presses de la Cité, 1950);

Les Petits Cochons sans queue (Paris: Presses de la Cité, 1950);

Poisoned Relations, translated by Sainsbury (London: Routledge & Kegan Paul, 1950)–comprises *Monsieur La Souris* and *Les Sœurs Lacroix;*

Tante Jeanne (Paris: Presses de la Cité, 1950); translated by Sainsbury as *Aunt Jeanne* (London: Routledge & Kegan Paul, 1953);

Les Volets verts (Paris: Presses de la Cité, 1950); translated by Varèse as *The Heart of a Man* (New York: Prentice-Hall / Toronto: McLeod, 1951); published in *A Sense of Guilt* (1955);

Maigret au "Picratt's" (Paris: Presses de la Cité, 1951); translated as *Maigret in Montmartre* in *Maigret Right and Wrong* (1954); translated by Cornelia Schaeffer as *Inspector Maigret and the Strangled Stripper* (Garden City: Doubleday, 1954);

Maigret en meublé (Paris: Presses de la Cité, 1951); translated by Brain as *Maigret Takes a Room* (London: Hamilton, 1960); republished as *Maigret Rents a Room* (Garden City: Doubleday, 1961);

Maigret et la grande perche (Paris: Presses de la Cité, 1951); translated by J. Maclaren-Ross as *Maigret and the Burglar's Wife* (London: Hamilton, 1955); republished as *Inspector Maigret and the Burglar's Wife* (Garden City: Doubleday, 1956);

Marie qui louche (Paris: Presses de la Cité, 1951); translated by Thomson as *The Girl with a Squint* (New York: Harcourt Brace Jovanovich, 1978);

Les Mémoires de Maigret (Paris: Presses de la Cité, 1951); translated by Stewart as *Maigret's Memoirs* (London: Hamilton, 1963);

Un Noël de Maigret (Paris: Presses de la Cité, 1951)—comprises *Un Noël de Maigret,* translated as *Maigret's Christmas* in *The Short Cases of Inspector Maigret* (1959), *Sept petites croix dans un carnet,* and *Le Petit Restaurant des Ternes;*

Le Temps d'Anaïs (Paris: Presses de la Cité, 1951); translated by Varèse as *The Girl in His Past* (New York: Prentice-Hall, 1952; London: Hamilton, 1976);

Une Vie Comme neuve (Paris: Presses de la Cité, 1951); translated by Joanna Richardson as *A New Lease on Life* (London: Hamilton, 1963; New York: Doubleday, 1963);

The Window over the Way, translated by Sainsbury (London: Routledge & Kegan Paul / New York: British Book Service, 1951)—comprises *Les Gens d'en face* and *Le Rapport du gendarme;*

Les Frères Rico (Paris: Presses de la Cité, 1952); translated as *The Brothers Rico* in *Violent Ends* (1954); published in *Tidal Waves* (1954);

The House by the Canal, translated by Sainsbury (London: Routledge & Kegan Paul, 1952)—comprises *La Maison du canal* and *Le Clan des Ostendais;*

Maigret, Lognon et les gangsters (Paris: Presses de la Cité, 1952); translated by Varèse as *Inspector Maigret and the Killers* (Garden City: Doubleday, 1954); republished as *Maigret and the Gangsters* (London: Hamilton, 1974);

La Mort de Belle (Paris: Presses de la Cité, 1952); translated as *Belle* in *Violent Ends* (1954); published in *Tidal Wave* (1954);

Le Revolver de Maigret (Paris: Presses de la Cité, 1952); translated by Ryan as *Maigret's Revolver* (London: Hamilton, 1956);

Antoine et Julie (Paris: Presses de la Cité, 1953); translated as *The Magician* in *The Magician* [and] *The Widow* (1955); published separately (London: Hamilton, 1974);

L'Escalier de feu (Paris: Presses de la Cité, 1953); translated by Ellenbogen as *The Iron Staircase* (London: Hamilton, 1963; New York: Harcourt Brace Jovanovich, 1977);

Feux rouges (Paris: Presses de la Cité, 1953); translated as *Red Lights* in *Danger Ahead* (1955); republished as *The Hitchhiker* in *Destinations* (1955);

Maigret a peur (Paris: Presses de la Cité, 1953); translated by Margaret Duff as *Maigret Afraid* (London: Hamilton, 1961; San Diego: Harcourt Brace Jovanovich, 1983);

Maigret et l'homme du banc (Paris: Presses de la Cité, 1953); translated by Ellenbogen as *Maigret and the Man on the Boulevard* (London: Hamilton, 1975); republished as *Maigret and the Man on the Bench* (New York: Harcourt Brace Jovanovich, 1975);

Maigret se trompe (Paris: Presses de la Cité, 1953); translated as *Maigret's Mistake* in *Maigret Right and Wrong* (1954); published in *Five Times Maigret* (1964);

Satan's Children, translated by Varèse (New York: Prentice-Hall, 1953)—comprises *La Vérité sur Bébé Donge* and *Les Quatre Jours du pauvre homme;*

Le Bateau d'Emile (Paris: Gallimard, 1954);

Crime impuni (Paris: Presses de la Cité, 1954); translated by Varèse as *Fugitive* (Garden City: Doubleday, 1954); translated by Tony White as *Account Unsettled* (London: Hamilton, 1962);

Le Grand Bob (Paris: Presses de la Cité, 1954); translated by Eileen Howe as *Big Bob* (London: Hamilton, 1954);

L'Horloger d'Everton (Paris: Presses de la Cité, 1954); translated as *The Watchmaker of Everton* in *Danger Ahead* (1955); published with *The Witnesses* (1956);

Maigret à l'école (Paris: Presses de la Cité, 1954); translated by Daphne Woodward as *Maigret Goes to School* (London: Hamilton, 1957); published in *Five Times Maigret* (1964);

Maigret chez le ministre (Lakeville, Conn., 1954; Paris: Presses de la Cité, 1955); translated by Moura Budberg as *Maigret and the Minister* (London: Hamilton, 1969); republished as *Maigret and the Calame Report* (New York: Harcourt, Brace & World, 1969);

Maigret et la jeune morte (Paris: Presses de la Cité, 1954); translated by Woodward as *Maigret and the Young Girl* (London: Hamilton, 1955); republished as *Inspector Maigret and the Dead Girl* (Garden City: Doubleday, 1955);

Maigret Right and Wrong (London: Hamilton, 1954)—comprises *Maigret au "Picratt's,"* translated by Woodward as *Maigret in Montmartre*, and *Maigret se trompe*, translated by Alan Hodge as *Maigret's Mistake;*

On Land and Sea, translated by Victor Kosta (Garden City: Hanover House, 1954)—comprises *Le Passager du "Polarlys"* and *Les Gens d'en face;*

Les Témoins (Lakeville, Conn., 1954; Paris: Presses de la Cité, 1955); translated as *The Witnesses* in *The Judge and the Hatter* (1956); published with *The Watchmaker of Everton* (1956);

Tidal Wave (Garden City: Doubleday, 1954)—comprises *Le Fond de la bouteille*, translated by Schaeffer as *The Bottom of the Bottle*, *Les Frères Rico*, translated by Ernst Pawel as *The Brothers Rico*, and *La Mort de Belle*, translated by Varèse as *Belle;*

Violent Ends (London: Hamilton, 1954)—comprises *Les Frères Rico*, translated by Pawel as *The Brothers Rico*, and *La Mort de Belle*, translated by Varèse as *Belle;*

La Boule noire (Paris: Presses de la Cité, 1955);

Les Complices (Paris: Presses de la Cité, 1955); translated as *The Accomplices* in *The Blue Room* [and] *The Accomplices* (1964); published separately (London: Hamilton, 1966);

Danger Ahead, translated by Denny (London: Hamilton, 1955)—comprises *Feux rouges* and *L'Horloger d'Everton;*

Destinations (Garden City: Doubleday, 1955)—comprises *Feux rouges*, translated by Denny as *The Hitchhiker*, and *L'Enterrement de Monsieur Bouvet*, translated by MacCown as *The Burial of Monsieur Bouvet;*

The Magician [and] *The Widow* (Garden City: Doubleday, 1955)—comprises *Antoine et Julie*, translated by Sebba as *The Magician*, and *La Veuve Couderc*, translated by Petrie as *The Widow;*

Maigret et le corps sans tête (Lakeville, Conn., 1955; Paris: Presses de la Cité, 1955); translated by Ellenbogen as *Maigret and the Headless Corpse* (London: Hamilton, 1967; New York: Harcourt, Brace & World, 1968);

Maigret tend un piège (Paris: Presses de la Cité, 1955); translated by Woodward as *Maigret Sets a Trap* (London: Hamilton, 1965; New York: Harcourt, Brace & World, 1972);

A Sense of Guilt, translated by Woodward (London: Hamilton, 1955)—comprises *Chez Krull* and *Les Volets verts;*

Un Echec de Maigret (Paris: Presses de la Cité, 1956); translated by Woodward as *Maigret's Failure* (London: Hamilton, 1962); published in *A Maigret Trio* (1973);

En cas de malheur (Paris: Presses de la Cité, 1956); translated by Sebba as *In Case of Emergency* (Garden City: Doubleday, 1958; London: Hamilton, 1960);

The Judge and the Hatter (London: Hamilton, 1956)—comprises *Les Fantômes du chapelier*, translated by Ryan as *The Hatter's Ghost*, and *Les Témoins*, translated by Budberg as *The Witnesses;*

The Sacrifice (London: Hamilton, 1956)—comprises *Les Fiançailles de M. Hire*, translated by Woodward as *Mr. Hire's Engagement*, and *Le Fils Cardinaud*, translated by Brain as *Young Cardinaud;*

The Witnesses [and] *The Watchmaker* (Garden City: Doubleday, 1956)—comprises *L'Horloger d'Everton*, translated by Denny as *The Watchmaker of Everton*, and *Les Témoins*, translated by Budberg as *The Witnesses;*

Le Fils (Paris: Presses de la Cité, 1957); translated by Woodward as *The Son* (London: Hamilton, 1958);

Maigret s'amuse (Paris: Presses de la Cité, 1957); translated by Brain as *Maigret's Little Joke* (London: Hamilton, 1957); republished as *None of Maigret's Business* (Garden City: Doubleday, 1958);

Le Nègre (Paris: Presses de la Cité, 1957); translated by Sebba as *The Negro* (London: Hamilton, 1959);

Le Petit Homme d'Arkhangelsk (Paris: Presses de la Cité, 1957); translated by Ryan as *The Little Man from Archangel* (London: Hamilton, 1957); published with *Sunday* (1966);

Maigret voyage (Paris: Presses de la Cité, 1958); translated by Stewart as *Maigret and the Millionaires* (London: Hamilton, 1974; New York: Harcourt Brace Jovanovich, 1974);

Le Passage de la ligne (Paris: Presses de la Cité, 1958);

Le Président (Paris: Presses de la Cité, 1958); translated by Woodward as *The Premier* (London: Hamilton, 1961);

Les Scrupules de Maigret (Paris: Presses de la Cité, 1958); translated by Robert Eglesfield as *Maigret Has Scruples* (London: Hamilton, 1959); published in *Versus Inspector Maigret* (1960);

Une Confidence de Maigret (Paris: Presses de la Cité, 1959); translated by Lyn Moir as *Maigret Has Doubts* (London: Hamilton, 1968; New York: Harcourt Brace Jovanovich, 1982);

Dimanche (Paris: Presses de la Cité, 1959); translated by Ryan as *Sunday* (London: Hamilton, 1960); published with *The Little Man from Archangel* (1966);

The Short Cases of Inspector Maigret, translated by Blochman (Garden City: Doubleday, 1959);

La Vieille (Paris: Presses de la Cité, 1959); translated by Stewart as *The Grandmother* (New York: Harcourt Brace Jovanovich, 1978);

Maigret aux assises (Paris: Presses de la Cité, 1960); translated by Brain as *Maigret in Court* (London: Hamilton, 1961);

Maigret et les vieillards (Paris: Presses de la Cité, 1960); translated by Eglesfield as *Maigret in Society* (London: Hamilton, 1962); published in *A Maigret Trio* (1973);

L'Ours en peluche (Paris: Presses de la Cité, 1960); translated by John Clay as *Teddy Bear* (London: Hamilton, 1971; New York: Harcourt Brace Jovanovich, 1972);

Le Roman de l'homme (Paris: Presses de la Cité, 1960); translated by Bernard Frechtman as *The Novel of a Man* (New York: Harcourt, Brace & World, 1964);

Versus Inspector Maigret (Garden City: Doubleday, 1960)–comprises *Les Scrupules de Maigret,* translated by Eglesfield as *Maigret Has Scruples,* and *Maigret et les témoins récalcitrants,* translated by Woodward as *Maigret and the Reluctant Witnesses;*

Le Veuf (Paris: Presses de la Cité, 1960); translated by Baldick as *The Widower* (London: Hamilton, 1961);

Betty (Paris: Presses de la Cité, 1961); translated by Alastair Hamilton (London: Hamilton, 1975; New York: Harcourt Brace Jovanovich, 1975);

Maigret et le voleur paresseux (Paris: Presses de la Cité, 1961); translated by Woodward as *Maigret and the Lazy Burglar* (London: Hamilton, 1963); published in *A Maigret Trio* (1973);

Le Train (Paris: Presses de la Cité, 1961); translated by Baldick as *The Train* (London: Hamilton, 1964);

Les Autres (Paris: Presses de la Cité, 1962); translated by Hamilton as *The Others* (London: Hamilton, 1975); republished as *The House on Quai Notre Dame* (New York: Harcourt Brace Jovanovich, 1975);

Maigret et le client du samedi (Paris: Presses de la Cité, 1962); translated by Tony White as *Maigret and the Saturday Caller* (London: Hamilton, 1964);

Maigret et les braves gens (Paris: Presses de la Cité, 1962); translated by Thomson as *Maigret and the Black Sheep* (London: Hamilton, 1976; New York: Harcourt Brace Jovanovich, 1976);

La Porte (Paris: Presses de la Cité, 1962); translated by Woodward as *The Door* (London: Hamilton, 1964);

Les Anneaux de Bicêtre (Paris: Presses de la Cité, 1963); translated by Stewart as *The Patient* (London: Hamilton, 1963; New York: Harcourt, Brace & World, 1964);

La Colère de Maigret (Paris: Presses de la Cité, 1963); translated by Eglesfield as *Maigret Loses His Temper* (London: Hamilton, 1964; New York: Harcourt Brace Jovanovich, 1974);

Ma Conviction profonde (Geneva: Cailler, 1963);

Maigret et le clochard (Paris: Presses de la Cité, 1963); translated by Stewart as *Maigret and the Dossier* (London: Hamilton, 1973); republished as *Maigret and the Bum* (New York: Harcourt Brace Jovanovich, 1973);

La Rue aux trois poussins (Paris: Presses de la Cité, 1963);

La Chambre bleue (Paris: Presses de la Cité, 1964); translated as *The Blue Room* in *The Blue Room* [and] *The Accomplices* (1964); published separately (London: Hamilton, 1965);

The Blue Room [and] *The Accomplices* (New York: Harcourt, Brace & World, 1964)–comprises *Les Complices,* translated by Frechtman as *The Accomplices,* and *La Chambre bleue,* translated by Ellenbogen as *The Blue Room;*

Five Times Maigret, translated by Woodward (New York: Harcourt, Brace, 1964)–comprises *Maigret au "Picratt's," Maigret se trompe, Maigret à l'école, Les Scrupules de Maigret,* and *Maigret et les témoins récalcitrants;*

L'Homme au petit chien (Paris: Presses de la Cité, 1964); translated by Stewart (London: Hamilton, 1965);

Maigret et le fantôme (Paris: Presses de la Cité, 1964); translated by Ellenbogen as *Maigret and the Ghost* (London: Hamilton, 1976); republished as *Maigret and the Apparition* (New York: Harcourt Brace Jovanovich, 1976);

Maigret se défend (Paris: Presses de la Cité, 1964); translated by Hamilton as *Maigret on the Defensive* (London: Hamilton, 1966); republished as *Maigret on the Defensive* (New York: Harcourt Brace Jovanovich, 1981);

Maigret Cinq, translated by Brain (New York: Harcourt, Brace, 1965)–comprises *Maigret et la vieille dame, La Première Enquête de Maigret, Maigret en meublé, Maigret et la jeune morte,* and *Maigret s'amuse;*

La Patience de Maigret (Paris: Presses de la Cité, 1965); translated by Hamilton as *The Patience of Maigret* (London: Hamilton, 1966); republished as *Maigret Bides His Time* (San Diego: Harcourt Brace Jovanovich, 1985);

Le Petit Saint (Paris: Presses de la Cité, 1965); translated by Frechtman as *The Little Saint* (New York: Harcourt, Brace & World, 1965; London: Hamilton, 1966);

Le Train de Venise (Paris: Presses de la Cité, 1965); translated by Hamilton as *The Venice Train* (London: Hamilton, 1974; New York: Harcourt Brace Jovanovich, 1974);

Le Confessional (Paris: Presses de la Cité, 1966); translated by Stewart as *The Confessional* (London: Hamilton, 1967; New York: Harcourt Brace Jovanovich, 1968);

La Mort d'Auguste (Paris: Presses de la Cité, 1966); translated by Frechtman as *The Old Man Dies* (New York: Harcourt, Brace & World, 1967; London: Hamilton, 1968);

Maigret et l'affaire Nahour (Paris: Presses de la Cité, 1966); translated by Hamilton as *Maigret and the Nahour Case* (London: Hamilton, 1967);

Sunday [and] *The Little Man from Archangel,* translated by Ryan (New York: Harcourt, Brace & World, 1966)–comprises *Dimanche* and *Le Petit Homme d'Arkhangelsk;*

Le Chat (Paris: Presses de la Cité, 1967); translated by Frechtman as *The Cat* (New York: Harcourt, Brace & World, 1967; London: Hamilton, 1972);

Le Déménagement (Paris: Presses de la Cité, 1967); translated by Christopher Sinclair-Stevenson as *The Neighbors* (London: Hamilton, 1968); republished as *The Move* (New York: Harcourt, Brace & World, 1968);

Le Voleur de Maigret (Paris: Presses de la Cité, 1967); translated by Ryan as *Maigret's Pickpocket* (London: Hamilton, 1968; New York: Harcourt Brace Jovanovich, 1968);

L'Ami d'enfance de Maigret (Paris: Presses de la Cité, 1968); translated by Ellenbogen as *Maigret's Boyhood Friend* (London: Hamilton, 1970; New York: Harcourt Brace Jovanovich, 1970);

Maigret à Vichy (Paris: Presses de la Cité, 1968); translated by Ellenbogen as *Maigret Takes the Waters* (London: Hamilton, 1969); republished as *Maigret in Vichy* (New York: Harcourt Brace Jovanovich, 1969);

Maigret hésite (Paris: Presses de la Cité, 1968); translated by Moir as *Maigret Hesitates* (London: Hamilton, 1970; New York: Harcourt Brace Jovanovich, 1970);

La Main (Paris: Presses de la Cité, 1968); translated by Budberg as *The Man on the Bench in the Barn* (London: Hamilton, 1970; New York: Harcourt Brace Jovanovich, 1970);

La Prison (Paris: Presses de la Cité, 1968); translated by Moir as *The Prison* (London: Hamilton, 1969; New York: Harcourt Brace Jovanovich, 1969);

Il y a encore des noisetiers (Paris: Presses de la Cité, 1969);

Maigret et le tueur (Paris: Presses de la Cité, 1969); translated by Moir as *Maigret and the Killer* (London: Hamilton, 1971; New York: Harcourt Brace Jovanovich, 1971);

Novembre (Paris: Presses de la Cité, 1969); translated by Stewart as *November* (London: Hamilton, 1970; New York: Harcourt Brace Jovanovich, 1970);

La Folle de Maigret (Paris: Presses de la Cité, 1970); translated by Ellenbogen as *Maigret and the Madwoman* (London: Hamilton, 1972; New York: Harcourt Brace Jovanovich, 1972);

Maigret et le marchand de vin (Paris: Presses de la Cité, 1970); translated by Ellenbogen as *Maigret and the Wine Merchant* (London: Hamilton, 1971; New York: Harcourt Brace Jovanovich, 1971);

Quand j'étais vieux (Paris: Presses de la Cité, 1970); translated by Helen Eustis as *When I Was Old* (New York: Harcourt Brace Jovanovich, 1971; London: Hamilton, 1972);

Le Riche Homme (Paris: Presses de la Cité, 1970); translated by Stewart as *The Rich Man* (London: Hamilton, 1971; New York: Harcourt Brace Jovanovich, 1971);

La Cage de verre (Paris: Presses de la Cité, 1971); translated by Antonia White as *The Glass Cage* (London: Hamilton, 1973; New York: Harcourt Brace Jovanovich, 1973);

La Disparition d'Odile (Paris: Club Français du Livre, 1971); translated by Moir as *The Disappearance of Odile* (London: Hamilton, 1972; New York: Harcourt Brace Jovanovich, 1972);

Maigret et l'homme tout seul (Paris: Presses de la Cité, 1971); translated by Ellenbogen as *Maigret and the Loner* (London: Hamilton, 1975; New York: Harcourt Brace Jovanovich, 1975);

Maigret et l'indicateur (Paris: Presses de la Cité, 1971); translated by Moir as *Maigret and the Flea* (London: Hamilton, 1972); republished as *Maigret and the Informer* (New York: Harcourt Brace Jovanovich, 1972);

Choix de Simenon, edited by Frank W. Lindsay and Anthony M. Nazzaro (New York: Appleton-Century-Crofts, 1972);

Les Innocents (Paris: Presses de la Cité, 1972); translated by Ellenbogen as *The Innocents* (London: Hamilton, 1973; New York: Harcourt Brace Jovanovich, 1973);

Maigret et Monsieur Charles (Paris: Presses de la Cité, 1972); translated by Marianne A. Sinclair as *Maigret and Monsieur Charles* (London: Hamilton, 1973);

A Maigret Trio, translated by Woodward (New York: Harcourt, Brace & World, 1973)—comprises *Un Echec de Maigret, Maigret et les vieillards,* and *Maigret et le voleur paresseux;*

La Piste du Hollandais (Paris: Presses de la Cité, 1973);

Lettre à ma mère (Paris: Presses de la Cité, 1974); translated by Ralph Manheim as *Letter to My Mother* (London: Hamilton, 1976; New York: Harcourt Brace Jovanovich, 1976);

Un Homme comme un autre (Paris: Presses de la Cité, 1975);

Des Traces de pas (Paris: Presses de la Cité, 1975);

A la découverte de la France, edited by Francis Lacassin and Gilbert Sigaux (Paris: Union Générale d'Editions, 1976);

A la recherche de l'homme nu, edited by Lacassin and Sigaux (Paris: Union Générale d'Editions, 1976);

Maigret's Christmas, translated by Stewart (London: Hamilton, 1976; New York: Harcourt Brace Jovanovich, 1977);

Les Petits Hommes (Paris: Presses de la Cité, 1976);

Vent du nord, vent du sud (Paris: Presses de la Cité, 1976);

A l'abri de notre arbre (Paris: Presses de la Cité, 1977);

L'Aîné des Ferchaux (Paris: Gallimard, 1977);

Un Banc au soleil (Paris: Presses de la Cité, 1977);

De la cave au grenier (Paris: Presses de la Cité, 1977);

Maigret's Pipe, translated by Stewart (London: Hamilton, 1977; New York: Harcourt Brace Jovanovich, 1978);

La Main dans la main (Paris: Presses de la Cité, 1978);

Tant que je suis vivant (Paris: Presses de la Cité, 1978);

Vacances obligatoires (Paris: Presses de la Cité, 1978);

A quoi bon jurer? (Paris: Presses de la Cité, 1979);

Au-delà de ma porte-fenêtre (Paris: Presses de la Cité, 1979);

Je suis resté un enfant de chœur (Paris: Presses de la Cité, 1979);

Point-virgule (Paris: Presses de la Cité, 1979);

Les Libertés qu'il nous reste (Paris: Presses de la Cité, 1980);

Maigret and the Mad Killers (Garden City: Doubleday, 1980);

On dit que j'ai soixante-quinze ans (Paris: Presses de la Cité, 1980);

Le Prix d'un homme (Paris: Presses de la Cité, 1980);

Quand vient le froid (Paris: Presses de la Cité, 1980);

La Femme endormie (Paris: Presses de la Cité, 1981);

Jour et nuit (Paris: Presses de la Cité, 1981);

Mémoires intimes (Paris: Presses de la Cité, 1981); translated by Harold J. Salemson as *Intimate Memoirs* (San Diego, New York & London: Harcourt Brace Jovanovich, 1984).

Collection: *Œuvres complètes*, 72 volumes, edited by Gilbert Sigaux (Lausanne: Rencontre, 1967-1973).

Georges Simenon, who fashioned a thousand violent and sordid—at best, pathetic—deaths for his characters, died in his sleep on 4 September 1989. For his life, in contrast with theirs, he had devised a structure of success and energy, and, in the last fifteen years, of serenity and fulfillment quite as realistic as their aridity, despair, and chronic failure. With Teresa at his side—the indispensable mistress/companion/nurturer of many years—he had retreated from the appurtenances and demeanor of success, not, to be sure, to the desolations of his fictions, but to his "little pink house" in Lausanne that had replaced the grandiose, automated mansion he had built at Epalinges, overlooking the Lake of Geneva, in 1964.

He had shut down Epalinges as he shut down his fiction enterprise ("l'usine Simenon," some called it though his highbrow admirers held, as Brendan Gill put it in his 24 January 1953 *New Yorker* profile, "that any resemblance between him and General Motors is unintentional, coincidental and too bad"). He had, one morning in 1972, begun a novel to be called "Oscar," then, asking himself why he was doing this, pulled the paper out of the typewriter and went to the Belgian consulate to have the designation in his passport changed from "novelist" to "retired." As it turned out, he immediately discovered the cassette recorder and produced an avalanche of reminiscences and reflections, promptly transcribed and published. In 1981 he handwrote the enormous *Mémoires intimes*, (translated as *Intimate Memoirs*, 1984), and swore that that was it. Except for the likely posthumous records, this time he kept his word. The *Mémoires* were occasioned largely by the tempestuous battle between him and his second wife, Denyse Ouimet (or "Denise," as he renamed her), who went to the trouble of suing him, assuring a final best-seller. (His first marriage, to Régine Renchon, had ended in divorce in 1949).

Before his "retirement," his life had been unstintingly active: traveling, partying, furnishing and unfurnishing mansions, carrying on with the ten thousand women he had once offhandedly estimated to his friend Federico Fellini as the number he had slept with–and writing, writing, writing. His enormous success in fiction had never, in fact, been part of his original life project. In his early teens Simenon began writing–in school and on his own–because he was good at it, and because he was a precocious and avid reader: writing fell into his lap, became part of his personal environment. This was the beginning of his serious writing. A little later he fell in with a bohemian crowd that might have been expected to nourish the idea of serious writing but instead had the opposite effect: sniffing out a depressing odor of failure among the bohemians, he kept his distance and went his own way.

His own way by then was mainly journalism, into which he had stumbled and which brought him rapid local success in Liège, where he had been born on 13 February 1903. Soon, a branch of his journalistic work–humor, at first–overflowed into fiction, which he could produce so fast that there was money in it: he had discovered commercial literature, which had not at all been part of his original plan but which soon expanded into every conceivable form of pulp fiction. "Serious" writing lay dormant in the 1920s:

he wrote for money because he found he could do it successfully but might as well have been doing anything else for money. He had always intended to reconnect himself with serious literature but had never thought of it as a way of making a living; that it turned out to be was something of an accident–which did not keep him from making the most of the accident.

In 1929 he invented his famous detective, then tried to leave Maigret behind and go on to other things. He indeed climbed the literary ladder, to the loud acclaim of many literati, but was only half-hearted in his attempt to shake off Maigret and was forever identified either as the man who wrote Maigrets or who had just written something other than a Maigret. This confused his status in the republic of letters no end, and for half a century one critic after another kept dissecting "le cas Simenon." The issue was not clarified by the fact that his "serious" fiction sometimes made as much money as his detective novels.

He himself discovered that literature was not only a way of making money but a mode of exploring experience, a mode of knowledge. He did not put it in those terms, but that is what he meant. He came to understand his literary project as a delving into man, which he found exhausting and anxiety-provoking. His explorations in literature paralleled his explorations in life and came from the same impulses–probably curiosity and discontent, which, in fiction, often became curiosity about discontent. His motivation, in the final analysis, was never really artistic. His underlying conviction when he wrote novels was not that he was composing works of art but that he was exploring life, and, furthermore, that there were more gratifying ways of doing so. Literary labor was that much effort drawn away from the business of living, and he was impatient to get it over with and go back to life. That is why he wrote so quickly and never revised, and that is why all of his novels are, to a greater or lesser degree, flawed. It is indeed an index of genius that, in these circumstances, he should have produced so many good novels, and a few masterpieces.

After his journalistic apprenticeship in Liège (and one Rabelaisian novella, *Au pont des Arches* [On the Bridge of the Arches], written when he was sixteen and privately published in 1921, subsidized by a rich woman whom, one assumes, he had been sleeping with), he abandoned small-city success for the big time, landing at the Gare du Nord in Paris on a bleak December morning in 1922 and swiftly elbowing his way to a preliminary kind of stardom as an unparalleled producer of pulp fiction. True stardom came with the first nineteen Maigrets (1931-1934), followed by a robust plunge into what he called variously *romans durs, romans-romans,* or *romans-tout-court,* to distinguish them from both pulps and Maigrets. Unable to shake off Maigret, he settled for an alternating production of Maigrets and straight novels, all produced at an astonishing rate, and all making him ever more rich and famous. His success backwardly progressed from financial to *d'estime,* as several men of letters (he detested the category), one after another, "discovered" him, André Gide heading the roster. They assured him he had the wrong public and praised, nudged, cajoled, and sometimes worried him about the straight novels. "I do not understand very well *how* you construct, compose, write your books," Gide mildly complained. Simenon sometimes manifested a certain frustration, anxiety, and confusion in his explanations. In a letter to Gide he fretted: "Intelligence frightens me terribly ... I try to feel rather than think. Or rather to think with ... (?) here we are! I would be hard put to say with what! A Rembrandt painting, a Renoir.... A little piece for harpsichord or violin that Bach would *piss* as a musical exercise for his kids." This note of worried earnestness emerged sporadically in the late 1930s and the 1940s but turned out to be a detour in the pattern of Simenon's literary career.

The mainstream of that career was a vast continued production of Maigrets and non-Maigrets, exhibiting a very wide range of literary quality and a narrower range of recurring themes, which have been frequently classified as alienation, flight, return, destiny, justice, destructiveness and self-destructiveness, desire, despair, hate, tenderness, envy. There are the couple, the family, the siblings, the parent and child (often father-son), the clan, the town, society, mankind, "them." Behind these, or beyond, there is solitude.

Most of Simenon's characters are radically alienated, either from the start or because something happens to dislocate them from their surroundings. The ubiquitous flight motif frequently ensues from this dislocation: one day the protagonist abandons all, hops on the train, and gets the hell out. Sometimes, without leaving physically, he is nonetheless in the same state of flight as his semblable on the train. Rather often, the flight is from a socially integrated situation to an alienated one, where the protagonist feels more at home and finds his real self; yet a constituent element of the alienated situation is a longing for what one is alienated from–that is, what one has fled from. There is a painful sense of exclusion, a sort of sad gazing into warm and cozy interiors from a cold outside. Some want out, some want in; wanting out and succeeding means being where, by definition, you want in.

Often, Simenon's characters try to build something, which turns out to be a house of cards on shifting sands; or they discover that such a structure is where they've been living all along. Add the closets, put in the skeletons, and you have the basic Simenonian habitat. The exceptions and alternatives are dotted around it, isolated specks in a sparsely populated region. The majority of Simenon's protagonists are propelled by inexorable destiny, as in classical tragedy, but with a stronger inmixture of futility and helplessness and a glaring absence of heroic resistance. Destinies are mostly carried out alone, occasionally in small groups. Rarely are the latter successful or harmonious, though some are enduring in their disharmonies.

Unhappy families are all alike in Simenon: anticouples, antipartners, antifamilies, stuck with each other. Sometimes Simenon liked to experiment with extreme situations compounding deep hostility, tight proximity, and isolation: islands, jungles, ships at sea–though an equally radical isolation can arise in city apartments or French provinces. Instances of love, tenderness, loyalty, respect, and responsibility sometimes provide relief from this bleak landscape but serve more often to define it.

In the straight novels, these preoccupations were insistently explored, beginning with *La Maison du canal* (translated as *The House by the Canal,* 1952), *Les Fiançailles de M. Hire* (*Mr. Hire's Engagement,* 1956), *L'Âne rouge* (*The Nightclub,* 1979), and *Le Coup de lune* (*Tropic Moon,* 1942), his first serious "tropical" novel–all written in 1932 and published in 1933. *Les Pitard* of 1935 (translated as *A Wife at Sea,* 1949), an uneven but sometimes very powerful sea story, with a superlative description, toward the end, of an attempted rescue of a trawler floundering in a hurricane, occasioned the first highbrow critical response, André Thérive's influential review in *Le Temps,* proclaiming that he had just read "a masterpiece in its pure state, in its basic state" ("à l'état pur, à l'état brut"). *L'Homme qui regardait passer les trains* (1938; translated as *The Man Who Watched the*

Trains Go By, 1945) is an archetypal "flight" story about a Dutch businessman who, ruined, takes flight to Paris, where he arrives at the Gare du Nord in a way very reminiscent of Simenon's arrival in 1922, and where it becomes increasingly clear that the flight is not really the result of a cause (the bankruptcy), but rather that the apparent cause merely reveals what he always knew—that his ordered, bourgeois life was a lie. *Le Bourgmestre de Furnes* (1939; translated as *The Bourgomaster of Furnes*, 1952) chronicles a "flight-standing-in-place" (the character does not actually leave but becomes as alienated as those who do) into sexual obsession and extreme social ostracism. About *Les Inconnus dans la maison* (1940; translated as *Strangers in the House*, 1951), Gide wrote, "I have read your astounding *Inconnus dans la maison*. Hadn't felt such lively interest in a long time.... You're on the right path.... Bravo!" It is the story of an alcoholic, isolated ex-lawyer, who rouses himself from his torpor to help clear an injustice, the dropout, this time, dropping back in. *La Neige était sale* (1948; translated as *The Snow Was Black*, 1950) is a tour de force that, against all expectations, manages brilliantly to transform one of Simenon's most odious characters (which is saying a lot) into an object of some compassion, certainly understanding, and possibly even admiration. This last, like many other books of that period, dramatizes an urgent need to understand—and not so much the understanding as the need, or not even the need so much as the urgency of the need. *Lettre à mon juge* (1947; translated as *Act of Passion*, 1952) is another.

Simenon continued to mine these and similar veins for the rest of his career and sometimes to explore new ones. In the 1950s and 1960s he wrote several novels about successful men painfully reappraising their lives. *L'Ours en peluche* (1960; translated as *Teddy Bear*, 1971) depicts a doctor who finds his successes to be masks and betrayals of the "little people" from whom he came and, himself betrayed by his mistress, hesitates between murder and suicide, opting, virtually by accident, for the former. In *En cas de malheur* (1956; translated as *In Case of Emergency*, 1958) a top lawyer opens a dossier labeled "me" and proceeds to extract the *real* truth from himself with the same tenacity he uses to pry the truth from his clients, who are always hedging. *Le Président* (1958; translated as *The Premier*, 1961), based on the life of Georges Clemenceau, examines with some subtlety an old man's loss of power. *Les*

Anneaux de Bicêtre (1963; translated as *The Patient*, 1963), Simenon's biggest success from these years, follows with remarkable precision the fractal contours of a press magnate's reckonings and summing up as he slowly regains consciousness after a heart attack.

In the latter half of this last decade of fiction Simenon wrote several well-known books notable for a more affirmative tone than was customary, associated with a relish of sensory experience. *Le Petit Saint* (1965; translated as *The Little Saint*, 1965) is a loosely narrated, essentially sensory biography of a fictional character, tracing the history of his sensual perceptions from infancy to old age, concentrating on his childhood. For background, Simenon had left the forbidding mansion at Epalinges for on-the-spot rummaging around the swarming, popular rue Mouffetard, one of his old haunts of the 1920s and, no doubt, Epalinges's antidote (keeping, nonetheless, his taxi waiting to take him back to the Hôtel George V). *La Mort d'Auguste* (1966; translated as *The Old Man Dies*, 1967), in an exceptionally well-articulated plot, depicts the conflict that ensues following the death of an old restaurateur, between the greedy, corrupt, and vacuous world of two of his sons and the community of decent men incarnate in the dead father and the third son—the community motif richly amplified by the warm communion of the old man with the "little people" of the neighborhood, portrayed in flashbacks and reaching a moving crescendo as the funeral procession winds through the heart of Les Halles. Simenon's last important novel was *Il y a encore des noisetiers* (There Are Still Hazel Trees, 1969), in which a wealthy, retired banker becomes absorbed in questions of generational continuity, and of family, lost and recovered—a man who has led a glamorous, agitated life but now realizes that it is the little things that count: doubtless a portrait, well fictionalized, of the older Simenon.

Then, of course, there are the Maigrets. When Simenon, who had been making large amounts of money with avalanches of pulp fiction written under eighteen or more pseudonyms, created Maigret in 1929, he had an inkling that he had hit upon something more than just another throwaway pulp figure. Being Simenon, he made the most of the inkling. He rushed to his publisher, Fayard, with the first "real" Maigret, *Pietr-le-Letton* (1931; translated as *The Case of Peter the Lett*, 1933), and proposed launching the new detective with fanfare. Fayard's response, according to Simenon's frequently related account, was that this was not a real detective story unraveling a mystery, with good guys and bad guys, and that there was no love interest, and besides, everything turned sour in the end. "We're going to lose a lot of money," he said, nonetheless adding, "but I'll try it anyway."

The young author became a whirlwind of energy. He was living on a converted trawler with his first wife, whom he called Tigy, and his servant/mistress Boule (her Christian name was Henriette–he had a penchant for renaming his women), and a Great Dane named (straightforwardly) Olaf, where, moored upstream from Paris, he dashed off four more Maigrets and plunged into promotion with irrepressible gusto. Fayard had proposed marketing the books at five francs, but Simenon had made his own calculations and concluded that six would yield maximum profits. It was he who decided to use photographed instead of drawn covers, and engaged two prominent photographers, one of whom was Man Ray. He himself went rummaging about the rue Mouffetard (as he would thirty years later for *Le Petit saint*) in search of an appropriate bum to pose for the third Maigret, *Le Charretier de la "Providence"* (1931; translated as *The Crime at Lock 14*, 1934). He also negotiated something above the normal 10 percent royalty, as he always did subsequently.

He went usually under the name "Georges Sim"–a reduced name, perhaps, for a reduced literature–and when the question arose of which of the eighteen pseudonyms to use, Fayard asked, "What *is* your real name, anyway?" "Simenon," he answered, and they decided that would do. By February of 1931 all was ready, and two of the books were chosen for a flamboyant release at the well-known Montparnasse nightclub, the Boule Blanche. It was dubbed a "bal anthropométrique," referring to police procedures for identifying and classifying criminals and suspects. The invitations were streaked with bloody fingerprints, and the guests themselves were fingerprinted at the door.

If the creation of Maigret were a lucky accident, Simenon seized upon the accident not only to make more money but also to start climbing some notches up that literary ladder toward a destination that has remained ambiguous to this day. During the prepublication hoopla, Simenon was developing a theory of the "semi-literary" novel, or, more earthily, "semi-alimentary." The theory was that he wrote pulps to make money, was aiming at "straight" novels but felt insecure about

"high" literature, and took up the detective story as a midway step. The pulp novel is easy to write because the writer is totally uninvolved, the straight novel difficult because he is wholly involved, to the point of exhaustion and nervous breakdown, and the detective story in-between, because, though involved, the writer has a set gimmick to structure his book and keep his reader interested: the crime to be solved and the detective who can come and go at will in solving it.

By the fall of 1931 Simenon was clearly an "item." The ever-alert Janet Flanner (who wrote as "Genêt" for the *New Yorker*) introduced Simenon to America in the "Paris Letter" of 24 October, anticipating that "Simenon" would become his permanent "pseudonym" and quoting him as saying, "My ambition is to arrive little by little in the class of a Jack London, or–who knows?–a Conrad," but gallantly adding, "he is already in a class by himself."

From a pyrotechnic phenomenon in the 1930s, Maigret in the 1940s had become an applauded revival and then turned into an institution, whether he is minimally or maximally evaluated as a literary creation, or somewhere in between. Minimally, Maigret is one of a score of famous detectives in a minor popular genre: that, indeed, is pretty much the status that he–and his creator as well–has for most of the public the world around. Maximally, Maigret is considered as a sort of émigré from a higher literary realm wandering in the world of detective fiction, which he transfigures.

What Simenon had created in 1929 was a well-defined, if rudimentary, figure: a stocky, high-ranking criminal police official in a bowler hat, an overcoat with a velvet collar, reasonably well-tailored suits of reasonably good wool, with neckties tending not to knot quite properly and pants a bit baggy: neither a dandy nor a slob, in short, but a man of the people who detests worldliness and luxury and exhibits a marked sympathy for his quarries. This basic figure was elaborated and fleshed out in many ways over the years.

One way was the accumulation or reiteration of more personal details about Maigret and his surroundings. Maigret has good eyesight, can fall asleep virtually anywhere, but tends to be short of breath when climbing stairs and suffers from claustrophobia. His files are disorganized, he often leaves his badge at home, but straightens pictures on walls. He is no good at picking locks and has never learned to drive a car, fearing that his mind might wander and he would for-

Simenon at Epalinges, circa 1966 (photograph by Alfredo Penicucci, Grazia; *courtesy of the estate of Georges Simenon)*

get he's at the wheel. Maigret, indeed, uses fewer police cars than might be expected, preferring taxis and even buses.

His pipes, of course, are legendary, though he may be discovered once smoking a cigarette and once, a cigar. He reads psychiatric treatises but finds them impractical in his work. He reads Alexandre Dumas but does not read detective stories. Similarly, when television makes its way into his world, he watches westerns and grade-B movies but dislikes detective shows. He and Mme. Maigret often go to the movies on rainy afternoons, seemingly indifferent to what is playing.

Maigret has two families, two households where he snuggles in comfort and warm intimacy: his home and his office. Home is the fifth floor of 130 boulevard Richard-Lenoir, Paris XIème, which he shares with the celebrated Mme. Maigret. She frequently worries about his getting wet and cold–for good reason, since he often catches cold. He never calls her Louise nor does she call him Jules. He calls her Mme. Maigret and does not use terms of endearment because he considers the two of them to be the same person. She cooks for him, of course, abundantly, even when the odds are that an investigation will keep him from coming home. She gives him grogs when he has a cold, and can be found knitting him a blue scarf. He tends to be undemonstrative, but his affection and appreciation are per-

vasively implicit and occasionally rise to consciousness and articulation: "He had rarely been so eager to go home and find his wife's tender and gay eyes"; and, a little later, at a restaurant, he says, "Nothing in a restaurant is better than at home."

Maigret's other family is the Police Judiciaire, where his lack of progeny (a great sorrow to him) is compensated for by his inspectors, whom he repeatedly calls "mes enfants," or "les enfants," as in, say, "au travail, les enfants" (let's get to work, kids). Professional teamwork is as unruffled at headquarters as domestic life at boulevard Richard-Lenoir. Maigret's associates acquire Homeric epithets: le *brave* Lucas, le *petit* Lapointe, le *gros* Torrence, and the ancient usher, le *vieux* Joseph; in the course of the saga, they develop personalities that seem less perfunctory than they are because of the charm of recognition the sympathetic reader feels every time they are described.

Among the small personal details that accumulate around Maigret, probably the most insistent (other than the pipes) are those having to do with food and drink, and one can do no better than draw up a kind of Rabelaisian catalog. Maigret can be found eating ris de veau, blanquette de veau, tête de veau en tortue (a Belgian specialty), tripes à la mode de Caen, filet de hareng, sole dieppoise, bouillabaisse, maqueraux au four, coquille de langouste, homard à l'américaine, escargots, rillettes, goat cheese, baba au rhum, coq au vin blanc, skewered robin redbreasts, and kilometers of andouillettes. Among Mme. Maigret's dishes are fricandeau à l'oseille (one of his favorites), pot au feu, raie au beurre noir, pintadeau en croûte, and quiche (one of which is getting cold in an extended sequence at the beginning of *Maigret et le client du samedi* [1962; translated as *Maigret and the Saturday Caller*, 1964]). Not to be ignored either are Mme. Pardon's boeuf bourguignon, cassoulet, couscous, brandade de morue, and rice pudding (the Pardons are the only family friends).

Maigret eats not only amply and well, but also knowledgeably. In *Le Voleur de Maigret* (1967; translated as *Maigret's Pickpocket*, 1968), for instance, we find him in a restaurant serving La Rochelle specialties such as "mouclade" and "chaudrée fourrasienne," which he correctly identifies to the impressed *patronne* as "an eel soup with little soles and cuttle fish." Gastronomy gives Maigret warmth, charm, and, so to speak, human substance; we enjoy watching him eat. His eating habits make him one of "the people," unlike Rex Stout's epicurean detective Nero Wolfe, who is merely a snob. (When the *New York Times* claimed that Maigret ate better than Nero Wolfe, Stout testily riposted, "Nonsense. The Wolfe/Breme diet is altogether more stimulating than *cuisine bourgeoise*.") But in both cases, the intention is to enliven and particularize the detective-hero, to make him more intimate to the reader by repeated exposure to his habits.

If Maigret's eating habits invite comparison with such "classical" holdovers as Nero Wolfe, his drinking is more in the I-can-hold-my-liquor-with-the-best-of-them vein of the hard-boiled school. He is most famous for his glasses of draught beer (most memorable as washing down sandwiches during long interrogations at the quai des Orfèvres), but he will drink anything alcoholic, even when he does not like it, such as whisky (Scotch *and* Bourbon) or champagne. Cocktails are not up his alley, but he will not turn down a very dry martini. He often drinks cognac ("une fine") and keeps a bottle in his office, usually for suspects or witnesses in need, but occasionally for himself. Among other brandies are marc (though he once couples it with kummel as another drink he dislikes—which does not keep him from savoring a 130-proof bottle), armagnac, many a calvados, and, at home, prunelle and framboise. Sweeter stuff is also not to his liking, and celebrat-

ing a promotion, he once got drunk on mandarincuraçao. Once in a while he can be caught with a hangover. Among apéritifs, pernod is the most frequent, but he will also indulge in such things as picon-grenadine. The catalog of wines is long and begins with the glasses of white wine, innumerable as the beers, drunk hurriedly at the bar ("sur le zinc"). With or without meals, he drinks, among other wines, Beaujolais, rosé de Provence (to wash away, incidentally, the taste of a Tom Collins), Chateauneuf-du-Pape, Chianti, Sancerre, and Vouvray.

These personal details are the classifiable items of that process of amplification in the Maigrets, of which deeper manifestations are Maigret's psychology and his philosophy. Maigret's psychology, like any psychology, is an epistemology: it has to do with truly *knowing* people—discovering the substance beneath the appearance. His philosophy has to do with justice, likewise a justice more substantive and more human than official justice. Thus both psychology and philosophy boil down to a matter of fellow feeling, of human sympathy, which is itself the core of the famous Maigret method: a Scotland Yard inspector comes to study the method and leaves concluding that there *is* no method. There is no method because Maigret works largely by improvisation and intuition. He gets on the right trail when the "déclic" occurs—something undefinable that clicks in his consciousness. After intuition, imagination takes over: little by little, the victim or the criminal becomes his intimate in imagination—and often in actuality as well. The method, or nonmethod, is remarkably like that of novel writing, particularly the writing of Simenon novels.

One of the more remarkable things about Maigret is the way Simenon juggled with his creature's social and professional status as he developed him over forty years. In contrast with the dominant detective-story mode, he made his hero a policeman of high enough rank to provide a reassuring sense of control and, more important, to reinforce the paternal qualities toward subordinates, victims, and criminals that are such an essential ingredient of the Maigret myth. But if his rank is high, his heart, so to speak, points downward, to the "little people." He is their protector; he is one of them. Private detectives, after all, tend to serve the rich people who hire them. Maigret is a public servant in the truest sense of the term.

On the other hand, it is clear that Simenon turns somersaults to dissociate Maigret from the judicial apparatus of which the police are necessarily a part. Not only does he wage a persistent guerrilla war with the higher echelons, but a great deal of the time he is acting, in fact, like a private detective, carrying on his own private investigation, paralleling, contravening, or ignoring the official inquest. It is no accident that the functionaries of the judicial apparatus are almost invariably of the upper classes–the ubiquitous *juge d'instruction* (something like a district attorney) Coméliau, who is Maigret's bête noire, or the young upstart judge Angelot with the handshake of a tennis player, or the obnoxious prefect in *Maigret se défend* (1964; translated as *Maigret on the Defensive*, 1966), who asks Maigret for his resignation (Angelot also plays tennis: tennis is the representative sport of such people, as bowling on the green is of the "little people"). What is wrong with these officials is precisely the converse of what is right about Maigret: they know their cases only from bureaucratic dossiers, he from feeling his way into the very substance of people's lives–the texture of their environment, the quality of their inner selves.

In the aggregate, the Maigrets depict many interesting major characters–beginning with the commissaire himself–and a panoply of delightful minor ones. There is at least a score of first-rate stories–*Le Chien jaune* (1931; translated as *A Face for a Clue*, 1939), *Les Caves du Majestic* (1942; *Maigret and the Hotel Majestic*, 1977), *Cécile est morte* (1942; *Maigret and the Spinster*, 1977), *Maigret et la jeune morte* (1954; *Maigret and the Young Girl*, 1955), *Maigret tend un piège* (1955; *Maigret Sets a Trap*, 1965), *Les Scrupules de Maigret* (1958; *Maigret Has Scruples*, 1959), *La Patience de Maigret* (1965; *The Patience of Maigret*, 1966)–merely to start a personal list. The Maigret saga is possessed of at least these qualities: charm, a generous humanism, and endurance.

After Simenon's literary retirement in 1972, Maigret in fact did not entirely disappear from his life, for he dreamed about him. In one dream he saw Maigret with a battered straw hat hoeing in his garden at Meung-sur-Loire, and Simenon felt he knew every nook and cranny of his little house intimately. Later, Maigret went to play cards at his usual café; he no longer went fishing because the water was too polluted. A few months later Simenon was moved to take a touching farewell of the character who had made him famous: "I leave him on the banks of the Loire,

where he must be retired, like me. He digs in his garden, plays cards with the townspeople and goes fishing . . . I wish him a happy retirement, just as mine is happy. We've worked together long enough that I may, with a twinge of emotion, bid him farewell."

Simenon said this in 1975, in one of the "Dictées" he was lavishing into his tape recorder. He kept up this mode of composition until 1980, then wrote his compendious *Mémoires intimes*, and stopped literary production, this time for good. In 1984, a brain tumor was diagnosed and successfully removed–an ordeal from which he recuperated with remarkable vigor, continuing for the next three years "a perfectly normal man's life," as he put it to his faithful office manager, Joyce Aitken. In time, though, he was plagued by headaches, then by a gradual paralysis of his left arm, then of his legs. He gave the last of his thousands of interviews in 1988, for Swiss television, declaring that the worst vice was pride, the highest virtue, humility. In his last year he became increasingly worn out and drowsy–"an old gentleman, very silent, very dreamy, absent," according to Aitken. He died quietly in his sleep in the night of 4 September 1989. His three sons, as forewarned, learned of their father's death from the press. "He would not submit to the hypocrisy of a public funeral," he had told them. His ashes were scattered in the yard of his little house. The mansion at Epalinges, empty, awaits disposition as part of the estate.

Bibliography:
Trudee Young, *Georges Simenon* (Metuchen, N.J.: Scarecrow Press, 1976).

Biographies:
Fenton Bresler, *The Mystery of Georges Simenon* (New York: Beaufort Books, 1983);
Stanley G. Eskin, *Simenon: A Critical Biography* (Jefferson, N.C. & London: McFarland, 1987)–includes bibliography of Simenon's pseudonymous publications.

References:
Lucille F. Becker, *Georges Simenon* (Boston: Twayne, 1977);
Michel Butor, *Repertoire, Etudes et conférences 1948-1959* (Paris: Editions de Minuit, 1960);
Carvel Collins, "The Art of Fiction IX: Georges Simenon," *Paris Review*, 9 (Summer 1955): 71-90;

Brendan Gill, "Profiles: Out of the Dark," *New Yorker*, 28 (24 January 1953): 35-45;

Francis Lacassin and Gilbert Sigaux, *Simenon* (Paris: Plon, 1973);

Michel Lemoine, *Index des personnages de Georges Simenon* (Brussels: Editions Labor, 1986);

Thomas Narcejac, *The Art of Simenon* (London: Routledge, 1952);

Maurice Piron, *L'Univers de Simenon* (Paris: Presses de la Cité, 1983);

John Raymond, *Simenon in Court* (New York: Harcourt, Brace & World, 1968);

Charles J. Rolo, "Simenon and Spillane: The Metaphysics of Murder for the Millions," in *New World Writing* (New York: New American Library of World Literature, 1952), pp. 235-245.

Papers:
Collections of Simenon's papers are held at the Centre d'Etudes Georges Simenon in Liege, Belgium, and at the Simenon Center, Drew University, Madison, New Jersey.

A TRIBUTE

from NICOLAS FREELING

Why should obituaries be such sad and silly stuff? I have read "Nearly a great writer." This is nonsense: he was a major writer who lived, worked and womanised on a disconcerting scale. If great then because paying no heed to the fashions in "detective stories" he maintained the classical crime-writing tradition of the last century, into present times.

We were not friends–do writers have friends? I knew him. Now, I honour a remarkable man; a masterly technician; an astounding creative inventor. Yes; he lived too long. So did Picasso.

A TRIBUTE

from HAMMOND INNES

I recall Simenon as a very quiet, very unassuming man. This was particularly noticeable at the unveiling of the Maigret statue at Delfzijl. This was the Black Bear express culmination of a three-day Maigret event at which the burgomaster announced that the city fathers had unanimously agreed to enter the birth of the great detective in the City Register 'Aged 42 years'–or whatever Maigret's age was at the time Simenon's boat broke down in the port.

A TRIBUTE

from PETER LOVESEY

In the character of Maigret, Georges Simenon gave to mystery fiction that rare creature–a believable detective. Astonishingly, Maigret, a man with concerns, tastes and flaws that we recognize as authentic, a real policeman in the real France, sprang to life as early as 1931, the heyday of Lord Peter Wimsey, Hercule Poirot, Miss Marple and Charlie Chan. Enough said?

Robert Penn Warren

(24 April 1905 - 15 September 1989)

Victor Strandberg
Duke University

See also the Warren entries in *DLB 2: American Novelists Since World War II*; *DLB 48: American Poets, 1880-1945*; and *DLB Yearbook: 1980*.

BOOKS: *John Brown: The Making of a Martyr* (New York: Payson & Clarke, 1929);

Thirty-Six Poems (New York: Alcestis Press, 1935);

An Approach to Literature, by Warren, Cleanth Brooks, and John Thibault Purser (Baton Rouge: Louisiana State University Press, 1936);

Night Rider (Boston: Houghton Mifflin, 1939; London: Eyre & Spottiswoode, 1940);

Eleven Poems on the Same Theme (Norfolk, Conn.: New Directions, 1942);

At Heaven's Gate (New York: Harcourt, Brace, 1943; London: Eyre & Spottiswoode, 1943);

Selected Poems, 1923-1943 (New York: Harcourt, Brace, 1944; London: Fortune Press, 1951);

All the King's Men (New York: Harcourt, Brace, 1946; abridged edition, London: Eyre & Spottiswoode, 1948);

Blackberry Winter (Cummington, Mass.: Cummington Press, 1946);

The Circus in the Attic and Other Stories (New York: Harcourt, Brace, 1947; London: Eyre & Spottiswoode, 1952);

Modern Rhetoric, by Warren and Brooks (New York: Harcourt, Brace, 1949);

World Enough and Time: A Romantic Novel (New York: Random House, 1950; London: Eyre & Spottiswoode, 1951);

Fundamentals of Good Writing, by Warren and Brooks (New York: Harcourt, Brace, 1950; London: Dobson, 1952);

Brother to Dragons: A Tale in Verse and Voices (New York: Random House, 1953; London: Eyre & Spottiswoode, 1954; new version, New York: Random House, 1979);

Band of Angels (New York: Random House, 1955; London: Eyre & Spottiswoode, 1956);

Segregation: The Inner Conflict in the South (New York: Random House, 1956; London: Eyre & Spottiswoode, 1957);

Robert Penn Warren (photograph by Robert A. Ballard, Jr.)

To a Little Girl, One Year Old, In a Ruined Fortress (New Haven: Yale School of Design, 1956);

Promises: Poems 1954-1956 (New York: Random House, 1957; London: Eyre & Spottiswoode, 1959);

Selected Essays (New York: Random House, 1958; London: Eyre & Spottiswoode, 1964);

Remember the Alamo (New York: Random House, 1958);

213

How Texas Won Her Freedom (San Jacinto Monument, Tex.: San Jacinto Museum of History, 1959);

The Cave (New York: Random House, 1959; London: Eyre & Spottiswoode, 1959);

The Gods of Mount Olympus (New York: Random House, 1959; London: Muller, 1962);

All the King's Men (A Play) (New York: Random House, 1960);

You, Emperors, and Others: Poems 1957-1960 (New York: Random House, 1960);

The Legacy of the Civil War: Meditations on the Centennial (New York: Random House, 1961);

Wilderness: A Tale of the Civil War (New York: Random House, 1961; London: Eyre & Spottiswoode, 1962);

Flood: A Romance of Our Time (New York: Random House, 1964; London: Collins, 1964);

Who Speaks for the Negro? (New York: Random House, 1965);

A Plea in Mitigation: Modern Poetry and the End of an Era (Macon, Ga.: Wesleyan College, 1966);

Selected Poems: New and Old, 1923-1966 (New York: Random House, 1966);

Incarnations: Poems 1966-1968 (New York: Random House, 1968; London: Allen, 1970);

Audubon: A Vision (New York: Random House, 1969);

Homage to Theodore Dreiser: August 27, 1871-December 28, 1945, On the Centennial of His Birth (New York: Random House, 1971);

Meet Me in the Green Glen (New York: Random House, 1971; London: Secker & Warburg, 1972);

Or Else: Poem / Poems 1968-1974 (New York: Random House, 1974);

Democracy and Poetry (Cambridge: Harvard University Press, 1975);

Selected Poems: 1923-1975 (New York: Random House, 1977; London: Secker & Warburg, 1977);

A Place to Come To (New York: Random House, 1977; London: Secker & Warburg, 1977);

Now and Then: Poems 1976-1978 (New York: Random House, 1978);

Being Here: Poetry 1977-1980 (New York: Random House, 1980; London: Secker & Warburg, 1980);

Jefferson Davis Gets His Citizenship Back (Lexington: University Press of Kentucky, 1980);

Rumor Verified: Poems 1979-1980 (New York: Random House, 1981; London: Secker & Warburg, 1982);

Chief Joseph of the Nez Perce (New York: Random House, 1983);

New and Selected Poems 1923-1985 (New York: Random House, 1985);

A Robert Penn Warren Reader (New York: Random House, 1987);

Portrait of a Father (Lexington: University of Kentucky Press, 1988);

New and Selected Essays (New York: Random House, 1989).

OTHER: "The Briar Patch," in *I'll Take My Stand: The South and the Agrarian Tradition*, by Twelve Southerners (New York: Harper, 1930);

A Southern Harvest: Short Stories by Southern Writers, edited by Warren (Boston: Houghton Mifflin, 1937);

Understanding Poetry: An Anthology for College Students, edited by Warren and Cleanth Brooks (New York: Holt, 1938; fourth edition, New York: Holt, Rinehart & Winston, 1976);

Understanding Fiction, edited by Warren and Brooks (New York: Crofts, 1943; third edition, Englewood Cliffs, N.J.: Prentice-Hall, 1976);

"A Poem of Pure Imagination: An Experiment in Reading," in *The Rime of the Ancient Mariner*, by Samuel Taylor Coleridge (New York: Reynal & Hitchcock, 1946), pp. 59-117;

An Anthology of Stories from the Southern Review, edited by Warren and Brooks (Baton Rouge: Louisiana State University Press, 1953);

Short Story Masterpieces, edited by Warren and Albert Erskine (New York: Dell, 1954);

Six Centuries of Great Poetry: From Chaucer to Yeats, edited by Warren and Erskine (New York: Dell, 1955);

A New Southern Harvest, edited by Warren and Erskine (New York: Bantam, 1957);

The Scope of Fiction, edited by Warren and Brooks (New York: Appleton-Century-Crofts, 1960);

Dennis Devlin, *Selected Poems*, edited by Warren and Allen Tate (New York: Holt, Rinehart & Winston, 1963);

Faulkner: A Collection of Critical Essays, edited by Warren (Englewood Cliffs, N.J.: Prentice-Hall, 1966);

Randall Jarrell: 1914-1965, edited by Warren, Robert Lowell, and Peter Taylor (New York: Farrar, Straus & Giroux, 1967);

Selected Poems of Herman Melville: A Reader's Edition, edited by Warren (New York: Random House, 1970);

John Greenleaf Whittier's Poetry, edited by Warren
(Minneapolis: University of Minnesota
Press, 1971);

American Literature: The Makers and the Making, 2
volumes, edited by Warren, Brooks, and
R. W. B. Lewis (New York: St. Martin's
Press, 1973).

Robert Penn Warren's life spanned almost
the whole twentieth century. When he died in,
the middle of his ninth decade, full of years and
honors, he bequeathed to posterity a towering
monument of creativity–including ten novels, sixteen volumes of poetry, a cycle of books relating
to the Civil War (*John Brown, Segregation, The Legacy of the Civil War, Who Speaks for the Negro?, Jefferson Davis Gets His Citizenship Back*), and several
book-length treatises on literature (*Selected Essays,
Homage to Theodore Dreiser, Democracy and Poetry*).
Draped like bunting over that long shelf of books
are the awards and honors that descended routinely upon them, including three Pulitzer Prizes
(for *All the King's Men, Promises*, and *Now and
Then*), the Bollingen Prize, the National Book
Award, the Shelley Memorial Prize, the Van
Wyck Brooks Award, the National Medal for Literature, the Emerson-Thoreau Award, the Copernicus Award, the Harriet Monroe Prize, a fellowship prize from the MacArthur Foundation, and
the Presidential Medal of Freedom. In 1986 Warren achieved the unique distinction of becoming
America's first poet laureate (by act of Congress).
In his later years he was declared, by authorities
as disparate as Harold Bloom and *Newsweek* magazine, America's greatest living man of letters.

Fully in the American tradition (one thinks
of Mark Twain and William Faulkner), his modest beginnings did not augur such distinction.
Raised in the small Kentucky town of Guthrie,
on the Tennessee border, Robert Penn Warren
was the oldest of three children born to Ruth
Penn and Robert Franklin Warren, a small-time
banker who went bankrupt in the Depression. As
a boy Warren spent idyllic summers in the countryside on the farm of his grandfather Gabriel
Thomas Penn (1836-1920), a Confederate veteran who himself as a boy had known veterans of
the American Revolution. This palpable contact
with the living past may have guided Warren's
later artistic orientation toward his most prevalent interest: the role of the past in the struggle
to realize a meaningful identity, both on an individual and a communal–including national–level.

With respect to his own past Warren developed a lifelong affinity for the small-town life
and rural landscape of his upbringing. "The
basic images that every man has, I suppose, go
back to . . . his childhood. He has to live on that
capital all his life," Warren said in an interview
with Richard B. Sale. Especially during his later
years, while a resident of New England, his poetry evoked that lost town of his childhood with a
power and precision reminiscent–as Floyd Watkins has remarked–of Wordsworth and Twain.

Warren displayed exceptional precocity as a
schoolboy. Quickly outstripping what the Guthrie
schools could offer him, he was sent to the much
larger high school in nearby Clarksville, Tennessee, where he graduated at age fifteen. About
this time Warren decided he wanted to be a
naval captain, and with some political assistance
from his father he obtained entrance to the naval
academy at Annapolis. While he was waiting to
meet the legal age requirement for this appointment, a tragic accident changed his plans: a stone
thrown over a hedge by his brother blinded his
left eye, making him unqualified for naval service. He thereupon decided to go instead to Vanderbilt University, where he began his studies in
1921, at age sixteen, intending to major in electri-
cal engineering.

At Vanderbilt a boring chemistry course combined with an exciting English course–taught by
John Crowe Ransom–to once again change Warren's plans. The talented literary group surrounding Ransom, notably including Allen Tate and
Donald Davidson, was just then launching a little
magazine, the *Fugitive*. That title, along with the
later designation for many of these people, the
Agrarians, indicates the fixation on the past that
affected Warren's initial intellectual orientation.
These writers meant to assert their status as fugi-
tives from the oncoming urban-commercial New
South, fleeing back to their rural-agrarian Old
South values. Although Warren never gave doctri-
naire allegiance to these notions, he did betray
Fugitive / Agrarian reflexes periodically throughout his career–in his portrayals, for example, of
American cities (especially New York) as cess-
pools of corruption and hypocrisy, as opposed to
his affectionate portrayals of rural life in Kentucky and Vermont.

At Vanderbilt Warren's literary education
was greatly enhanced by the guidance of his two
most eminent mentors–Ransom, who excited Warren's interest in the traditional mainstream of literature (including Ransom's own poetry); and Tate,

who attuned his young friend ("the most talented man I ever met," Tate later called him) to the modernist avant-garde then entering its glory years. Dante, Donne, Shakespeare, Milton, and Thomas Hardy (the primary model for Warren's early poetry) were particularly strong, traditional influences, while in the avant-garde vein T. S. Eliot was the leading master. Warren claimed that he and his college mates memorized the entire *Waste Land* as soon as it was published in 1922, and Tate remembered Warren drawing scenes from that poem (most notably a rat crawling through vegetation) on his dormitory walls.

After graduating summa cum laude from Vanderbilt in 1925, Warren did graduate study at Berkeley. Here the program of literary studies proved disappointingly retrograde compared to what he had enjoyed in the Fugitive circle, but before moving on to Yale he met and wooed a talented, vivacious Italian-American student named Emma Brescia, whom he married in 1930. While at Yale in 1927 Warren learned that he had been chosen to receive a Rhodes Scholarship for the state of Kentucky, and he went on to earn his B.Litt. at Oxford in 1930.

By age twenty-four Warren had two major projects at the printer's. In November 1929 Payson and Clark published *John Brown: The Making of a Martyr*, a biography written with the intention of correcting a fabulous misuse of the past. The ignorance in the North about this man—whose "truth goes marching on" according to the "Battle Hymn of the Republic" brought forth a rejoinder from Warren that echoed through all of his subsequent work. The real truth was that Brown was a murderous fanatic who slaughtered whole families, including infants, in the Kansas-Nebraska conflict and whose favorite Bible verse was "there is no remission of sin without the shedding of blood." For Warren, as Allan Nevins has noted, John Brown "was no hypocrite, but a man of enormous and criminal egotism," becoming thereby a prototype of the American man who tires of palaver and reaches for meat-ax or shotgun to uphold his version of truth and idealism. Percy Munn in *Night Rider* (1939), Adam Stanton in *All the King's Men* (1946), Jeremiah Beaumont in *World Enough and Time: A Romantic Novel* (1950), and Lilburne Lewis in *Brother to Dragons: A Tale in Verse and Voices* (1953)—these are some of the fictionalized descendants of Warren's John Brown. At the end of this study in American fanaticism, Warren strikes a chilling note by resting his focus on one of the soldiers standing at atten-

tion during the hanging of John Brown, a private named John Wilkes Booth.

The other major project at the printer's in 1929 was Warren's first book of verse, "Pondy Woods and Other Poems," which Payson and Clark accepted but could not publish because of bankruptcy following the stock market crash that fall. In the early 1930s, as Warren began his teaching career (in Renaissance literature) at Vanderbilt, he continued to work primarily as a poet, producing two more unpublished collections—"Kentucky Mountain Farm and Other Poems" (1930) and "Cold Colloquy" (1933)—until at last, after some fifteen years of poetry writing, *Thirty-Six Poems* was published in 1935. Although it displays occasional fingerprints of Donne, Milton, Hardy, Eliot, and Hart Crane, this collection clearly voices an original talent, especially in its rendering of the lapsarian theme. Broken relationships—"Letter of a Mother," "For a Self-Possessed Friend"—underscore the theme of loss, as do the many titles reflecting the book's autumnal mood: "So Frost Astounds," "Aged Man Surveys the Past Time," "Croesus in Autumn," "Problem of Knowledge." The book's most important and prevalent motif is the speaker's lost doppelgänger, his Jungian anima that flees back toward a lost paradise at the lapsarian moment, leaving an empty husk in search of identity. Especially memorable from this volume are "Kentucky Mountain Farm," a lyric-philosophical poem set against a backcountry landscape; and "The Return: An Elegy," which hauntingly portrays a son's mixed feelings on his way to his mother's funeral. (It was written two years before Ruth Warren's death in 1931.)

Exploiting Governor Huey Long's generosity to Louisiana State University, where he taught Renaissance literature from 1934 to 1942, in 1935 Warren cofounded with Cleanth Brooks one of the most distinguished literary journals of that time, the *Southern Review*. Partly through this organ, but primarily through the sale of anthologies and textbooks, he and Brooks were largely responsible for engineering a transformation in the teaching of literature. *Understanding Poetry: An Anthology for College Students* (1938) and *Understanding Fiction* (1943), which brought the New Criticism into American classrooms for a third of a century, were the most influential of Brooks and Warren's formalist, text-centered works of criticism, but Warren also at this time began composing his classic modernist essays on recent or contemporary literature. Among his most brilliant and influential such studies, which were later gathered in *Selected Essays* (1958), were his analyses of William Faulkner, Joseph Conrad, Ernest Hemingway, Robert Frost, and (as a proto-modern) Samuel Taylor Coleridge.

Not content with these achievements, Warren also ventured into play writing in the late 1930s, producing a play that (thanks to some helpful discouragement from the players' group at Bennington College) he later turned into *All The King's Men*, and some short stories, the most important of which, "Prime Leaf," gave impetus to Warren's first published novel–*Night Rider*. Set against the Kentucky tobacco wars of the early 1900s, this novel establishes several of the ground themes for Warren's later work as both poet and novelist. Like Eliot's Hollow Men trapped in a Waste Land, Warren's protagonist, Percy Munn, suffers from loneliness, dread, and a lack of beliefs to live by. Whereas Eliot overcame this condition by joining the Anglican Church, Munn (like many 1930 intellectuals) seeks a cure by joining a political group–the tobacco farmers whose struggle for economic justice might answer Munn's search for a meaningful life. As the group's prospects become desperate, however, it resorts to murderous vigilante action, and Munn–again like many others in those years of global fanaticism–finds in violence the means to fill his inner vacancy. Predictably, as the book ends, Munn himself is fatally caught in the web of violence, alone and mortally wounded, encircled by a posse, alienated, and devoid of any sense of life's meaning.

In the early 1940s, as Warren's career in letters was about to ascend, Louisiana State University failed to match an offer of a promotion and raise of a few hundred dollars from the University of Minnesota. From this time forward Warren was to live far north of his native region, though the South would continue to be the predominant focus of his novels, poems, and historical studies during his sojourns in Minneapolis (1942-1950) and New England (1950-1989), where he divided his time between teaching at Yale, near his home in Fairfield, Connecticut, and writing at his backcountry hideaway near Stratton, Vermont.

In 1942 and 1944 two collections of poetry revealed remarkable new developments in Warren's style and prophetic imagination. Although *Eleven Poems on the Same Theme* extended the Waste Land mentality of the 1930s in poems about alienation ("Monologue at Midnight"), mortality ("Bearded Oaks"), and the Fall ("Picnic Remembered," "End of Season"), the newer poems in the collection indicated the onset of some sort of conversion experience. Densely written, with a lessened fidelity to standard forms but heightened complexity of sound texture and image patterns, such poems as "Crime," "Pursuit," "Terror," and "Original Sin: A Short Story" traced the persona's attempt to escape a polluted alter ego, only to discover that his search for identity could be satisfied only through reconciliation with that zone of the psyche represented by Freudian id or Jungian shadow.

In *Selected Poems, 1923-1943* this theme culminates in Warren's single most crucial poem, "The Ballad of Billie Potts" (1943). Here the theme of "Original Sin"–"not hereditary sin; it is original with the sinner and is of his will," Warren later explained–applies initially to Little Billie, whose father augments his income by killing the guests at his inn for their money. After bungling a homocide meant to assist his father's business, Billie flees west for ten years and returns, bearded and unrecognized, to his parents' inn. Because Billie withholds his identity so as to tease them, they follow their standard practice and kill him for his money. At this point Warren's true protagonist, "you," takes over Billie's quest for identity, enabling the poet to move the poem toward a climactic reconciliation of "you" with a sullied self and a fallen world. That union between zones of the psyche and between the unified psyche and the outer world leads to the poem's concluding vision of a universal quest for meaning, here figured as a return to home (that is, eternity): "The bee knows, and the eel's cold ganglia burn, / The sad head lifting to the long return, / Through brumal deeps. . . . / Carries its knowledge, navigator without star." The poem's ultimate reconciliation, bridging time and eternity, comes about through an acceptance of mortality within "the sacramental silence of evening": "the salmon heaves at the fall, and, wanderer, you / Heave at the great Fall of time. / Back to the silence, back to the pool, back / To . . . the unmurmuring dream." Later, in an essay entitled "Knowledge and the Image of Man" (1955), Warren termed this pantheistic insight the "Osmosis of Being," which evokes "such a sublimation that the world which once provoked . . . fear and disgust may now be totally loved." According to William James's *The Varieties of Religious Experience* (1902), this movement from a Sick Soul condition to a world that may be totally loved is the essence of a conversion experience, especially when it occurs in connection with an influx of cosmic consciousness.

After "Billie Potts," Warren published no verse for ten years, turning his creativity instead to his most celebrated achievements in fiction. *At Heaven's Gate* (1943), a novel patterned after Dante's circle of sins against nature, features a remarkably large and varied cast of characters arranged in dialectical counterpoint. Themes that were to become standard in Warren's work abound in this book, represented by Jerry Calhoun's search for an acceptable father figure, Slim Sarrett's discovery of his own criminal potentiality, and Duckfoot Blake's philosophy of pragmatism. Eventually the corrupt business magnate Bogan Murdock is done in by his opposite counterpart, a lowly backcountry fellow named Ashby Windham whose confessional monologue vividly prefigures the Cass Mastern story in Warren's next book, the Pulitzer Prize-winning *All the King's Men*.

During the half-century since it appeared, this novel has become Warren's most acclaimed achievement, a masterwork that may well stand with *Moby-Dick* (1851), *Adventures of Huckleberry Finn* (1884), and *The Great Gatsby* (1925) as an American classic. Begun when Warren was living in Mussolini's Rome in 1939, it depicts the political rise and fall of Willie Stark, a state governor partly modeled after the assassinated Louisiana kingfish, Huey Long. By the time Warren completed the book in Minnesota in 1946, the world had changed radically, and Warren himself had changed his worldview. His central character now was not the governor but the narrator, Jack Burden, whose conversion to a new view of life comprises the central design of the narrative. Like a modern Oedipus, Jack is an investigator who, assigned to dig up hidden crimes of others, comes to discover his own complicity in his father's death, achieving self-knowledge at a tragic cost. Warren brings his narrator through a series of Sick Soul ideologies reflecting the philosophical crisis of the age: naturalistic determinism (the Great Twitch episode), escapism (the Great Sleep), solipsism (during the flight west), hedonism (Jack's marriage to Lois), and black humor (Jack's corrosively cynical tone in chapters 1-7).

In his preface to the Modern Library edition of *All the King's Men*, Warren describes the long gestation of this novel as having been affected by his readings in Machiavelli, Dante, Spenser, Coleridge, and William James. From Cole-

ridge and other Romantic poets he evidently derived confirmation of his pantheist insight that figured into Cass Mastern's Great Web of Being. As James H. Justus has written, Warren also derived from Coleridge's Mariner the concept of the individual who, through confession and remorse, seeks expiation for a primal crime—a concept portrayed in Willie Proudfit in *Night Rider*, Ashby Windham in *At Heaven's Gate*, Cass Mastern and Jack Burden in *All the King's Men*, and Jeremiah Beaumont in *World Enough and Time*. From William James, Warren derived justification for his narrator's movement from the Sick Soul condition to the philosophy of pragmatism and pluralism—that is, from "naturalistic determinism" to a belief in "history and the awful responsibility of Time."

In 1947 Warren published his only collection of short stories, *The Circus in the Attic and Other Stories*. (Warren later explained that his short stories kept turning into poems; hence the solitary volume.) The title story, staged as a play in 1987 during the Robert Penn Warren Home Town Symposium in Clarksville, Tennessee, was favorably compared by some theatregoers with Thornton Wilder's *Our Town* (1938). The book also contains the much-anthologized "Blackberry Winter," a quintessential initiation story in which a nine-year-old boy moves from innocence to knowledge of reality in the aftermath of a giant storm, primarily through his encounter with a penniless, wandering bum hired (and shortly fired) by the boy's father to clean up the storm's debris.

As illustrious as his career had been up to this point, it turned out that the 1950s were in several ways Warren's most momentous decade. In 1950 his marriage to Emma Brescia ended and he accepted a professorship at Yale. Two years later he married the writer Eleanor Clark, who bore him a daughter, Rosanna, in 1953 and a son, Gabriel, in 1955. Perhaps under the stimulus of this rejuvenation, Warren resumed his career as a poet, after a ten-year hiatus, by publishing *Brother to Dragons*, a book-length narrative poem that earned lavish praise from a chorus of eminent voices including Randall Jarrell, Delmore Schwartz, and Robert Lowell. Based on a historical incident—the vivisection of a slave by Thomas Jefferson's nephew, Lilburn Lewis—this work brought Warren's grand theme of man confronting his own capacity for evil to a culmination of epic style and magnitude. Initially a believer in human grandeur, Jefferson is brought to a Sick

Soul condition by his nephew's crime, as exemplified in his image of the minotaur at the center of the psyche's labyrinth: "In the blind dark, hockdeep in ordure, its beard / And shag foulscabbed, and when the hoof heaves– / Listen!– The foulness sucks like mire." But eventually, through the persuasion of his sister Lucy and of Warren's narrative persona, R. P. W., Jefferson achieves a reconciliation with the reality of evil within his kindred blood: "We must strike the steel of wrath on the stone of guilt, / And hope to provoke, thus, in the midst of our coiling darkness / The incandescence of the heart's great flare. / And in that illumination I should hope to see / How creation validates itself."

Throughout his career Warren continued to portray "Original Sin" in various manifestations, but in the later decades this theme yielded center stage to hard-earned affirmations. Although this change seemed to weaken his fiction in the view of some critics, it gave a widely acclaimed new thrust to his poetic creativity. Directly responding to his long-delayed fatherhood, Warren's *Promises* (1957), which won his first Pulitzer Prize for poetry, consists of two sets of lyric poems dedicated to his two infant children. Among the plethora of forms gathered here–sonnets, terza rima, lullabies, ballads, and suites–perhaps the most remarkable entry is "Ballad of a Sweet Dream of Peace," a seven-part suite of poems in which a young initiate travels across the dusky border between life and death to discover Warren's eschatological insight that "all Time is a dream, and we're all one Flesh, at last." In this triumphant new start as a lyric poet, Warren used personal materials as never before: children, wife, friends, ancestors, boyhood memories, and always his own vulnerable self. From this point on such materials were to comprise the foundation of his major poetic volumes, and partly (it seems) as a result Warren's verse gained far more acclaim than his fiction.

At the start of the next decade *You, Emperors, and Others: Poems 1957-1960* (1960) met a disappointing reception after the high success of *Promises*, though in hindsight it now appears that this volume includes several of Warren's finest poems. One of these, "The Letter about Money, Love, or Other Comfort, if Any," is particularly notable for its form–eight rhyming eleven-line stanzas making up a single sentence–and for its portrayal of the artist-speaker (with letter–art, identity–in hand) relentlessly tracking down a bestial alter ego. His "Two Pieces After Suetonius," about the sadistic emperors Tiberius and Do-

mitian, extend his "Original Sin" theme into a classical rather than Judeo-Christian setting. And his monologues by Civil War soldiers, Union and Confederate, make the companion poems in "Two Studies in Idealism" a gem of ironic portraiture. Vividly realized also is the suite of poems about the death of his father (deceased in 1955), entitled "Mortmain." The terminal image of this sequence, in which the poet imagines his father's boyhood, exemplifies the intensity and vividness of the whole poem cluster: "I strive to cry across the dry pasture, / But cannot. . . . The boy / With imperial calm, crosses a space, rejoins / The shadow of woods, but pauses, turns, grins once, / And is gone. . . ."

During the 1950s Warren also published an important nonfiction book, *Segregation: The Inner Conflict in the South* (1956), a southerner's response to the Supreme Court's desegregation order of 1954, and three major novels. Inaugurating the decade for Warren was *World Enough and Time*, a novel historically grounded in the celebrated Sharp-Beauchamp murder in 1820s Kentucky. Subtitled *A Romantic Novel*, this book employs the richly textured style of its historical setting to explore the problems of identity that bemuse its protagonist, Jeremiah Beaumont. Unable to mediate between idealism and reality, the young man avenges a woman's honor by murdering his fatherly benefactor, Senator Fort, despite the latter's remorse for his act of seduction. A. B. Guthrie, Jr., rightly called this work "an arresting and provocative book, . . . a book of immense and mature disillusion."

Band of Angels (1955), another historical novel set in nineteenth-century America, complicates Warren's recurring theme of identity by employing a protagonist-narrator who is both black and female. Despite some memorable characterizations and gripping episodes, including a slaver's raid into the African interior, critics such as Allen Shepherd and James Justus have judged the book flawed because the narrator is too weakly drawn to elicit much interest or sympathy. Critics have stated similar misgivings toward several of Warren's later novels, alleging that while his minor characters have often been superbly realized, some of his central characters have lacked the precise and vivid definition that marked his portraits of Jack Burden and Willie Stark. As with *Band of Angels* these later protagonists may have been too far removed from Warren's realm of personal experience: an immigrant Jew in *Wilderness: A Tale of the Civil War* (1961), an immi-

Warren (standing) with Allen Tate, Merrill Moore, John Crowe Ransom, and Donald Davidson in Nashville, 4 May 1956, at a reunion of the Fugitive poets (photograph by Joe Rudis)

grant Italian in *Meet Me in the Green Glen* (1971), and a movie director in *Flood: A Romance of Our Time* (1964).

In *The Cave* (1959) Warren finessed the problem of a dominant protagonist by sharing the central role among seven characters, four of them members of the Harrick family. In a new refinement of Warren's father-son theme, Jack Harrick, dying of cancer, has to come to terms with his envy of his son Jasper's youth and health, leading him to want Jasper to die in the cave in which he has become trapped while exploring. Justus has noted how the entombment motif, objectifying the idea of a buried self, is "the chief orienting symbol by which an individual's sense of his own identity is tested." The book's title also evokes Plato's parable of the cave as a paradigm of the human consciousness trying to distinguish between reality and its shadows.

In the early 1960s the centenary of the Civil War coincided with the rise of the Civil Rights movement to reinvigorate a circuit of historical interest that began with *John Brown*, extended through *Segregation* and *Who Speaks for the Negro?* (1965), and concluded with *Jefferson Davis Gets His Citizenship Back* (1980). At the center of these studies loosely associated with the Civil War is the 1961 discourse, *The Legacy of the Civil War: Meditations on the Centennial*. In this work Warren argues that the Civil War divided American intellectual history into two conflicting segments: before the war, the North had espoused higher law, the doctrine notably expounded in Henry David Thoreau's "Civil Disobedience" that every man's final allegiance must be solely to his own conscience, while the South had espoused the opposite doctrine of legalism, which claimed that anything the Constitution permitted, including

DLB Yearbook 1989

slavery, remained forever beyond the realm of change or even discussion. Rather than resolve this conflict, Warren says, the war merely produced new ideologies of escape from reality. In the North such issues as child labor and exploitation of immigrant workers were subsumed under a Treasury of Virtue, which postulated that the North had won the battle for truth and need take no further interest in social justice. The South in turn lapsed back into its disastrous Great Alibi, the assertion that the woes of the region were none of its fault, having arisen from the iniquities perpetuated by the victorious Northerners during Reconstruction. The answer to this impasse, Warren went on to explain, was the major contribution made by Americans to world philosophy, pragmatism. Citing William James and C. S. Pierce in philosophy, and Abraham Lincoln (who had proposed to purchase the slaves' freedom) and Franklin Delano Roosevelt in politics, Warren makes an eloquent plea for the wisdom of pragmatism in America's ongoing social and ideological struggles.

In 1961, the same year that Warren published these meditations on the centennial, he also published a novel set against the Civil War entitled *Wilderness*. Although the title refers to one of the great battles of the war, it more largely designates the moral confusion that encompassed the whole era. Epitomizing that confusion is Warren's vivid rendering of a major, horrifying episode that is rarely mentioned in traditional histories of the war: the draft riots of July 1863 in New York City. Sparked by resentment against forced service in the Union Army, thousands of rioters looted, committed arson, and murdered freely for most of a week before battalions of soldiers suppressed the insurrection. Many of the rioters were recent immigrants fleeing from military conscription in Europe, and many of their victims were Negro men, women, and children who were caught and hanged from the city's lampposts for being the root cause of this war. The book's protagonist, a young German-Jewish immigrant who witnesses these atrocities, can hardly be blamed for the ideological muddle that subsequently affects his life as a Union soldier.

In 1965 Warren extended these studies in the legacy of the war with *Who Speaks For the Negro?*, a collection of interviews amplified by analyses of the major Civil Rights leaders of that turbulent era. Martin Luther King, Jr., James Baldwin, and Stokely Carmichael are among the figures astutely interviewed and analyzed in these pages,

but probably the most arresting interview is with Malcolm X, who was assassinated soon after. Although Malcolm had to figure as the most John Brown-like fanatic of the group, Warren established such a rapport with him that the interview was extended by several hours and Malcolm invited his guest to come along on his rounds of Harlem the next day. (Although very eager to do so, Warren was committed to fly to Italy instead, to his immense regret after the Malcolm X murder.)

From mid decade on, the 1960s were given over to poetry. In *Selected Poems: New and Old, 1923-1966* (1966) Warren added to his poetic oeuvre a hundred pages entitled "Tale of Time: New Poems 1960-1966." Of the six suites gathered here the most deeply affective are the title suite, "Tale of Time," which hauntingly evokes his lost mother; "The Day Dr. Knox Did It," which recounts his boyhood initiation into the world's stew on account of a doctor's suicide; and the ecstatic set of lyrics entitled "Delight," which terminate the "Tale of Time" purporting to imply its meaning. About this time George Palmer Garrett, Jr., was the first to declare Warren's late-flowering creativity of equivalent value with that of Yeats, Stravinsky, and Picasso.

Though plausible enough at the time, this judgment came to seem premature, engulfed by Warren's subsequent massive surge of creativity. In 1968 Warren published a book of poems called *Incarnations: Poems 1966-1968*, containing long suites focusing variously on Mediterranean civilization, a doomed prisoner, a fatal automobile accident, and epiphanies of the world's beauty. In 1969 he finished a work of twenty-five years' gestation, *Audubon: A Vision*, which was hailed by many critics as a masterpiece of American mythmaking. Typifying many responses was Helen Vendler's remark that "these striking vignettes of a man questionlessly happy in his environment map out for us a possible happiness." What broke the poet's creative block in this instance was Warren's notion of structuring the poem as a series of "shots," or illustrative episodes from the life of the great naturalist. The central episode, Audubon's rescue from a murder plot, was revised by Warren from Audubon's original testimony (in which he was pleased to see the perpetrators, an "infernal hag" and her sons, hanged for attempted murder) so as to afford the artist-observer "a new definition of beauty" in the old woman's willful courage during her hanging. The essential thing for both Audubon and Warren in this poem is the sufficiency of the world's beauty, which in effect restores the lost anima to the psyche during the observer's state of heightened consciousness.

Although poetry had now become Warren's predominant genre, there yet remained two large-scale novels in his matrix of creativity. *Meet Me in the Green Glen*, "a remarkably pure poetic distillation of Warren's typical themes and materials" in John W. Aldridge's view, forces the "inwardness" of its characters to surface when an outsider–a wandering Sicilian named Angelo–is executed by the townspeople for a murder he did not commit. *A Place to Come To* (1977) completes Warren's career as a novelist with the most autobiographical protagonist in all his fiction. Jed Tewksbury, commanded by his mother to get out of the small back-country town of his birth, goes to Nashville and Chicago and abroad for his higher education, becomes a professor of history, and in the end returns to the hometown in an effort to still his hunger for identity.

From the mid 1970s to the mid 1980s, while passing through his seventies, Warren produced an autumnal harvest of rarely (if ever) equaled dimensions. In addition to *A Place to Come To*, there was *Democracy and Poetry* (1975), his book-length treatise on the political psychology of fictive writing; *Jefferson Davis Gets His Citizenship Back*, his terminal entry in his Civil War cycle of works that began in 1929 with *John Brown*; and an astounding output of new poetry: *Or Else: Poem / Poems 1968-1974* (1974); *Selected Poems: 1923-1975* (1977), including ten new poems gathered under the title "Can I See Arcturus From Where I Stand?: Poems 1975"; *Now and Then: Poems 1976-1978* (1978); *Brother To Dragons: A New Version* (1979); *Being Here: Poetry 1977-1980* (1980); *Rumor Verified: Poems 1979-1980* (1981); *Chief Joseph of the Nez Perce* (1983); and–published on 24 April 1985, the poet's eightieth birthday, *New and Selected Poems 1923-1985*, including new poems gathered in a section entitled "Altitudes and Extensions: Poems 1980-1984." Among the numerous shorter pieces also belonging to this late harvest, one in particular requires closing mention: *Portrait of a Father* (1988), Warren's admiring and affectionate family memoir. It seems characteristic of Warren–an inveterate portrayer of the father-son theme–to close out his distinguished career in letters with a tribute to his father.

Warren's final years, though graced with high laurels, were a time of long, debilitating struggle with bone cancer. Although the condition caused him to resign his poet laureateship after barely a year, he maintained a courageous and generous spirit to the end. He died on 15 September 1989 and was buried, after an Episcopal service, in Vermont. Warren's final resting place is of course the living mind of his readership. In some unpredictable measure, that readership will reexperience what James Dickey found in Warren's work, "the sense of poetry as a thing of final importance to life." Underneath its irony and erudition, its enormous sweep of forms and genres and subject matter, Warren's oeuvre in the end reenacted art's ancient imperative of seeking how to establish a viable self, how to align that self with the larger world, and how to reconcile one's self to mortality. From the closing lines of "Myth of Mountain Sunrise"–the final poem of "Altitudes and Extensions"–the aged poet's last testimony is rejuvenescent with pantheistic vitalism, portrayed in the rising sun taking a tree like an ardent lover:

> Think of a girl-shape, birch-white sapling, rising
>   now
> From ankle-deep brook-stones, head back-flung,
>   eyes closed in first beam,
> While hair–long, water-roped, past curve, coign,
>   sway that no geometries know–
> Spreads end-thin, to define fruit-swell of haunches,
>   tingle of hand-hold.
> The sun blazes over the peak. That will be the old
>   tale told.

For all his mastery of language he reached at last for something beyond language, the "unwordable" meanings radiating out of nature that were capturable only in images. "Man lives by images," he said; "They / Lean at us from the world's wall, and Time's." One of those images, of the fallen soul striving to rejoin its fleeing anima (in "Heart of Autumn," the terminal poem in *Now and Then*), seems particularly relevant to this poet's passage from time to eternity. For us as for the watcher of geese in flight, it suggests an annealing end:

> . . . and I stand, my face lifted now skyward,
>   Hearing the high beat, my arms out-
> stretched in the tingling
>   Process of transformation, and soon tough
> legs,
>
> With folded feet, trail in the sounding vacuum of
>   passage,
> And my heart is impacted with a fierce impulse
> To unwordable utterance–

Toward sunset, at a great height.

References:

George Garrett, "The Recent Poetry of Robert Penn Warren," in *Robert Penn Warren: A Collection of Critical Essays*, edited by John L. Longley, Jr. (New York: New York University Press, 1965), pp. 223-236;

James H. Justus, *The Achievement of Robert Penn Warren* (Baton Rouge: Louisiana State University Press, 1981);

Richard B. Sale, "An Interview in New Haven with Robert Penn Warren," *Studies in the Novel*, 2 (1970): 325-354;

Allen Shepherd, "Warren's *Audubon*: 'Issues in Purer Form' and 'The Ground Rules of Fact,' " *Mississippi Quarterly*, 24 (Winter 1970-1971): 47-56;

Floyd Watkins, *Then & Now: The Personal Past in the Poetry of Robert Penn Warren* (Lexington: University Press of Kentucky, 1982).

A TRIBUTE

from STANLEY BURNSHAW

It was during my years at the Henry Holt publishing house that I first met Robert Penn Warren. Strange though it sounds, the long-past fact that we'd occupied opposite sides of the barricades during the nineteen-thirties seemed to have made us almost at once unexpectedly friendly. And I soon came to admire one of his earlier selves as befitting the Worried Conservator, as I do to this day, though the Poet-Critic Warren is the figure that looms with his name.

A series of unpredictable meetings arose in the wake of the 85th Robert Frost Birthday dinner at which Lionel Trilling shocked the guests—including the guest of honor—by extolling "the public man whom the nation adored" as "a poet who terrifies." Twelve hours later I accompanied a surprisingly unperturbed Frost to his interview on "The Craft of Poetry" that Warren and Brooks were recording for their *Understanding Poetry*. Though some of the poet's assertions seemed at odds with the New Criticism, Cleanth and Red took care to assure Frost of their high delight with everything he had said. Then the four of us set forth to lunch at the Century Club in the course of which the poet regaled us with mimicking Yeats's talk of "the agony that each of [his] lyrics had cost him."

The words had odd repercussions. Agony? Can one "worry" a poem into being (Frost)? What of the lines "that simply come" (Eliot)? What of the poems born not of words but of wordless rhythms (Valéry)? Warren and I had occasionally shared our views of the body's involvement with the poet, the poem, and the reader. Though the question had not been explored in ways that I thought essential (and would follow in *The Seamless Web*), André Spire, the poet-critic on whom I had written my earliest book, had published a lengthy work on this subject in French. Before I had finished conveying to Red the main ideas of *Plaisir Poétique et Plaisir Musculaire*, I was stopped: Would I summarize what Spire had said about rhythm in verse and its bodily "echoes" in the poet and the reader? I might try, I said, but what would you want it for? It's important for students to know, he explained, and a new edition of *Understanding Poetry* was being prepared. (The end-result I described as a "telescoped translation" of Spire's own words in a footnote that appeared in the editors' Foreword on Metrics.)

I apologized to Red for my summary's brevity: the galleys of my new book of verse were causing some "problems." He turned to me: "I'd be very happy to read the proofs." I was startled—delighted—and quite unprepared for what finally came of his offer. He had made very careful notes on 25 of the 41 new poems. . . .

When I learned of his death, some of the comments he made during the hours we spent on *Caged in an Animal's Mind* started to ring in my head. I almost could feel his presence: standing beside me, turning his eye from his penciled lines to the lines of print—at one point saying about a word that I wanted to keep: "Let it stand if you feel that you have to, but I *implore* you to—" The word he had urged me to find struck me in time. . . . Never before had I felt the force of such feeling-full thought. It led me to think then as it makes me feel now of "sympathy" as Shelley had used the term: as a "going out, a reaching out, from the self."

A TRIBUTE

from RICHARD EBERHART

Robert Penn Warren may be compared with Edgar Allan Poe in the nineteenth century. Red belonged very much to the twentieth. Poe wrote short stories, critical articles, and poetry. They were very different in appearance and personality but both were Southerners. Once Poe got to Yaddo at Saratoga Springs, stood beside a melancholy tarn near the mansion, and was heard to say, "Nevermore." This is fantasy but if my friend Red Warren had assumed the same posture, which he would not, I should think he would have left off the first letter.

A TRIBUTE

from PAUL ENGLE

Red Warren was as good a companion as he was a writer. The words came out as lively and as harmonious in his talk as they did in the books. They were considered words, full of human warmth and humor. I brought him to teach in the Writers Workshop at the University of Iowa when I was director of it. He was a superb teacher, full of shrewd insight into why a student text lacked insight. He was sympathetic to stories and poems which deserved minimal sympathy. His criticism always built up the text. I never saw him tear down a writer, even one who was about to fall down for his own inadequacies. About one episode in a story about a character who had committed a cruel act and been reproved, the student-author asked Red, "What would you have done with that guy down south?" A judicious pause, and then came the calm answer, "Wal, I reckon we would have shot him like the varmint he was."

He was a gentle person who understood violence. I never heard him make one cruel remark. Unlike many writers, he never cared about the sort of messy, petty scene which disfigures too many writers. When he spoke kindly about a person or a piece of writing (as he usually did), it was like a laying on of hands.

A TRIBUTE

from RICHARD WILBUR

Warren's works are so diverse and of such quality that every literate American is somehow in his debt. Of the many specific debts which poets owe him, let me mention three. His 1938 textbook *Understanding Poetry* (done with Cleanth Brooks) was of immeasurable value, helping to form the tastes and standards of at least one generation of educated poets and readers. His 1942 volume, *Eleven Poems on the Same Theme*—with its vigorous yoking of the terrible and the comic, its bridging of lexicons, its moral penetration—had a galvanizing effect on many poets whom I know, myself included. And he was in his dealings a decent, straightforward, delightful man, unfailingly generous—as not all are—toward his fellow-writers.

A TRIBUTE

from JAMES WILCOX

As a teacher Robert Penn Warren touched not just the minds, but it seemed the souls themselves of his students. His very presence in the classroom or at one of his unforgettable, joyous parties, was enriching—memories that have nourished me over the years. He brought everything to bear on the study of literature, not just a daunting intellect, but also a heart as wise and noble as that of the timeless masters he taught.

Literary Awards and Honors Announced in 1989

ACADEMY OF AMERICAN POETS AWARDS

LAMONT POETRY SELECTION
Minnie Bruce Pratt, *Crime Against Nature* (Firebrand).

HAROLD MORTON LANDON
TRANSLATION AWARD
Martin Greenberg, *Five Plays*, by Heinrich von Kleist (Yale University Press).

PETER I. B. LAVAN YOUNGER
POET AWARDS
Melissa Green, Jeffrey Harrison, William Logan.

WALT WHITMAN AWARD
Martha Hollander, *The Game of Statues* (Atlantic Monthly).

NELSON ALGREN AWARD
FOR SHORT FICTION
Geoffrey Becker, "Bluestown."

AMERICAN ACADEMY AND INSTITUTE OF ARTS AND LETTERS AWARDS

AWARD OF MERIT FOR THE SHORT STORY
Doris Betts.

MICHAEL BRAUDE AWARD FOR
LIGHT VERSE
X. J. Kennedy.

WITTER BYNNER FOUNDATION
POETRY PRIZE
Mary Jo Salter.

E. M. FORSTER AWARD
A. N. Wilson.

GOLD MEDAL FOR FICTION
Isaac Bashevis Singer.

IRVING HOWE AWARDS IN LITERATURE
Richard Ford, Martin Greenberg, Ron

Hansen, Herbert Morris, Gregory Rabassa, David R. Slavitt, Arturo Vivante, Joy Williams.

SUE KAUFMAN PRIZE FOR FIRST FICTION
Gary Krist.

ROME FELLOWSHIP IN LITERATURE
Bob Shacochis.

RICHARD AND HINDA ROSENTHAL
FOUNDATION AWARD
James Robison.

JEAN STEIN AWARD
Rodney Jones.

HAROLD D. VURSELL MEMORIAL AWARD
Oliver Sacks.

MORTON DAUWEN ZABEL AWARD
C. K. Williams.

AMERICAN ACADEMY OF ARTS
AND SCIENCES
EMERSON-THOREAU MEDAL
Norman Mailer.

BANCROFT PRIZES

Eric Foner, *Reconstruction: America's Unfinished Revolution, 1863-1877* (Harper & Row).

Edmund S. Morgan, *Inventing the People: The Rise of Popular Sovereignty in England and America* (Norton).

BAY AREA BOOK REVIEWERS
ASSOCIATION AWARDS

FRED CODY MEMORIAL AWARD FOR
LIFETIME ACHIEVEMENT
Gary Snyder.

FICTION
Alice Adams, *Second Chances* (Knopf).

Peter Dexter, *Paris Trout* (Random House).

Ehud Havazelt, *What Is It Between Us?* (Scribners).

NONFICTION
Timothy Ferris, *Coming of Age in the Milky Way* (Morrow).

Beverly Cleary, *A Girl from Yamhill* (Morrow).

POETRY
Philip Levine, *A Walk with Thomas Jefferson* (Knopf).

CURTIS G. BENJAMIN AWARD FOR CREATIVE PUBLISHING

Edward E. Booher.

IRMA SIMONTON BLACK AWARD

Bonnie Pryor, *Porcupine Mouse*, illustrated by Maryjane Begin (Morrow Junior Books).

ELMER HOLMES BOBST AWARDS

CRITICISM
Elizabeth Hardwick.

FICTION
William Styron.

HISTORY
C. Vann Woodward.

POETRY
Adrienne Rich.

BOLLINGEN PRIZE FOR POETRY

Edgar Bowers.

BOOKER PRIZE
Kazuo Ishiguro, *The Remains of the Day* (Faber).

BOSTON GLOBE-HORN BOOK AWARDS

FICTION
Paula Fox, *The Village by the Sea* (Orchard / Jackson).

NONFICTION
David Macaulay, *The Way Things Work* (Houghton Mifflin).

PICTURE BOOK
Rosemary Wells, *Shy Charles* (Dial).

RANDOLPH CALDECOTT AWARDS

CALDECOTT MEDAL
Stephen Gammell, illustrator of *Song and Dance Man*, by Karen Ackerman (Knopf).

CALDECOTT HONOR BOOKS
James Marshall, *Goldilocks and the Three Bears* (Dial).

Jerry Pinkney, illustrator of *Mirandy and Brother Wind*, by Patricia McKissak (Knopf).

Allen Say, *The Boy of the Three-year Nap* (Houghton Mifflin).

David Wiesner, *Free Fall* (Lothrop, Lee & Shepard).

CANADA-AUSTRALIA LITERARY PRIZE

Elizabeth Jolley.

CAREY-THOMAS PUBLISHING AWARD

Thunder's Mouth Press.

COMMONWEALTH WRITERS PRIZE

Janet Frame, *The Carpathians* (Century Hutchinson).

JOHN DOS PASSOS PRIZE FOR LITERATURE

Shelby Foote.

GOLDEN KITE AWARDS

FICTION
George Ella Lyon, *Borrowed Children* (Orchard / Jackson).

ILLUSTRATION
Susan Jeffers, illustrator of *Forest of Dreams*, by Rosemary Wells (Dial).

NONFICTION
James Giblin, *Let There Be Light* (Crowell).

THE GOVERNOR GENERAL'S LITERARY AWARDS

CHILDREN'S LITERATURE
(ILLUSTRATION)
Kim LaFave, illustrator of *Amos's Sweater*, by Janet Lunn (Douglas & McIntyre).

CHILDREN'S LITERATURE
(TEXT)
Welwyn Wilton Katz, *The Third Magic* (Douglas & McIntyre).

DRAMA
George F. Walker, *Nothing Sacred* (Coach House).

FICTION
David Adams Richards, *Nights Below Station Street* (McClelland & Stewart).

NONFICTION
Anne Collins, *In the Sleep Room* (Lester & Orphen Dennys).

POETRY
Erin Mouré, *Furious* (House of Anansi).

TRANSLATION
Philip Stratford, *Second Chance*, by Diane Hébert (Lester & Orphen Dennys).

DRUE HEINZ LITERATURE PRIZE

Maya Sonenberg, *Cartographies* (University of Pittsburgh Press).

O. HENRY AWARD

Ernest J. Finney, "Peacocks" (*Sewanee Review*, Winter, 1988).

CLARENCE L. HOLTE LITERARY PRIZE

Arnold Rampersad, *The Life of Langston Hughes, Volume 1, 1902-1941: I, Too, Sing of America* (Oxford University Press).

HUGO AWARDS

JOHN W. CAMPBELL AWARD FOR THE
BEST NEW WRITER
Michaela Roessner.

NOVEL
C. J. Cherryh, *Cyteen* (Warner).

NOVELETTE
George Alec Effinger, "Schrodinger's Kitten" (*Omni*, September 1988).

SHORT STORY
Mike Resnick, "Kirinyaga" (*Magazine of Fantasy and Science-Fiction*, November 1988).

INGERSOLL PRIZES

T. S. ELIOT AWARD FOR
CREATIVE WRITING
George Garrett.

RICHARD M. WEAVER AWARD FOR
SCHOLARLY LETTERS
Edward O. Wilson.

IOWA SHORT FICTION AWARD

Marly Swick.

JANET HEIDINGER KAFKA PRIZE

FOR FICTION

Kathryn Davis, *Labrador* (Farrar, Straus & Giroux).

ROBERT F. KENNEDY MEMORIAL BOOK AWARDS

Neil Sheehan, *A Bright and Shining Lie: John*

Paul Vann and America in Vietnam (Random House).

Jonathan Kozol, *Rachel and Her Children: Homeless Families in America* (Crown).

RUTH LILLY POETRY PRIZE

Mona Van Duyn.

LOS ANGELES TIMES BOOK PRIZES

Taylor Branch, *Parting the Waters: America in the King Years, 1954-1963* (Simon & Schuster).

Neal Gabler, *An Empire of Their Own: How the Jews Invented Hollywood* (Crown).

Donald Hall, *The One Day: A Poem in Three Parts* (Ticknor & Fields).

Frans de Waal, *Peacemaking Among the Primates* (Harvard University Press).

Fay Weldon, *The Heart of the Country* (Viking).

Tobias Wolff, *This Boy's Life* (Atlantic Monthly).

ROBERT KIRSCH AWARD
Karl Shapiro.

JOHN D. AND CATHERINE T. MACARTHUR FOUNDATION FELLOWSHIPS

Jay Cantor, Allen Grossman, Aaron Lansky, Errol Morris, Richard Powers, Ellendea Catherine Proffer, Bernice Johnson Reagon, Theodore Rosengarten, Claire Van Vliet, Eliot Wigginton.

EDWARD MACDOWELL MEDAL

Stan Brakhage.

HARRIET MONROE POETRY PRIZE

Edgar Bowers.

NATIONAL BOOK AWARDS

FICTION
John Casey, *Spartina* (Knopf).

MEDAL FOR DISTINGUISHED CONTRIBUTION TO AMERICAN LETTERS
Daniel J. Boorstin.

NONFICTION
Thomas L. Friedman, *From Beirut to Jerusalem* (Farrar, Straus & Giroux).

NATIONAL BOOK CRITICS CIRCLE AWARDS

BIOGRAPHY / AUTOBIOGRAPHY
Richard Ellmann, *Oscar Wilde* (Knopf).

CITATION FOR EXCELLENCE IN REVIEWING
William Logan, *Chicago Tribune, New York Times Book Review, Washington Post, Times Literary Supplement.*

CRITICISM
Clifford Geertz, *Works and Lives: The Anthropologist as Author* (Stanford University Press).

FICTION
Bharati Mukherjee, *The Middleman and Other Stories* (Grove Press).

GENERAL NONFICTION
Taylor Branch, *Parting the Waters: America in the King Years, 1954-1963* (Simon & Schuster).

POETRY
Donald Hall, *The One Day: A Poem in Three Parts* (Ticknor & Fields).

NATIONAL JEWISH BOOK AWARDS

AUTOBIOGRAPHY / MEMOIR
Natan Sharansky, *Fear No Evil* (Random House).

CHILDREN'S LITERATURE
    Jane Yolen, *The Devil's Arithmetic* (Viking Kestrel).

CHILDREN'S PICTURE BOOK
    Barbara Diamond Goldin, *Just Enough Is Plenty: A Hanukkah Tale*, illustrated by Seymour Chwast (Viking Kestrel).

CONTEMPORARY JEWISH LIFE
    Jonathan Kaufman, *Broken Alliance: The Turbulent Times between Blacks and Jews in America* (Scribners).

FICTION
    Aharon Appelfeld, *The Immortal Bartfuss* (Weidenfeld & Nicolson).

HOLOCAUST
    Christopher Simpson, *Blowback: America's Recruitment of Nazis and Its Effect on the Cold War* (Weidenfeld & Nicolson).

ISRAEL
    Haim Chertok, *Stealing Home: Israel Bound and Rebound* (Fordham University Press).

JEWISH HISTORY
    Michael A. Meyer, *Response to Modernity: A History of the Reform Movement in Judaism* (Oxford University Press).

JEWISH THOUGHT
    Michael Rosenak, *Commandments and Concerns: Jewish Religious Education in Secular Society* (Jewish Publication Society).

SCHOLARSHIP
    Moshe Idel, *Kabbalah: New Perspectives* (Yale University Press).

VISUAL ARTS
    2000 Years of Hebrew Books and Illuminated Manuscripts, edited by Leonard Gold (New York Public Library / Oxford University Press).

NEBULA AWARDS

GRAND MASTER AWARD
    Ray Bradbury.

NOVEL
    Lois McMaster Bujold, *Falling Free* (Baen).

NOVELLA
    Connie Williams, "The Last of the Winnebagos" (*Isaac Asimov's Science Fiction Magazine*, July 1988).

NOVELETTE
    George Alec Effinger, "Schrodinger's Kitten" (*Omni*, September 1988).

SHORT STORY
    James Morrow, "Bible Stories for Adults, No. 17: The Deluge" (in *Full Spectrum*, edited by Lou Aronica and Shawna McCarthy (Bantam Spectra).

JOHN NEWBERY AWARDS

NEWBERY MEDAL
    Paul Fleischman, *Joyful Noise: Poems for Two Voices* (Harper & Row).

NEWBERY HONOR CITATIONS
    Virginia Hamilton, *In the Beginning: Creation Stories from Around the World* (Harcourt Brace Jovanovich).

    Walter Dean Myers, *Scorpions* (Harper & Row).

NOBEL PRIZE FOR LITERATURE

Camilo José Cela

SCOTT O'DELL AWARD FOR HISTORICAL FICTION

Patricia Beatty, *Charley Skedaddle* (Morrow).

PEN LITERARY AWARDS

FAULKNER AWARD FOR FICTION
    James Salter, *Dusk and Other Stories* (North Point Press).

ERNEST HEMINGWAY
FOUNDATION AWARD
Jane Hamilton, *The Book of Ruth* (Ticknor & Fields).

PEN / BOOK-OF-THE-MONTH CLUB
TRANSLATION PRIZE
Matthew Ward, *The Stranger*, by Albert Camus (Knopf).

PEN / JERARD FUND AWARD
Shelley Rice.

PEN / MARTHA ALBRAND AWARD
FOR NONFICTION
Merrill Gilfillan, *Magpie Rising: Sketches from the Great Plains* (Pruett).

PEN / NELSON ALGREN FICTION AWARD
FOR A WORK IN PROGRESS
Carolyn Page, "Prologue."

RENATO POGGIOLI TRANSLATION AWARD
FOR A WORK IN PROGRESS
Philip Parisi, English-language versions of the poetry of Alphonso Gatto.

**PEN-NEW ENGLAND AWARD FOR
LITERARY EXCELLENCE**

Marge Piercy.

ØBK'S CHRISTIAN GAUSS AWARD

Harold Bloom, *Ruin the Sacred Truths: Poetry and Belief from the Bible to the Present* (Harvard University Press).

EDGAR ALLAN POE AWARDS

BIOGRAPHICAL / CRITICAL STUDY
Francis M. Nevins, Jr., *Cornell Woolrich: First You Dream, Then You Die* (Mysterious Press).

ELLERY QUEEN
Richard Levinson and William Link.

FACT CRIME
Harry N. MacLean, *In Broad Daylight* (Harper & Row).

FIRST NOVEL
David Stout, *Carolina Skeletons* (Mysterious Press).

GRAND MASTER
Hillary Waugh.

JUVENILE NOVEL
Willo Davis Roberts, *Megan's Island* (Atheneum).

MYSTERY NOVEL
Stuart M. Kaminsky, *A Cold Red Sunrise* (Scribners).

ORIGINAL PAPERBACK
Timothy Findley, *The Telling of Lies* (Dell).

SPECIAL EDGAR
Joan Kahn.

YOUNG ADULT NOVEL
Sonia Levitin, *Incident at Loring Groves* (Dial).

**PRESENT TENSE / JOEL H. CAVIOR
LITERARY AWARDS**

BIOGRAPHY / AUTOBIOGRAPHY
Betty Jean Lifton, *The King of Children: A Biography of Janusz Korczak* (Farrar, Straus & Giroux).

CHILDREN'S LITERATURE
Barbara Rogasky, *Smoke and Ashes: The Story of the Holocaust* (Holiday House).

CURRENT AFFAIRS
Jonathan Kaufman, *Broken Alliance: The Turbulent Times between Blacks and Jews in America* (Scribners).

FICTION
Harold Brodkey, *Stories in an Almost Classical Mode* (Knopf).

HISTORY
Christopher Simpson, *Blowback: America's Recruitment of Nazis and Its Effect on the Cold War* (Weidenfeld & Nicolson).

RELIGIOUS THOUGHT
Moshe Idel, *Kabbalah: New Perspectives* (Yale University Press).

SPECIAL CITATION FOR LIFETIME
ACHIEVEMENT
    Arthur Hertzberg.

PULITZER PRIZES

BIOGRAPHY
    Richard Ellmann, *Oscar Wilde* (Knopf).

DRAMA
    Wendy Wasserstein, *The Heidi Chronicles.*

FICTION
    Anne Tyler, *Breathing Lessons* (Knopf).

GENERAL NONFICTION
    Neil Sheehan, *A Bright Shining Lie: John Paul
    Vann and America in Vietnam* (Random
    House).

HISTORY
    Taylor Branch, *Parting the Waters: America
    in the King Years, 1954-1963* (Simon &
    Schuster).
    James M. McPherson, *Battle Cry of Freedom:
    The Civil War Era* (Oxford University Press).

POETRY
    Richard Wilbur, *New and Collected Poems*
    (Harcourt Brace Jovanovich).

REA AWARD FOR THE SHORT STORY

Tobias Wolff.

REGINA MEDAL

Stephen Kellog.

WHITBREAD BOOK OF THE YEAR AWARD

Paul Sayer, *Comforts of Madness* (Constable).

WHITING AWARDS

Ellen Akins, Russel Edson, Ian Frazier,
Mary Karr, Natalie Kusz, Luc Sante, Tim-
berlake Wertenbaker, Marianne Wiggins,
Tobias Wolff, C. D. Wright.

LAURA INGALLS WILDER AWARD

Elizabeth George Speare.

Checklist: Contributions to Literary History and Biography

This checklist is a selection of new books on various aspects and periods of literary and cultural history, including biographies, memoirs, and correspondence of literary people and their associates.

Backscheider, Paula R. *Daniel Defoe: His Life*. Baltimore: Johns Hopkins University Press, 1989.

Baker, James Robert. *Citizen Welles: A Biography of Orson Welles*. New York: Scribners, 1989.

Baker, Russell. *The Good Times*. New York: Morrow, 1989.

Berg, A. Scott. *Goldwyn*. New York: Knopf, 1989.

Boswell, James. *Boswell: The Great Biographer*. Edited by Marlies K. Danziger and Frank Brady. New York: McGraw-Hill, 1989.

Branden, Nathaniel. *Judgment Day: My Years with Ayn Rand*. Boston: Houghton Mifflin, 1989.

Carpenter, Humphrey. *A Serious Character: The Life of Ezra Pound*. Boston: Houghton Mifflin, 1989.

Charyn, Jerome. *Movieland: Hollywood and the Great American Dream Culture*. New York: Putnam's, 1989.

Chatwin, Bruce. *What Am I Doing Here?* New York: Viking, 1989.

Cheever, John. *The Letters of John Cheever*. Edited by Benjamin Cheever. New York: Simon & Schuster, 1989.

Conn, Peter. *Literature in America: An Illustrated History*. New York: Cambridge University Press, 1989.

Craddock, Patricia B. *Edward Gibbon, Luminous Historian: 1772-1794*. Baltimore: Johns Hopkins University Press, 1989.

Crane, Stephen. *The Correspondence of Stephen Crane*. Edited by Stanley Wertheimer and Paul Sorrentino. New York: Columbia University Press, 1989.

Crouthamel, James L. *Bennett's New York Herald and the Rise of the Popular Press*. Syracuse: Syracuse University Press, 1989.

Darnton, Robert, and Daniel Roche, eds. *Revolution in Print: The Press in France, 1775-1800*. Berkeley: University of California Press, 1989.

Dickey, James. *The Voiced Connections of James Dickey: Interviews and Conversations*. Edited by Ronald Baughman. Columbia: University of South Carolina Press, 1989.

Dillard, Annie. *The Writing Life*. New York: Harper & Row, 1989.

Doll, Mary Aswell, and Clara Stites, eds. *In the Shadow of the Giant: Thomas Wolfe. Correspondence of Edward C. Aswell and Elizabeth Nowell, 1949-1958.* Athens: Ohio University Press, 1989.

Drew, Bettina. *Nelson Algren: A Life On the Wild Side.* New York: Putnam's, 1989.

Dunaway, David King. *Huxley in Hollywood.* New York: Harper & Row, 1989.

Forster, Margaret. *Elizabeth Barrett Browning: A Biography.* New York: Doubleday, 1989.

Frank, Anne. *The Diary of Anne Frank: The Critical Edition.* Edited by David Barnouu and Gerrold van der Stroom. Translated by Arnold J. Pomerans and B. M. Mooyaart-Doubleday. New York: Doubleday, 1989.

Fraser, Rebecca. *The Brontës: Charlotte and Her Family.* New York: Crown, 1989.

Gerassi, John. *Jean-Paul Sartre: Hated Conscience of His Century. Volume One: Protestant or Protester?* Chicago: University of Chicago Press, 1989.

Gibson, Ian. *Federico García Lorca: A Life.* New York: Pantheon, 1989.

Gill, Stephen. *William Wordsworth: A Life.* New York: Oxford University Press, 1989.

Goytisolo, Juan. *Forbidden Territory: The Memoirs of Juan Goytisolo, 1931-1956.* Translated by Peter Bush. Berkeley: North Point, 1989.

Greenfield, George. *Scribblers for Bread: Aspects of the English Novel Since 1945.* New York: Norton, 1989.

Handke, Peter. *The Afternoon of a Writer.* Translated by Ralph Manheim. New York: Farrar, Straus & Giroux, 1989.

Hartill, Rosemary. *Writers Revealed.* New York: Peter Bedrick, 1989.

Heilbrun, Carolyn G. *Writing a Woman's Life.* New York: Norton, 1989.

Hirsch, E. D., Jr., ed., with the assistance of William G. Roland, Jr., and Michael Stanford. *A First Dictionary of Cultural Literacy: What Our Children Need to Know.* Boston: Houghton Mifflin, 1989.

Hersey, John. *Life Sketches.* New York: Knopf, 1989.

Holroyd, Michael. *Bernard Shaw. Volume Two: 1898-1918. The Pursuit of Power.* New York: Random House, 1989.

Jones, James. *To Reach Eternity: The Letters of James Jones.* Edited by George Hendrick. New York: Random House, 1989.

Karl, Frederick R. *William Faulkner: American Writer. A Biography.* New York: Weidenfeld & Nicolson, 1989.

Kennedy, Emmet. *A Cultural History of the French Revolution.* New Haven: Yale University Press, 1989.

London, Jack. *The Letters of Jack London. Volume One: 1896-1905. Volume Two: 1906-1912. Volume Three: 1913-1916.* Edited by Earle Labor, Robert C. Leitz III, and I. Milo Shepard. Stanford: Stanford University Press, 1989.

L'Amour, Louis. *Education of a Wandering Man.* New York: Bantam, 1989.

Lawrence, T. E. *The Selected Letters.* Edited by Malcolm Brown. New York: Norton, 1989.

Lottman, Herbert. *Flaubert: A Biography.* Boston: Little, Brown, 1989.

Makowsky, Veronica. *Caroline Gordon: A Biography.* New York: Oxford University Press, 1989.

Marcus, Greil. *Lipstick Traces: A Secret History of the Twentieth Century.* Cambridge: Harvard University Press, 1989.

Mencken, H. L. *The Diary of H. L. Mencken.* Edited by Charles A. Fecher. New York: Knopf, 1989.

Miles, Barry. *Ginsberg: A Biography.* New York: Simon & Schuster, 1989.

Miller, Donald L. *Lewis Mumford: A Life.* New York: Weidenfeld & Nicolson, 1989.

Mudge, Bradford Keyes. *Sara Coleridge, a Victorian Daughter: Her Life and Essays.* New Haven: Yale University Press, 1989.

Nabokov, Vladimir. *Selected Letters 1940-1977.* Edited by Dmitri Nabokov and Matthew J. Bruccoli. San Diego, New York & London: Harcourt Brace Jovanovich / Bruccoli Clark Layman, 1989.

The Oxford English Dictionary, Second Edition. Prepared by J. A. Simpson and E. S. C. Weiner. New York: Clarendon Press / Oxford University Press, 1989.

Price, Reynolds. *Clear Pictures: First Loves, First Guides.* New York: Atheneum, 1989.

Proust, Marcel. *Selected Letters: Volume Two, 1904-1909.* Edited by Philip Kolb. Translated by Terrence Kilmartin. New York: Oxford University Press, 1989.

Reynolds, Michael. *Hemingway: The Paris Years.* New York: Blackwell, 1989.

Riggs, David. *Jonson: A Life.* Cambridge: Harvard University Press, 1989.

Russo, John Paul. *I. A. Richards: His Life and Work.* Baltimore: Johns Hopkins University Press, 1989.

St. Clair, William. *The Godwins and the Shelleys: The Biography of a Family.* New York: Norton, 1989.

Samuels, Ernest. *Henry Adams.* Cambridge: Harvard University Press, 1989.

Sawyer-Lauçanno, Christopher. *An Invisible Spectator: A Biography of Paul Bowles.* New York: Weidenfeld & Nicolson, 1989.

Schatz, Thomas. *The Genius of the System: Hollywood Filmmaking in the Studio Era.* New York: Pantheon, 1989.

Shelden, Michael. *Friends of Promise: Cyril Connolly and the World of Horizon.* New York: Harper & Row, 1989.

Sherry, Norman. *The Life of Graham Greene, Volume I: 1904-1939.* New York: Viking, 1989.

Spalding, Frances. *Stevie Smith: A Biography.* New York: Norton, 1989.

Steinbeck, John. *Working Days: The Journals of "The Grapes of Wrath," 1938-1941*. Edited by Robert DeMott. New York: Viking, 1989.

Stevenson, Anne. *Bitter Fame: A Life of Sylvia Plath*. Boston: Houghton Mifflin, 1989.

Sunstein, Emily W. *Mary Shelley: Romance and Reality*. Boston: Little, Brown, 1989.

Thurber, James. *Collecting Himself: James Thurber on Writing and Writers, Humor and Himself*. Edited by Michael J. Rosen. New York: Harper & Row, 1989.

Troyat, Henri. *Gorky: A Biography*. Translated by Lowell Blair. New York: Crown, 1989.

Updike, John. *Self-Consciousness: Memoirs*. New York: Knopf, 1989.

Villard, Henry Serrano, and James Nagel, eds. *Hemingway in Love and War*. Boston: Northeastern University Press, 1989.

Weatherby, W. J. *James Baldwin: Artist on Fire*. New York: Fine, 1989.

Wilson, Charles Reagan, and William Ferris, eds. *Encyclopedia of Southern Culture*. Chapel Hill: University of North Carolina Press, 1989.

Wilson, Rosalind Baker. *Near the Magician: A Memoir of My Father, Edmund Wilson*. New York: Grove Weidenfeld, 1989.

Wolff, Tobias. *This Boy's Life: A Memoir*. Boston: Atlantic Monthly Press, 1989.

Woolf, Leonard. *Letters*. Edited by Frederic Spotts. San Diego, New York & London: Harcourt Brace Jovanovich, 1989.

Necrology

Edward Abbey–14 March 1989
Richard Armour–28 February 1989
Oriana Atkinson–31 July 1989
Carlos Barral–12 December 1989
Donald Barthelme–23 July 1989
Samuel Beckett–22 December 1989
Dahn Ben-Amotz–20 October 1989
Irving Berlin–22 September 1989
Edward Brecher–15 April 1989
Sterling A. Brown–13 January 1989
Gerald Carson–4 December 1989
Graham Chapman–4 October 1989
Bruce Chatwin–17 January 1989
Malcolm Cowley–27 March 1989
Nigel Forbes Dennis–19 July 1989
Birago Diop–25 November 1989
Walter Farley–17 October 1989
Berry Fleming–15 September 1989
Gertrude T. Friedberg–17 September 1989
A. Bartlett Giametti–1 September 1989
Stella Gibbons–19 December 1989
Eric F. Goldman–19 February 1989
Lorenz Graham–11 September 1989
Bill Gunn–5 April 1989
William Haines–18 November 1989
Robert Halsband–25 October 1989
Michael Harrington–31 July 1989
Harold Hayes–5 April 1989
Nathan I. Huggins–5 December 1989
C. L. R. James–31 May 1989
Emily Kimbrough–11 February 1989
Hans Helmut Kirst–23 February 1989
Norma Klein–25 April 1989
Herman Kogan–8 March 1989
Seymour Krim–30 August 1989
Delia W. Kuhn–16 December 1989
Margaret Leonard–19 January 1989

Alpheus Mason–31 October 1989
Daphne du Maurier–19 April 1989
Mary McCarthy–26 October 1989
Aubrey Menen–13 February 1989
Alice-Leone Moats–14 May 1989
Richard B. Morris–3 March 1989
Scott O'Dell–15 October 1989
Stanley Olson–9 December 1989
Frank O'Rourke–27 April 1989
Robert Phelps–2 August 1989
Judson Philips–7 March 1989
Frederic Prokosch–2 June 1989
Priscilla Robertson–26 November 1989
Zola Helen Ross–20 November 1989
Francis Russell–21 March 1989
Leonardo Sciascia–20 November 1989
George Selden–5 December 1989
Georges Simenon–4 September 1989
John Steptoe–28 August 1989
I. F. Stone–18 June 1989
Irving Stone–26 August 1989
May Swenson–4 December 1989
Sir Ronald Syme–4 September 1989
Virgil Thomson–30 September 1989
Barbara Tuchman–6 February 1989
Harry Tugend–11 September 1989
John Unterecker–9 January 1989
Nick Virgilio–3 January 1989
Robert Penn Warren–15 September 1989
Edward A. Weeks–11 March 1989
Christine Weston–3 May 1989
Arnold Whitridge–29 January 1989
Ron Whyte–13 September 1989
Dan Wickenden–27 October 1989
Bart Winer–19 February 1989
Margot Zemach–21 May 1989

Contributors

Jack Armistead...*University of Tennessee at Knoxville*
Hans Bak ....*Catholic University of Nijmegen*
Richard R. Centing..*Ohio State University*
Lucile C. Charlebois...*University of South Carolina*
Stanley G. Eskin ....*Samois-Sur-Seine*
George Garrett ....*University of Virginia*
George Greenfield ....*London*
R. S. Gwynn ....*Lamar University*
Mark A. Heberle.....................................*University of Hawaii at Manoa*
Howard Kissel ....*New York Daily News*
Ronald Meyer..*Ardis Publishers*
Joel Myerson..*University of South Carolina*
G. Ross Roy ....*University of South Carolina*
J. D. Stahl...................*Virginia Polytechnic Institute and State University*
Victor Strandberg ....*Duke University*
Henry Taylor ....*Lincoln, Virginia*
George A. Test ....*State University of New York College at Oneonta*
Stanley Trachtenberg..*Texas Christian University*

Cumulative Index

Dictionary of Literary Biography, Volumes 1-94
Dictionary of Literary Biography Yearbook, 1980-1989
Dictionary of Literary Biography Documentary Series, Volumes 1-7

Cumulative Index

DLB before number: *Dictionary of Literary Biography,* Volumes 1-94
Y before number: *Dictionary of Literary Biography Yearbook,* 1980-1989
DS before number: *Dictionary of Literary Biography Documentary Series,* Volumes 1-7

A

B

Cumulative Index

E

F

G

Cumulative Index

H

I

J

L

Cumulative Index

M

N

P

Q

R

S

U

V

W

(Continued from front endsheets)

71: *American Literary Critics and Scholars, 1880-1900*, edited by John W. Rathbun and Monica M. Grecu (1988)

72: *French Novelists, 1930-1960*, edited by Catharine Savage Brosman (1988)

73: *American Magazine Journalists, 1741-1850*, edited by Sam G. Riley (1988)

74: *American Short-Story Writers Before 1880*, edited by Bobby Ellen Kimbel, with the assistance of William E. Grant (1988)

75: *Contemporary German Fiction Writers*, Second Series, edited by Wolfgang D. Elfe and James Hardin (1988)

76: *Afro-American Writers, 1940-1955*, edited by Trudier Harris (1988)

77: *British Mystery Writers, 1920-1939*, edited by Bernard Benstock and Thomas F. Staley (1988)

78: *American Short-Story Writers, 1880-1910*, edited by Bobby Ellen Kimbel, with the assistance of William E. Grant (1988)

79: *American Magazine Journalists, 1850-1900*, edited by Sam G. Riley (1988)

80: *Restoration and Eighteenth-Century Dramatists*, First Series, edited by Paula R. Backscheider (1989)

81: *Austrian Fiction Writers, 1875-1913*, edited by James Hardin and Donald G. Daviau (1989)

82: *Chicano Writers*, First Series, edited by Francisco A. Lomelí and Carl R. Shirley (1989)

83: *French Novelists Since 1960*, edited by Catharine Savage Brosman (1989)

84: *Restoration and Eighteenth-Century Dramatists*, Second Series, edited by Paula R. Backscheider (1989)

85: *Austrian Fiction Writers After 1914*, edited by James Hardin and Donald G. Daviau (1989)

86: *American Short-Story Writers, 1910-1945*, First Series, edited by Bobby Ellen Kimbel (1989)

87: *British Mystery and Thriller Writers Since 1940*, First Series, edited by Bernard Benstock and Thomas F. Staley (1989)

88: *Canadian Writers, 1920-1959*, Second Series, edited by W. H. New (1989)

89: *Restoration and Eighteenth-Century Dramatists*, Third Series, edited by Paula R. Backscheider (1989)

90: *German Writers in the Age of Goethe, 1789-1832*, edited by James Hardin and Christoph E. Schweitzer (1989)

91: *American Magazine Journalists, 1900-1960*, First Series, edited by Sam G. Riley (1990)

92: *Canadian Writers, 1890-1920*, edited by W. H. New (1990)

93: *British Romantic Poets, 1789-1832*, First Series, edited by John R. Greenfield (1990)

94: *German Writers in the Age of Goethe: Sturm und Drang to Classicism*, edited by James Hardin and Christoph E. Schweitzer (1990)

Documentary Series

1: *Sherwood Anderson, Willa Cather, John Dos Passos, Theodore Dreiser, F. Scott Fitzgerald, Ernest Hemingway, Sinclair Lewis*, edited by Margaret A. Van Antwerp (1982)

2: *James Gould Cozzens, James T. Farrell, William Faulkner, John O'Hara, John Steinbeck, Thomas Wolfe, Richard Wright*, edited by Margaret A. Van Antwerp (1982)

3: *Saul Bellow, Jack Kerouac, Norman Mailer, Vladimir Nabokov, John Updike, Kurt Vonnegut*, edited by Mary Bruccoli (1983)

4: *Tennessee Williams*, edited by Margaret A. Van Antwerp and Sally Johns (1984)